BELINDA J. Oxford. She is u. *Large* (1999) and (2005).

The Woman Reader

BELINDA JACK

YALE UNIVERSITY PRESS
NEW HAVEN AND LONDON

For Eliza

For information about this and other Yale University Press publications, please contact:
U.S. Office: sales.press@yale.edu   yalebooks.com
Europe Office: sales@yaleup.co.uk   www.yalebooks.co.uk

Typeset in Minion Pro by IDSUK (DataConnection) Ltd
Printed in Great Britain by Hobbs the Printers Ltd, Totton, Hampshire

Library of Congress Cataloging-in-Publication Data

Jack, Belinda Elizabeth.
   The woman reader / Belinda Jack.
      pages cm
Includes bibliographical references and index.
   ISBN 978-0-300-12045-5
   1. Women–Books and reading–History. 2. Women—Books and
reading–Social aspects—History. 3. Girls—Books and reading—History.
4. Girls—Books and reading—Social aspects–History. I. Title.
   Z1039.W65J33 2012
   028.9 082–dc23

                                                        2012002608

A catalogue record for this book is available from the British Library.

ISBN 978-0-300-19720-4 (pbk)

10 9 8 7 6 5 4 3 2 1

Hetty had never read a novel; how then could she find a shape for her expectations?
GEORGE ELIOT, *Adam Bede*

Literature is my Utopia. Here I am not disenfranchised. No barrier of the senses shuts me out of the sweet, gracious discourse of my book-friends. They talk to me without embarrassment or awkwardness.
HELEN KELLER

Reading makes immigrants of us all. It takes us away from home, but more important, it finds homes for us everywhere.
HAZEL ROCHMAN

Fiction reveals truth that reality obscures.
JESSAMYN WEST

Contents

—◦◦◦—

List of Illustrations

Acknowledgements

Many individuals and institutions have helped me with this book. I am grateful to Christ Church, University of Oxford, for providing resources for travel and research assistance, and periods of leave from teaching. Librarians and curators offered invaluable expert help at the Fondation Martin Bodmer, Geneva, the Bibliothèque Nationale François Mitterrand, Paris, the British Library, London, the National Library of Scotland, Edinburgh, and the Taylorian, English Faculty, History Faculty and Bodleian libraries, Oxford.

It would be invidious to distinguish between friends and colleagues – and inappropriate. I am lucky to know so many knowledgeable and kindly people. I would like to thank the following for their considerable help, especially their reading of one or more chapters: Kate Bennett, Marianne Fillenz, Vincent Gillespie, Peter Hawkins, Martha Klein, Diarmaid MacCulloch, Jane Nelson, Richard Rutherford, Sally Thompson, Catherine Whistler and Jonathan Wright. Any errors in the book are the fault of the author, of course.

Emily Baragwanath, Alan Bowman and Bruno Currie all made excellent bibliographical suggestions and steered me towards research-in-progress that proved most useful. I would also like to thank my sons, John, Jamie and Nick, and Allan and Colin, for reading draft material, for encouragement, and for many useful suggestions. Two women readers, Eleanor Parker and Karen Park, worked with me as research assistants. Their enthusiasm for, commitment to and pleasure in the book sustained me for a number of years. I'd like warmly to acknowledge their contributions. My editor at Yale, Heather McCallum, has been both highly professional and great fun to work with, and Rachael Lonsdale, also at Yale, has been energetic and helpful throughout. Finally I'd like to make known my gratitude to my agent, Felicity Bryan, who believed in the book from the moment I suggested it.

Introduction

From clay tablets to papyrus, from manuscripts to printed books, from pamphlets to manifestos and advertisements, from newspapers to illustrated magazines, from the logos on T-shirts to computer screens, from text messages to the advent of e-readers, reading has gone on for millennia. Its story could hardly be more intriguing and varied across time and space. Nor is it a simple chronicle of a steady progression gradually involving more and more readers and increasing amounts of reading matter; there have been stagnant times and periods of reversal when literacy rates dropped or access to reading material declined. The censorship of reading for religious or political reasons has been, and remains, another strand in the history. But the story of the woman reader has a certain coherence.

Women's access to the written word has been a particular source of anxiety for men – and indeed some women – almost from the very beginning. Through the centuries there have been many and various attempts to control literacy or access to reading material and, of course, counterforces, such as the vigorous individual and collective campaigns to promote women's literacy and free access to books which, in some parts of the world, remain the *sine qua non* of women's greater social and political equality. For much of history it was this fear of women assuming greater power that caused the most unease. One strategy was – and is – to deny women education, but with the passage of time women in many parts of the world did become numerate and literate. This did not mean that they had free access to the material they most wanted to read, of course. The revolutionary moment, for the woman reader, comes in those parts of the world where women were both able to read, and had free access to a significant range of material. In many cases what mattered most was to be able to use libraries. The writer Doris Lessing, who grew up in colonial Rhodesia (now Zimbabwe), makes the point very clearly: 'With a library you are free,' she writes, 'not confined by temporary political climates'. For Lessing, who saw in South Africa a regime's appalling attempts to deny freedom to the majority, access to books is the most fundamental human right. The library, she goes on to say, 'is the most democratic of institutions because no-one – but no-one at all – can tell you what to read and when and how'.[1] The history of the woman reader is in large part one of societies' attempts to control the freedom Lessing identifies, and women's rebellion against those constraints. And although Lessing is right that no-one can tell us *how* to read, all manner of forces both social and psychological, conscious and unconscious, make a difference to the process.

For one thing, women's reading has been overtly or covertly associated with moral corruption for a very long time, and this remains the case today. The prestigious French publisher Gallimard recently advertised their summer holiday novels with seductive images of an array of lone men and lone women reading. The images of the women readers were all suggestive of reading's potentially corrupting forces. One advertisement included a snake and an apple, those age-old symbols of temptation, making the book – as so often with women readers – forbidden fruit. The props in the images of men reading were well-known symbols of machismo: motorbikes and oversized expensive watches. No doubt some of this is sophisticated parody but the fact remains: women readers have long been associated with sexual illicitness and moral degeneration, and male readers with power and authority.

In relation to the licentious and corrupting effects of reading fiction in particular, some women have been quite as vociferous as men in expressing their anxieties. Anna Seward (1742–1809), poet and correspondent, in a letter penned on 17 August 1789, expressed a not atypical point of view, however comically overblown it may be: 'The contemptible rage for novel-reading, is a pernicious and deplorably prevalent taste, which vitiates and palls the appetite for literary food of a more nutritive and wholesome kind. It surprises me that superior genius stoops to feed this reigning folly, to administer sweet poison for the age's tooth'.[2] Reading was often likened to a form of consumption, sometimes fortifying, sometimes a noxious comestible. The rise of women's literacy led many to try to control women's reading and steer them towards the 'nourishing'. By the late eighteenth century, commercial forces in much of Europe and elsewhere were too strong to stem the tide, hence Seward's alarmed and alarming hyperbole. Nor is it altogether coincidental that Seward was writing in the year of the French Revolution. Reading – and the novel in particular – was very much associated with the promotion of ideas which might lead to fundamental changes in the status quo, including the position of women.

This has been the case all over the world. In Japan, in the early seventeenth century, the rise of print culture caused anxieties about the increasingly affordable reading material available to women. In Kyoto, women's classical court poetry was abridged, or published in new editions with glosses, which made them easier for girls and women to read without the help of a tutor. The erotic content of much of this poetry, especially *Genji Monogatari* and *Ise Monogatari*, elicited widespread warnings against allowing girls and women access to them. One of many writers on education, Yamaga Soko (1622–85), wrote: 'It is common in our country to give girls ... *Genji Monogatari*, *Ise Monogatari*, and such like books.... In my opinion ... [these] pursue the emotional relationships of the sexes and principally concern the sensual; consequently, ethics are forgotten, and the essential relationships between lord and retainer, father and son, husband and wife fall into disarray.'[3] There were women, however, who took a different line. Nonaka En (1660–1725), a doctor who also wrote an advice book for a friend about to marry, encouraged reading, lamenting that too many contemporary young women paid attention to their hairstyles and fashion rather than books that could offer valuable moral lessons, including the *Genji*.

Children's reading, particularly girls', has been informally censored usually by their reader-mothers throughout history and across the globe, although all women readers also know – often to their delight – how counterproductive this can be. In eleventh-century Byzantium, Anna Komnene was given a wide education by her royal parents but forbidden to read ancient poetry because of its erotic content. She promptly ensured that one of the imperial court's eunuchs, one of her official tutors, helped her illicitly to read and understand the banned material.

The story of formal censorship, from classification (in lists like the Catholic Church's *Index of Prohibited Books*) to book-burnings, has almost as long a history as that of reading itself, and testifies to the dangers of reading that leaders fear.[4] The pioneering feminist Simone de Beauvoir (1908–86) is one of the most notable women authors on the *Index*. Her argument for women's emancipation arose from the claim that women's social and political inequality was based only on biological difference; the advent of the contraceptive pill and free state childcare would allow women to be sexually free and to be mothers without prejudicing their careers. De Beauvoir's writings could hardly have been more threatening to the Catholic Church. While there are relatively few women authors on the *Index*, the volume of censored material that relates to women and which might have encouraged women readers to question the Church's perceptions and expectations of them, is enormous.

The *Index* is of particular relevance to women's reading because of the centrality of sexual morality and its importance in terms of the power relations between men and women, embracing key concerns about contraception and abortion, marriage and adultery, and the roles of men and women within the family.

Since time immemorial, reading has been deemed subversive, disruptive, or threatening to the stability of a relationship, a community, even a nation or a worldwide Church. Momentous episodes of censorship and book-burnings span human history.[5] The specific control of women's reading has often been more private and subtle but motivated by similar convictions about the potentially dangerous influence of reading. Certain kinds of reading material can spark and fuel dissent and revolution, whether small-scale and domestic, or large-scale and political. The competing ideologies of the world's religions and their founding writings have often been the focus of attention in relation to women's reading. At the time of the Reformation in Europe there was great resistance to the idea that the Bible should be made available in the everyday language of the vernaculars and therefore accessible to those who knew no Latin, including large numbers of women. The reformers argued differently. Erasmus declared: 'I wish that they [the Epistles of Paul] were translated into all the languages so that they might be read and understood'. And he was equally clear about the importance of a female readership: 'I wish that even the weakest woman should read the Gospel'.[6] The atmosphere of general scepticism encouraged many women involved in the religious controversies of the day to call for fundamental enquiry into all manner of things. Jane Anger referred to the need to 'question that now which hath ever been questionless'.[7] Needless to say it was her reading that had given her this kind of intellectual self-confidence.

What has been deemed 'acceptable' women's reading, on the other hand, has often been the same across time and space. In ancient Rome, women's literacy was tolerated or even encouraged provided it constituted a moral training (including strictures on virginity or marital fidelity), or led to women more able to fulfil their role as teachers, particularly of their sons, or if it made them more competent managers of sometimes large households. At the same time there was a widespread awareness that literate women were proof of their father or husband's social status, as they were evidence of the family wealth that had provided both tutors and, more importantly, the leisure time necessary for reading. These same criteria applied to women's reading in Europe and the New World in the nineteenth century. Being seen to be reading the right kind of book became something of considerable social importance. The writer Harriet Martineau (1802–76) was typically forthright in her contempt for this: 'She [a woman of a certain class] was expected to sit in her parlour with her sewing, listen to a book read aloud, and hold herself ready for [female] callers. When the caller came conversation often turned naturally on the book just laid down, which must therefore be very carefully chosen lest the shocked visitor should carry to the house where she paid her next call an account of the deplorable laxity shown by the family she had left.'[8]

Some brave women (and, of course, some men) have repeatedly questioned the inequalities that strictures about propriety and sexual morality bring in their wake. This has often been motivated by their reading. Olympe de Gouges (1748–93) was a political pamphleteer and supporter of the French Revolution who published *Déclaration des droits de la femme et de la citoyenne* (*Declaration of the Rights of Woman and the Female Citizen*) in outraged reaction to reading the marquis de Lafayette's *Declaration of the Rights of Man*, one of the founding documents of post-Revolutionary France. Olympe also denounced Maximilien Robespierre's Reign of Terror. In 1793, the year of Olympe's execution, Robespierre ordered the destruction by fire of religious libraries, as well as the burning of those books supporting or glorifying the French monarchy or the idea of royalism – books that were considered 'inimical towards reformed France'.

The execution of writers, the destruction of libraries and the burning of books may be more or less calculated. Relatively recently, in the wake of the 2003 invasion of Iraq, both the National Library and Archive and a nearby Islamic library in central Baghdad were burned and destroyed. The National Library housed several rare volumes and handwritten documents from as far back as the sixteenth century, including entire royal court records from the period when Iraq was part of the Ottoman Empire. In the conflagration of the Islamic library one of the oldest surviving copies of the Qur'an was also lost. These may be acts of unthinking vandalism but they show a conscious or unconscious association of repositories of knowledge and history with power and authority. In the case of these two libraries, the erasure of the historical record includes evidence of the very considerable respect shown to educated literate women during some periods in the Islamic past, in contrast to the heavy policing of women's reading in some areas of the Muslim world today.

Censorship and book-burnings may be symbolic displays of rage and contempt which go beyond the practical business of preventing the reading of certain books, or they may be deliberate attempts to 'forget', but whether symbolic or pragmatic (or both) they reveal the perceived supremacy of the written word to encapsulate and spread certain ideologies, whether secular or religious; to record the past, or a version of it; and to present a vision of what life is or could be like. It is these powers that have made the particular question of women's literacy and access to written material so controversial. But quite as crucially, it has to do with the ultimate secrecy of reading: no-one outside the reader can know what is going on in the reader's mind, or indeed body, and no-one can know what difference the reading experience may make to his or her thoughts or behaviour. Lone reading is an inherently antisocial activity and the onus on women has been, and often remains, to be sociable and to facilitate easy human relations. Reading is intensely private and literally self-centred.

Alan Bennett brilliantly dramatises the silent and secret exchange of reading in his witty novella *The Uncommon Reader*.[9] (The title is a teasing allusion to Virginia Woolf's *The Common Reader*.) In Bennett's story, the Queen is trying to bring the unruly royal corgis to heel and comes across a mobile library at the back of Buckingham Palace, unaware that it visited. She apologises to the driver-librarian for the dogs' barking and then feels that it would be impolite not to avail herself of a book. She is not a reader and selects an Ivy Compton-Burnett, remembering that she made her a dame. She returns the book the following Wednesday:

> 'How did you find it, ma'am,' asked Mr Hutchings.
> 'Dame Ivy? A little dry. . . '
> '. . . How far did your Majesty get?'
> 'Oh, to the end. Once I start a book I finish it. That was the way one was brought up. Books, bread and butter, mashed potato – one finishes what's on one's plate.'[10]

Once her reading habit is established, the nation is on a slippery slope, but I would not want to spoil the ending for those who have not yet read the book.

Although an entertaining farce, Bennett's tale provides succinct insights into what reading is – and does – for one woman. The Royal Household, especially her private secretary Sir Kevin, is deeply suspicious of the Queen's new passion, while she regrets not having read works by the many writers she has met including John Masefield, Walter de la Mare, T.S. Eliot, J.B. Priestley, Philip Larkin and 'even Ted Hughes'. She makes the mistake of mentioning this to Sir Kevin. ' "But ma'am must have been briefed, surely?" "Of course," said the Queen, "but briefing is not reading. In fact it is the antithesis of reading. Briefing is terse, factual and to the point. Reading is untidy, discursive and perpetually inviting. Briefing closes down a subject, reading opens it up." '[11] The more she reads, the more penetrating the insights become:

The appeal of reading, she thought, lay in its indifference: there was something undeferring about literature. Books did not care who was reading them or whether one read them or not. All readers were equal, herself included. Literature, she thought, is a commonwealth; letters a republic. . . . All readers were equal, and this took her back to the beginning of her life. As a girl, one of her greatest thrills had been on VE night when she and her sister had slipped out of the gates and mingled with the crowds. There was something of that, she felt, to reading. It was anonymous; it was shared; it was common. And she who had led a life apart now found that she craved it. Here in these pages and between these covers she could go unrecognised.[12]

In *The Uncommon Reader* the Queen is cast as rebellious because she finds a private space which is paradoxically and in her own words (or Bennett's) 'common'. She is part of a community of readers and writers and no longer the isolated monarch positioned above the rest. Time and again, women have expressed similar ideas in relation to the experience of community provided by their reading.

Bennett's protagonist recognises that the magic of a book lies not simply in itself but in the conjuring powers of the reader. The philosopher Hans-Georg Gadamer, in his essay 'On the Problem of Self-Understanding', puts it this way: 'The understanding of a text has not begun at all as long as the text remains mute. But a text can begin to speak.'[13] To be a reader, whether a woman or a man, you need to be literate and have access to the written word. But beyond these, and if you are to begin to get something back from a more complex work, you need to be able to enter into a conversation with what you are reading. The text needs to be allowed to 'begin to speak', and you need to allow yourself to answer. Reading comes to life in an act of engagement. It involves an individual consciousness with particular knowledge, experience, and a unique make-up engaging with writing at a particular time, in a particular place, in a particular mood.

Nor can one really force someone to read in a particular way. One cannot ensure that someone, simply by reading, will take seriously material in which they do not believe or do not want to believe. This makes the history of reading a complex one and distinct from other related areas such as the histories of the book, libraries, printing and publishing, education, and so on. As the eighteenth-century writer Georg C. Lichtenberg baldly stated, 'A book is a mirror: when a monkey looks in, no apostle can look out', or as the nineteenth-century writer and moralist Ralph Waldo Emerson put it more succinctly, ' 'Tis the good reader that makes the good book'.[14] When Ovid was sent into exile from Rome, in part because he was accused of writing material unsuitable for women readers, his defence was similar: 'But it is not a crime to unroll tender verse. Chaste women may read of many things which they may not do.' In other words, morally upright women readers will not be corrupted by their reading or encouraged to behave improperly. Discussions of foolish and wise readers, or of good (with moral overtones intended) and bad readers, have concerned women a great deal more than men from virtually the very beginning of the history of reading, and have spawned a diverse range of literary and visual representations.

In Edmund Spenser's *Faerie Queene* (1590) we come face-to-face with a female monster, half-woman, half-serpent, 'Most loathsome, filthie, foule, and full of vile disdaine'.[15] She battles against the noble Redcrosse Knight, and vomits a mixture of books, papers, frogs and toads – an extraordinary image of the dangerous effect of indiscriminate and indigestible reading. Of course this monstrous figure is a metaphor for what Spenser saw as the dangers of an unregulated printing industry, spreading misunderstanding, alarm and confusion among its readership, both female and male. And yet it serves as one of the myriad potent images discouraging the woman reader from exploration and experimentation.

Blatantly misogynist tracts continued to be published well into the seventeenth century and women who read these works often took up the pen to refute them. One of the last of these overtly woman-baiting compositions was Jacques Olivier's seventeenth-century *Alphabet of the Imperfection and Malice of Women*, which provides an unpleasant female attribute as a gloss for every letter of the alphabet. The entries are in Latin, followed by a French translation: 'Advissimum animal, animal très avide [rapacious animal]; Bestiale baratrum, abîme de bêtise [abyss of stupidity]; Concupiscentia carnis, concupiscence de la chair [lust of the flesh]; Duellum damnosum, duel dommageable [harmful duel]', and so forth. The book went into seventeen editions and was translated into English in 1662 by an anonymous author.[16] Thereafter women were much less likely to read such exaggerated and explicit condemnation of their sex.

Women readers and intellectuals, however, had been vilified in the ancient world and this deep prejudice continued. When girls have had the opportunity of education there have been subtle ways of discouraging serious reading. One was to promote an image of the serious woman reader as manly, androgynous, or simply unattractive. This goes back a very long way. The Roman historian Sallust (86 BC–35 BC) condemned learned women. He described the noblewoman Sempronia as 'well read in Greek and Latin literature' and associated this with her 'masculine' daring and promiscuity: 'her desires were so ardent that she sought men more often than she was sought by them'. A little later, the Roman poet Juvenal revealed how male pride can easily be knocked by educated women: 'I loathe the woman ... who quotes lines I've never heard'. Some women have pointed out the absurdity of all this and often with considerable humour. The writer Elizabeth Asquith Bibesco was forthright: 'You don't have to signal a social conscience by looking like a frump. . . . You can ban the bomb in a feather boa just as well as without, and a mild interest in the length of hemlines doesn't necessarily disqualify you from reading *Das Kapital* and agreeing with every word.'[17]

Once women were reading in significant numbers – and this is true across cultures – reading material telling them how to behave appeared more or less simultaneously. The 'conduct book', which first appeared in the sixteenth century, advised women how to be spiritually acceptable, good wives, perfect mothers, managers of the household, and so on. But we also have plenty of evidence in the form of letters and literary works, in particular, that some women were not having any of it. There are wonderful parodies of the conduct book written by women. Jane Collier's mock advice manual, *An Essay on the Art of Ingeniously Tormenting* (1753), brilliantly satirises the conduct book by offering advice on how to be a totally infuriating wife and intolerable employer.[18]

Collier's real interest is in unequal relationships and how dependants can be abused. The 'how-tos' of her book are ingenious. If you have a friend whom you want to annoy, for example, Collier suggests that you make it unpleasant for her to be with you, while 'upbraiding' her for avoiding you. Tell her the 'spiteful stories' you have heard, she advises, while of course claiming not to believe them. Collier parodies the conduct book but also exposes how easy it is for those in a position of authority – mostly men – to make life wretched for others, be they women or servants.

Other forms of advice books were volumes of sermons which were particularly popular in the eighteenth century. Dr James Fordyce's *Sermons to Young Women* (1766) was a famous two-volume compendium of sermons compiled by a tedious Scottish clergyman, which encouraged female subjugation and a feminine manner of speech, action and appearance.[19] They appeared at a time when debates about what constituted moral and immoral reading for women were particularly rife: what would have a positive effect on women's behaviour, and what a negative effect? That some women did not take *Fordyce's Sermons* seriously – if they ever had – is suggested in Jane Austen's *Pride and Prejudice* (1813), where Mr Collins, the buffoonish clergyman, selects them for reading aloud to his young female cousins. Lydia Bennet cannot bear to hear another word and interrupts the sanctimonious Mr Collins in full flow.

Austen's satirical point is characteristically succinct. She was a great admirer of the Irish writer and Whig politician Richard Sheridan who, in his

1775 comedy *The Rivals*, had invented the wonderful Lydia Languish who reads nothing but romantic fiction when she can lay her hands on it. Austen must surely have chosen her 'Lydia' as a tribute to Sheridan. In his play Sheridan repeatedly alludes to Lydia's addiction to the Local Lending Library, an obvious sign of her unharnessed erotic appetites. The headstrong Lydia wants nothing whatever to do with the morally edifying works (including *Fordyce's Sermons*, this time less than ten years after their publication) that her elders put her way. At one point, hearing them about to breach the relative sanctuary of her boudoir, she addresses her maid excitedly:

> Here, my dear Lucy, hide these books. Quick, quick – Fling *Peregrine Pickle* under the toilet – throw *Roderick Random* into the closet – put *The Innocent Adulterer* into *The Whole Duty of Man* – thrust *Lord Aimworth* under the sofa – cram *Ovid* behind the bolster – there – put *The Man of Feeling* into your pocket, so so – now lay *Mrs Chapone* in sight, and leave *Fordyce's Sermons* open on the table.[20]

The *frisson* of nearly being caught in the act itself becomes a source of mild erotic excitement for the audience. The elders, the potential voyeurs, then enter the stage and the scene is one of apparently serene compliance with their prescribed order; Sheridan has ensured that the audience, on the other hand, is delightedly in the know. *The Rivals* dramatises how, where, what and with whom women read.

Throughout the history of women's reading there are colourful examples of women who were not prepared to toe the line. Marie Anne de Vichy-Chamrond, later marquise du Deffand (1706–49), like most of her contemporary female compatriots, was educated at a convent school.[21] Here she preached irreligion to her classmates. The abbess, somewhat in desperation, sent for the then-celebrated and very pious Jean Baptiste Massillon. The abbess's hope was that the learned bishop would be able to offer advice as to what the rebellious child should be given as appropriate reading to tame her. The bishop and the schoolgirl conversed in private for some time while the abbess waited impatiently. When the bishop finally emerged, the famous saviour of souls said only, 'She's delightful'. When pressed by the abbess about suitable reading to convert the dangerous force corrupting her convent, the bishop simply suggested 'a cheap catechism'. As an adult Mme du Deffand read widely and educated herself in literature, history and mathematics with the help of several hired tutors. She maintained a prolific correspondence with numerous famous men, exchanging some 840 letters with the English dandy, politician and man of letters, Horace Walpole. She also corresponded regularly with the sceptical French philosopher Voltaire. In one letter, late in her life, she asks Voltaire for reading material: 'Send me, sir, a few trifles to read, but nothing about the prophets: everything they predicted I assume to have happened already.' At the end of her life Mme du Deffand gave religion another go, hoping that it might bring solace as it seemed to do for many of her friends. She had her maid read her St Paul's epistles but grew impatient with the apostle's style, finally interrupting to ask, 'Can *you* make head or tail of it?' She did allow a father confessor into her house when she was dying, but with strict instructions: 'Father, you must be very pleased with me; but I ask of you just three things: no questions, no reasons, no sermons.' Mme du Deffand was from a noble family. She was married off by her parents against her will but was able to separate from her husband in 1722. She knew her own mind, and read what she wanted, when she wanted, and according to her own lights.

Nora Barnacle – the name could so easily be a fictional invention – was James Joyce's wife.[22] She represents a rather different kind of woman reader, one who refused to read material that she might well have felt obliged to read. The Joyces spent a great deal of time apart, he in Dublin, she in Trieste, Italy, where they usually lived. Like so many women readers from antiquity to the present day, she was as good as obliged to read her husband's letters. These are more than a little prying, sometimes dwelling on Joyce's interest in slightly soiled women's underwear and his scatological-erotic interests, or delving into Nora's experience of sexual abuse as a girl. One wonders as to Nora's reaction, given that she was constrained to read the correspondence for the practical information within it. Nora once described Joyce as 'a fanatic' and she never bothered to read one of Europe's greatest modern novels, her husband's *Ulysses*. She may have had to read his letters, but she clearly felt under no obligation to read the fiction for which she had been repeatedly asked to provide sordid autobiographical detail. Women have always resisted reading material they have not wanted to read, and have withstood being persuaded by it.

From ancient times on, when not altogether convinced or charmed by their reading, some women readers have been prompted to write, modifying a vision or proposing a radically different one. Some of the most fascinating traces of women's reading are in their rewritings, often of works by men. Early on we find only a lucky few who were both literate and in a position to write – often a queen, a princess, or a woman living in a religious community. But even when and where women had been fortunate enough to receive an education, there were specific reasons preventing them entering the public domain as writers. In early modern England, for example, there was a clear association between speaking publicly or writing, and harlotry. Women were brought up to inhabit a sphere of domestic piety. Silence – as opposed to speech and other forms of self-expression – was promoted as a feminine ideal. More subtly but quite as crucially, the mastery of rhetoric was regarded as first and foremost a male puberty rite. But some women found ways to make their thoughts known and left writings to be read by their sons and daughters. These works were known as 'mothers' legacies' and were particularly popular in the seventeenth century. They were sometimes written during pregnancy when women naturally feared for their lives, and as such they assumed much of the form and style of a last will and testament. They were seen as essentially private documents and so were generally deemed to be an acceptable form of women's writing. Elizabeth Grymeston wrote her *Miscelanae, Meditations, Memoratives* in 1604, explaining: 'I resolved to break the barren soile of my fruitless braine, to dictate something for thy direction, the rather for that as I am now a dead woman among the living'. In a similar vein Elizabeth Joceline wrote *The Mothers Legacie to her Unborn Child* in 1624: 'I could not chuse but manifest this desire in writing . . . lest it should please God to deprive me time to speak'.[23] Legacies were one of the earliest forms of writing that women could acceptably author, and no doubt one of the most moving kinds of reading for daughters and sons, particularly if their mother died in childbirth.

Examples of a diverse range of real women readers from different periods and living within different cultures are a major part of this story. The woman reader is not a single type but distinguished by her individual experience, her social and economic position, and so much more. And what is read is a unique tangible object: a particular edition with a particular typeface and even a distinctive smell. It may have been a gift and maintain a certain sentimental value, or a prize, or stolen. And all this affects the reading and re-reading of it.

But the woman reader is not only a reality. She is also a striking invention of the male imagination, a crucial aspect of men's desire to worship or condemn the mysteries of the 'opposite sex'. For a long time the woman reader was more often an idea or a symbolic construct rather than real, during stretches of history when few, if any, women were literate. At the same time men's visual representations of women reading have had a profound but to some degree incalculable effect on women readers, serving either as an encouragement to read or an alarming warning against reading. The visual legacy is a vivid reminder of the myriad role models offered to woman readers.[24] And the history of this legacy in the fine arts is much more intriguing than its male counterpart. Men have generally enjoyed greater freedoms, a consequence being that their reactions to reading have (allegedly) been more cerebral and less psychologically charged. So it is that the iconography of the male reader is less complex and loaded. Women (and for that matter, men) have not shown much interest in the male reader: he is by no means as beguiling as the woman reader. By and large the book or other document he holds alerts the viewer to the man's religious or scholarly seriousness, his profession, his status – and not much else. Images of women reading are more numerous, more varied and often more enigmatic. They may conjure an aura of piety, virtue, maternal responsibility, privilege, luxury, scholarly learning or social status. But they may also be richly suggestive of idle leisure, frivolity or erotic temptation.

The dominant image of the woman reader in the Western tradition, based on work by male artists, is of the Virgin Mary with a book, often at the scene of the Annunciation. The Italian Renaissance was the high point for images of this kind, which encourage pious reading and submission to scripture.

In Simone Martini's fourteenth-century painting Mary appears timid. She has been interrupted in her reading and the way in which she is holding her book to mark her place is delightfully familiar. Artists continue to seek to represent this extraordinary scene, so central to the Christian story.

1 *The Annunciation and Two Saints* by Simone Martini, 1333. Mary's reading has been interrupted, but although her posture suggests that she has been startled, she has not lost her place in her book.

2 In *The Annunciation* by John Collier, Mary could be a suburban schoolgirl but the lilies, symbolising purity, and the winged Gabriel (here resembling a Catholic priest) belong to tradition.

John Collier depicts Mary as an unprecocious teenager, surprised but attentive to the messenger. She has not altogether dropped her guard and her book is held up as something of a shield. Annunciation images show Mary acceding to an absurd request: to be the mother of God. It is an image of the wholly submissive woman reader, agreeing to do as she is told.

At the opposite extreme is the image of the woman reader reading for pleasure, a surprisingly recent idea, emerging only in the mid-seventeenth century. Pierre Antoine Baudouin's *The Reader* (*c.* 1760) is richly suggestive of precisely what that pleasure might be. The painting is both risqué – the woman's right hand is under her skirts and between her legs – and with this, mildly peepshow-erotic. The viewer is a voyeur, looking in on the woman in her private and sumptuously decorated boudoir. She has fallen into a swoon

3 Pierre-Antoine Baudouin's *The Reader*, c. 1760. Here the boudoir is unambiguously a place where a woman can enjoy reading in private.

and has cast aside the book in her left hand. In contrast to the large, learned tomes beside the globe on the side-table, her reading is of a small volume, presumably a novel. Women's interest in the novel and the idea of sexual self-sufficiency were sometimes, alarmingly, considered to be related.

Paintings of women readers by women artists make for interesting comparisons. As early as 1554, Sofonisba Anguissola (*c.* 1535–1625) painted a self-portrait in which she holds a small book in her hand.

Sofonisba was unusual in many ways: she was well educated and enjoyed much more encouragement and intellectual support than the average woman of her day. However, she was unable to follow the kind of training open to her male counterparts, which included anatomy and life drawing. Her most celebrated works were her portraits, including many self-portraits, and the straightforwardness and relative informality of her paintings were distinctive. In this one she holds an open book and the page reads, 'I Sophonisba, a virgin, made this, 1554' – a forthright declaration of her authorship.

Among the most beautiful and complex images of women readers are those by the turn-of-the-century Welsh painter Gwen John. Her extensive series of

4 Sofonisba Anguissola, *Self-Portrait*, 1554. The book's small size indicates that it is a devotional work, or possibly a book of love sonnets like those by Petrarch. Either would have been appropriate reading material for a woman of her social standing.

5 Gwen John, *The Precious Book*, *c.* 1926. John captures the unique combination of relaxation and attentiveness that reading stimulates.

paintings of women with books draws on a long tradition and can be seen as something of a crystallisation of the iconography of the serious woman reader. No other woman artist has engaged with the subject of the woman reader so obsessively as to suggest desperation. The sequence of closely related paintings is disturbing; one senses an urgency, an almost manic desire to get something absolutely right but which fails each time, compelling another attempt. The reading matter is placed centre-stage in a still, subtly toned and textured composition: the real drama is in the unfathomable act of intimate encounter between woman and written materials.

The Precious Book is a tantalising title for a painting in which reading is the focus of attention. What confronts the viewer first and foremost is the question of what is being read, what has been read and what will be – there is another book on the table at her side. Is this woman's reading a means of imaginative escape, or distraction? Is it devotional, as the reverent atmosphere and cloth covering her hands might suggest – or is that simply a napkin? The point is that the image cannot be read in the relatively straightforward way that was possible with earlier genre paintings. And ambiguity, variety and richness, as the novelist Elizabeth Hardwick put it, characterise modern women's reading experiences: 'The greatest gift is the passion for reading. It is cheap, it consoles, it distracts, it excites, it gives you knowledge of the world and experience of a wide kind. It is a moral illumination.' All this is beautifully and subtly suggested in Gwen John's magnificent paintings.

Images of women readers give us some insights into the story, but we know about the history of women's reading from a wide range of sources: from ancient inscriptions and tablets, paintings and cartoons, literature and letters, library catalogues and the evidence of wills and dedications, and much more. Had it not been for the existence of a number of histories of reading (men and women's), particularly those by Alberto Manguel and Steven Roger Fischer, both entitled *A History of Reading*, and *A History of Reading in the West*, a collection of essays edited by Guglielmo Cavallo and Roger Chartier, I would not have had the nerve to work on what appeared to be fewer than half their stories. These three remarkable works include references to the woman reader, of course, but sometimes there is no way of knowing whether 'the reader' is a man or a woman. These books provided fascinating insights and essential maps of various areas, but there were more obscure regions that also called out to be explored. Robert Darnton's works, including *The Forbidden Best-Sellers of Pre-Revolutionary France*, as well as Kate Flint's *The Woman Reader, 1837–1914*, Paul Saenger's chapter 'Reading in the Later Middle Ages' in Cavallo and Chartier's aforementioned book, and David Vincent's *The Rise of Mass Literacy* are all important scholarly works that have proved an inspiration. The newly published *Oxford Companion to the Book* is a remarkable reference work and I wish it had come out before the final stages of writing this history. There are many more books, articles and databases on which I have drawn and which I include in the Endnotes. But there is no history of women's reading to date and, as Walter Benjamin famously declared, we write the books that we write because we cannot find them elsewhere.

Previous histories are, naturally, highly selective. Any comprehensive history, were such a thing possible, would run to innumerable volumes and in its scope would be virtually unreadable. This history is equally selective but it aims to do a slightly different job. In choosing material I have tried to provide typical as well as unusual examples of women readers so as to sketch some sort of overall geography. I have included telling vignettes of individual and quirky women readers too. But the availability of research on and about women's reading remains patchy, and a large proportion of book history, or that of publishing, or libraries, does not distinguish between male and female readerships. As reading is by and large a private, even secret experience, records of reading provide a diverse but not altogether straightforward pool of historical information. So while I have proceeded with a method, serendipity has also played a part and I have come across material about women's reading in all manner of unexpected places. Absence of hard data on women's reading, particularly in the early periods, has led to a good deal of conjecture and to more or less plausible hypotheses. These themselves are not wholly without relevance to the history of women's reading and some I have included.

Proust claimed, 'In reality every reader is, while he is reading, the reader of his own self. The writer's work is merely a kind of optical instrument which he offers to the reader to enable him to discern what, without this book, he would perhaps never have perceived in himself.'[25] Proust was of course referring both to male and female readers and it is this kind of self-discovery that gradually asserts itself over time. In the modern period much reading may be practical or 'easy', such as that done while navigating the Internet, or reading escapist fiction. But difficult reading goes on too, drawing us into challenging or disconcerting conversations with our inner selves, but helping us to make some sense of what we, and life, are about.

It is this sort of engagement that so many readers have wanted to encourage in others and into which so many readers have sought to enfranchise others. In 1923, the American writer Jesse Lee Bennett wrote a guide to reading with the somewhat worthy title, *What Books Can Do for You: A Sketch Map of the Frontiers of Knowledge, with Lists of Selected Books*. Not surprisingly, it has long been out of print, but it articulates a belief in the power of books, a belief that many still hold even as countless other media for learning about the self and the world now compete with, or complement, reading. Her idea was to provide 'a guide to books which can give such a realistic understanding of the essentials of knowledge as will permit the individual to adapt himself more happily and satisfactorily to life because he will have gained new understanding of life and of himself.' 'Books', she claimed in wonderfully outdated poetic language, 'are the compasses and telescopes and sextants and charts which other men have prepared to help us navigate the dangerous seas of human life.'[26] By 'men', she no doubt meant 'men and women'.

CHAPTER 1

⟨⟨⟨⟩⟩⟩

Primitives, Goddesses and Aristocrats

THE very earliest 'reading' of man-made markings was of those on cave walls, and notches on sticks and bones. And the making of these images, in relation to women and men, may have been different from the start. Were women as much involved in creating them – and 'reading' them – as men?

As image-making is a sign of sophistication in primitive peoples, providing a record of life beyond immediate survival in real time, the degree to which women may have participated is bound up with the possible status of women within these most remote human societies. Archaeologists' discussions about who made these images may to some extent be rooted in their desire to confirm or refute the idea that men and women have lived differently from the very beginning of time. Prejudices and anachronistic assumptions based on gender relations among later peoples may also play a part. And when the transition from image-making to writing occurs, women's involvement or exclusion is often assumed to be a litmus test of women's position within a society and therefore a key and contested subject.

The most ancient images are hand and foot prints and representations of animals and people. The archaeologists who first discover these describe their feelings of awe, sensing a remote but tangible connectedness with peoples of our most distant past. French caves in the Ariège region of south-west France, on the edge of the Pyrenees, were used as burial chambers for men, women and children, and date from 30,000 BC. In one cave the skeletons of a man and woman have been found entwined. The paintings and markings in the famous Lascaux caves date from roughly 28,000 BC. In those caves where conditions have allowed, human markings, mostly hand and foot prints, have survived covering the entire surface of the cave wall up to four metres in height, which would have necessitated a ladder of some description or, less likely, feats of remarkable group acrobatics. We know from the sizes of the hand and foot prints that men, women and children were all involved in this image-making activity. There have been claims that the images of hunters with their weapons, for example, are the work of men, and the animals the work of women. There is little real proof, simply speculation based on anthropological comparisons with other later primitive peoples.[1]

There are striking depictions of pregnant women as well as animals. A woman's footprint has been identified in the highly decorated cave called Pech Merle, near Cabrerets. A grave in the Dordogne called 'L'Abri du Cap Blanc' contains the remains of a female skeleton and the walls surrounding her are covered in images of animals and symbols, the latter bearing striking resemblance to images on later Neolithic pottery which was certainly the work of women. Not dissimilar symbols can be found among tribes south of the Sahara, and among the so-called Amerindians. There is a reverence in the depictions of animals that differentiates them from the images of animals in hunting scenes; some depictions of male bison (often associated with

6 Silhouette of a woman, perhaps after childbirth, found in the Cussac Cave, Dordogne, France. The images and bones discovered here could be 28,000 years old.

virility and strength) when not being hunted show a creature both calm and gentle.[2] But there is nothing to prove that these differences mean the images were made by men or by women, or, further, to suggest that men and women's roles were fundamentally different, or their vision of things distinct, however tempting it might be.

In any case, cave art made and 'read' by Palaeolithic peoples has survived across time and we are able to 'read' it, to wonder at it and to speculate about its makers' world-view – but all this through a glass darkly. In terms of women's reading what is striking is the liveliness of the archaeological debate about the extent to which men and women might have been involved, despite having so very little to go on. The mysteries of creating and reading images, and men's and women's participation, raise crucial questions, so far largely unanswered, which set the scene for the history of women's reading – and men's attitude towards it.

The process of decoding images is highly significant in terms of human intellectual development and clearly separates us from the animals. A key feature is a shift in the relationship with time. He – or she – now has the capacity to operate both in the here-and-now, and better to imagine, contemplate, record, plan or hallow. In other words, notions of a present, past and future become real. But what exactly is this process of 'decoding', or mentally identifying the 'real' thing evoked by the image? And how is this process related to reading?[3] We know that the Neanderthals, early *Homo sapiens* and primitive peoples read notches on bones that meant something to them. Primitive man also read more complicated picture messages on bark and leather. The Incas read detailed colour-coded quipus knots as evidence of trade deals and the ancient Polynesians used string-and-notch records to keep track of the generations. All these systems require the reading of a conventional symbol in order to understand events (the hunting scenes in cave paintings), number values (as in different shapes of notch in a tally), or names (in notches or strings).

But true reading, as opposed to looking at or viewing, generally means making sense of a more complex *sequence* of meaningful signs. These functions as the graphic representation of human speech or thought. This kind of 'complete reading' was a remarkably long time in coming. And the reading of long works of poetry and prose, as opposed to records of deals done, or agreements set down to last across time, comes much later. Our notion of being blissfully 'lost' in a book which, as we read – and even for breaks in between – may seem more real than reality itself, comes later still. That the characters' lives, their loves and fears may seem more important than our own, is a very recent phenomenon, relatively speaking.

The process that turned fragmentary signs into a continuous system that functioned as a substitute for speech, occurred in stages. There are a few markers along the way: in ancient Mesopotamia, fragmentary pictograms became both standardised and, crucially, abstract, while retaining their phonetic value. The big shift happened when a sign was interpreted exclusively for its *sound* within a *standardised system of signs*. Whole texts could suddenly be read, not as isolated words carrying a one-to-one relationship between sound and object, but as a logical sequencing which replicated human speech. Reading no longer had to do with pictures, but with the representation of oral language. This key shift, of such fundamental importance to human development, happened in Mesopotamia only some 6,000 years ago. The idea of producing standardised conventions to stand for the sounds of human speech spread west to the Nile and east to the Indus (in today's Pakistan), where different languages and different kinds of societies demanded different graphic expressions.

Rockall, Dogger, German Bight: the mysterious names that are broadcast on BBC Radio 4's Shipping Forecast whisk us off on an imagined and perilous sea voyage around the British Isles. Although some areas are known and could readily be identified on a map, others remain familiar but more fictional than real. The names of the world's ancient languages, likewise, bring us into direct but strange contact with the peoples and places of our distant past. Some of these languages are relatively familiar to us because we know a little of their cultures: Ancient Egyptian, Hebrew, Phoenician, Aramaic, Attic Greek, Old Persian, Latin, Ancient Chinese and Old Tamil. Others are less well-known: Elamite, Hurrian, Urartian, Akkadian, Ugaritic, Ge'ez, Hittite, Luvian, Middle Indic and so many more. It is only because these languages exist in written form that they are known to us at all; more mysterious are the languages that remain undeciphered and wholly impenetrable. The earliest is known as Proto-Elamite and is from the fourth millennium BC. We may never discover whether women were literate in this language. But we do know that some women were fully involved in certain literary activities from the very beginning of human history.

Reading and writing first emerged in the late fourth millennium BC in the context of temple bureaucracies in the towns and cities in southern Mesopotamia, now southern Iraq.[4] A very small number of accountants used word and number signs to record assets: land, labour and, most importantly, animals. They wrote on small clay tablets about the size of a cigarette packet. By the third millennium BC accountants were joined by scribes and writing expanded to include records of legal transactions. But across the next thousand years much more exciting material also started to be written down – and read. This includes dramatic tales of political events and hymns to the deities who were often women. And there were authors too, who drew on their imaginations and depended on the scribes.

Remarkably, the first author we know of to sign a work was a woman. Princess Enheduanna was the daughter of the great Sargon of Akkad in Mesopotamia. She was born around 2300 BC and was high priestess of Nanna the moon god and, in effect, the earliest poetess in human history. Over a period of forty turbulent and warring years she established her position as holder of the most important religious office in ancient Sumer. A large number of compositions have been attributed to her, many dedicated to the sacred temples, their occupants, and the deities to whom they were consecrated.[5] One of the curiosities of her hymns is that some are written in the third person but others in the first – the voice of the poetess herself – and this sets them apart from works likely to have been authored by men. Enheduanna read or listened to hymns in the votive tradition and she responded to them in innovatory ways. There are three hymns to Nanna and three others to Inanna, Enheduanna's personal goddess. One of these, 'The Exaltation of Inanna', has been collated from around fifty clay tablets and 153 lines restored. This is remarkably extensive and complete evidence compared with what little we have of Sappho, for instance, who comes more than sixteen centuries later.

'The Exaltation of Inanna' is a hymn to the goddess Inanna which celebrates her many attributes, and makes intriguing, albeit obscure, allusions to Enheduanna herself. Within the Sumerian tradition, Inanna is usually praised for her feminine qualities. But Enheduanna casts her as a goddess of war, as well as of love and fertility as was the convention. Feminine and masculine qualities are combined, and in one striking image Inanna is likened to a great bird, swooping down to scare away the lesser gods. The hymn then continues as the poetess's own account of her past triumphs and present difficulties. As high priestess she has been sent into temporary exile from Uruk as a result of the actions of Lugalanne, possibly her brother-in-law. She begs for help to crush a rebellion against her father, Sargon. Under the leadership of Lugalanne, the rebels have destroyed the temple of Eanna, one of the greatest in the ancient world. Lugalanne has also dared to claim he is her equal. Furthermore, in what must be the earliest written accusation of sexual harassment, Enheduanna describes the inappropriate advances that he has made towards her: 'He has wiped his spit-soaked hand/ on my honey-sweet mouth'. Lugalanne has also threatened her with a ritual dagger (such as was sometimes used to castrate priests) and he tells her, 'it becomes you'. The symbolism of the dagger is two-fold: as an instrument of castration it mocks Enheduanna's loss of power, and as a phallic symbol it may also suggest that she has been raped.[6] She remains determined not to submit and begs the goddess to overthrow her usurper and abuser: 'O my divine ecstatic wild cow/ drive this man out/ hunt him down/ catch him'. She appeals to her as it is she who 'crush[es] rebellious lands . . ./ smash[es] heads' and 'gorge[s] on corpses like a dog'. By the end of the poem Enheduanna has triumphed: 'the holy heart/ of Inanna/ returns to her'.[7]

The precise nature of Enheduanna's literacy remains a vexed question, as is the distinction between written and oral literature generally in Mesopotamia. By the middle of the second millennium, poems, like parts of the *Epic of Gilgamesh*, were being composed by literate people in a scholarly environment. But whether Enheduanna wrote her poems herself or a scribe or scribes worked with her is unknown. Kings of the period do occasionally boast that they can write, but this may have been a metaphorical literary conceit to do with authority and the permanence of the historical record. The question also arises whether we can sensibly talk about one person developing a poem and writing it down or dictating it to an individual scribe. A more persuasive picture is perhaps that a commission was given to a 'scribal school' or some other college of scribes to put together a series of Enheduanna's poems. But in any event what is ascribed to Enheduanna was written by her or others – to please her.

Whether or not she could read we cannot know. But the literary devices she exploits in her compositions draw on other Sumerian writings which she must have known. Her 'Exaltation' is highly structured and divided into three parts: an exhortium (or introduction), an argument, and a peroration (or forceful conclusion). Each part is made up of eighteen units, like a stanza, and most of these are three lines long. To have been able to compose as she did, Enheduanna must have been familiar with the literary conventions, including formal poetic structures, of her time. In this sense a link can be drawn between Enheduanna and women thousands of years later, who read or had read to them what was available and felt moved, as a result, to compose themselves. Their compositions sometimes refuted aspects of a tradition and presented something new, often relating to the supposed differences between the sexes and men and women's allegedly innate characteristics. In Enheduanna's case we can see the powerfully androgynous way that the goddess Inanna is portrayed. In one of her hymns, 'Lady of the Heart', Inanna delights in violence – 'fighting is her play/ she never tires of it' – and she 'goes about' to the tavern (or brothel). Her ultimate, all-consuming powers are summed up in the lines that describe her wearing 'the carved out ground plan/ of heaven and earth'. Not only is Enheduanna one of the earliest known composers of literary material, she was also devising characters which departed from the tradition. Her poems remain extremely unusual, not only because they are ascribed to a specific author, but also because of their striking originality. Enheduanna was a major literary influence for some 500 years.

Under the Akkadians, properly 'literary' writing appeared from around 2500 BC, but unlike the 'Exaltation', these are mostly unascribed. However, they do offer interesting insights into the position of women and the qualities sometimes associated with them, irrespective of their social position. In the main these literary pieces are hymns to the gods and goddesses, songs to the king, cult dirges and exorcisms of evil spirits. Others are myths which often bear striking resemblance to classical myths: one tells of the goddess Inanna's travels into the underworld, for example, not unlike the story of Persephone's descent into Hades. Other stories memorialise the divine order of the world and tell of Uruk's kings – Enmerkar, Lugalbanda and most famously, Gilgamesh. The role of women in this epic is striking.

There are a number of versions but each is essentially an adventure story and, in the telling, an exploration of some of the fundamental aspects of human life: the human propensity for ambition, the values of love and friendship, the experience of loss and the knowledge of our mortality. Gilgamesh is at once man, hero, king and god, and must discover how best to live and how best to prepare for death. In each version the basic structure is the same: Gilgamesh must leave Uruk, undertake a journey, experience trials, successes and failures, and then return home. In one version he loses his dearest friend, Enkidu, and despairs. He gives up all idea of achieving fame and sets out to discover the secret of immortality. It is a woman, a tavern-keeper, who tries to bring him to his senses:

> Gilgamesh, where are you hurrying to? You will never find that life for which you are looking. When the gods created man they allotted to him death, but life they retained in their own keeping. As for you, Gilgamesh, fill your belly with good things; day and night, night and day, dance and be merry, feast and rejoice. Let your clothes be fresh, bathe yourself in water, cherish the little child that holds your hand, and make your wife happy in your embrace; for this too is the lot of man.[8]

Gilgamesh's friend Enkidu, earlier in this version, was humanised by a prostitute, and here Gilgamesh is encouraged to accept normal life by a barmaid. Ordinary, even despised women represent good sense and extol the virtues of mundane life as opposed to the quest for heroism and immortality which flirts constantly with death.[9] Alongside hymns to goddesses are stories that tell of remarkable but humble women, which must have pleased the illiterate women who had these tales told to them or read aloud.

The early literary writings from this part of the world exist thanks to scribes. Who were they – and could one of them be our first identified woman reader? It is an intriguing question, and one that we can in fact answer. Records for the Babylonian city-state of Sippar between 1850 BC and 1550 BC include the names of its official scribes. In Mesopotamia scribes provided their writings with their own 'colophon', a unique inscription at the end of the document giving name, place of drafting, and the date. Of the 185 scribes who are named, fourteen were women. A further nine named scribes appear in a ration list (for oil) from the Mari palace in the same period. There is also a personnel list from the palace which mentions six female scribes employed there.[10] And as it is reasonable to assume that writers must have had at least a limited reading ability, one of these – the first of them to learn to write – is probably our first known woman reader.[11]

The training of professional scribes was rigorous. It began at the age of seven and continued until the age of eighteen. The day was long, beginning early and finishing in the late afternoon. In addition, schooling took up twenty-four days in every thirty. Pupils learned defunct Sumerian as well as their native Akkadian. They also studied history, mathematics, religious literature, and the drafting of legal contracts. The basis of the training was reading and writing but a good deal of the material was oral, as much of Babylon's factual knowledge and social ideology was never recorded in clay. Tablets have been discovered that allow us to understand that reading was taught through a simultaneous process of reading and writing. The teacher wrote a sign on one side of a small tablet, beginning with the smallest graphic fragments, and then showed it to the pupil who had to reproduce the same sign on the other side. Gradually signs were built up into words and finally into short proverbial sentences or lists of names, for example. In this way the memory was trained as literacy developed. The method was, of course, primarily visual rather than phonetic – the earliest incarnation of the reading method rediscovered by educationalists in eighteenth-century Europe, now known as 'whole-word recognition'.

We do not know whether girls attended scribal schools alongside boys, nor can we know on what basis the much smaller number of women became involved in the business of writing and reading. Perhaps they were highly intellectually gifted and so given access to education as exceptions to the rule. But the female scribe was not a wholly marginal phenomenon and the training of women must have demanded the investment of time by some schools. The women scribes may have worked at the same jobs, in the same manner, on the same terms, as their male counterparts. Such equality, if it existed, is a rare occurrence in the long and twisted tale of the woman reader.

Scribes were readers for the illiterate. They maintained responsibility for interpreting written records. Sumerian scribes often acted as arbiters of the law, with their interpretation of a written text settling disputes over accounts or some legal article. Scribes also functioned as notaries, accountants, archivists, secretaries and bureaucrats. But more interestingly, they also acted as paid readers, working for their non-literate patrons and superiors: an architect or an astronomer, a merchant, a shipper or a priest. Those who were gifted mathematicians became surveyors. Even those who showed little academic ability beyond their basic literacy could make a decent living as letter-writers and readers operating from market stalls. Literacy seems to us so fundamental to authority and power, and to all kinds of non-manual jobs that it is hard to understand a society in which the literate, including some women, were seen merely as servants or craftspeople in an otherwise almost exclusively oral culture. Oratory, rhetoric, wide knowledge (dependent on a highly trained memory): these were the prized intellectual qualities.

We also know that women scribes, like their male counterparts, were valued members of the community, performing an essential function. It was common for colophons to be followed by the maxim: 'Let the literate instruct the illiterate, for the illiterate may not see.'[12] Although the vast majority of early writing and reading was administrative, mostly to do with finances and the economy, scribes were also teachers, with all the power associated with that profession, and some of them may well have been women.[13] The deity responsible for the protection of scribes was not a god but a goddess, Nisaba. Her symbol or attribute was a stylus, suggesting that writing and recording were the scribe's primary activity. But the goddess Nisaba, along with the later Greek sibyls and Roman muses, are also to some degree abstractions, created by men's imaginings. Throughout the history of women's reading the real woman reader has lived alongside male fantasies of idealised literate women and sometimes, paradoxically, during periods when women's literacy was exceptional and discouraged.

The other important centre of civilisation in the Near East was Egypt. Here writers wrote on perishable papyrus paper, rather than clay tablets, so much has been lost. As elsewhere in the Near East the literary culture was above all oral; the written word was not an end in itself but a means to a practical end. But by around 2150 BC several categories of written text existed: contracts between individuals, laws, decrees and legal proceedings, letters and religious writings. Reading, as elsewhere in the ancient world, was very much a minority activity. In fact for most of the country's ancient history it is unlikely that more than 1 per cent of its population was literate. They were largely members of the elite and, unlike in Mesopotamia, they held specific administrative offices. There were, however, village scribes who were available to the illiterate 99 per cent. Very broadly speaking, one can contrast the freelance artisan-scribes of Mesopotamia, with the elite civil servants in ancient Egypt.[14]

It may be that because literacy was also associated with professional advancement it was more highly regarded in Egypt than in Mesopotamia and, perhaps, therefore an activity from which women were excluded. Young men were encouraged to read and write in the interests of preferment. The Egyptian bureaucrat Dua-Khety, writing to his son, advised him:

> Set your thoughts just on writings, for I have seen people saved by their labour. Behold, there is nothing greater than writings. They are like a boat on water. Let me teach you to love writing more than [you love] your mother. Let me encourage its beauty into your sight. For it is greater than any office. There is nothing like it on earth.[15]

Some scribes went on to become palace officials and ministers and thus took their places among the richest and most powerful men in ancient Egypt. Most, however, were mere subordinates carrying out the mundane business of the realm. In neither category, it seems, were there women; yet the relative dearth of what has survived of the vast ancient Egyptian administrative papyri trail means we can probably never be sure. What is left, apart from rare papyri, are the inscriptions in stone on and in temples, and on tombs and other monuments. These will have had few actual readers and none of them is likely to have been a woman. The inscriptions would have meant something symbolic to women, as signs to be revered, to be held in awe, to be mystified by – but not to be decoded, that is, read.

But Dua-Khety's letter does reveal how much women were respected and loved. Women in ancient Egypt, unlike elsewhere, had equal status and responsibilities in law. They were in charge of running the home and for the wealthy this meant directing numerous servants. The largest estates had male scribes, overseen by women, to keep inventories up to date. Women also served in the temple. They may not have been literate, but this did not mean, as so often in history, that they held inferior status, lacked authority, or were excluded from important areas of life. In the modern world we may associate illiteracy with forms of disenfranchisement and powerlessness. This was not invariably the case in the ancient world.

In the Middle East, thousands of clay tablets are still to be discovered. Many lie buried beneath miles of territory made inaccessible to archaeologists by war. But we know that a small number of women played a part in the early literacy of peoples in the region. These civilisations came to an end, and so did their libraries and, to a large degree, the practice of literacy itself. The rapid decline of the Assyrian Empire was probably due to civil war. There are no extant inscriptions after 640 BC. With the Greeks and Romans, on the other hand, their written cultures were to radiate far from their centres.[16]

The Greeks, like the Romans, recognised the power of writing long before literacy had been achieved by any save a tiny minority. The Greeks had been reading since around 2000 BC when the idea of syllabic writing arrived from Canaan. But it took a thousand years for people to develop a consonantal alphabet. These were descendants of the Canaanites, the Phoenicians. The Greek scribes of Cyprus developed a complete consonant and vowel alphabet like our own. To begin with this new system simply speeded up and tidied up – in the sense of making less ambiguous – the syllabic writing that had previously been used. The same material was produced: accounts, delivery notices and correspondence which were mainly written on skins. Then the idea of writing on other materials – vases, metals, potsherds (broken fragments of clay pots) – began to catch on and written pieces gradually became more extended and complex. But what did it mean 'to read' in Greek? And who were the chosen readers in a largely illiterate society?[17]

The Greek verb *anagignosko* meant 'I read' as well as 'I recognise' and, in Ionian Greek, 'I convince, I persuade (someone to do something)'. So the emphasis remained on spoken competence: the power of the enunciated word to hold sway, to exert power over another. The decisive moment, although primarily symbolic rather than pragmatic, came in the seventh century BC when laws started to be written in stone, a metaphor we still use today to refer to unchangeable authority. Laws became visible in public architecture, for all to see, but for few to read and understand. The primary purpose of the written word, however, as in Mesopotamia and Egypt, was to suggest the authority of the state, rather than to communicate details. Inscriptions, whether or not you could decode them, reeked of authority.

Before around 600 BC we know that very few Greeks could read. But as writing began to be used more and more, both in public places and in the decorative arts, so reading began to percolate through society. By *c.* 480 BC, possibly as many as 5 per cent of Greeks had attained a level of literacy, including slaves – and women. It may be that as many as one in ten Athenians could read with varying degrees of efficiency, although this is one of the more extravagant estimates. Some famous intellectuals viewed these changes with distrust and fear. Plato (428/427 BC–348/347 BC), for example, was only one of a significant number of ancient writers who regarded literacy with deep suspicion. In his *Phaedrus* he has Socrates declare: 'Every word [*logos*], when

once it is written, is bandied about, alike among those who understand it and those who have no interest in it, and it knows not to whom to speak or not to speak. ... When ill-treated or unjustly abused it [the *logos*] always needs its father to help it; for it has no power to protect or help itself.[18] For Plato, as for many other ancients, only 'spoken discourse' is the 'discourse of truth'. In part this is because the spoken word chooses its audience or interlocutors, and can respond to reactions, questions or attacks by explaining, elaborating or shifting its ground. Writing, on the other hand, exists without controls and cannot know who will deliver it or give it voice, or what meanings a reading will draw out. Every act of reading is an interpretation conditioned by the reader. This is the danger that Plato identified: readers can fundamentally *misread*, that is to say misinterpret, and miss the truth the author wanted tell. Women, as they gained access to literacy, were often treated with gra suspicion because they might 'misinterpret' their reading in their own int ests, and get ideas about assuming new powers within marriage, the famil in society more broadly.

The most famous and intriguing female literary figure from ancient Gr was Sappho and she was also an inspiration to other literary women formed a group around her.[19] Sappho composed her poetry in the cont an intimate circle of women friends whom she called 'companions' in poems, while in several late poems she speaks to a group of younger or girls whom she addresses as 'children', aware of their joyful and dancing in contrast to her own heaviness of heart and slowness movement, characteristic of old age.[20] She was born around 620 the ancients praised her in hyperbolic fashion, some regarding h tenth Muse. Hundreds of years after her death (which was around Strabo, the Greek Stoic scholar (*c*. 63/64 BC–*c*. AD 24) wrote, 'in t span of recorded time we know of no woman to challenge her even in the slightest degree'. In the medieval period, Christine de Sappho in her *Le Livre de la Cité des Dames* (*The Book of the Cit* as one of the eighteen – and the most ancient – proofs that we intellectually able as men.[21] In the early Renaissance, Raph Sappho in his painting of Parnassus; she is the only woman included aside from the subjugated and passive muses. Even 3 Sappho was most frequently named in a poll undertaken by *Gazette*, asking readers to name the twelve most import history.[22]

What Sappho knew of other literary work has to be inf writings as today we have only tantalising fragments of her ni side quotations and references to her in ancient authors, and

7 Detail of Sappho from Raphael's *Parnassus*, c. 1510.

papyrus and parchment copies, mostly from the Roman period. These limited remains number 264 fragments in modern editions but only sixty-three contain complete lines and only twenty-one contain complete verses. Just four poems have survived in sufficient completeness for us to have a real sense of Sapphic poetic structure.

Nevertheless what little we have of Sappho distinguishes itself from work by her male contemporaries, like Hesiod and Alcaeus. A distinctively feminine voice comes through. There is a striking emotional range, reservations about war and violence are expressed, and a powerful sense of individuality is voiced. Sappho's portrayal of women also departs from conventional traditions. Take fragment 16 about Helen of Troy's love of Paris: 'Some say an army of horsemen, some an army on foot/ and some say a fleet of ships is the loveliest sight/ ... but I say it is what-/ ever you desire'. Helen of Troy is

8 Remaining fragment of a poem by Sappho.

described by Sappho as desiring a man who was not her husband, and her passion is presented as more rational than men's passions for fleets of ships. On the other hand, the lyric poet and Sappho's contemporary, Alcaeus, wrote bluntly of Helen, 'But through Helen, the Trojans perished/ and all their city'.

Sappho continues to fascinate us because she is such an early literary figure; Homer's writing was not committed to the written record until some hundred years after her. But she also intrigues us for somewhat paradoxical reasons. Unlike many of her male contemporaries, and Homer most obviously, whose works remain as good as intact, Sappho is something of a clean slate onto which others can project, and have projected, myriad reconstructed images. And the echoes of Sappho in poets from Ovid to Baudelaire to T.S. Eliot create an extraordinarily rich afterlife for her across the millennia.[23] Perhaps one should go further and say that she has been used, re-invented, and even almost erased as a unique voice in others' subsequent readings of her. Infinitely more has been written eulogising her, dismissing her and speculating about her sexuality, than the written record we have of her in her own words.[24]

Catullus imitated her – a sure sign of respect. During the Renaissance, writers recorded the Church's public burnings of her writings. Mme de Scudéry was known as the 'French Sappho' and Katherine Philips was her English counterpart, allusions to their not-so-private lives. Attacking Lady Mary Wortley Montagu, Pope described her not only as a promiscuous Sappho but a syphilitic one into the bargain. But by the nineteenth century women were boldly reading Sappho as a feminist originator and Germaine de Staël, Caroline Norton and Christina Rossetti cited her as a role model. During the same period men read Sappho rather differently; Baudelaire and Swinburne saw her as a sadomasochistic and androgynous *femme fatale*.

The varying representation of women readers – both real and symbolic – begins very early. We can trace one interesting development as far back as the fifth century BC. The Etruscans had established a stable civilisation in northern Italy. Funerary design had been festive, including dancers and apparently realistic representations of married couples happily tucked up under bedclothes atop the tomb. But a period of extreme austerity seems to have changed the previously optimistic Etruscan world-view. This change is visible in a cinerary container carved soon after 400 BC.

The realistic female figure is no longer in the man's arms but now sits at the foot of a couch, and she is no longer the young man's wife; her wings indicate that she is the spirit of death, and she is reading a scroll, the record of the fate

9 An Etruscan funerary carving. The reading material – the small scroll held by the angel – immediately captures the viewer's attention.

of the deceased. The young man is reaching for the scroll as though to accept his fate: 'Behold my time has come, I go'. The happy wife accompanying her husband at the moment of death has been transformed into a symbolic representation of death. Literate Etruscans were aware of the power of reading: here, woman is cast as the reader and the conduit of fearful wisdom.

Literate women, and women who have contributed to the written record, have been controversial virtually from the beginnings of civilisation in ways that are not true of their male contemporaries. They have been ridiculed, criticised often in hyperbolic terms, and faced with denials that their genius was actually their own, while at the same time celebrated and heralded for their contributions. They have also been represented as erotically desirable. These extremes of reaction and invention are distinct from the parallel history of literary men. They are also considerably more intriguing.

The Romans read Sappho and other Greek authors for new insights into human life and human feeling. Reading had become more than a matter of practical utility (*utilitas*); like the Greeks, the Romans frequently referred to reading as a matter also of pleasure (*voluptas*). This great innovation in terms of reading in the ancient world had to do with the gradual rise of non-essential reading.

For an extraordinarily long time reading was an awkward business. For roughly the first three thousand years of reading, the 'book' would almost always have taken the form of deciphering words from a clay tablet or roll of papyrus. Innovations took place quite suddenly which significantly aided

10 Sarcophagus relief of a learned woman holding a scroll. The child is trying unsuccessfully to attract her attention.

readers. There was the dramatic invention, around the first century AD, of the *codex*, or bound volume of papyrus, which was relatively cheap to produce and which made surreptitious reading possible. Then vellum was introduced, which was much more durable than papyrus. From here it is only a relatively small step to the paperback hidden in the handbag.

In ancient Rome women could be more or less lucky in terms of their access to literacy once codices began to circulate. This varied greatly from one period to another, from place to place and from social group to social group. What we have to go on is patchy and sometimes contradictory. Girls from privileged families in the early republic learned to communicate lucidly, even elegantly, and were taught spinning, weaving and cookery. In wealthy homes at least, girls may well have shared their brother's tutors or have been tutored by their mother. Early unusual examples of educated women from the first century BC are Gracchi's mother Cornelia, and her daughter Sempronia.[25] Both of their educations were unusually extensive. This was a function of high social standing overruling the conventional restrictions placed on women. Given Cornelia's status as a member of a family of the highest nobility, maintaining family prestige was paramount and her education served this end. She is also the earliest known Roman patroness of literature and learning.

Cornelia's father was P. Cornelius Scipio Africanus Maior, famous above all for his victory over Hannibal. He was one of the very first Roman aristocrats to take Greek culture and learning seriously. He built up an extensive library of Greek works and Cornelia is the first known Roman woman to have been well-read in both Latin and Greek. She also ensured that her daughter, Sempronia, received a good education and she too read widely in both languages. Cornelia taught her two famous sons, Tiberius and Gaius – who would later both serve as tribunes – apparently without the help of any tutor in the early years. It may be that the education she gave her sons was idealised by authors of the republican and imperial periods who emphasised the intimacy of Cornelia's relationship with her sons and admired the fact that she had not handed them over to the care of others. One wrote, 'we have read the letters of Cornelia, mother of the Gracchi; they make it plain that her sons were nursed not less by their mother's speech than at her breast.' Because Cornelia knew Greek well she was able to choose the best possible tutor for them later on: 'Gracchus, thanks to the affectionate pains of his mother Cornelia, had been trained from boyhood and was thoroughly grounded in Greek letters. He had always enjoyed the instruction of Greek teachers carefully chosen [by his mother].'[26] Descriptions of Cornelia emphasise that her learning mattered first and foremost in relation to the education of her sons. She is an exemplary case of the acceptance of a woman reader in ancient Rome. Her reading is presented as having formed her moral training (her commitment to her husband and then her sons), shaped her approach to her maternal duties (as the carer and teacher of her children, particularly her sons), and as providing evidence of her social status. Nowhere is it suggested that her reading did anything other than to encourage her to be the kind of woman advocated by male-dominated Roman society.

There were writers, however, who wrote potentially more subversive material and very much with the woman reader in mind. At the turn of the millennium, Ovid (43 BC–AD 17/18) provides a very particular insight into the rise of the woman reader.[27] He was aware that a significant proportion of his audience were women and he responded with extraordinary sensitivity – and daring. In the *Metamorphoses*, his character Byblis is a symbolic figure, a frustrated woman writer who struggles to articulate and thereby understand her own experiences. She is tormented by an incestuous love for her brother Caunus, and equally by her incapacity faithfully to describe her tumultuous and insane passion. She writes her story on a wax tablet, but dissatisfied and frustrated, she rubs it out and rewrites it. The implication is that she is unable to find the words to describe her forbidden feelings. She can consummate her love neither verbally nor physically. Caunus is so disgusted by his sister's declaration of love that he leaves home to found a new city. Byblis follows him but fails to find her beloved brother. She sits down in a meadow and weeps. A nymph appears and turns her into a spring.

In Ovid's work, Byblis fails, but her struggle is a wonderful founding story of the woman writer-reader. It is a striking way of making concrete the idea that insightful reading and experience are locked together. We cannot read and understand experience that is wholly unknown to us, nor can we understand experiences for which we have no context. Byblis's story would have been heady stuff for the growing number of women readers and her tragic tale has inspired numerous and increasingly romanticised images across the centuries.

Another of Ovid's women characters, Philomela, must have been equally compelling. Her sister, Procne, marries Tereus and the two leave Philomela behind in Athens and return to his home in Thrace. Procne misses her sister greatly and later Tereus returns to Athens to collect her and bring her to visit Thrace. He had, however, and unbeknown to Procne, fallen madly in love with her sister. Before returning home he takes Philomela to a secluded cottage, rapes her and leaves her incarcerated there.

Philomela vowed to tell all of her abuse and so Tereus cut out her tongue at the root. He tells Procne that he arrived in Athens to discover that Philomela had died. The silenced Philomela turns to the ladylike pastime of weaving and, whilst in captivity, weaves the details of her terrible story into images in her cloth. The cloth finds its way to Procne who 'reads' her sister's woes. During the festival to celebrate Bacchus, Procne goes into the woods and manages to find her sister and take her home. Further violence ensues. What matters here is that Ovid once again dramatised the subject of women's need for free expression and their determination to tell their story against all the odds. Byblis attempts to express the inexpressible but fails to explain her feelings to her brother. Philomela, although rendered dumb, succeeds in telling her tale to her sister and, in the end, takes her revenge against her brother-in-law.

Some of Ovid's writing was explicitly produced for a female readership. His book on love, *Remedia amoris* (*Love's Remedy*), is a parody of that genre of books that still dominates the self-help section of any bookshop. His *Medicamina faciei femineae* (*Women's Facial Cosmetics*), similarly, is in essence a make-up manual for women, another popular and resilient genre. The third book of his, *Ars Amatoria* (*The Art of Love*), is addressed to women and includes advice to read the poets.

When Ovid was exiled from Rome he wrote some remarkable poems exploring the consequences of how his writings had been received in the city.[28] In one of the *Tristia* (*Sorrows* or *Lamentations*) he complains that his *carmen* (songs) – which have proved popular with both men and women – influenced Caesar's reading of his *Ars Amatoria* and led in turn to his banishment and wretchedness: 'My songs have brought about that men and women should wish to know me, which portended nothing good for me. My songs have brought about that Caesar should censure me and my way of life from the *Ars Amatoria* which had already been published'. Allegations that his writings have a corrupting effect on women readers are also countered in Ovid's exile poetry: 'But it is not a crime to unroll tender verse. Chaste women may read of many things which they may not do.' He also counters the claim, 'But a poem corrupts some women', in *Tristia* II: 'Whoever thinks this is wrong, and ascribes too much power to my writings.' Ovid's argument is that the morally upright woman will not be corrupted by her reading. It is the virtue of the reader, and not her reading, that matters.

Ovid was writing at a time when other popular types of books emerged and some of them were types still familiar to the consumer book market today: escapist poetry, history written in abridged forms, or the lives of great men. Cookery books also started to appear, and guides to sports, games and pastimes, erotica, horoscopes, books about magic and works essentially of popular psychology, for example guides to the interpretation of dreams. Adventure stories also emerged as a highly popular genre, essentially stories of love and danger with twisting plots and stereotypical characters. There is little hard evidence about the readership of these various genres but some have claimed that poetry, cookbooks and adventure stories where romantic love dominates, appealed particularly to women.

Ovid had remarkable insight into the reading public. Others who were equally astute and more overtly commercial in their ambitions soon joined him. Martial (AD 40–c. 103) was a Latin poet from Hispania (on the Iberian Peninsula) and is best known for his twelve books of *Epigrams*, published in Rome between 86 and 103. He was supported by more than sixty wealthy patrons, four of whom were women who clearly admired his wisdom and overlooked some aspects of his writing. In his witty poems he satirises the scandalous activities of his urban acquaintances and makes much of the merits of his provincial upbringing. The butts of his satire are city-dwellers and sometimes women and homosexuals. But despite his misogynism, Martial was read by women as well as men. In a telling example he jokes that *matronae* (women) will eagerly peruse the second (obscene) section of the book. This is one of a number of instances that suggest that women probably made up a sizeable part of his readership.[29]

Reading aloud gradually became an increasingly common source of entertainment among certain social groups and women were by no means excluded. Few may yet have been readers, but they were fully involved as listeners. Pliny the Younger (61–c. 112), the Roman writer and administrator, recorded that, 'At dinner, when my wife is present or a few friends, I have a book read aloud; after dinner a comedy or lyre playing; afterwards a stroll with my people, among whom are erudite individuals. Thus the evening passes in varied discussion, and even the longest day is quickly seasoned.'[30] In his letters he frequently mentioned his wife, Calpurnia, and her literary abilities although his praise is, simultaneously, self-flattery: 'Her affection for me has given her an interest in literature. My writings are continually in her hands; she reads them again and again and even learns them by heart. … When I recite my works, she sits nearby, concealed behind a curtain, and greedily drinks in my praises.'[31] In Pliny's descriptions of his devoted and modest wife there is nowhere mention of the impressive education that Calpurnia received at her aunt's house. Her understanding of literature may well have been due to a grammarian employed by her aunt to teach her as a girl.

Pliny's letters were selected and possibly partially rewritten for publication. His concern would seem to be to portray his marriage as meeting the contemporary ideal. The husband, superior in education and age, moulds his younger wife so as to live harmoniously the life he wants and enjoy his literary tastes.

Calpurnia was clearly an intelligent woman reader but the record of her reading is exclusively from a man's perspective – her husband's.

Some men were undoubtedly staunch advocates of women's literacy. The best case for educating women of the elite was made by the Roman rhetorician Quintilian (c. 35–c. 100) in his *Institutio Oratoria*. He argued that since the early education of children took place in the home it was important for their mother to be as educated as possible.[32] Women readers were rare in republican Rome and they were tolerated first and foremost because of their role as teachers of male children.

Practices slowly started to change as literacy spread. Lucian (125–after 180), the author of biting satires, draws a portrait of a second-century reader not unlike Jane Austen's 'silly reader' hundreds of years later. His reader collects books as an outward sign of status but reads without understanding or discrimination. He is unable 'to know the merits and defects of each passage', nor can he 'understand what every sentence means'. In short he is a 'silly ignorant fellow'.[33] Snobbery, in relation to reading, became more prevalent as poetry and more difficult prose started to be tackled by a more cultivated public. Less sophisticated readers were often ridiculed. And as the imperial age was also a time of women's increasing access to the written word, they too were often the butt of the joke.

Satire VI – also known as 'Against Woman' – by Juvenal (first and second centuries AD) serves as an excellent example, brimming with hostile metaphors of women as vipers, poison and so on. Women who participate in the public sphere are cast as gossips and scandal-mongers. Women who considered themselves orators and grammarians, daring to dispute literary points and pointing out their husbands' grammatical slips, were repulsive: 'I loathe the woman who is forever referring to Palaemon's *Grammar* and thumbing through it, observing all the laws and rules of speech, or who quotes lines I've never heard, a female scholar'.[34] In fact men were specifically warned against marrying women readers of any sophistication and advised that 'there should be something in her reading which she doesn't even understand'. Literate women were one thing, critical women readers were another.

During the first century AD Greek culture spread through Roman society, despite efforts to stem what was seen by some as a luxurious and even effeminising influence. Greek scholars served in wealthy households, and libraries proliferated. Growing numbers of upper-class women and well-educated women within the imperial family, like Augustus's sister Octavia and her daughter Antonia, were keen readers. Education, even of women, was seen as a mark of high social status and well-to-do women of more modest descent started to take seriously their education and that of their children. Educated

11 Detail of a first-century fresco in the Villa of the Mysteries, Pompeii. The woman's right hand rests on the child's shoulder, gently touching his ear and cheek as though to encourage his reading.

women also shared this skill with Greek freedwomen, including actresses and courtesans. We also know that Athenian prostitutes read and graffitied on a cemetery wall in the city.[35] This is a salient reminder that reading and writing, until quite late in Antiquity, were seen merely as practical crafts in societies dominated by oral communication, and not necessarily a mark of social status. It was only when women's education was perceived to be exclusively in the interests of their family that most literate women were held in any esteem. But there were notable exceptions.

Octavia, the sister of Emperor Augustus, was in a privileged position and she took both education and patronage very seriously indeed. She acted as a kind of broker between the talented and the wealthy, securing support for the architect Vitruvius by mediating with her brother. Likewise she sought to ensure that Athendorus was properly supported as court philosopher, and he dedicated a book to her. Her most lavish patronage, however, was a library of Greek and Latin literature, almost certainly paid for from her own resources. Her commitment to literature is beyond question.[36]

Empress Julia Domna, wife of Emperor Lucius Septimius Severus (193–211), another patron of learning, was the most influential adviser to her son, Caracalla (211–17), throughout much of his reign as emperor. She positioned herself at the centre of a circle of Roman and Greek philosophers, principally the sophists. Disappointed in the books available to read, and unable to find the books she wanted, she commissioned authors to write. Most notably, she had Philostratus write (or rewrite) the *Life of Apollonius*. In his introduction he wrote: 'As I belonged to the circle of the empress – for she was a devoted admirer of all rhetorical exercises – she commanded me to rewrite and edit these essays [a biography supposedly written by a disciple of his, Damis of Nineveh] and to pay special attention to style and diction; for the man of Nineveh had told his story clearly enough, but not very skilfully.'[37] Julia Domna was also a keen admirer of the sophist Philiscus of Thessaly. In 212, during Caracalla's reign, Philiscus travelled to Rome. As Philostratus recorded, 'there he attached himself closely to Julia's circle of geometricians and philosophers, and obtained from her with the emperor's consent the chair of rhetoric at Athens.' Like Octavia before her, Julia was able, through her family connections, to ensure that the philosopher whom she most admired be appointed to the most sought-after imperial chair.

Upper-class women were also able to exert some influence as patronesses of literature and learning as these forms of patronage were based in people's homes. But, needless to say, women played a much less influential role than their male counterparts. As they were excluded from political office they had reduced means to offer support in the form of sinecures, for example.

Their education was also mostly a matter of luck. And of course women had less control over their wealth – until their husbands died. Widows, with their greater financial independence, stand out as some of the most notable patrons: Cornelia, Octavia and Julia made their greatest contributions after the death of their spouses.

Other women were beginning to enjoy fiction. By the second century, romances started to appear to feed the growing market for women's reading, and this kind of fiction may have been read by a range of women across the social classes.[38] Novels like Achilles Tatius's *Leucippe and Clitophon,* Longus's *Daphnis and Chloe,* and Heliodorus's *Aethiopica* – fast-paced love stories full of twists and turns, shifting in tone from tragic to comic, optimistic to pessimistic, religious to gently erotic, and arousing a helter-skelter of emotions – may have appealed particularly to women. It is even possible that the readership of the novel in the ancient world consisted mostly of women. But some of the arguments offered to support this line seem to issue from prejudice and snobbery; novels that are considered unoriginal and crudely imitative of other writings, or highly sentimental, have been construed as appropriate only, or at least mainly, to a female readership. The implication is that any 'discerning' reader – that is, the male reader – would have been uninterested. More sophisticated claims for a female readership have been made, based on an analysis of the various representations of strong and sexually powerful women in these books, which, it has been argued, would have appealed to women readers' fantasies about female emotional and erotic omnipotence.[39] Trying to establish what in a novel might be more or less appealing to women or men remains tricky. But it is easy for a modern woman reader to be struck, for example, by Melite, the central character in *Leucippe and Clitophon,* who displays a wonderful independence and sense of the comic in her clever seduction of the eponymous hero. She may well have been attractive to Roman women more than, or even rather than, men.

We know from the Late Hellenistic images from Pompeii, which usually depict seated women reading a book scroll, that women read in a domestic setting, and generally alone. But there are also intimations that women read in public. Lucian's description of a woman reader is intriguing: 'She had a scroll in her hands, with both ends of it rolled up, so that she seemed to be reading the one part and to have already read the other. As she walked along, she was discussing something or other with one of her escorts.'[40]

As in ancient Greece, the Roman Empire also had libraries filled mostly with serious reading matter – that is, Greek scrolls. The Romans had sacked many Greek libraries, the Royal Macedonian Library being the most celebrated. By the fifth century some country houses had their own libraries of Latin works, with the classics for the men, and devotional works for women. Some intellectual women were able to contribute to the founding of educational institutions. In 425, Eudocia was almost certainly responsible for re-founding (notionally with her husband) the so-called University of Constantinople.[41] Educated women also established monasteries and nunneries with particular concerns for education, like Melania the Younger (c. 385–439) in the fifth century. She was made a saint and was celebrated as a great reader by Gerontius, a Roman scholar who wrote her life, *Vitae S. Melaniae Iunioris* (*The Life of Melania the Younger*).

Melania was a member of the famous and extremely wealthy family of Valerii. Little is known of her childhood, but she submitted to her parents' desire that she marry one of her relatives, Pinianus, a patrician. They had two children but both died. Melania then persuaded her husband to renounce earthly possessions and little by little they gave their wealth away. He became a brotherly companion and supported her in all her efforts towards sanctity. In 410 she went to Africa where she became a close associate of St Augustine. She devoted herself to works of charity and piety, and later founded a nunnery of which she became mother superior, and a cloister which her husband oversaw. On her return to Jerusalem she lived in a hermitage near the Mount of Olives for twelve years, and here Melania founded other monastic foundations. After her husband's death, in 438 Empress Eudocia, wife of Theodosius, travelled to Jerusalem to meet Melania, such was her celebrated reputation both for scholarship and patronage. All Melania's work was sustained by wide reading. Gerontius described Melania's bookish, intellectual hunger: 'She would go through the *Lives* of the fathers as if she were eating dessert.' He also wrote:

She read books that were bought, as well as books she chanced upon, with such diligence that no word or thought remained unknown to her. So overwhelming was her love of learning that when she read Latin, it seemed to everyone that she could not know Greek and, on the other hand, when she read Greek, it was thought that she did not know Latin.[42]

Another interesting insight into reading practices, specifically relating to women, comes from St Cyril, Bishop of Jerusalem (c. 315–86), addressing women parishioners, asking them to read 'quietly . . . so that, while their lips speak no other ears may hear what they say'.[43] At this point writing had not yet been broken up into words – that occurred only in the ninth century. It may be that the mouthing of words, 'lips speaking silently', facilitated the recognition of where one word ended and the next began. What St Cyril describes also suggests that there was a high degree of literacy among the women of Jerusalem and that, perhaps, the parish was wealthy enough to supply each woman with her own copy of a prayer book. St Cyril had dictated their reading to them and although they read silently, they were all reading the same material.

Equally unexpected, given the suspicion that women readers and writers sometimes aroused, is the esteem in which the Greek books of the Sibylline Oracles continued to be held. The Sibylline Oracles (also known as the 'pseudo-Sibylline Oracles') are a collection of Greek hexameters ascribed to the Sibyls or prophetic priestesses who uttered divine revelations in a possessed state.[44] There are twelve books, made up of oracular utterances composed between the middle of the second century to the fifth century AD. The original Sibylline Books were closely guarded scrolls written by the Sibyls in the Etruscan and early Roman era as early as 6 BC. The Sibylline Books or *Libri Sibyllini* were a collection of oracular utterances supposedly bought from a Sibyl by Tarquinius Superbus, the last king of Rome, and consulted at moments of crisis throughout the history of the Roman Republic and Empire.

12 Michelangelo's *Erythraean Sibyl* painted on the ceiling of the Sistine Chapel, Rome. Not only is she depicted as a reader – she is extraordinarily muscular too.

They were almost all destroyed in a fire in 83 BC, and what remained was burned by order of the Roman General Flavius Stilicho (AD 365–408).

The original contents of the Sibylline Books remain something of a mystery. The texts that exist today were probably composed between the second and sixth century AD. They claim to predict events which were already history or mythological history at the time they were written, as well as including less specific predictions, especially in relation to Rome and Assyria. They are a motley assortment of Hellenistic and Roman pagan mythology, including Homer and Hesiod. There are also Jewish legends, such as the Garden of Eden, Noah and the Tower of Babel. Historical figures are also alluded to: Alexander the Great, Cleopatra, and an extensive list of Roman emperors. Finally, Gnostic and early Christian writings are included, all in an apparently random order. Whether some of the original Sibylline Books have found their way into this peculiar hotchpotch of writing is uncertain. But they nevertheless tell us a good deal about classical mythology and early Gnostic, Jewish and Christian beliefs in the first millennium. Some apocalyptic passages bear close resemblance to some of the themes of St John's Book of Revelation.

The Sibylline Books and, later, Oracles, were part of a strange phenomenon. They were read not for direct guidance, but for insights and inspiration. Because they were written in Greek, those who consulted them relied on official translators. Like the cleverly written horoscope today, they were constructed in such a way as to encourage the reader to find pertinence to his or her life – and unconsciously to disregard anything that does not ring true. The Roman rulers who appealed to the Sibylline Books were setting great store by the mysterious prophesies of women, and at a time when women were largely excluded from politics and power, with limited freedom of movement and a generally minimal education compared to that of boys. In addition, the tiny number of more intellectually sophisticated women were treated with suspicion, if not ridicule. But a very select number of women, both alive and dead, mostly prophetesses, poets and saints, were deemed to have a wisdom and insight beyond the vast majority of men. Within the later Christian tradition women mystics, too, would be held in high regard while the institution of the Church excluded women from the priesthood.

The public readings that had flourished in the early empire came to an end in the sixth century. This was a time of demographic change with large numbers of patricians moving out of the towns and cities in fear of Germanic invasions. Education also suffered and, with it, the book trade. Women's relations with the book suffered still more as a result of the corruption of Latin. Greek reading was in decline and vernacular, spoken Latin changed and gradually became distinct from written Latin. This meant that the Latin of the Church was not necessarily comprehensible to the literate. The language of Christian worship became increasingly alien to the populace. In time, specially trained readers had to be prepared by the Church to interpret on behalf of the people. They were a special caste, *presbyters*, or 'priests'. Women were excluded from this position. Through a strange concatenation of circumstances, women's reading went into a sudden decline.

The resurgence of the book and the rise of Christianity went hand in hand. And the question of the kind of access to the Bible that women should or should not have would become one of the greatest debates in the story of women's reading. The Bible is, of course, the most ubiquitous book in history, translated into more languages than any other. The Latin translation of the Bible from the original Hebrew and Greek was fundamental to the medieval Church. From the fifth century on, other liturgical works appeared in churches in large format: missals containing the liturgy for the year, hymn books and psalms. Reading these works was a group activity.

Around the same time, silent reading began to emerge as a new and innovative way of engaging with writing. As early as AD 384, Augustine described his teacher's practice of silent reading. Of St Ambrose, Bishop of Milan, Augustine wrote:

> when he was reading, he drew his eyes along over the leaves, and his heart searched into its sense, but his voice and tongue were silent. Oft-times when we were present . . . we still saw him reading to himself, and never otherwise . . . . But with what intent soever he did it, that man certainly had a good meaning in it.[45]

Augustine obviously had not seen anyone reading silently before, given the detail of his description and the sense of his surprise that it conveys. He goes on to consider the motives for Ambrose's unusual practice: 'Perhaps he was afraid that if he read out loud, a difficult passage by the author he was reading would raise a question in the mind of an attentive listener, and he would then have to explain what it meant or even argue about some of the more abstruse points.'[46] Augustine recognises the idea of an intense personal engagement with what is being read, in which concentration and attention are key. This kind of private, individualistic reading would only become widespread in the Middle Ages. But even in those rare cases where silent reading was preferred or recommended there are only very occasional intimations, as in the writings of Augustine, of a fundamentally new practice, one in which the reader participates in an intense and individualistic engagement with what he or she is reading. This kind of secret reading was what some people were most determined to prevent women from practising.

It is only in later centuries that fundamental changes in religious and philosophical outlook encouraged this very different kind of private reading. During the Middle Ages the amalgam of Greek, Jewish and Latin cultures with Christianity fed into the idea of individual faith and a personal, unique relationship with God, which in turn affected reading. Silent, solitary reading of scripture became the basis of the contemplative life. But for a long time, within the Christian tradition, parallel practices coexisted. In religious communities reading aloud during mealtimes, for example, suggested a communal learning – or indoctrination, even – while the individual 'study' of religious texts was beginning to develop alongside. This latter engagement was one from which women were, unsurprisingly, largely discouraged.

But whatever the prevalent cultures, as silent, solitary reading established itself as the more common practice, there were always women readers who were going to do their best to subvert the dominant order and read for themselves, sometimes with the support of men. In so doing, these women contributed to, and reflect, more fundamental changes to the status quo.

—*๛*—

CHAPTER 2

Reading in the Not-So-Dark Ages

W HAT were women reading in the murky half-light of the so-called 'Dark Ages' which followed the collapse of the Roman Empire around AD 600 and lasted until the turn of the second millennium? This pejorative term, originally coined because relatively little was known of the period, is now less often used – although some historians refer instead to the 'Silent Ages', particularly when discussing women's lives.[1] But over recent decades ever-increasing amounts of exciting material have come to light. Archaeologists, historians and others – including many women excited by the likelihood of discovering more about women's unwritten history – have been delving deeply.

What kinds of access did women have, in different parts of the world, to writing in this broad period? Can we know *how* women read? And what difference did their reading make to their own lives and the lives of others? Amid the apparent silence, more than murmurings can be heard and they alert us to various connections between women and books. There are wills detailing gifts or loans of books to daughters and women friends, and records of bequests of books given by women to nunnery libraries. There are letters by women that reveal their reading, and tracts that include calls for the promotion of women's literacy. Tradeswomen, in particular, participated in the world of book- and record-keeping. There are books written in thanks for commissions from women patrons and, as in earlier periods, there is teasing iconography and archaeology associated with women's reading. Beyond the West there is evidence that women provided financial support to Buddhist monks to sustain them while they undertook lengthy public readings of holy writings. And in the Muslim world there were certainly women scholars, however little we know about them. Most striking, however, are the books written by women and largely for women in the West – some with reading itself as their subject. All this suggests that the 'silence' of the period was far from universal.

Some early medieval aristocratic women, others in religious communities, and a still smaller number of tradeswomen were to varying degrees proper readers and they participated in the world of manuscripts, books and records in ways not dissimilar to their male counterparts. In fact, women in communities across the world frequently had more time for reading than men, mostly due to the hours they spent in a more private sphere. Letter-writing facilitated contact with other women and men in otherwise cut-off communities, and sometimes opened lines of communication with men of influence in public political worlds. Lack of certain freedoms gave a small number of women access to reading and so to discoveries and explanations about human life in all its myriad forms, on which they could reflect at leisure. Religious communities were often relatively isolated from the wider world and so, despite the violence and instability of the early medieval period, there were safe places for women to read.

For most people their lives were characterised by drudgery and poverty with little time for anything other than long hours of exhausting manual work, and sleep. Illiteracy prevailed, and for the masses of illiterate women, like the masses of illiterate men, 'reading' meant the interpretation of often complex images rather than language. The highly influential Gregory the Great (c. 540–604), who oversaw the ambitious task of converting the Anglo-Saxons to the Christian faith, was very clear about the importance of making images 'readable' by the people:

> It is one thing to worship a picture, it is another to learn in depth, by means of pictures, a venerable story. For that which makes writing present to the reader, pictures make present to the illiterate, to those who only perceive visually, because in pictures the ignorant see the story they ought to follow, and those who don't know their letters find that they can, after a fashion, read. Therefore, especially for the common folk, pictures are the equivalent of reading.[2]

Gregory's concern that visual literacy should be learning 'in depth' and result in 'following' example, is obviously a step along the way to literacy proper. And interestingly, the notion that real reading was primarily a visual, rather than intellectual activity, persisted for a very long time among small groups of reading women. As late as the fifteenth century, the nuns at Syon Abbey were expected to read in a particular way. The purpose was to become the 'living images' of St Bridget, and reading was seen above all as a visual act, rather than an intellectual endeavour. The words on the page were to be absorbed rather than pondered, which was then followed by spiritual contemplation. A kind of holy cloning would occur through an uncritical visual act of reading.[3]

For the vast majority during the Early Middle Ages, 'reading' meant looking at images or, and more importantly, listening to others reading aloud. Just as Gregory the Great emphasised the need to make pictures 'readable', so his contemporary, the Spanish theologian Isidore of Seville (c. 560–636), one of the greatest and most original minds of the time, wrote about reading and being read to as a complex range of processes. He offered insights into the peculiar and distinctive merits of silent reading, about reading as communication across space and time, and about the training necessary to ensure that lectors in church exercised their reading ministry with due wisdom and integrity. Of silent reading he advised that it was 'without effort, reflecting on that which has been read, rendering their escape from memory less easy.' According to his contemporary St Augustine, Isidore also emphasised what now seems obvious – that reading allows a conversation with those not there: 'Letters have the power to convey to us silently the sayings of those who are absent.'[4] In relation to lectors reading aloud to the illiterate, including large numbers of women, Isidore maintained:

> Whosoever is promoted to a rank of this kind shall be deeply versed in doctrine and books, and thoroughly adorned with the knowledge of meanings and words, so that in the analysis of sentences he may understand where the grammatical boundaries occur: where the utterance continues, where the sentence concludes. In this way he will control the technique of oral delivery without impediment, in order that he may move the minds and feelings of all to understand, by distinguishing between the kinds of delivery, and by expressing the feelings of the sentences: now by the tone of one expounding, now in the manner of one who is suffering, now in the manner of one who is chiding, now in the manner of one who is exhorting, or by those according to the kinds of appropriate delivery.[5]

What Isidore underscores is the importance of reading in terms of *meaningful* delivery. It is not enough simply to 'sound out' the words; the lector must understand both the grammar and syntax of the writing, and its argumentative and emotional force. All this depends on being educated in grammar, and being well read. Women were, of course, prevented from rising to the 'rank' of lector, so the power inherent in reading as interpretation remained almost exclusively the preserve of men and with it, to a large extent, control of meaning.

Changes in reading practices were naturally as multiple as their contexts. Differences in reading practice and reading material in the Early Middle Ages were closely associated with place. Whether in a cloister, a castle, a small town or a village, people lived communally. A basic aspect of medieval life which is easy to overlook is that most people were hardly ever alone. In gardens and private halls, romances and epics were read by family members rather than, as in the ancient world, servants or slaves; and in the marketplaces, travelling entertainers continued to address large bawdy crowds who made their admiration or displeasure abundantly clear. These were very much group events where the mood and size of the audience would have a direct effect on what and how the reader or storyteller performed. The biblical readings that occurred in churches, and the reading to monks and nuns at mealtimes to ensure that their minds were not taken up by inappropriate daydreams, were, in contrast, relatively passive.

In most medieval European languages, the verb 'to read' means 'read aloud, recite, broadcast, announce'. But for the vast majority, listening to a storyteller reciting tales from memory in the marketplace was not supplemented by listening to a formal, authoritative public reading. The last occurred in only five specific places: church, religious community, court, private residence and university. Most ordinary people were debarred from all but the first, and women were excluded from the universities until as late as the end of the nineteenth century. The notion of a 'Silent Age' in relation to the majority of women readers seems in many ways true.

But throughout the medieval period there were dramatic clashes between the oral, the reading of images and symbols, and varying degrees of literacy proper. Gradually literacy came to dominate, and with it a shift from social, communal forms of reading to more private kinds. The fascinating and most imponderable transformation was when reading as a solitary and secret means of entering the world of writing – as something that needs to be *interpreted* by the individual – began to take hold. The reader can establish his or her own tempo and re-read, reflect, and sometimes make marginal notes. Whereas the listener has limited control over the speed of delivery, and so of comprehension, the reader can choose his or her own pace, savouring, reflecting, questioning or memorising. It is a moment of profound change, and one bound up with the development of a radically new notion of the individual, and a new sense of self. Alone, in private, no longer subject to censorship (except perhaps in some internalised form), the reader engages with words that may, for example, focus on a relationship with God, or with other 'characters', sometimes real, as in the case of letters from a correspondent, or historical, fictional or mystical. Ideas and theories can be quietly ruminated. This is an entirely new engagement with words, and it is hard, at this distance in time, to imagine its revolutionary novelty.

The gradual shift from group consumption to private reading occurred from the top down in society. First were the aristocracy and the clergy, as they had both the necessary wealth to purchase manuscripts and books, and the leisure that afforded them the privacy and time to read. Women were numbered among both groups.

Despite widespread illiteracy, and the deliberate exclusion from increasingly formalised education, very different kinds of women, for different reasons, became influential readers: women religious, mostly nuns, and aristocratic ladies for whom some education was deemed appropriate. In fact until the founding of the great European universities, noblemen and women often received similar educations. Girls, like boys, were taught to ride so as to be able to join the hunt, and literacy and numeracy skills formed the basis of their formal education. But there were, of course, some women who took their intellectual pursuits much more seriously than others. And there is plenty to go on that allows us to glimpse not simply what these more ambitious women read, but how, and with what intent.

13 Caesarius of Arles emphasising the importance of Scripture to the nuns. The angle of their heads is wonderfully suggestive of their compliance with his instructions.

A lucky few were encouraged by enlightened churchmen. Bishop Caesarius of Arles (468/470–542) believed that nuns' varied reading, as well as prayer, provided spiritual sustenance of the soul.[6] Writing to the sisters of St Jean he stipulated: 'Apply yourselves to reading and prayer . . . . In particular . . . accustom yourselves to reading . . . and dedicate the better part of the day to spiritual works.' *Lectio divina* ('holy reading') was not simply a matter of reading, but also of interpretation, as nuns were expected to consider the significance of scripture for their own lives. In many of his sermons Caesarius declared *lectio* to be a requirement for everyone, laity, clergy and monastics alike. In the Rule he wrote for the sisters, the *Regula sanctarum virginum* (*Rule for Virgins*), he quite simply advised, 'All should learn to read', and girls were only to be accepted as novices when they had become literate. In the *Vitae Cesarii* (*Life of Caesarius*), a huge collection of his sermons and other writings, he extols the exemplary lives of the sisters of St Jean: 'Her [Caesaria II, Mother Superior] work with her companions is so outstanding that in the midst of psalms and fasts, vigils and readings, the virgins of Christ beautifully copy out the holy books, with their mother herself as teacher.'[7] In Caesarius's writings there is nothing to suggest that he considered the nuns under his care any less intellectually capable than their male counterparts. Indeed, the scholarly diligence of the sisters made a deep impression on him. These women were, however, relatively detached from the world. Other women found themselves in more politically involved positions and assumed rather more active involvement in reading.

The same Caesarius also made a significant contribution to the extraordinary life of the sixth-century Frankish princess Radegund. She was born in Thuringia, a principality in central Germany. Her uncle had murdered her father, who ruled the region. Clothar (also called Clotaire or Lothar), King of the Franks, conquered Thuringia in 531 and slaughtered virtually every member of the royal house. Radegund and her only surviving brother were captured and the princess was brought up as Clothar's future bride, so as to make legitimate his claim to Thuringia's throne. In 538 they married but had no children. Clothar, for reasons that are disputed, then arranged for the murder of Radegund's brother. Radegund obviously decided that enough was enough and fled. Sporadic attempts were made to bring her back, but to no avail; nevertheless, her husband continued to support her financially until his own death in 561.

While Clothar was still living, Radegund lit upon the idea of founding a women's community in Poitiers under the Rule of Caesarius, and her husband provided funds. At its height the nunnery housed some 200 educated women. Poitiers was an important region of the Frankish kingdom and Radegund's presence and initiative further attracted religious and indeed literary men to the area. Radegund also drew high-ranking as well as well-educated women to her community. Her biographer, the nun Baudonivia (fl. 600–2), describes Radegund's understanding of her own peculiar status:

> She was always solicitous for peace and worked diligently for the welfare of the fatherland. Whenever the different kingdoms made war on one another, she prayed for the lives of all the kings, for she loved them all. And she taught us also to pray incessantly for their stability.
>
> Whenever she heard of bitterness arising among them, trembling, she sent such letters to one and then to the other pleading that they should not make war among themselves nor take up arms lest this land perish. And, likewise, she sent to their noble followers to give the high kings salutary counsel so that their power might work to the welfare of the people and the land.[8]

Despite her apparent withdrawal from the world, Radegund, like many other monastic leaders, abbesses above all, had merely found a position from which participation in an interesting range of assumed duties was possible through correspondence. From time to time, in exchanges of letters, Radegund challenged her bishop's authority, on the assumption that this was her queenly right. Although she refused to be abbess in name, she guided her community, led a prayerful life, and advised and counselled among warring groups, both secular and religious. Her confidence was in part a function of her high birth, but it was also derived from her reading.

Three Latin verse epistles by Radegund survive, and indicate that she was well versed in both classical and Germanic poetry. She blended these, both to provide traditional laments for the dead, and to describe her own personal pain, particularly in relation to her brother's death. In them there are echoes of Virgil's *Aeneid* and the laments of Propertius and Ausonius, Ovid's fictive epistles, the *Heroides*, and the plaintive tone of the Germanic lament. In a letter-poem to Hamalfred, her cousin, living in exile in Constantinople, she wrote:

> Why are you silent about the murder of my brother, the deep pain
> how innocent he fell by a treacherous ambush? . . .
> A gentle boy with a downy beard, he was pierced through,
> Absent, I, his sister, did not see his cruel death.[9]

The lament in a woman's voice was a feature of the Anglo-Saxon tradition which Radegund drew on, merging it with the exaggerated rhetoric of the classical corpus. Radegund was evidently highly sensitive to reading that

14 Illuminated image of Radegund, from the *Life*. Her influence spread beyond the walls of her community.

allowed her to make sense of her own experience – and to articulate it effectively to others. Her writing has the power both to move and to assert her erudite authority as a queen, despite her loss of noble status. Much has been made of Radegund's life in women's history, and rightly so. She is a relatively rare but crucially important example of a learned, intelligent and shrewd woman reader.

That we know so much about Radegund is thanks to another thoughtful, but less strident, woman reader-writer. Baudonivia's *Life* was written between 600 and 602, some thirteen years after Radegund's death. The author was undoubtedly herself a reader as her writing demonstrates a sure grasp of the traditional form of a life. At the same time she offers the conventional humble apologies for her temerity in embarking on a very different and presumptuous act: that of writing, rather than 'merely' reading:

> I can as easily touch heaven with my fingers as . . . write something about the life of the holy Lady Radegund. . . . This task should be assigned to those

who have fountains of eloquence within them. . . . I am the smallest of the small ones she nourished familiarly from the cradle as her own child at her feet . . . so that I may . . . compose, . . . so that I may offer a public celebration of her glorious life to the ears of her flock, in devout though unworthy language, I pray that you will aid me with your prayers, for I am more devoted than learned.[10]

Elsewhere she describes her prose as 'rustic rather than refined language'. Baudonivia had certainly read Bishop Fortunatus's life of Radegund as she writes, near the beginning, when describing the scope of her own work: 'In this book we will not repeat what the apostolic Bishop recorded of her blessed life.' For all her projected humility, Baudonivia displays her wide reading and an intelligent approach in memorialising another extraordinary woman's life, one that would have been impossible had it not been for her peculiar status, and education.

Radegund was one of a small number of women who participated in the Anglo-Saxon Renaissance and this drew on an important Celtic tradition in which women intellectuals had participated. New material is regularly coming to light dispelling assumptions about the apparent 'silence' of Irish women in these early centuries. The lives of St Darerca and her sister scholars provide remarkable evidence of women's education.[11] Darerca went on to educate three bishops. When integrated with findings from other medieval Irish writings, like chronicles, devotional works and poetry, it becomes apparent that education was available to at least some girls and women under both male and female teachers. Schools were both mixed and single-sex from the earliest days of the Irish church in the fifth century until the mid-fifteenth. Irish women, then, were far from excluded from literacy and, in the main, were highly respected by men. Many functioned as founders and benefactors, and many were made saints. And there were keen readers in each of these groups.

The religion of pre-Christian Ireland had its brutish sides, such as the glorification of the warrior. The figure of the Virgin Mary was seen, in some ways, as a new and humane goddess. No doubt because of their prominent position in the Celtic Church, women were afforded considerable status in the Roman Church and it may be that they held quite senior positions. We know that Brigit of Ireland (453–523), who would inspire women religious for centuries, had considerable responsibility within the church structures. (Brigit had been influenced by the other Bridget, St Bridget of Sweden, another semi-literate aristocratic woman for whom some autograph pages survive.)[12] In the emerging Christian communities of Ireland, women could participate as doctors or healers, scholars, arbitrators or judges, deacons, and perhaps even bishops. But living in community meant foregoing considerable freedoms. Or did it? Irish women of this period lived in fear of war and rape. The brutalities of life could be avoided by commitment to a religious foundation and the Church hierarchy. Furthermore, entrance to these communities offered educational opportunities which were otherwise rarely available. The Church here, as elsewhere, fostered women's literacy and many women were keen to benefit from it.

In Ireland there had been notable female monasteries at Kildare, Sliab Cuilinn and Cluain-Credhuil. At the last, there was a school for boys which educated many of the influential ecclesiastics of the next generation. Monasteries for both men and women often played an important educational role and there is evidence that there was instruction in rhetoric, grammar, mathematics and some secular Latin authors.[13] Educated women nuns were respected and asked for help by men. Brendan of Clonfert, for example, approached Brigit of Kildare for instruction at the end of the fifth century.[14] We may have relatively little to go on, but it is clear that literate women played an important role in early Irish monastic education.

Aspects of Celtic culture came to Britain as a result of a request made by King Oswald in 635. According to the Venerable Bede, in his *Ecclesiastical History of the English People*, Oswald wrote to Irish Elders whom he knew from his time in Ireland, 'asking them to send him a bishop whose teaching and ministry' would benefit the English. Aidan was sent and built his community on the island of Lindisfarne, and other foundations were established by Irish missionaries in Northumberland and East Anglia, also at Oswald's bidding. It was Bishop Aidan of Lindisfarne who summoned Hilda, a nun in the Frankish monastery of Chelles, and she became abbess of the monastery of Heruteu, now Hartlepool in Northumbria.

Her most important foundation was at Whitby. Here she established her reputation and with this came considerable influence within the local religious structures. She even hosted the Synod of 664 that saw the adoption of Roman practices, which emphasised the importance of education, in Northumbria. Bede recorded that 'those under her direction were required to make a thorough study of the Scriptures'. Bede devoted an entire chapter of his *History* to her life, which includes a discussion of her role in the Synod of Whitby.[15] He also recounts Hilda's contribution to Caedmon's education. Caedmon was a stable-hand who went on to became a monk at Whitby and, inspired by Hilda, the earliest author of vernacular Christian poetry. An anonymous life of Gregory the Great was also written at Whitby under Hilda around 704, the first book written by an Englishman.[16]

Bede chose to write about Hilda at length because she was much more than a holy cloistered nun – of whom there were many. She was the most remarkable of the royal-aristocratic abbesses of her day, and her sway on the seventh-century English Church was enormous. In addition to being highly respected within the Church she became a national religious figure of immense spiritual influence. This was evidently a time when religious women, at least those well born, were in a position to operate with energy and vision. Men listened to Hilda with awe and reverence; kings and bishops consulted her, and monks, clerics and leading churchmen kept up correspondence with her. Her commitment to learning was profound. As abbess of Whitby, she built up the library and school and she was an open and highly persuasive advocate of women's literacy. She was also immensely humane in her oversight of the community and believed in encouragement rather than punishment. This is thrown into stark relief by some of her male counterparts. Benedict Biscop (c. 628–90; also known as Biscop Baducing), an Anglo-Saxon abbot, founded Monkwearmouth-Jarrow Priory where his student Bede would write the remarkable history that includes the chapter on Hilda. According to Benedict, the Divine Office was the work of God and it took precedence over everything else. If a nun arrived late to choir, or made a mistake in the recitation of the Office, she was punished in such a way as to humiliate her before the entire community. Girls were regularly flogged. Hilda's approach was gentle and she lived by example. At the very end of her life Bede tells us that 'she never ceased to give thanks to her maker or to instruct the flock committed to her'.[17]

Hilda's life was intimately bound up with the lives of men as well as women and in this she was not unique. A contemporary of Bede's, Aldhelm (639– 709), was the first known English writer and one of his works, *In Praise of Virginity*, was written for the well-educated nuns at Barking; he names ten of them in his work. He applauded their intellectual commitment and celebrated their 'erudition in the sacred sciences', describing them as 'scholars as wise as the ancient philosophers'. Aldhelm was one of the most-read people in Europe, second only to Isidore of Seville, so his assessment is high praise.

Another important figure, St Boniface (c. 680–755), was also deeply involved with educated women of the time, often nuns, frequently writing to ask to borrow books from them. He was appointed as a missionary by Pope Gregory II in 719 and charged with preaching in Germany 'to those people who are still bound by the shackles of paganism'. In carrying out his task he was particularly dependent on Abbess Leoba of Tauberbischofsheim. In her *Life*, there are extensive descriptions of her intellectual acumen and Boniface was clearly aware that he needed to draw on her wisdom if he was successfully to convert the people. 'So great was her zeal for reading,' her *Life* states, 'that she discontinued it only for prayers or for the refreshment of her body with food and sleep'. She read extensively – 'The scriptures were never out of her hands' – but she also read 'the writings of the Church Fathers, its decrees of the councils and the whole of ecclesiastical law'. The respect that intellectual nuns were afforded by their male counterparts during this period is striking, and it is founded on the authority women commanded as a function of their extensive and attentive reading. It was a time in which men and women worked collaboratively, together establishing the foundations of medieval culture: reading and writing were fundamental to the project.

Although the women who participated in this way were not numerous, their influence was very great. And this extended out from the Celtic and Anglo-Saxon worlds to Burgundy and the northern territories of the Germanic peoples, fuelling the Carolingian Renaissance. As both the quality and quantity of intellectual activity increased, women readers were again fully involved. Abbesses as well as abbots established libraries, and letters and biographies reveal how important reading was to their lives. The biographer of two eighth-century women, Herlindis and Reglindis, emphasises their careful study of 'divine doctrine, human arts, religious studies, and sacred letters'.[18] Educational initiatives were stimulated by Charlemagne's political vision. He was responsible for what is widely considered to be a ninth-century reading revolution in Europe. At the end of the eighth century he decreed that all churches and cathedrals in the Frankish Empire should organise educational systems and teach reading, writing, arithmetic and chanting. Charlemagne's greatest conviction was that widespread literacy – men's and women's – was necessary for the cohesion of society. In his *Admonitio generalis* (*General Exhortation*) of 789, he detailed new legislation for improving education, most particularly reading and writing. His intentions were a complex blend of the political, the cultural, and above all the ecclesiastical. The Frankish Church was in desperate need of literate priests if the institution was to hold together. While correspondence between the Frankish kingdom's larger monasteries, and the exchange of manuscripts, continued, thus preserving at least a skeletal tradition of reliable scholarship, priests (unlike the monks, nuns, abbots and abbesses) were only poorly educated, often illiterate, and peripatetic. And in terms of getting their message across, they were up against stiff competition from roving storytellers.

The Church tried to suppress these performers and their largely secular tales. In the Germanic lands the courtly *scoph* had long spoken and sung, and the Celtic bards had performed a similar role. Much of their material was ancient, the same tales their ancestors had heard, but adapted here and there. In the eighth and ninth centuries, travelling minstrels took to the stage, to be joined, in the tenth, by itinerant clerics later known as *vagantes* ('wanderers'), storytellers, jesters and public entertainers. Some were literate and added classical, theological and even heroic tales to their repertoire.

Charlemagne's reforms, particularly the prominence given to encouraging reading, made a vast difference to girls' and women's literacy. Large numbers of scribes set about copying every conceivable work of literature with minute attention to detail. Libraries swelled with the influx of books. Catalogue fragments show that some classical works survived only in a Carolingian edition, later to be printed. These scribes were the custodians of the Western written tradition. And the burgeoning numbers of scriptoria sprung up in women's monasteries as well as men's. One of the most productive was at Chelles, where Charlemagne's sister Gisela was abbess. Charlemagne also

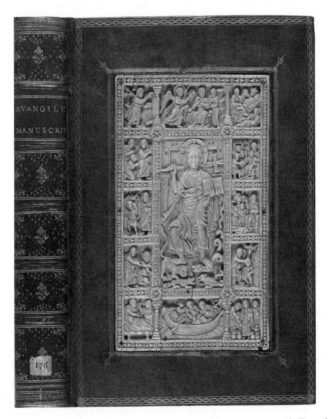

15 A Latin Gospel Lectionary, made around 800 for Gisela's monastery at Chelles, which would have been read aloud in church. The ivory inset, added later, shows a triumphant Christ trampling on a lion and a serpent, surrounded by scenes from his life.

invited foreign scholars to his court, including Alcuin of York. One of his projects was to revise the Vulgate so as to eliminate the numerous discrepancies between different translations. Many educated women corresponded with him and these exchanges of letters reveal just how serious many women readers of the time were, including Charlemagne's sister, his two daughters, his fourth wife and large numbers of nuns and abbesses both on the Continent and in England.

The educational advances promoted by Charlemagne were widespread and some bishops and councils called for universal education for all children. Lay men and women also began to participate in intellectual life outside religious establishments. One woman who was to embrace these new opportunities with unusual commitment was a lay aristocratic woman, Dhuoda. She was the author of the *Liber Manualis* (known as *The Manual for my Son*) which, among other things, dramatises the personal transformation brought about by reading, and the role reading might have in shaping the conscience of an aristocratic son with particular responsibilities incumbent on rank. Her work also exudes a wild optimism about the power of literacy and books.

Dhuoda was married to Bernard, Duke of Septimania (the son of Charlemagne's cousin, William of Gellone) in Aachen on 30 June 824. She had two sons, William, born in 826, and a second, born around the time she embarked on writing her treatise in 841. In it she advises, quite simply, that one learns about God, and gains wisdom, from reading books. Over and over again she insists that William read the books she sends him. An injunction to read Gregory the Great and Isidore of Seville is particularly pronounced. Dhuoda's Latin is literate but not really literary, suggesting that her education may have been patchy. But she was, without doubt, a keen reader with enormous faith in the accumulated truths of the written word. Most unusually for a woman writing in the ninth century, Dhuoda embraces not only the writings of the Church but also stresses the need to recover the classical wisdom of the ancient Christian past. (This was very much in line with the Carolingian ideal and the tradition of the bishops of Uzès, where she wrote her remarkable book. The city also gave greater social freedoms to women, which goes some way to explaining Dhuoda's life and work.) Dhuoda worked systematically on earlier and traditional material which, she believed, constituted an authentic, if not exhaustive, explanation of the divine mysteries. Like most early medieval writers, she quotes extensively, revealing her remarkably wide reading, including biblical material (particularly from the Psalms), grammarians like Aelius Donatus, poets like Prudentius (she quotes passages from his *Liber Cathemerinon*), and the Fathers of the Church, particularly St Augustine and St Gregory. Among her contemporaries whom she read and was impressed by were Ambrose

Autpert, abbot of San-Vincenzo on the Volturno; Alcuin; and Rabanus Maurus, archbishop of Mainz. Among other things, Dhuoda's book is evidence that learning, based on a wide range of authors, had spread at least to some extent to aristocratic lay women in the North of Gaul.[19]

It is also clear that Dhuoda envisioned a wider readership – including women – than simply her own son, as she presents herself, in the tenth chapter, not only as William's 'counsellor' but also as a 'teacher' of both men and women. What is most striking is Dhuoda's cool assumption that women will, increasingly, participate more fully in public roles. This was at a time when involvement was closed to women both by custom and law. But throughout the *Liber*, and with increasing confidence as it unfolds, she assumes the role of public writer, counsellor and educator. Her competence is, of course, grounded in her literacy and wide reading and the implication is that with increasing enfranchisement into education, women will be able, more and more, to participate essentially as intellectuals in the public domain. No doubt Dhuoda was a remarkable and bold woman, but she had also been born in a particularly liberal place at a particularly liberal time, where public opinion cautioning against women's involvement in social and religious debate was not strong enough to deter her from reading, and writing, according to her own convictions. It was, of course, a very long time indeed until Dhuoda's bold vision of a future in which women would participate in learning as fully as men became anything like a reality.

Dhuoda's reflections on the art of writing are intimately bound up with reading, particularly its critical and selective basis. 'If all the people born into the cultures of the world were to be made writers by a sudden increase in human genius', she muses, not everything they wrote would capture the grandeur of God; rather, it requires 'sharpness of mind'. On every page of her book Dhuoda's careful quotations and paraphrases offer a constant example to the reader of the importance of these critical faculties. But writing is, she asserts, 'a perilous public contest'. This gives an impression of the life of the intellectual as comparable to the competitor in tournaments and public debates where humiliation, as well as possible triumph, may result. This striking image goes some way to explaining Dhuoda's unusualness. Few women were minded to enter a dangerous competitive arena that was generally assumed to be exclusively male.

Some have cast Dhuoda as an exceptional Carolingian bluestocking. But there are fragments of works dedicated to laywomen, or commissioned by them, which suggest a not negligible community of women readers contemporary with Dhuoda. This is further buttressed by evidence of women's book ownership, and records of book-borrowing and gifts of books to and from women. Wills and library documents suggest that the practice of lay people borrowing from, and donating to, monasteries and large churches, was common. It is possible that Dhuoda might have had her own library containing most if not all of the material on which she draws in her manual. She was a rare, but by no means unique, example of an educated Carolingian lay woman deeply committed to reading.

Dhuoda finished her *Liber Manualis* at a crucial moment, 2 February 843, the year in which the Carolingian Empire was divided into three kingdoms. The political stability of the empire was weakened by foreign invasion by the Magyars (a Finno-Ugric people who form the ethnic core of the Hungarian nation), Muslims and Scandinavians. Schools, religious foundations and religious buildings were destroyed, but new foundations were also established, including monasteries for women in England and France. But the greatest concentration of religious houses for women was in north-west Germany, at Gandersheim, Essen, Quedlinburg and Nordhausen. The abbesses responsible for these foundations were well aware of the importance of scholarship and learning, and they commissioned histories, often written by women. There are manuscripts from Essen filled with marginalia which testify to the religious women's sophisticated reading skills.

They read both Latin and the vernacular. We also know that girls were educated in these institutions, but not bound to commit to the religious life and could return to their parents once their education was complete, later to

16 One of the Essen manuscripts contains this handwritten petition from a student to her teacher: '... give me leave to keep vigil this night ... and I affirm and swear to you with both hands that I shall not cease either reading or singing on behalf of our Lord the whole night through.'

become teachers to their children, boys and girls. Some women, however, committed to the religious life and enjoyed the intellectual possibilities it offered. Hrotsvit (also known as Hroswitha, Hrosvit, Roswitha and Hroswitha, c. 935–after 973) was a monastic Christian poet who lived and worked in Gandersheim (now Lower Saxony). She was born into a noble family and chose to enter the local Benedictine abbey. There she continued her studies, reading, and writing a number of works which show us both what she read and *how*. She knew the works of the Church Fathers, but also classical poetry, including Virgil, Horace, Ovid, Plautus and, most importantly, Terence. Hrotsvit studied under Gerberga II, the daughter of Henry of Bavaria and niece of Otto I, the founder of the Holy Roman Empire.

Hrotsvit's writings are fascinatingly innovative. The plays of Terence, which had been used since antiquity to encourage good vocal delivery and eloquence, were frequently copied in monasteries in the ninth and tenth centuries. (The irony of using pagan material to teach people how to communicate the word of God effectively seems to have passed many churchmen by.) Hrotsvit, on the other hand, decided to rewrite Terence to provide her sisters with more spiritually nourishing reading material.[20] She felt that his dramas were wholly inappropriate and found their depictions of violence and their unsympathetic representation of women offensive to her sensibility. Interestingly, Hrotsvit's reading is hyperbolic: there is relatively little of what she describes as the 'shameless acts of licentious women' to be found in Terence's plays.[21] In fact the female characters are relatively token. In *The Girl from Andros* the 'girl' does not appear on stage at all; her labour screams are heard off-stage and used to comic effect. The two women who do appear are a drunken woman of loose morals and a slave girl who is exploited by Darus, a male slave. Within the classical tradition adhered to by Terence women are relatively invisible and their behaviour is often described by men rather than enacted. Women are commodities within the plot for the men to trade and the best outcome for women is marriage. In Hrotsvit's rewritings, women's actions are at the centre of the drama and the ways in which they respond to male aggression accounts for the core of the plot.

Hrotsvit claimed that her concern was to substitute the erotically wanton Roman women with examples of feminine holiness.[22] To encourage her nuns to read aloud clearly and persuasively, she wrote her own Christian, mildly feminist versions of Terence. In all she wrote sixteen works which do two things. On the one hand, they elaborate her ideas on the spiritual life of the individual, and on the other, the spiritual lives of the politically powerful.

Hrotsvit's interpretations of scripture are sometimes surprising and original. Her short tale of Christ's ascension is written as an assertion of the beauty and dignity of man (and woman). Her rewriting of the story of Agnes demonstrates the spiritual worth of martyrdom over virginity, an argument that went against the obsession with bodily purity that was rife among the sisters at Gandersheim, as in other communities in the Carolingian Empire. And the importance of virginity, for unmarried women, would long remain a matter of the utmost significance in patriarchal societies. Hrotsvit saw things differently and sought to emphasise the importance of women's religious commitment and involvement in the world, rather than their purity. In addition, in a number of her plays about the rise of Christendom women are shown to be actively involved in the promotion of religious practices. Mary is depicted as the victim of weak, if not flawed teachers. Most remarkable is Hrotsvit's treatment of Thaïs. According to legend she was an aristocratic Egyptian who became a courtesan, later repenting of her lifestyle and entering a convent where she was walled up for some years, dying only days after her release from her anchorite existence. In Hrotsvit's more psychologically-charged version, Thaïs is shown forgiveness as a function of her recognition of guilt which brings a successful balance of mind and body, and peace before her death. In short, women should never be represented as beyond redemption, whatever their sins.

Hrotsvit also wrote two historical poems based on her response to contemporary history, in particular her disappointment with Otto's politics after his coronation in 962.[23] Before his assumption of power, the society of Gandersheim is shown to be one in which the secular and religious authorities worked cooperatively and tolerantly for the shared good. Thereafter, it is a story of political wheeling and dealing with the arrival of Otto I and his son Otto II as successive emperors. In this period, Church structures became increasingly rigid and presided over by bishops and abbots. The secular authorities lost power and women, aside from those of the royal family and the aristocracy, were systematically disenfranchised from positions of authority.

Hrotsvit's story is one of a highly able and well-educated woman. Her noble background gave her a sense of obligation and power both to act in ways she thought fit and to express her ideas. As a woman writer, her works allow us to see how discriminating she was in her reading, how she borrowed, adjusted and renewed the writings of others, so as to provide better reading material for the women for whom she was responsible. She was also prepared to cast an eye back over recent history, no doubt hoping that the future might be brighter.

Hrotsvit was only one of a large number of educated Carolingian and Ottonian women. In Ottonian manuscripts, illustrations of intellectual women – albeit aristocratic women – appear much more frequently than in Carolingian manuscripts.[24] There is little doubt that educated royal women contributed to the intellectual atmosphere in which the Ottonian Renaissance developed. Otto I, in

17 Albrecht Dürer's woodcut of Hrotsvit presenting her book to Otto the Great.

particular, presided over a new prosperity in which a particular and centralised intellectual life flourished. It may have been more limited than the Anglo-Saxon and Carolingian renaissances, but it was neither a time of darkness nor of silence. And all three renaissances of the Early Middle Ages were intellectual periods in which women readers made significant contributions. What is equally notable is the respect that educated women enjoyed, by and large: a deference that women readers had often been denied, and would be again.

The relative prestige of some women in the West was not unique in the world. Widespread assumptions about women's exclusion from the structures of other world religions, Islam in particular, have often been over-hasty. There is a long-lost tradition of Muslim women teaching the Qur'an, transmitting *hadith* (deeds and sayings of the Prophet Muhammad) and even making Islamic law as jurists.[25] Biographical dictionaries, classical writings, chronicles and letters contain fleeting references to women readers. It is likely that there were at least 8,000 female *hadith* scholars, dating back to the seventh century. One of the earliest was from Medina, a woman who reached the rank of jurist and issued *fatwas* on *hajj* rituals (those associated with the annual pilgrimage to Mecca). A tenth-century Baghdad-born woman jurist travelled through Syria and Egypt, teaching other women. So here, in perhaps one of the least likely parts of the world, and very early on, we discover women reading and, what is more, functioning in society as respected, educated members of the community, and with this, exerting considerable power.

Women have been book patrons from the beginning and, again, in many different places in the world. This kind of charitable giving brought respect and emphasised status, but it would be churlish not to accept that it was also bound up with the patron's faith in the importance of books and learning. Evidence of its significance has been found near Turfan, an oasis in Xinjiang lying on the Silk Road between China and India, where there is the remarkable Astana-Karakhoja tomb complex. The tombs have been excavated by treasure-seekers and archaeologists since the beginning of the twentieth century, and have been found to contain the mummified remains of a range of Gaochang citizens, from aristocrats to commoners, alongside papers, shoes, belts and hats, all buried from around 273 in the Western Jin dynasty to 778 in the Tang dynasty, and remarkably well preserved by the dry desert climate.

The tombstones and associated documents lend new insights into women's lives and concerns.[26] In the main, tomb epigraphs are as formulaic, not to say sentimental and clichéd, as those to be found in contemporary civic cemeteries around the world. But there are some fascinating cases where both a tomb inscription and written documentation have been found. Lady Dong Zhenying's tomb indicates that she died in the year 667, aged fifty-one. The manuscript discovered in her tomb is entitled a 'list of merit-earning good deeds'; unfortunately, there are gaps. But she is identified as a 'faithful follower of the Buddha and a pure female believer'. The manuscripts she copied are listed. She also sponsored numerous public readings of the *sutra* (Buddhist texts). Mention is also made of the generous support she offered to 300 Buddhist monks. Similar lists of merit-earning good works survive for other women, along with documents describing the religious activities of women in Gaochang. One remarkably long list of good deeds (comprising ninety-four lines) celebrates a woman who donated a horse, clothing and a silver plate to Buddhist monks, and sponsored a Buddhist ceremony, including public readings, to expiate the sins of her dead father-in-law. She was obviously a pious adherent to Buddhism and also paid for the copying of manuscripts. These Gaochang women were wealthy and belonged to the highest economic and social class. But they believed in the importance of the written word, the need for it to be enunciated to the illiterate, and the importance of its preservation for future generations.

The alleged 'silence' of women in the Early Middle Ages was only relative. The period was broken by bold whisperings in many parts of the world and these would gradually become louder. Early Christian aristocrats and holy women like Radegund, lay women like Dhuoda, Hrotsvit the playwright, and women monastics in Ireland like St Darerca, or Hilda of Whitby in England, and Buddhist noblewomen like Lady Dong Zhenying and Muslim women scholars in the East, provide varied examples of women readers who in turn inspired the reading of others, often women.

Broadly speaking, the intellectual renaissances of the Early Middle Ages were intimately linked with arguments about reading. Veneration of the Bible lies at the heart of the Christian tradition. Alongside the spread of scriptural reading came earnest and lively debates about interpretation. Indissolubly bound up in these debates were questions as to women's exegetical competence, or capacity properly to understand scripture. Hilda of Whitby commanded great respect, but she was unusual. An awareness of the dangers of misreading would become an increasing preoccupation during the medieval period. It marks the beginning of Christian hermeneutics. Gregory the Great had argued that reading was simply a conversation between the individual and the book, but some scholars became more technical, and fascinating treatises on the understanding of metaphor and allegory, for example, also appeared at this point, revealing an increasing awareness of the complexities and ambiguities of language and the scholarly need to trace authoritative understanding.

The Christian Church, in all its variety, was the crucial force in the drive towards both greater visual literacy as well as reading proper. Furthermore, whereas in antiquity the highest culture was the reserve of a social elite, Christians of all social classes were encouraged to read. Monks and nuns were charged with learning to read in order to preserve and promote the Christian faith. Literate mothers taught their children with one clear aim in view: the salvation of the soul. The Psalter became the child's copy book and the ability to read the Psalms became a basic test of literacy for many centuries.

These two phenomena – the awareness of the complexities and dangers of the reading process, and the continuing spread of literacy – overlapped. But it was the status of the woman reader and the power she might assume or should be denied, that would focus the greatest attention.

CHAPTER 3

—◦/◦/◦—

History, Mystery and Copying

Time, which flies irresistibly and perpetually, sweeps up and carries away with it everything that has seen the light of day and plunges it into utter darkness, whether deeds of no significance or those that are mighty and worthy of commemoration. . . . The science of History is a great bulwark against this stream of Time; in a way it checks this irresistible flood, it holds in a tight grasp whatever it can seize floating on the surface and will not allow it to slip away into the depths of Oblivion.[1]

THE idea that the worlds of writing and reading transcend the death of the author may be an insight which becomes a cliché over time, but this early description written by the Byzantine princess and scholar, Anna Komnene (1083–1153), has a striking freshness. Anna was the daughter of the Byzantine emperor Alexios I Komnenos and Irene Doukaina, and she became a historian like her northern sister, Hrotsvit of Gandersheim.

Anna must have been not only one of the best educated women of her time, but one of the most roundly educated too. She was born in the palace of Constantinople, the eldest of nine children. Like her brother and sisters she received a wide education, reading Greek philosophy and history, and studying maths and science. But she was also drawn to reading ancient poetry. Her parents considered this kind of literature, in which the gods' libidinous desires are violently or pleasurably satisfied, to glamorise role models inappropriate for a princess, and they feared the scenarios might entice, influence and perhaps even lead Anna astray. Like so many women readers throughout the world in every millennium, their attempts at censorship proved counterproductive. Under the able guidance of one of the imperial court's eunuchs, who also acted as one of her official tutors, she illicitly studied the prohibited poetry. Royal women of earlier and later periods, like many women in religious communities, received privileged educations. But women in court circles, unlike their religious counterparts, also witnessed first-hand the power struggles and political intrigues. Anna's reading gave her insights into the differences between the lives of women and men within ruling families. She knew she could not be a direct player in the politics of her family. History, she knew from her own reading, would forget her, as so many women before her had been forgotten.

Anna Komnene was accused of involvement in a plot to murder her brother and fled to the monastery of Kecharitomene in Constantinople. Here she was placed under house arrest and her life thereafter was circumscribed. But it gave her time and peace to write a learned history, the *Alexiad*. It is a remarkable work which tells the story of her father's reign between 1081 and 1118, describing his career as a highly successful military leader and founder of the Komnenian dynasty. In the preface she writes:

> I, Anna, daughter of the Emperor Alexios and the Empress Irene, born and bred in the purple [of royal birth] not without some acquaintance with literature – having devoted the most earnest study to the Greek language, in fact, and being not unpractised in Rhetoric and having read thoroughly the works of Aristotle and the dialogues of Plato; . . . I desire now by means of my writings to give an account of my father's deeds, which do not deserve to be consigned to silence nor to be swept away on the flood of Time into an ocean of obscurity.[2]

But she knew that in the very act of authoring a history, she too might be spared from the anonymity of oblivion. Aware that active political involvement was denied her because of her sex, Komnene, like so many women across time and space, asserted her identity and left her mark – as an author. Had she not read widely and intelligently her writings might have been forgotten, but, nourished by her extensive reading, she produced a history which survived and is regarded as one of the most accomplished writings by a woman author before the Renaissance.

The *Alexiad* is written in Homeric epic style and Anna's first-person interjections give it a powerful and unusual directness. Her obvious fascination with human psychology and motivation give it a peculiarly intimate quality. The plot is carefully crafted and the twists and turns in the story add pace and excitement. Much of it is an ingenious reworking of formulae borrowed from the *Iliad* and the *Odyssey*, works that Anna had obviously read and re-read. Her self-consciousness is still more intriguing. Anna often mentions both her own appetite for knowledge and her confidence in her own native intelligence. But she also acknowledges the example and guidance given to her, especially by other women and her mother in particular. All this is carefully spelled out in the *Alexiad*: 'Many a time when a meal was already served I remember seeing my mother with a book in her hands, diligently reading the dogmatic pronouncements of the Holy Fathers, especially of the philosopher and martyr Maximus.'[3] If Anna was confused or unsure in her reading of a book she knew her mother had already read, she would appeal to her: 'How could you of your own accord aspire to such sublimity? For my part, I tremble and dare not consider such things even in the smallest degree. The man's writing, so highly abstract and intellectual, makes the reader's head swim.'[4] What Anna is initially disconcerted by in her reading is the hypothetical, the probing quest for wisdom. When there is a good deal to puzzle over, Anna's mother's response is at once understanding and encouraging: 'I myself do not approach such books without a tremble. Yet I cannot tear myself away from them. Wait a little, and after a close look at other books, believe me, you will taste the sweetness of these.'[5] In other words, books are part of large jigsaw puzzle; no single work shows a complete picture, but as they become part of wider reading, they become intelligible.

Anna Komnene accomplished three things: she wrote her father's history, she demonstrated that women writers could achieve a form of immortality, and she explained how she had achieved these. Her extensive accounts of her reading and her mother's guidance would serve as an encouragement to other mothers and daughters. Reading is presented as a difficult challenge but one that girls and women should not shy away from. Furthermore, reading will inevitably throw up contradictions, but these should be confronted and can be resolved through more patient reading.

Women members of royal households, like Anna, form an important group of women readers in Byzantium during this period; the other was made up of nuns. At around the same time scholarly study became more institutionalised within all-male preserves. Some women were increasingly aware of their status as outsiders and sought to find ways of participating in fields that were apparently closed to them. Texts in the vernacular were becoming increasingly available, which was particularly important to those women readers who knew no Latin. Some women writers were themselves among the vanguard, often explicitly concerned to communicate the wisdom of classical writings to less-educated readers, including large numbers of women.

Nuns in the Middle Byzantine period (843–1204) tended to stay within the confines of their monastery unlike many nuns in the West who often went on pilgrimages or travelled widely. The wisdom of the Byzantine nuns was based on reading rather than lived experience and their influence seldom spread beyond their communities. But by the thirteenth century, education came to dominate nuns' lives and their importance spread beyond the confines of the monasteries. Their religious and scholarly enthusiasms were made possible by the division of women in religious communities into two distinct classes: church nuns, also called psalming nuns or choir nuns, and labouring nuns. The church nuns usually came from a more privileged social background, hence their higher levels of literacy and education; most women of aristocratic background came to the convent with knowledge of the Scriptures and the ability to read and write. The abbess, needless to say, was chosen from among the church nuns. The labouring nuns were the servants of the community, tending the gardens, preparing and serving food, working in the infirmary, making candles, spinning and embroidering, and keeping things clean and orderly. Women found themselves in nunneries for a variety of reasons, but for those able to enter the community as church nuns, it offered remarkable opportunities for learning, given the enormous household support provided by the labouring nuns. Some arrived very well educated, having received the tutelage of their fathers or, sometimes, household tutors. Among the abbesses, there were prolific letter-writers, poets and writers of hymns. For many women it was a sociable retreat from the world offering few responsibilities, comfortable surroundings and plenty of intellectual stimulus. Others were widows with little means of support.

The growing literacy among the church nuns in the Late Byzantine period (1204–1453) was part and parcel of a growing written tradition that recorded the vision of abbesses for their communities.[6] Theodora Synadene and her daughter Euphrosyne were both abbesses at a convent in Constantinople. Euphrosyne's written record of her vision for the community is based on her reading of her mother's text, and shows significant shifts of policy particularly in relation to women's education: the practice of educating lay girls living in the vicinity of the monastery was to come to an end. This had been a crucial contribution in terms of improving their literacy and, of course, giving them access to books and reading. Although the number of manuscripts available within communities was small, these could nevertheless be a crucial resource for girls who would otherwise have been completely divorced from the world of reading. But in Euphrosyne's so-called 'second typikon' (*hupotyposis deutera*, second book of rules), she stipulates that, contrary to the way things worked during her mother's time as abbess, the practice of educating local girls was to cease:

I absolutely forbid the admission of lay children for the sake of being educated and learning their letters or anything else. For I find that it is a pernicious influence on the morals and habits of the nuns. For anyone who has renounced the world once and for all, and then comes into contact again with lay people and assumes responsibilities incongruous with our vows, and thus causes confusion within himself and obscures the light of under-standing ... should not have entered a monastery nor donned monastic habit in the first place. .... But if certain girls should wish to be enrolled among the nuns, but want first to be educated, and learn lessons which contribute to the monastic rule, with the intention of being tonsured years later and numbered among the nuns, I fully approve and consent.[7]

For the girls living around Euphrosyne's abbey, access to the world of reading came at the price of withdrawal from that other world. For many it must have been an agonising choice. And, presumably, girls who had been under instruction must one day have been told, no doubt unexpectedly, that unless they intended to enter the community as nuns later on, they were no longer welcome in class. Some may have decided that it was a price worth paying and made their commitment. Others may simply have borne the brutal expulsion, aware that the life of community was not for them even if that meant an end to their formal education. The tale of this community is a reminder that the story of women's reading is not simply one of slow and steady progress. Even in parts of the world in which women readers continued to live and work in more stable and safe communities, the question of reading and the teaching of literacy could excite strong views and sudden changes of policy and opinion.

In very rare cases, women of the period assumed men's clothing in order to enter monasteries, sometimes to be close to their husbands and sometimes to benefit from the greater freedoms that monks enjoyed, particularly the opportunity to leave the community to travel. There are ten examples of such women in the *Bibliotheca Hagiographica Graeca*, lives of the saints estab-lished from ancient Greek sources and first compiled at the end of the nineteenth century.[8] For all the daring subversiveness of these women's lives, we know little about their reading and the importance it may have had for them.

Byzantine culture was to have an important influence on the Slavic tradi-tion. At some point around the seventh century the Slavs had adapted Byzantine Greek cursive letters so as to be able to write Scripture in their own language. But reading and writing remained almost exclusively the activity of churchmen. More extensive Russian writings emerged during the Kievan period (907–1169) such as lives of the saints, sermons and religious tracts. Literacy levels in Western Europe pale into insignificance when compared with the medieval Russian aristocracy. They read in Latin and Greek (not Russian) and, as Russia was a player in the European dynastic networks comprising England, France, Germany, Sweden, Hungary and Byzantium during the eleventh and twelfth centuries, Russian princes and princesses regularly married into the ruling houses elsewhere in Europe.[9] Russian women aristocrats were almost always highly literate and took their reading skills into sometimes hitherto illiterate royal families. Anna, the daughter of the Kievan Prince Yaroslav, married King Henri I of France on 19 May 1051 and, of the entire French royal family, she was the only literate member. State documents that had previously been signed by royal notaries were signed in her fair hand.[10]

Occasional works addressed to women, at least in part, also appeared. Grand Prince Vladímir Monomákh (1053–1125) wrote *His Instruction to his Children*, an autobiography addressed to both his sons and daughters.[11] Among his recommendations for a godly life is the need for education so as to facilitate understanding between peoples:

> But the main thing is that you should keep the fear of the Lord higher than anything else. If you should forget this, read this often; then shall I have no shame, and all will be well with you. Whatever good you know, do not forget it, and what you do not know, learn it; just as my father had learned, staying at home, five languages, for this makes one honoured in other lands. Indolence is the mother of all vices: what one knows, one forgets, and what one does not know, one does not learn.[12]

Here again, within a royal household, and at one remove, we glimpse women readers being encouraged to engage with writings in numerous languages. Most written material of the period, however, was in the form of epics recording triumphs in wars, and the Grand Prince includes much on his own military successes in his *Advice*.

Anna Komnene and Hrotsvit before her were not alone in taking a keen interest in history. They recognised the importance of recording the past. Other women looked to the need to establish seats of learning in order both to further education and to found libraries to preserve history. We know little of Abbot Hugues de Fleury except through his writings. But his pioneering *Historia Ecclesiastica* (*History of the Church*) was dedicated to a woman, the Countess Adela, daughter of William the Conqueror. In his epilogue Fleury wrote: 'Incited by the reputation of your generosity, venerable countess, I gathered these things from ancient historians, like a bee collecting honey from different flowers.' Unlike most of her contemporaries, Adela was a fluent reader of Latin and highly knowledgeable about the history of the Church. Another Adela, the daughter of the French king Robert II, took a deep interest in his politics of Church reform. Her second husband, Baldwin V of Flanders, was a great believer in the importance of education within the Church and Adela was behind her husband's founding of several collegiate churches. She was more or less directly responsible for establishing the colleges of Aire (1049), Lille (1050) and Harelbeke (1064), as well as the abbeys of Messines (1057) and Ename (1063). She withdrew to the abbey at Messines after her second husband's death.

Two of the most important centres of learning in twelfth-century England were Campsey Priory and Barking Abbey. Activities here were supported by the surrounding local communities, and it is likely that Isabella, Countess of Arundel, may have commissioned the saints' lives associated with both Campsey and Barking. This is the largest surviving account of the lives of Anglo-Norman saints and virgins. Clemence of Barking probably wrote the *Vie d'Edouard le confesseur* (*The Life of Edward the Confessor*) in the second half of the twelfth century. Clemence also translated a life of St Catherine, explaining her undertaking with uncomplicated frankness. She did this simply 'because she wanted to'.[13]

There were other women from less privileged backgrounds who were equally influential and in many ways more daring. Some women religious of the period spoke out against what they saw as the discriminatory views of the Church that kept women on the margins of the establishment proper. These women were almost invariably great readers but their reputations were often based on other aspects of their lives. This was largely because their images, after their deaths and sometimes even before, depended on how they were perceived by men. Their male contemporaries were intrigued by what they saw as the peculiarly feminine dimensions of their characters. Some women, knowingly or not, colluded in these men's inventions of them.

Hildegard of Bingen (1098–1179), an abbess but also a poet, composer and highly respected mystic, argued, somewhat extravagantly and often unsubtly, that the weakness of the Church was essentially a matter of men's inability to take charge on their own. Women, she argued, were necessary to fill a vacuum that men were incapable of filling. On the whole, her ideas were not gratefully received by churchmen, no doubt in part because of the vociferousness of her arguments. But she was not alone in her claims for women's greater natural closeness to Christian ideals including humility and compassion – claims that were based on her careful reading of Scripture. Hildegard was an extensive letter-writer and corresponded with notable churchmen of her day, including

Bernard of Clairvaux, Guibert of Gembloux and Pope Eugene III. She wanted, above all, to be taken seriously. But Hildegard and her protégée, Elisabeth of Schönau, were intensely aware of how they were ridiculed for their accounts of their mystical visions, which Hildegard frequently sketches out in her letters.

The apparent artlessness of her style is in fact carefully calculated. Her accounts of her visions obliquely sanction, and in some cases implicitly advocate, an understanding of the characteristics of men and women in which reversals of convention take place. The roles of men and women in the society in which she lived were not, in her view, in keeping with the roles of women in her reading; in some cases God's movements in the world are associated with conventionally feminine qualities, including gentleness. There is often a clever disingenuousness in her writings dependent on a developed understanding of rhetorical devices. She portrays men as weak and lacking in conscience, while women emerge as blessed with prophetic powers on which they are willing to act. She implies that 'learning' – that is, the more 'sophisticated' learning enjoyed by churchmen – has in some way alienated them from God, or at least inhibited their direct communication of spiritual experience. Not so for herself:

> The things that I write in vision I see and hear; nor do I add words, for that which I hear and make known are not elegant Latin words. . . . For in this vision I am not taught to write as philosophers do; and the words in that vision are not like words which resound from the human mouth, but like a sparkling flame and clouds moved through clear air.[14]

Hildegard presents herself as a naïve conduit for the pure transmission of God's will. It is an absurd pose given her carefully considered style, and one which could only derive from thorough and intelligent reading.

At the same time she suggests that the intellectual formation of her male counterparts, from which she has been excluded, leads to a deformation of, or at least a distancing from, God's message, as described by male visionaries. Her own reading was clearly extensive, but she strove to suggest that her lack of formal education allowed her to approach her experiences with an open mind:

> In this vision I understood without any human instruction the writings of the prophets of the Gospels, and of other saints and of certain philosophers, and I expounded a number of their texts, although I had scarcely any knowledge of literature since the woman who taught me was not a scholar. I also

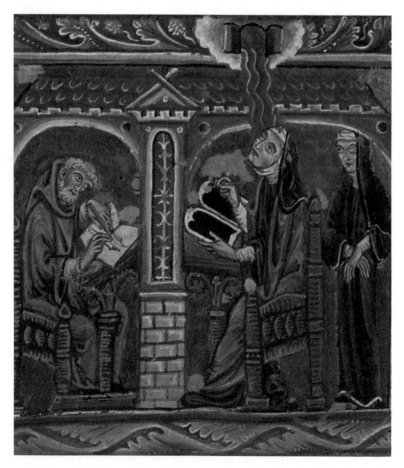

18 Volmar, Hildegard and Richardis. The wavy lines descending on Hildegard's head indicate heaven-sent inspiration.

composed and sang chant with melody, to the praise of God and his saints, without being taught by anyone, since I had never studied neumes [musical notation] or any chant at all.[15]

Hildegard's writings included music and songs, as well as works that discuss medicine and science. She did not claim that her thoughts in relation to these last two were inspired by visions, so her knowledge of written material must have extended beyond the narrowly religious.

Much of Hildegard's concern was to impress on churchmen the need to view women with greater respect and to allow them more involvement in the Church. Women would therefore need to be better educated, although Hildegard does not imply that this would lead women to record their religious experiences in a way that deformed their immediacy – a paradox she never explained. Instead she sought to impress others, in part arguing that her achievements were due to her innate abilities and her natural spiritual bent. Unlike Dhuoda and Hrotsvit, Hildegard's reputation was impressive, but only for a relatively brief period. Perhaps only Bernard of Clairvaux rivalled her in terms of her influence on her contemporaries. Men and women, royal and religious, corresponded with her from Rome, Paris, Constantinople and every other corner of the Holy Roman Empire. Typical of her correspondents' estimation of her was Hermann's, Bishop of Constance: 'the fame of your wisdom has spread far and wide and has been reported to me by a number of truthful people.'[16]

Undoubtedly, Hildegard was intellectually highly able. She had a thirst for knowledge and read widely. Her importance, however, diminished sharply after her death. Her community at Bingen did not develop into the intellectual centre it might have become. Responsibility for the community fell to Elisabeth of Schönau who was to prove more narrowly concerned with visions, rather than formal theology, philosophy or other intellectual disciplines. Elisabeth's account of her spiritual life, *Liber viarum Dei* (*Book of the Ways of God*), shows her to have been an attentive reader of Hildegard's writings, but what she authored is imitative rather than innovative. Like many educated women before her, it was her mystical gifts that inspired others.

The same had been true of Hildegard whose otherworldliness, rather than her educated humanity, had intrigued many of her contemporaries and prompted so many to correspond with her. There are many ironies here. In part she had sought subtly to present the world as one in which women as well as men might contribute to the religious life and religious understanding in complementary ways. In her visions Hildegard asserted that women could display characteristics conventionally associated with men, in particular conscience and courage. But she seems to have supposed that she would be most likely to attract the attention of others by presenting herself as a holy woman, rather than as a well-read intellectual. Her works were written so as to be read as spiritually reassuring and inspiring, as opposed to scholarly and authoritative. Perhaps she knew that it was best if she avoided what might be seen as a challenge to the male-dominated discipline of institutional theology, although she openly criticised aspects of it.

In many ways Hildegard was on the cusp of two worlds. Goddesses, prophetesses and princesses had been revered in earlier cultures, often in part because of a perceived superhumanity. Myths further ennobled them in the human memory. Hildegard tried to be both woman and divine, if not a prophetess. In some ways she succeeded. But the early medieval fascination with the unexplained and the mysterious soon gave way, in formal intellectual circles, to other approaches, often Aristotelian and scholastic, which integrated metaphysics, morality, aesthetics, logic, science and politics. Hildegard's writings inherently demonstrated her interest in aspects of these but her writing strategies obscured much of her wisdom. Did Hildegard seriously misjudge the influence she might have asserted more permanently? Or was her moment one in which she had no choice?

One of Hildegard's many correspondents was Peter Abelard, a canon of Notre Dame in Paris. He continued to advocate and promulgate one important aspect of Hildegard's thinking: the question of men and women's innate qualities and the importance of women being fully involved in religious education so as to broaden the wisdom of the Church. This emerges in the moving correspondence between Abelard and Heloïse, his former pupil and later abbess of the Paraclete, north-west of Troyes.[17] Peter had allegedly seduced Heloïse when she was in his charge, and was castrated for the offence. He was also prohibited from teaching and writing by Pope Innocent II. Exchanging letters with his love, he explored his conviction that women were, by nature, closer to Christ and Christian ideals. Men's tendency to involve themselves in violence and war, and their obsession with ideas of valour and power, all run contrary to the teachings of Jesus. Women's greater gentleness means they are able to communicate with God in an intimate friendship. The Church needed well-read, educated women. Still more controversially, he was one of a growing number of men and women of the Church who encouraged critical reading: 'By doubting we come to inquiry and by inquiry we perceive the truth.'[18] This is very much the kind of critical reading that Anna Komnene had advocated. Abelard's letters must have made encouraging reading material for Heloïse, and inspired her to greater boldness in the management of her abbey. She was particularly committed to education and learning for the women in her charge.

Heloïse had first come to Abelard's attention because of her reputation as an astute reader and scholar. A contemporary wrote that she 'was exceedingly erudite in both Hebrew and Greek letters'. This was at a time when Greek, and still more, Hebrew, was known to very few. Abelard's view was that 'in the extent of her learning she stood supreme'.[19] What we know of her independent thinking is contained in three letters to Abelard and the so-called *Problemata*,

19 A medieval illuminated manuscript depicting Abelard and Heloïse in conversation, *c.* 1483.

forty-two theological questions which she addressed to him. Heloïse emerges from her writings as an intellectual but also as a humanist. This is most visible in her denial of a separation between body, mind and spirit. Abelard was tormented by the 'obscene pleasures' of their love affair which he describes as having begun 'all in fire with desire'. And he considers his punishment to be appropriate: 'It was wholly just and merciful ... to be reduced in that part of my body that was the seat of lust and sole reason for those desires'. Heloïse's reading had led her to believe that the self was an indivisible whole. Abelard's castration was an injustice and she refers to God, 'whom I always accuse of the greatest cruelty in regard to this outrage'.[20] Heloïse's torments were intellectual. Most telling is her linguistic sensitivity in questioning her reading: 'We also ask how the Evangelists could have written so differently. ... What did the Lord want with all his diversity of Expression?'[21] God's truth, she believed, had been only mysteriously communicated. She repeatedly described her own interpretive frustrations and those of the women for whom she was responsible, and again there are echoes of Anna Komnene's reading experience: 'We are disturbed by many questions, we become sluggish in our reading, and are led to love less what we are most ignorant of in the sacred world, until we feel unfruitful the labour in which we are engaged.'[22] The community, she recognised, needed more intellectual enlightenment. She did not seek answers from Abelard, but the opening of an intense and extensive dialogue in which she would maintain a certain control. Heloïse would pose the questions.

Many of Abelard's letters were inspired by Heloïse's awareness of religious contradictions in her reading and were written at her request. Her position is very much one of an educated humanist of the late eleventh and early twelfth centuries, which drew upon an amalgam of classical and scriptural writing, and the early Christian writings of the Church Fathers like St Augustine and St Ambrose. Above all, Heloïse seeks to make sense of the relationship between her learning and how life should be lived. She was an intellectual and highly critical and astute reader, but she also articulated her understanding of selfless love between real people in the world: 'I wanted simply you, nothing of yours. I looked for no marriage bond, no marriage portion, and it was not my own pleasures and wishes I sought to gratify, as you well know, but yours.'[23] And it is this simple declaration that sowed the seed of her image as a perfect lover. All else was for a very long time forgotten. Petrarch read the correspondence between Abelard and Heloïse at some point between 1337 and 1343. His jottings on the flyleaf of the manuscript record nothing of his response to Heloïse's probing ideas: he was simply struck by the nature of her selfless love for Abelard. Like so many great women readers and intellectuals before her, she quickly attained a near-mythical status as the idealised lover of the great Abelard. Heloïse the great reader was for a long time overlooked.

Of course the lives and contributions of Hildegard and Heloïse, while not altogether exceptional, were nevertheless highly unusual compared to the vast majority of medieval women. Outside religious communities, the gradual rise of church schools in England, for example, went hand in hand with the discussion of curricula and, in particular, what was or was not desirable for girls to know. Gradually an accepted method for teaching literacy and other subjects was established. The first texts used for reading were Latin prayers: the Lord's Prayer, the Hail Mary and the Apostles' Creed. By the age of eleven or twelve, when pupils were properly literate, they would concentrate on the *trivium* (the arts of grammar, rhetoric and logic). A year or two later they would be ready for university where they would either take one of the subjects of the *trivium* to a higher level, or go on to the *quadrivium* which included arithmetic, geometry, astronomy and music, or specialise in medicine or law.[24] This 'scholastic method' was designed for boys but girls could advance as far as the *trivium*, and sometimes further. A virtual reading curriculum gradually evolved. For grammar, the works of Priscian and Donatus were primary. For maths and astronomy the key authors were Euclid, Ptolemy and Boethius. For civil law, as opposed to ecclesiastical law, the *Corpus iuris civilis* was the authority, and for canon law Gratian's *Decretum* and Alexander III's decretals. For knowledge of medicine pupils studied Galen, Hippocrates and the *Liber pantegni*. The Bible was naturally central to the study of theology along with Peter Lombard's twelfth-century *Sententiae*. The core works in Latin were by Virgil, Ovid, Cicero, Juvenal, Lucan, Livy, Seneca, Horace, Sallust, Martial and Petronius, among others. The founding of church schools gained momentum from the mid-twelfth century on.[25] These 'grammar school' pupils, girls and boys, came from a wide variety of backgrounds including the gentry, citizens, yeoman and the poor, providing they had well-to-do patrons.[26]

The rise of education was part of the so-called twelfth-century 'renaissance', with all its connotations of reading and scholarship. C.S. Lewis was one of the first to make a claim for this early renaissance but his highly persuasive arguments are largely bound up with what he saw as the crucial cultural changes brought about by scholasticism. The word comes from the Latin, *scholasticus*, which means 'that (which) belongs to the school', and it was a method of learning taught by the scholastics ('schoolmen') of medieval universities from around 1100 to 1500. Women were excluded from these institutions, although there were women who read independently and seriously; there are also some remarkable examples of women cross-dressing in order to gain access to a university. In Krakow, Poland, towards the end of the fourteenth century, a young woman inherited a large fortune probably as a result of the death of her husband. Wealthy, and liberated from marriage, she disguised herself as a man and studied for two years in the Faculty of Arts at Krakow University. She was quickly recognised as a conscientious and highly able student, but just before receiving her degree, her cover was blown by a soldier who had recognised her ruse and was no doubt jealous of her keen intelligence. She was taken before a tribunal and when asked by the judge why she had behaved as she had, she replied simply and movingly, 'Amore studii' – for the love of learning. He was struck by her story and all ended happily enough. She chose to be sent to a convent where she rose to the rank of abbess and strongly encouraged reading and learning among those in her charge.[27]

Concurrent with the growth of scholasticism were developments in Jewish thinking, notably in the writings of Maimonides (1135–1205), one of the outstanding legal scholars and philosophers of the Middle Ages, who lived in

Egypt. The position of women was not one of his great concerns but in his major legal code, *Mishneh Torah*, he sets out women's entitlements within a marriage and supports women's rights to leave the home, both of which went against prevailing custom. He did not, however, go so far as to advocate women's education explicitly. Innovations in the Islamic tradition at this time also bear comparison with aspects of scholasticism. For instance, from the eighth century on, the Mutazilite school of Islam with whom the great thinker Averroes was associated, pursued a rational theology, 'ilm al-Kalam, in the face of the prevailing orthodox Islam. This can be seen as a development not unlike Western scholastic theology, and here women were significantly involved.[28]

As early as the ninth century, women played a key role in the establishment of a number of Islamic educational foundations.[29] Fatima al-Fihri (d. 880) was responsible for what was later known as the University of Al-Karaouine which opened in 859. Her father was a wealthy entrepreneur and she migrated with him from Qairawan (in today's Tunisia) to Fes (Morocco). After his death she used her inheritance to found the university. She was a devout Muslim and apparently fasted while the building work was underway. During the Ayyubid dynasty in the twelfth and thirteenth centuries, women were responsible as patrons for a large number of mosques and *madrasah*, educational institutions which were both religious and secular. Some but not all of these women patrons were members of royalty.

By the twelfth century there were also growing opportunities for women's education and women could qualify as scholars and teachers having received *ijazahs* (academic degrees). Among the higher social classes there was concern that both sons and daughters obtain the highest possible level of education. Female education in the Islamic world was inspired by Muhammad's wives: Khadijah, a successful businesswoman, and Aisha, a renowned scholar of Muhammad's writings (*hadith*). Muhammad held the women of Medina in high esteem because of their desire for religious knowledge: 'How splendid were the women . . .; shame did not prevent them from becoming learned in the faith.' Women were rarely allowed to attend formal classes but were permitted to attend lectures and teaching provided in public places, mosques in particular.

There were, needless to say, those that opposed women's education for reasons which may or may not have been spurious. The North African writer Muhammad ibn al-Hajj (d. 1336) alleged that the women who attended his lectures were disruptive:

> [Consider] what some women do when people gather with a shaykh [Sufi teacher] to hear [the recitation of] books. At that point women come, too, to

hear the readings; the men sit in one place, the women facing them. It even happens at such times that some of the women are carried away by the situation; one will stand up, and sit down, and shout in a loud voice. [Moreover,] her *'awra* [parts of the body that must be covered in Muslim law] will appear; in her house, their exposure would be forbidden – how can it be allowed in a mosque, in the presence of men?[30]

But there are vivid accounts of the impression some women scholars made on men. A female scholar, or *muhaddithat*, in twelfth-century Egypt, made a deep impact on her male students and they marvelled at her thorough knowledge of a 'camel load' of reading material.[31] It is a wonderful image that conjures their awe of the sheer weight of her scholarship.

Up until the twelfth century, women amounted to no more than roughly 1 per cent of Muslim scholars. But they were highly respected. The Sunni Islamic scholar Ibn Asakir (1106–75) was the author of the *History of Damascus* (*Tarikh Dimashiq*), one of the key Islamic histories of Syria. It is largely a biographical work but also contains a number of Arabic poems. Ibn Asakir claimed that he had studied under eighty different female teachers in his time.[32]

In Western Europe in the Early Middle Ages, women readers in religious communities also found themselves in positions not dissimilar to their male counterparts, although they remained more financially dependent on bequests.[33] Monks were generally able to buy the books they had heard about and were interested in, whereas roughly a fifth of the books in medieval nunneries were bequests and often unsolicited. Prayers were often requested in exchange. Gifts to nunnery libraries came from outside communities, but also through the Church.

Among the more optimistic and practical communities were those of the Dominicans, and they offered girls a relatively sophisticated literary education, not unlike that offered to some noblewomen. The level of education varied from nunnery to nunnery and naturally depended on the qualifications and abilities of the nuns. Three languages were involved: Latin, French and English. In Dominican nunneries and other pockets of the community, the importance of women's literacy was clearly recognised and as new evidence emerges, the impression of the High Middle Ages as a period in which men's literacy far outweighed women's, may be revised. It may well be that those women who could read were more highly informed in their reading than men who read merely for practical reasons. The Dominican Order took reading very seriously and virtually all nuns were literate and dedicated to religious study. These communities were almost exclusively based in towns, and from the fourteenth century on, started to promote girls' education. The level of analysis with which they went about biblical exegesis was far more intellectually rigorous than the equivalent study in the local boys' grammar schools.

The importance of the book for the Dominicans is well illustrated by the impact of the arrival in 1428 of ten sisters from Schönensteinbach, Alsace, at the community of St Catherine's Convent in Nuremberg. They had been sent to introduce the reformed Dominican life to the convent, one aspect of which was greater emphasis on learning. The arrival of the new nuns marked a turning-point in the convent's intellectual history as the new arrivals set about establishing a library. This was not unusual, but what is extraordinary, in the case of St Catherine's, is that a remarkable number of detailed fifteenth-century book lists survive.[34] One details the books privately owned by the sisters, another those belonging to the convent. Two further lists record the table readings (delivered during meals) for the years 1429–31 and 1455–61. Before the reform the library contained forty-six books, mostly comprising sermons, tracts and prayers. Interestingly there were no manuscripts describing the Dominican rule or its constitutions.

Central to the reform was the systematic collecting of books to regulate and stimulate the spiritual life of the community. By the end of the fifteenth century the library contained a remarkable 500–600 books. These served a number of purposes. First and foremost extracts from them provided meal-time readings. The senior cleric, Bartholomäus Texery, whose *Ordination* set out the reforms to be put in place, had stipulated: 'Thus I prescribe that you always have table readings during meals . . . in German in the morning and, in the evening, partly in Latin and partly in German.' Interestingly the sisters did not follow his prescriptions to the letter and dispensed with readings in Latin. Extracts were taken from the Bible alongside interpretations, mostly Wilhelm Durandus's *Rationale divinorum officiorum*, sermons (particularly Johannes Tauler's), tracts and saints' lives. The nuns were also expected to read in private after meals. They could borrow books from the library but some nuns arrived at the convent with books of their own, on average a dozen or so. The extensive library at St Catherine's was central to the lives of the nuns but important beyond the community too. Other convents that were reformed by the Nuremberg sisters, at Altenhohenau and Frauenaurach, were given books copied by them for their libraries. The majority of the books in the library of St Catherine's were copied by nuns known as *scriptrices*. They were exempt from manual work and had their own private rooms where they could work in peace. Other books were given to the library by nuns' family members, as many of them came from the upper classes. Friends, both secular and clerical, also gave to St Catherine's.

The Nuremberg sisters took books and reading very seriously indeed. They were fundamental to the reformed Dominican way of life. While there was considerable variety in the library collection, each work was chosen exclusively on the basis of its potential to help the nuns in the Divine Service which was the focus of their lives.

Elsewhere there were similar practices. We know that in England some books were given or left to the nuns by local aristocratic women. In 1399, Eleanor, Duchess of Gloucester (*c.* 1400–52) left a collection of seven books in French to her daughter Isobel, a nun of the London Minoresses.[35] Since the owning of personal property was, at least in principle, forbidden, the books found their way into the library. Occasionally an inscription indicates that an individual nun had temporary ownership of a volume, *ad terminum vitae* ('until life's close'). Thereafter the book would become the property of the library.

The libraries of English nunneries started to grow significantly in the late-fourteenth and fifteenth centuries, but what motivated aristocratic women to

20 A fourteenth-century illumination of a woman arriving at a convent.

give to nunnery libraries often remains obscure. Given the instabilities of medieval society some no doubt wanted to ensure that a book that deeply mattered to them was deposited in a relatively safe place. A certain status also came with an ability to make bequests. And some women were concerned to provide their counterparts with works which they themselves had found spiritually nourishing. But how much were these works read and studied by the nuns? There is a lack of marginalia in the written material that was held in nunnery libraries compared to that in male communities. Were women readers more respectful of the works they read, and more reluctant to deface them with their own jottings? Or were the books simply much less read?[36]

The question is a vexed one, but the story of what nuns may or may not have read pales into relative insignificance as the number of other women readers begins to grow. What they read and the effects that their reading had on them is a new chapter in the story. And they read and wrote more and more in the everyday vernaculars.

CHAPTER 4

—❦❦❦—

Outside the Cloister

OUTSIDE religious communities, educational initiatives were slowly percolating through the social system. Some women of the merchant classes were gradually becoming literate, although for them developed numeracy skills were more essential. Merchants and artisans taught women members of the household so that they could work unpaid in the family business. If the man of the household became incapacitated for any reason, or died, women often assumed a rare control and responsibility involving increased understanding of the business.

The growth in international trade encouraged new kinds of writing to support increasingly complex forms of administration. At the same time a new form of public entertainment began to flourish and one which would come to revolutionise – some would say dominate – women's private reading for hundreds of years. The tales of the Latin-trained goliards (mostly members of the clergy) were being pushed out of the market by new kinds of stories. Their subject was, almost exclusively, romantic love. Muslim-influenced Spain was the crucible of this new genre, and the stories spread from Spain across the Pyrenees to southern France and then panned out across Europe. The *jongleurs*, itinerant public entertainers, quickly picked up the new material and in marketplaces, fairs, manor houses and castles, they pronounced their love poetry in exchange for a few coins. The twelfth-century poet Petrus Pictor remarked on the widespread popularity of the unrefined *jongleurs*, adding that some churchmen of high rank seemed more drawn to this new fast-growing tradition than his own more elevated verses. Still more influential than the new tellers and tales was the fact that the best of the material started to be written down, the Arthurian legends most famously. These were in turn translated from Old French into Latin and numerous vernacular versions.[1]

The division between written religious material and the classics on the one hand, and oral literature in the vernacular on the other, blurred as the oral traditions were gradually committed to paper in the spoken languages familiar to everyone. Many of these incorporated a good deal of what is dismissively called 'folk' religion. Stories and poems that had long been enjoyed within the oral tradition were transcribed into many languages: Old French, Middle High German, Middle English, Old Norse, Old Spanish and many others. Some of the preciousness fell away in the process. Oral literature was often full of redundant stylistic repetitions – rhymes, clichés and ornate but meaningless flourishes. Written prose had a clarity and precision and a new realism: stories took place in a particular environment at a particular time involving characters who were infinitely more believable than the 'types' of the oral tradition.

As writing in the vernaculars emerged, some women sought to make their contribution, producing reading material that could be read by less-educated women, particularly those who knew no Latin. One of the most influential lay women was Marie de France (*c.* 1139–1216), perhaps the illegitimate sister of King Henry II of England.[2] Marie is generally assumed to be the first woman writer in France, author of her famous *Lais* ('lays', or short narrative poems), 103 animal fables, and the earliest vernacular version of an account of a pilgrimage to St Patrick's Purgatory. She was a highly sophisticated woman reader and her writing had a profound effect on other women readers. We know little about her but we can be sure of some of her reading. She read in a number of languages: English, French, Latin, as well as Breton, Welsh and Celtic. She knew the so-called 'Romances of Antiquity', especially *Le roman d'Enéas*, a medieval French romance based on Virgil's *Aeneid*. She had also clearly read the anonymous *Roman de Thèbes* (*Novel of Thebes*) and Benoît de Sainte-Maure's *Roman de Troie* (*Novel of Troy*).

But much of the imaginative colour and mystery, the fantastic boats and strange creatures, the metamorphosing birds, werewolves and fairies, were innovative in terms of their striking vividness. Some of the richness of the *Lais* came from both written and oral sources. Sometimes Marie is explicit about these. In 'Chevrefoil' ('Parsley'), the story of Tristan and Isolde, she claims that 'many people have recited it to me and I have also found it in a written form'.[3] Whatever her sources, Marie radically transformed the story. From the very beginning her readers, both men and women, recognised something original in her writing – a humanity and an absence of bullying argument. Her stories tell of human adventures and loves which are more realistic than those of earlier stories. Most importantly, from the point of view of her women readers, they explore relationships between men and women that are equal.

But there is something much more important about her writing in terms of her women readers' experience. What we read in the prologue to the *Lais* is a statement of the role of the individual psyche in the interpretation of his or her world. Marie asserts the idea of the individual, rather than group-belonging, as the bedrock of identity. With this came personalised notions of sin and penance, and in the parallel secular world, of personal legal responsibility. Marie's new preoccupation with the experience of the individual is also visible in the wandering lonely heroes of romance, in the anguished voice of the love lyric.

As a woman writer, Marie also explores sexual difference and integrates the feminine into the wholly male world of the epics of the first feudal age. Joseph Bédier (1864–1938), one of the great French medieval scholars, echoed the Anglo-Norman monk and poet Denis Piramus's assessment of Marie:

> E si en aiment mult l'escrit
> E lire le funt, si unt delit,
> E si les funt sovent retreire.
> Les lais solent as dames pleire:
> De joie les oient e de gré,
> Qu'il sunt sulum lur volenté.

21 A manuscript illumination from Marie de France's *Fables*. Marie is shown on the first page as author of the work.

And they [counts and barons and knights] greatly love her writing, they have it read aloud, they have them [lays] often told, and they take delight. For lays are used to pleasing ladies: they hear them willingly and in joy, for they suit their taste.[4]

Marie wrote, 'When a truly beneficial thing is heard by many people, it then enjoys its first blossom.'[5] This is a remarkably modern idea: the meaning of stories belongs to the reader (or listener) and is created in the act of engagement between the reader (or listener) and the writing. Marie's audiences clearly felt that they were hearing 'a truly beneficial thing', her women readers above all. For the first time they recognised a world in which women's individual consciousness was convincingly brought alive, along with its consequences: the difficulties and challenges of living in a male-dominated world. Marie de France's reputation spread widely. Her work was translated into other languages during the Middle Ages, including Italian, German, Old Norse and English. Interestingly – reversing the usual flow of the tide – she was also translated into Latin.[6] Marie's writing deserves a key chapter in the history of Western feminism.

Some women readers had access to other works in the vernacular, including those of an English mystical tradition. These were often written by women who themselves drew on their own reading of a diverse and international body of other women authors. One notable example is the anonymous *Ancrene Wisse* or *Guide for Anchoresses*, a monastic rule (or manual) written in the early thirteenth century in English based on a West Midlands dialect.[7] Another manuscript contains a guide, together with a set of texts that have become known as the 'Katherine Group': 'Katerine', 'Margerete', 'Iuliene', 'Hali Meidhad' and 'Sawles Warde'.[8] Writings of these kinds by holy women spread throughout Europe thanks to the Franciscans. The *Ancrene Wisse* is full of encouraging aphorisms: 'From little grows much'; 'Hope keeps the heart in health, whatever the flesh may suffer'; ' "Without hope," as they say, "the heart would break" '; 'What is a word but wind?' One of its many authors also appeals to his or her future readers: 'Read some of this book at your leisure every day; and I hope that if you read it often it will prove very profitable to you; otherwise I shall have spent my long hours very ill. I would rather, God be my witness, set out on foot for Rome than begin the work over again!'

There are echoes in the *Ancrene Wisse* of the work of Marie d'Oignies and St Elizabeth of Hungary, which remind us that a small elite group of women readers and writers were bound together in what was essentially a remarkable international reading group, enlightening and stimulating interested women.

22 The enclosure of an anchoress by the bishop, from an illustrated Pontifical.

Nevertheless despite this small but significant revolution within the vernacular traditions, most true reading was still of Latin texts, and largely ecclesiastical. Intimately related to this was the use of Latin in schooling and scholarship. A tension developed between the 'authority' of the Church's writing, and the traditions of the lively oral patrimony of particular regions. This conflict between churchmen and laity persisted for a very long time and some women, like the anonymous author of the *Ancrene Wisse*, attempted to mediate between the two. But prejudice against women's reading remained rife. Philip of Novara was explicit about what he saw as the pernicious consequences of a girl learning to read, except within the setting of a religious order: 'It is not appropriate for girls to learn to read or write unless they wish to become nuns, since they might otherwise, coming of age, write or receive amorous missives.'[9] It seems not to have occurred to the honourable Philip that men should be denied access to literacy so as not to be in a position to write to – or read letters from – ladies in the first place. The likes of St Thomas Aquinas and St Bernard of Siena, those formidable misogynists and arch-conservatives of the Church, argued that intellectual curiosity, and women's above all, was a sin.[10] What more evidence was needed than the story of Eve tasting the forbidden fruit of the tree of knowledge?

Whereas in Central Europe aristocratic women were readers of religious material above all, in Northern Europe political changes had no doubt unforeseen effects on women's literacy and involvement with the book. Some reading material, as elsewhere in Europe, was provided by liturgical books in Latin such as missals and breviaries. As early as 1200 certain members of the aristocracy, including women, had their own prayer books for private use. Ten psalters owned by Scandinavians are known from the period 1150–1350. They were all imported from France, England or Flanders. But other material was also available to women. In Norway, around 1200, the king initiated a separation of state and church, establishing an administration made up largely of literate laymen. A parallel development was the transformation of the traditional *hirð* ('court') of warriors and priests into a group where literate men and women of the laity had a place. But this new elite obviously had little sense of a tradition, nor any keen sense of an associated identity. The kings' sagas, which were essentially vernacular stories in Old Norse recounting Norway's history from the ninth century onwards, were an attempt to fill the void. They were commissioned by monarchs and wealthy Icelandic patrons who visited the courts. The reading of the sagas, and discussion of them, involved both men and women.[11]

The widespread rise of the vernaculars, so crucially important to women readers, is sometimes visible within a single work which passed between multiple owners. By the High Middle Ages, books, although rare, had become more common possessions among the rising middle classes in Western Europe. The Bible, psalters and lives of saints, were produced in the largest quantities. Most Bibles included psalters, while editions of the Psalms also included hymns, songs and dirges, eulogies and forms of royal praise. Within nunneries and monasteries these psalters lay at the heart of the liturgical *horae* ('hours'), the seven times of day when nuns and monks gathered to say the Divine Office. In manor houses and castles with their own chapel secular devotions took place, again using the psalter as the principal order of service. This practice was more often than not overseen by the lady of the house and we know from wills that psalters were very often the property of the lady.

By far and away the most popular books were Books of Hours. These were in effect liturgical scrapbooks, hotchpotches made up of the 'Little Office of the Blessed Virgin Mary' (a collation of brief services) designed to be said at various points throughout the day, and including psalms, hymns, prayers and, very often, a calendar of saints. Material could be added by readers, and in some cases removed or defaced. In this way readers were also to varying degrees the creators of their Books of Hours. These could be humble and crude or lavish depending on the wealth of the owner. They were generally small, easily portable and designed to accompany the owner to church or chapel, to be left on the bedside, or taken on walks and journeys. Books of Hours proved most popular with women and were sometimes beautifully illuminated wedding gifts to brides. What is particularly significant about the adoption of Books of Hours by women is that to some extent they allowed an independent relationship with God, without the mediation of a priest, or the Church. Reading gradually came to be perceived as a private and individual act of devotion. Equally significant is the fact that each Book of Hours was unique. This, combined with the emphasis on private devotion, reflects an important shift: the growing prominence of women's individuality.

Books of Hours certainly proved highly influential in the development of women's literacy as regular listening to, and reading of, one specific text encouraged reading generally. Women might not only establish an independent relationship with the Divine, but could also access other texts – independently. On the other hand Books of Hours sometimes also functioned as medieval status symbols or fashion accessories. Although only a small percentage of Books of Hours has survived, some are in remarkably good condition, suggesting minimal use. These books were sometimes no more than outward signs of religious humility; for others, they were genuinely intellectually and spiritually nourishing.

Books of Hours first appeared in the thirteenth century. An early example, known as the Murthly Hours, was written in the 1280s.[12] (Murthly is an estate in Perthshire, Scotland, owned by a family who inherited the book.) It is a stunning example and includes finely painted initial letters showing figures and scenes and a wealth of other detailed decoration in the margins including dragons, birds and beasts. It is attributed to a group of very highly skilled Parisian illuminators of the Cholet Group. Of great interest in and of itself, this particular Book of Hours also provides vivid insight into the piety, beliefs and literacy of its owners, some of them women, over three centuries. Sometime after it was first produced a set of full-page miniatures of Old and New Testament subjects painted by thirteenth-century British artists was bound in.

We cannot ever know the name of the first owner of this beautiful book, but we do know that she was a woman. It was conventional to include a portrait of the owner in one of the initials. She is clearly a female member of the nobility living in England and she is shown as a finely dressed young woman reading a book.

The earliest addition to the text in Anglo-Norman was probably made for her. It provides a striking example of the secular belief in the power of the Virgin Mary to protect 'from shame and ill repute [and] from sudden death and from all ills and from the pains of hell.' What follows, suggesting that

23 The opening of the Gradual Psalms in the Murthly Hours is marked with a decorated initial. It shows the owner kneeling and reading her Book of Hours while Christ looks down upon her.

these additions were almost certainly for a woman, is a prayer to be said by a woman to her guardian angel. Slightly later, around 1400, Gaelic additions were made including Folk-Christian protective charms. At the end of the calendar of the Christian year are two obituary notices that connect the families of the MacDougalls and the Stewarts of Lorne. The book may have belonged to Joan de Valence, the half-niece of Henry III of England, a woman of sufficient standing to have a luxurious Book of Hours.

Other clues to later owners are in the form not of additions but erasures – attempts at censorship. The face of Cain and the genitals of the drunken Noah – which we can imagine may have been more likely to offend a woman's sensibility – have been obliterated. In the fifteenth century an owner saw fit to include prayers to Scottish saints, St Duthac and St Boniface, possibly personal or family patrons.

The Murthly Hours survived the Reformation purges of popish books in private family ownership. During this period English captions were added, mostly correctly, to identify the subjects of the thirteenth-century miniatures.

This seems to have been the last chapter in the book's life as a family prayer book. When it was discovered in the nineteenth century it had become a highly collectable artefact of medieval antiquity. It is now in the National Library of Scotland and perused and studied by women and men readers alike.

The additions to the Latin in the Murthly Hours trace a shift from Anglo-Saxon to vernacular English. Over the same period the growing awareness of languages and their ambiguities led, little by little, to challenges to Latin as the supreme 'scholarly' language. The Italian lyric poet and scholar Petrarch (Francesco Petrarca, 1304–74) claimed that no more than a handful of his contemporaries knew Greek, which he saw as essential to real scholarship. In the history of reading, however, Pertrarch matters far more as a reader-harvester. Whereas most readers considered a text an indivisible whole, Petrarch counselled a selective approach: 'When you come to any passages that seem to you useful, make a firm mark against them, which may serve as lime in your memory, lest otherwise they might fly away.'[13] To some extent this approach to reading marks the beginning of the end for the scholastic tradition and heralds 'humanist reading', where the reader becomes, in a sense, the author of his or her own work, built on the fragments that he or she has selected from the literature he or she has read.

Reading gradually emerged, among other things, as a way to make sense of how to live, particularly in the face of terrible events. The Black Death, which devastated Europe in the mid-fourteenth century, was just such a catastrophe. Although some chroniclers spoke of the plague as an apocalyptic moment at the end of the world, and medicine remained primitive, there is evidence that people retained an optimistic outlook, continuing to believe that the Black Death was part of God's benevolent plan, and a sign of a new beginning. Their reading may have helped them; cataclysmic events have the effect of creating an atmosphere in which people look to stories that explain them and offer consolation. Another consequence of the Black Death was the sudden drop in populations throughout Northern Europe, which meant a growing number of books and other written materials were available to a smaller audience. People were drawn to works in the vernacular which offered insights and comfort. Julian of Norwich (1342–c. 1416), who lived through eight outbreaks of plague, continued to declare 'all shall be well' with the world.

Julian herself was a great reader and a busy harvester of material that inspired her. Her own writings were highly influential.[14] Considered to be one of the greatest English mystics, she experienced visions over a period of some twenty years and these formed the basis of her major work, *Sixteen Revelations of Divine Love* (c. 1393), one of the very first books written by a woman in the English language. Little is known of Julian's life and even her name is uncertain; her modern appellation comes from the Church of St Julian in Norwich where, in an adjoining cell, she lived as an anchoress. Aged thirty, she was struck down by illness and thought that she would die. This is when her intense visions began – and they continued until 13 May 1373, when her illness finally abated. Julian was well known throughout England as a spiritual authority and many visited her, including Margery Kempe.

Julian's theology was one of God's love and compassion. Suffering might be a punishment from God, but it was also a means of being drawn closer to him. Her famous saying, 'Sin is behovely but all shall be well, and all shall be well, and all manner of things shall be well', sums up her theology and has become one of the most famous lines in Catholic theological writing. By describing sin as 'behovely' she expressed her view that it was part of the natural order of things, but her faith was based on an essential optimism. Although Latin was the language of religion at the time, Julian wrote in a straightforward Middle English. She describes herself in her *Revelations* as 'a simple creature unlettered', but this belies the power and directness of her writings. She supposes that her readers will be 'mine evenchristen' ('other Christians') or those who are 'contemplative' (meaning nuns). Like so many early women readers and writers, her life and work have been the subject of heated disputes. Some argue that Julian was guided by male spiritual advisers. More recently, evidence of an informal collective of women exchanging knowledge and inspiring each other has been proposed.[15] Julian, as a woman reader, like so many others, continues to arouse controversy – even hundreds of years after her death.

Julian is famous for her faith in a better future and in that she was not alone, despite the extraordinary uncertainties of the time. But her popularity was also due to her sensitivity to what her readers wanted. This relationship between the vernacular writer and the reader was encouraged by the growing affordability of books. These would become significantly cheaper because of changes in manuscript production. Making parchment was a long, slow, smelly business but by the thirteenth century techniques for making paper travelled from China via the Arabs to Spain and Italy. By about 1330 there were paper mills in France and by 1390 in Germany. The first paper mill in England dates from 1495, meaning that paper no longer had to be imported from the Continent. The price of paper decreased and by around 1500 an average skin cost about the same as 100 sheets of paper. Parchment did continue to be used (for example, in service books) because of its extraordinary durability. By this point a number of English medieval nunnery libraries, most notably Barking (Essex), Shaftesbury (Dorset) and Syon (Middlesex) had impressive holdings.[16]

A number of women readers were inspired to write in vernaculars. Christine de Pizan (*c.* 1364–1430), who was born in Venice, wrote French ballads, *rondeaux*, lays and a remarkable biography of Charles V of France.[17] Her father was Tommaso di Benvenuto da Pizzano (Thomas de Pizan), a physician, professor of astrology, and councillor of the Republic of Venice. He was appointed astrologer to Charles V while Christine was still a small child and they moved to Paris. She spent the rest of her life in France. She was well educated in languages, literature, science and geometry. At the age of fifteen she married Etienne de Castel and they had three children. After the death of her husband she turned increasingly to writing, producing ballads and, later, books.

Just as women patrons provide insights into their desires for their reading, so women writers often wrote in response to reading works with which they found fault or, more often, which deeply offended them. Stung and dismayed by her reading of *Lamenta*, a tirade against women by the caustic cleric and poet Matheolus, Christine completed *Le Livre de la Cité des Dames* (*The Book of the City of Ladies*) in 1405.[18] (Matheolus had been translated into French by Jean le Fèvre de Ressons in 1370 and he, cunningly perhaps, also published his own work, *Book of Joy*, a refutation of Matheolus and a work in praise of women.) Christine begins with what mystifies her about men's vision of women:

> an extraordinary thought became planted in my mind which made me wonder why on earth it was that so many men, both clerks and others, have said and continue to say and write such awful, damning things about women and their ways. I was at a loss as to how to explain it. It is not just a handful of writers who do this. . . . It is all manner of philosophers, poets and orators too numerous to mention, who all seem to speak with one voice and are unanimous in their view that female nature is wholly given up to vice.[19]

The women in Christine's imagined city are noble through cultivated reading rather than by birth. They are exemplars of women who attain both grace and distinction while also contributing to society. The book also contains a number of didactic dialogues between Reason, Honesty and Justice, the last of whom requires Christine to construct the allegorical city that the women will inhabit. Christine asks why women should not receive the same education as men and why this idea is so abhorrent to men. She discusses the criminality of rape, women's innate political skills and above all their natural capacity for reading and study.

In the pre-print era, manuscripts like Christine's were copied and circulated by scribes. One consequence was that authors lost control of their writing and many were effaced altogether. Numerous women writers may have been

24 Christine de Pizan, *Le Livre de la Cité des Dames*. On the left, Christine with her books receives the three figures of Reason, Honesty and Justice; on the right, Christine sets about building her City of Women, aided by the figure of Justice.

erased from history, but not Christine. Her work is a pre-eminent early example of a woman advocating women's education and this first and foremost through reading. She is also an exemplary early case of a woman who was intolerant of misogyny, and recognised that one way of combating it was through women's literacy. Most tellingly, when Jean de Meun produced his continuation of Guillaume de Lorris's famous poem *Roman de la Rose*, she was dismayed. She considered it both immoral and misogynistic; de Meun's work slanders all womankind, and Christine and some of her contemporaries read it as a *summa* of a long tradition critical of women. In her book *L'Epistre au Dieu d'amours* she took a strong stand against de Meun, espousing women's achievements and innate moral virtues. In 1415 Christine retired to a convent where she continued to write.[20] Christine is an important type of woman reader who emerges across time and space. She read and was shocked by her reading, and wrote to encourage other women to read, and through their reading to counter sexual prejudice.

With the proliferation of writings in the vernaculars, attitudes to women's literacy became increasingly varied and complex. Women readers were seen by many as a potential threat to the status quo. This led some women readers to feign illiteracy, while others were no doubt illiterate but absorbed a good deal from listening to books being read aloud to a point where it is hard to believe that they were actually unable to read. As women's literacy became an increasingly contentious subject, so the record of women's reading becomes more obscure, adding to the difficulty of establishing reliable patterns during the period.

Margery Kempe (c. 1373–1438), was the supposed author of *The Book of Margery Kempe*, a remarkable work of late medieval spiritual literature and the first autobiography in the English language. She had to attempt to prove that she was a non-reader when her obvious intimate knowledge of the gospels made the authorities in York suspect her as a Lollard, a group which held, among other things, that everyone should have access to a Bible in the vernacular.[21] Kempe was subject to pressures from both the Church and civil authorities and was tried a number of times for allegedly preaching and teaching in public. She was also tried for wearing white, which was deemed hypocritical for a married woman. In each case, remarkably, she was able to defend herself and prove her innocence. Kempe's *Book* only came to light in 1934. It is one of the twentieth century's most important finds relating to early women writers in the vernacular and provides a fascinating account of an intelligent woman of relatively humble birth.

She was born Margery Brunham in King's Lynn (then Bishop's Lynn), Norfolk, and married John Kempe when she was twenty. They had fourteen children. After the birth of her first child Margery fell seriously ill and feared for her life. She suffered a bout of self-described madness, and then had a vision that called her to leave aside the vanities of this world. Margery committed to a more devout life, but she continued to be tempted by sexual stirrings for many years. Eventually she succeeded in turning her back on worldly pleasures and dedicated herself completely to the spiritual calling that she felt her earlier vision had demanded. She finally persuaded her husband to agree to a chaste marriage and set off on numerous pilgrimages around Europe to holy sites at Rome, Santiago de Compostela and in Norway and Jerusalem. Margery was also concerned to meet influential clerics and divines in England, and between 1413 and 1420 she travelled the country, visiting the Bishop of Lincoln, the Archbishop of Canterbury and Julian of Norwich. Much of her experience of her travels, including her persecution by both religious and civil leaders, became the material for her *Book*, with a final section made up of prayers.

Part of what is remarkable about Margery Kempe's writing is its autobiographical style. Her *Book* offers an extraordinary and rare insight into the life and experience of a middle-class woman in the Middle Ages. Kempe has often been cast as distinctly peculiar, and even mad (although in comparison to popular theologies of the time she is less a case apart than one might think), but today her *Book* is generally regarded as a considered commentary on the spiritual and social practices of her era. During her lifetime Lynn was one of the most important towns in England and, as elsewhere in Norfolk, it was unusual in its early adoption of the vernacular. Documentation relating to Norfolk guilds, for example, shows the early abandonment of the official use of Latin and French. In fact Norfolk was notorious for its ignorance of French. Kempe was living in a society where the vernacular was commonly used and this explains, in part, why the first true autobiography in English came from this part of the country.

Kempe had two amanuenses to whom she dictated her visions. Whether or not she was a reader is an interesting puzzle which tells us a good deal about how women's reading generally was viewed at the time. It is possible that she was a reader, but not an expert one. She may have had pragmatic literacy for business purposes – members of her family were in the import and export trade – but the books she knew are unlikely to have circulated among her social group. If she had only limited reading skills, she must have been read to, perhaps by priests who translated out of Latin for her.

But Kempe's *Book* is clearly influenced by the English mystic Walter Hilton's *Scale of Perfection*. (The Latin title *Scala perfectionis* is found in several other manuscripts and has the meaning of a ladder or stairway to perfection.) It is addressed to a female who has taken religious vows, and is part of an extensive body of writings in the Western European tradition directed at women and intended to offer devotional or spiritual guidance. Some were written in Latin, others in the vernacular. The most notable works are the *De institutione inclusarum* (*Rule of Life for Recluses*) by Aelred of Rievaulx (d. 1167), translated from Latin into Middle English in the fourteenth century; the *Ancrene Wisse*; and above all the widely read *Meditationes vitae Christi* (*Meditations on the Life of Christ*) which exists in a number of fifteenth-century English translations of the thirteenth-century Latin original.

Kempe was also clearly aware of Richard Rolle of Hampole's devotional works. One of the distinctive features of his writing was to describe God's physical presence as a sensory experience. He refers to 'real warmth, not imaginary' in his heart when conscious of the Divine. Likewise, Kempe describes awareness of God in terms of the physical senses, often hearing: 'she heard a melodious sound so sweet and delectable that she thought she had been in paradise.'[22] Rolle's originality was met with hostility from the clergy. He was wary of his relationships with women religious, although at the end of his life he lived in a cell near the Cistercian nunnery of Hampole. Here he wrote *The Form of Living* and an English psalter for a nun there, Margaret Kirkby (who later took up a similar life to Rolle, as an anchoress), and *Ego Dormio* (*I Sleep*) for a nun at Yedingham.

The most obvious influence on Kempe was St Bridget of Sweden (1303–73) whose work was translated into numerous languages including English. Kempe had clearly been profoundly swayed by both St Bridget's style and, equally, by her devotional life. Given how little reading material would have been available to Kempe (she was illiterate in Latin), something as accessible and as close to her own life as St Bridget's writings, would have had enormous force to move. Just as in the *Ancrene Wisse*, there are echoes in Kempe's writing of the work of Marie d'Oignies and St Elizabeth of Hungary. Mystical texts by holy women were spread throughout Europe by monks. Kempe's visions are comparable to other penitential writings associated with the holy women of the Low Countries, Germany and Sweden, a tradition based on the visualisation and imaginative re-experience of the life and death of Christ, the despair and joys of the Virgin Mary, and conversation with the saints and God.

Aside from the allusions to others' writing, Kempe's love of words – for repartee and a wide range of genres, including argumentative sermons and vivid accounts of her revelations – suggest someone capable of reading. We know that she was tutored by learned men over many years at Lynn, although the precise nature of what she learned from them remains obscure, in part because the risks of charges of heresy being brought were very real; as late as 1520 seven people were burned at Coventry for teaching their children and family the Lord's Prayer and the Ten Commandments in English.[23] Margery's confessors and amanuenses may well have thought it prudent to insist that she was dependent on the priesthood as censors and a channel for her own authorship. Two quotations from her writing may, however, give the game away. In one account she describes a stone falling on her in St Margaret's Church while she is kneeling at her prayers and holding a book in her hand. More forceful is her description of a revelation in which God tells her that he is not displeased with her whether she is praying with her mouth, thinking with her heart, reading or being read to. Margery is an important example of the relationship between women readers and the rise of literacy and writing in the vernaculars. Many feared that the Church would lose control over the dissemination and interpretation of scripture, while other writings that undermined the authority of the Church could also circulate among an increasingly broadening readership.

Some educated lay women of the period saw their vocation as one of promoting piety and scholarship outside religious communities. Lady Margaret Beaufort (1443–1509), mother of Henry VII, was both one of the most committed readers of the period and one of the most dedicated to encouraging scholarship.[24] Not only did she read widely, she also commissioned, promoted, bought, gave and translated material for others to read and benefit from intellectually and theologically. Her relationship with books was 'for her exercise, & for the profyte of others': both a personal spiritual matter, and of spiritual benefit to other readers. In the last years of her life, Margaret became an increasingly important patron of learning, founding both Christ's College and St John's College in Cambridge, and supplying the former with large numbers of books. During these years she was in close touch with printers who were keen to publish in the areas which were of special interest to her, principally devotional works. She supported the book trade and through her purchase of books, often in large quantities, disseminated learning through a variety of outlets. Her reading kept her up-to-date with contemporary scholarship and she promoted its publication. She herself also translated European devotional works, particularly those familiar to the Carthusian and Bridgettine orders, possibly encouraged by John Fisher, her confessor. These she distributed both within and outside the cloister. Fisher spoke of the remarkable impact she made on those who knew her, of her brilliant intellect and her energy. She was one of the pre-eminent women readers of her age and equally pre-eminent in her championing of books and learning.

Margaret was undoubtedly an earnest individual but we know that she also read lighthearted books and had them read to her at mealtimes. In a contemporary account we hear that she is 'joyous' at dinner 'with tales that were honest to make her merry'.[25] The earliest non-devotional work in which we know she took an interest was the French romance *Blanchardyn and Eglantine*, a chivalric tale that she bought from the printer William Caxton, probably in the early 1480s, which he translated and printed for her in 1488. She would have been in her mid-forties. But her interest in less-serious works seems to have ended abruptly: there is no evidence that she ever read a romance thereafter. Various explanations for this can be imagined, among them being Margaret's uncertainty about Caxton's vigorous promotion of his publications among the merchant classes who read as a means of assimilating more aristocratic ways.

Caxton used various shrewd strategies to sell *Blanchardyn and Eglantine* and other romances. In his prologues he suggests that the books are designed for an elite readership, generally members of the nobility. He makes much of this publication being at the behest of the virtuous Lady Margaret and reminds readers 'that the story of hit [sic] was honeste and joyefulle to all virtuous yonge noble gentylmen and wymen for to rede therin for their passe-time.' Caxton's tactic was akin to modern publishers' use of a celebrity endorsement. But the physical evidence of particular copies suggests that whatever Caxton's purported strategy, his romances were read by a much wider readership. Annotations suggest that the principal owners included merchant-class circles in London and Antwerp, provincial gentlewomen and Oxford clerics. On occasion the books found their way to the Tudor court but the notes within them imply that they were read by servants rather than the nobility.[26]

Books like *Blanchardyn and Eglantine* found a ready market across a wide spectrum of readers. Those in authority in all denominations of the Christian Church saw 'false fonde bookes, ballades and rimes' as attacking the roots of social stability.[27] Their objections were both moral and political. Literacy had come to be seen as a means of educating the laity, men and women, young and old, in their religious and political obligations, but there was a concomitant problem of control.

From the fifteenth century on, most Church traditions doggedly encouraged literacy for both boys and girls, and parents were enjoined to provide their children and other members of their household with a Christian education. Mothers and fathers, women and men, daughters and sons, were treated equally. And of course the practice of learning the Ten Commandments, of reciting psalms and prayers, and becoming familiar with Bible readings, all encouraged broader reading skills. William Caxton's *Boke of Good Manners* (1487), something of an early bestseller, had a section on 'How the father and the mother ought to teach their children'.[28] In more affluent households, a domestic chaplain not only led the family worship but also educated the children and servants. All this would feed into growing lay literacy.

Particularly significant are examples of literate women in the publishing trade who had varying degrees of control over what was produced for their readerships. Women had, of course, been involved in the making of books and printing from the beginning. Even before the advent of movable type, there was a tradition of women producing manuscripts in Western European religious houses. The first documented evidence of women working as printers is from the convent of San Jacopo di Ripoli in Florence in 1476.[29] Elsewhere, girls and women were often trained by their fathers or husbands to help out in the family business. The degree of involvement clearly varied significantly. But there is some documentary evidence that gives us a clear idea of just how equal women's involvement could be. Estellina, wife of the printer Abraham Conant, proudly announces in a Hebrew book, *Behinat 'olam*, published in Mantua around 1477, that 'she, together with one man, did the typesetting'.[30]

Craftsmen's houses in fifteenth-century Italy were usually two- or three-storey buildings. The ground floor served as the shop or studio, with the living quarters above. The free labour provided by wives and children was very welcome. In the event of the death of the master printer, wives or daughters frequently stepped into his shoes.[31] There are some fascinating stories, not simply of widows taking over and keeping businesses afloat, but of innovative and entrepreneurial women turning fortunes around. Anna Giovanni, of Vicenza, ran her former husband's printing and bookselling business, and expanded her financial control by buying her own paper mill so as not to be at the mercy of an unstable paper market. As paper was the biggest capital outlay, this shows considerable business acumen. In 1517, after her husband's death, Caterina De Silvestro added italic type to the existing stock of gothic and roman type so as to have an edge on her competitors. Italic type had only arrived in Italy in 1501. There were women printers in Mantua, Siena, Venice, Rome, Florence, Trino and Naples.[32] Nuns were also involved in the new technology of the *ars artificialiter scribendi* ('artificial craft of writing'). The remarkable diary of the Florentine press of the convent of San Jacopo di Ripoli records the work done by Dominican nuns as compositors under two monks who managed the press. Their first publication was *Donatus* in 1476, and they went on to produce works by Plutarch, Suetonius, Augustine and Petrarch. Most surprisingly, considering its bawdiness and eroticism, two sisters also produced Boccaccio's *Decameron*.

Women were also active in the book trade. Angela and Laura Bianzago, for instance, managed Bernadino Benali's bookshop in Padua. For women to be involved in the book business required that they be literate in the vernacular if not in Latin too. Few printers could afford to hire a private tutor for their children and most were educated by their parents. In some cases the teaching they received was extensive. Christophe Plantin, an Antwerp printer, taught his five daughters to read before they reached the age of five. Four later worked as proofreaders for him. His eldest daughter had a reading knowledge of Hebrew, Chaldean, Syriac, Greek and Latin which she needed when Plantin was working on a polyglot Bible.[33]

Members of Italy's printing families often intermarried, and presses were clustered in neighbourhoods. In Florence, for example, the presses were centered around the Badia where the city's paper merchants were also based; this remains the area for stationers and engravers today. In the fifteenth and sixteenth centuries there were enclaves in many cities where women worked alongside men in the book trade. These were well-educated women whose reading was part of their work. But they no doubt enjoyed discussing their reading with other women in the vicinity, many of whom were also intimately bound up in the book business.

Italy was also ahead of the game with respect to reading glasses.[34] A monk, known as Spina, in the last quarter of the thirteenth century was probably the first to make glasses and teach others how to produce them. By 1301 the Guild of Crystal Workers in Venice was producing glasses for the burgeoning number of readers. But it was not until after the invention of the printing press and the huge growth in book production that reading glasses really took off. Strasbourg became the new spectacle mecca, the first specialist shop opening in 1466. Spectacles were for a long time the supreme symbol of scholarship. Women scholars, as well as men, wore glasses. One image of the Holy Kinship from the fifteenth century shows St Anne with her spectacles lying on the page of an open book in front of her.

By the end of the fifteenth century, women's literacy was taking hold and women were beginning to wield increasing influence within religious institutions and a growing international network of more or less formal communities of educated women outside them. More women were beginning to write and to advocate more widespread reading for women, often with the support of like-minded men. Women writers were becoming bolder and their numbers steadily increased, provoking growing opposition from various groups who felt threatened. The contentiousness of the subject of women's reading – and education more broadly – is visible in the radically changing versions of various stories of educated women from the past.

St Catherine of Alexandria was one of the most popular early Christian martyrs. Her story emerges only in the ninth century, and its historical accuracy is doubtful. But what matters is the light thrown on women readers by the fluctuating versions of her story. According to the legend, St Catherine was an extremely learned and intellectually able girl of noble birth. She vociferously protested against the persecution of Christians under the Roman emperor Maxentius, and she succeeded in converting his wife. Maxentius summoned the most eminent scholars to oppose her views, but they failed. She was sentenced to death all the same. The spiked wheel she was strapped to (and the origin of the 'Catherine wheel' firework) was supposed to kill her but it broke, and she was then beheaded.

Whether apocryphal or not, her popularity in the medieval period and the successive tellings of her story are intriguing. In earlier versions she is described as being instructed by numerous learned men. Clemence of

Barking's *Life* presents Catherine as a woman intellectual of an earlier period as a precedent to justify Clemence's own work as a woman writer. In later representations, Catherine is an autodidact: she reads books alone and on the basis of her own private study is emboldened to argue with male pagan scholars. The shift may have represented changing patterns of women's reading, or at least changing aspirations in relation to women's self-education.

As women readers became more numerous, so they also started to appear *within* writing, as exemplary figures to be emulated by other women. In Geoffrey Gaimar's *L'Estoire des engleis* (*c.* 1150), Dame Constance reads *The Life of Henry of England* in her private chamber, and one of Marie de France's lays, 'Yonec', includes an old lady reading her psalter alone in her quarters.[35] Not only were there growing numbers of women readers, certain types of woman reader gradually became widespread symbols of the exemplary woman.

This becomes all the more evident in the growing number of visual images of women readers.

25 Fresco in the Barda Castiglioni Chapel of San Clemente showing the disputation between St Catherine of Alexandria and pagan philosophers before the emperor.

26 Detail of a woman reading, from the *Seven Sacraments Altarpiece* by Rogier van der Weyden, *c.* 1445–50.

This is a relatively rare image of a real woman – as opposed to a biblical figure – engrossed in reading. The sight of women reading Books of Hours, in particular, influenced representations of the Virgin Mary, her mother Anne, and Mary Magdalen. There are, of course, no biblical references to Mary reading: it is a later invention based on real women reading Books of Hours, and bound volumes of psalms and prayers, projected backwards in time. Images of this kind exerted a powerful incentive to women to read Scripture, both as an act of devotion in itself and as an inspiration to a particular way of life.

One of the most ubiquitous images of the woman reader of the period is of the Virgin Mary at the moment of the Annunciation. The story of the Annunciation is told in Luke 1:26–38, with additions in the apocryphal gospel of James the Lesser that find their way into visual representations. Mary goes outside to fill a jug with water when she hears the initial words of the angel's greeting. She goes back inside and attends to her spinning, when the angel Gabriel appears in the house and delivers the rest of his message. A further apocryphal gospel from the third or fourth century, the Gospel of the Nativity of Mary, includes an additional detail – the strong light that fills the room – and sometimes a beam of light is seen to enter the domestic space and connect to the middle of Mary's body, indicating the moment of conception. There is no mention anywhere of Mary's literacy or of books. Yet in paintings of the Annunciation, Mary's spinning or sewing is gradually replaced by reading. Sometimes she is kneeling at a *prie-dieu* (a prayer desk) with a volume of scripture on the book rest.

Van Eyck's painting is typical in its layered meaning: Mary's reading has been interrupted and she holds up her hands, showing total acceptance of the angel's message. This indicates the perfect correspondence between what was foretold in the Bible and its fulfilment in the birth and life of Jesus. And Mary *is* herself the 'book' in which the Church reads the ways of God. She is the

27 Jan Van Eyck, *The Annunciation, c.* 1434–36.

servant, 'the hand-maiden of the Lord'. Her submission to the Word is total. In the Christian world, Mary is the archetypal and exemplary woman reader: wholly submissive and wholly obedient. Women were encouraged to follow her example and to submit to pious reading.

In the fourteenth and fifteenth centuries, the infant Jesus, sometimes as 'baby reader', has been added to the scene, suggestive of the importance of the maternal duty to encourage children to read the Scriptures. Images of Anne, Mary's mother, also begin to emerge, spreading from England to France, then to Rome and Florence, and on to Spain. It is much more common to see Anne with a book in images from Northern Europe – and indeed women's reading was more prevalent in those regions. The depictions are remarkably various. In many fifteenth-century manuscripts, Anne is shown patiently listening to Mary as she reads aloud. Other images suggest a prescient St Anne, considering the adult life for which the child will be chosen, foretelling the Annunciation yet to come. These images are not biblically based, and in that sense are not 'true' representations. Yet they emerge at a point where real women *are* readers. They conflate, then, what artists witnessed all around them with the key stories of biblical women. Their effect is to sanction certain kinds of women's reading and to promote women as teachers of literacy, at least for devotional and spiritual purposes.

Images of religious scenes became increasingly popular and inspired large numbers of donor portraits and reflective representations of women readers in emulation of biblical women. One particularly striking example is a book commissioned by Mary of Burgundy around 1477.[36] The miniature within it shows Mary in the foreground of the frame, holding a book, with a cloth protecting it from her hands, suggesting that it is a holy work and revered. So here we have an illustration for a book, commissioned by a woman, which itself shows the donor reading. This is a further and particularly powerful representation of women's interest in books and reading and the prestige associated with them.

Images of great women readers can be more straightforward, but equally magnificent. Eleanor of Aquitaine, who died in 1204, is entombed in Fontevraud Abbey in the Loire Valley in central France. She was highly educated and famous for her wide reading. What could be more natural than for her tomb effigy to show her holding a book? She was also the patroness of such literary figures as the Anglo-Norman poet Wace, Benoît de Sainte-Maure and Chrétien de Troyes, a poet and a troubadour. Women patrons constitute an important group of women readers as they were able to commission writing; in other words, they paid to have written what they wanted to read and to have others read.

28 Mary of Burgundy's Book of Hours, by a Netherlandish miniaturist. The piece plays with the idea of the book as a window onto another world.

29 Eleanor of Aquitaine's tomb effigy, Fontevrault Abbey, *c.* 1210.

This is the beginning of one of the most exciting periods in the history of women's reading. But the visual record could be misleading. What we lack are representations of the growing number of humbler women being read to and reading works in the vernacular. Pious reading and the reading of Scripture to children was clearly encouraged as these artworks demonstrate. Certain kinds of scholarly women readers were also recognised and memorialised. But alongside this kind of reading was the dramatic rise of reading in everyday languages. Stories were being written in the vernaculars, and romantic stories would develop into the most enjoyable, and at the same time worrying, of all women's reading material: the modern novel. Somewhat paradoxically it would be the Church – and the splits within it – that would further encourage both widespread literacy and the publication of works that it would abhor.

CHAPTER 5

'To Reade Such Bookes ... My Selfe to Edyfye'

T HE question of the woman reader was central to many intellectual and
religious debates of the sixteenth century. In 1592, at the end of a century
of growing scepticism, the engagingly immoderate Moderata Fonte was
emboldened to voice some frank opinions in her work, *The Worth of Women
– Wherein is Clearly Revealed Their Nobility and Their Superiority
to Men*:

> Do you really believe ... that everything historians tell us about men – or
> about women – is actually true? You ought to consider the fact that these
> histories have been written by men, who never tell the truth about anything
> except by accident. And if you consider, in addition, the envy and ill will
> they bear us women, it is hardly surprising that they rarely have a good word
> to say for us, and concentrate instead on praising their own sex in general
> and particular members of it, as a way of praising themselves.[1]

Here was a woman reader with an emphatically incredulous approach to
reading, at pains to encourage other readers – women most particularly – to
adopt a similarly sceptical stance. Moderata (a pseudonym for Modesta
Pozzo) was a Venetian noblewoman and she dramatically delivered both her
book and a baby on her deathbed at the age of thirty-seven – or so the story
goes. We know of her thanks to her sympathetic male friend and biographer
Giovanni Doglioni, who recognised her intellectual skills grounded in her
wide and critical reading, and deplored contemporary Venetian attitudes
to women. What he particularly regretted was a culture in which it was
considered unbecoming for women to demonstrate competence other than in
repetitive domestic tasks. Combined with the burdens of childbirth and

bringing up children, most women continued to be inhibited from contributing to intellectual and cultural debate. Needless to say, Moderata has been taken up by modern feminists because she articulates, albeit in a different style, the arguments of contemporary feminist historians: everything written about women by men needs to be treated with caution. Her delightfully direct *The Worth of Women* takes us to the heart of the subject of the sixteenth-century woman reader.

Moderata was conscious that men maintained something close to a monopoly on the production of reading material, and this in the wake of Gutenberg's printing revolution and the rise of print culture. The debates of the Reformation and the Counter-Reformation were intimately bound up with questions about women's status and role in society, and particularly their education. There were increasingly lively exchanges between men and women, much of it related to what women should or should not read, and to differences in men's and women's interpretations of books, particularly the Bible. Women read about themselves variously described as malicious, deceitful, witchlike, vain and mad, but also as gentle, submissive and closer to God. The 'war between the sexes' gets properly underway in the sixteenth century. Moderata Fonte was one of the boldest on the women's side.

The conflict between men and women varied across the century and from place to place, in response to changing times and circumstances. Protestant and Catholic women found themselves in rather different reading contexts, and external forces – plague, disease, wars and economic changes – sometimes had the effect of encouraging women into a more public arena. However, women's education continued to lag behind men's and the mastery of rhetoric in particular was seen more and more as a male puberty rite. In addition, an association arose between women speaking publicly and harlotry; the domestic sphere and domestic piety were still the focus of women's education; and silence – as opposed to speech – remained one facet of the feminine ideal. But women were by no means everywhere dominated by oppressive men or ideologies. For most there were fundamental inequalities, but women exerted a profound influence, not just as exceptional heroines. Some were martyrs to their Protestant faith, at the heart of their allegedly subversive commitments being a belief in the right to read the Bible, often in the vernacular, and to express their interpretations of it. There were expectations, prohibitions and controls, but women readers, not infrequently encouraged by men, found ways of living within these constraints, and their reading nourished their desire to transcend them, and sometimes to endeavour to change them.

Much of the background of women's reading in the sixteenth century is provided by the changes brought by the Reformation and Counter-Reformation.

Religious controversies not only had a huge effect on people's faith, but on their lives more broadly. The Reformation was far more than a matter of dry doctrinal debate; key questions about our humanity, individual conscience, how life should be lived and societies organised, were repeatedly asked. The discussions these questions prompted were religious first and foremost, but they were also political, radically changing, for instance, the understanding of what it was to be a woman, and what women's rights and status should be. Initially this touched the lives of only a limited number of women, but the Protestant reformers' emphasis on the importance of literacy, with the Catholic Church following suit, gradually drew more and more women into reading. It is not too extravagant to suggest that the Reformation changed women's lives far more profoundly than men's; it stimulated the rise of women's literacy and their increased access to a growing range of material, some of it highly controversial. During this period printing gradually lowered the cost of books, coinciding serendipitously with the religious controversies of the day, and questions of women's roles and capabilities were argued out in private and in public – and in print.

The Reformation is sometimes known as the 'daughter of Gutenberg', highlighting the relationship between profound religious change and the ascendancy of print culture. Printing brought about far-reaching changes in terms of the availability of reading material (in the form of pamphlets and broadsheets) and the increased number of serious books published. In addition, the Rhine offered an easy means of transport to other parts of Europe, allowing Gutenberg's Bible to travel widely. But what matters goes beyond an increase in the availability of reading material. A key change, intimately bound up with the debates of the Reformation, concerned *how* men and women read. Fresh ideas circulated regarding the relationship between the individual and his – or her – personal reading.

It remains the case, of course, that from the fifteenth century in Europe, and right up until the eighteenth century, the vast majority of readers were members of the aristocracy, the clergy, doctors and wealthy merchants. Around the time of the Reformation, the overall picture was not so different from that of the Middle Ages and, although there were some notable and colourful exceptions, by and large women still belonged to only two of those groups: the nobility and religious communities. But a literate 'middle' class slowly emerged. Crudely speaking, the end of the Middle Ages marked the beginning of the gradual rise of a middle class that controlled new economic and commercial enterprises. With wealth came an increased desire to play a part in political processes and a wish to participate in cultural activities which had previously been the exclusive privilege of the classically educated aristocracy.

The fifteenth-century European printing phenomenon gradually spread.[2] By 1539 printing had been established in Mexico City, and in Russia by 1550; by the end of the century it had arrived in China and Japan. The impact of printing was gradual as to begin with the *ars artificialiter scribendi* was modelled very closely on the crafts associated with manuscript production. The realisation that mechanical reproduction could be something new and very different from the complicated craft of imitating handwritten manuscripts was relatively slow in coming. The printed book acquired a personality and conventions of its own at some point between 1520 and 1540, with a title-page and standardised and simplified typeface with fewer ligatures (joined letters as in handwriting). Print shops multiplied, spreading from Germany to Italy, France and the rest of Europe. By the middle of the sixteenth century it was only 'isolated' areas that still awaited the revolutionary potential of numerous printing presses: England, the Iberian Peninsula, Central Europe and Scandinavia were all poorly catered for. Germany, France, the Seventeen Provinces of the Netherlands and Italy, on the other hand, all had dense networks of printers. Yet despite all this industrial activity it remained the case that few people owned books, and those that did owned only small numbers.

Wills provide a reliable source for the tracing of book ownership. In fifteenth-century Florence, between 1413 and 1453 only 3.3 per cent of those who died leaving a child or ward passed on books. Between 1467 and 1520, after the introduction of printing, that fell to 1.4 per cent, but between 1531 and 1569 it rises to 4.6 per cent and between 1570 and 1608 to 5.2 per cent – still less than twice the percentage of a century and a half earlier.[3] Why? As the book became more common – and a less unusual possession – records at death bothered less with the careful inventorying of them. The patterns of book ownership in Spain were much the same, although in a university town such as Valladolid in the north-west, briefly Spain's capital, there was a brisker trade, particularly in devotional works, classical, travel and law books, and chivalrous stories.[4]

The city of Strasbourg was unusual in that literacy had permeated the strata of society further than in many other European cities. There is varied evidence of ordinary burghers' book ownership available from will inventories. Although we lack full notarial records for the period 1500–80, there is sufficient material to deduce the broad patterns of women's book ownership and reading and not just for the wealthy. The really poor died intestate, but the sample we do have includes a magistrate, civil servants, and more surprisingly a miller, a mason, a day-labourer, a fisherman, several gardeners, a boatman, and a man who made wooden lasts (those devices shaped like a

human foot, used in making and repairing shoes). Of the sample of 100 individuals, forty-four owned at least one book, suggesting that books were in the
possession of 40 per cent of the population, including artisans and workmen.
Women artisans who owned books included Anna Madnew, widow of a mine
foreman, Sara Trens, a tanner's wife, Barbara Wüchterin and Künigund Kraut,
both shoemakers' widows, Salome Schwinger, a furrier's wife, and Salome
Schmid, a cloth-dyer's wife. The most commonly owned book was, of
course, the Bible, but if there was more than one book in the household, the
clerk would tantalisingly record simply 'three old books', not specifying the
titles. We know that Appolonia Stöckler, a stonemason's wife, owned a
German Bible. And here and there a book on embroidery or some other practical manual is on the list, suggesting that some reading was gradually
becoming an important activity for women, even among the poorer levels of
society.[5]

Alongside the relatively inconspicuous and gradual social change
associated with the rise of printing were the events of the Reformation. These
were particularly exciting and encouraging for women readers: a large
number of women became martyrs, or were educated readers sustaining the
Protestant reformers both intellectually and in material ways, or were writers
advocating change.

In 1519 the Roman theologian Sylvester Prierias declared that the Bible had
to remain a 'mystery' and could be truthfully transmitted only through the
power and authority of the Pope. Luther and others of like mind, most particularly in Germany, the Netherlands and Switzerland, argued that everyone –
man and woman – had the 'divine right' to read the Bible in their own mother
tongue, and without the interpretive participation of anyone else.

What Luther argued was not new, but the conditions within which he
promoted his arguments were. Luther claimed that God's grace descended as
a function of individual faith and not through the agency of the Church. This
had been argued before, by the twelfth-century martyrs in particular. But the
invention of printing, on the one hand, and the German princes' desire to
break free from the controlling power of Rome, on the other, conspired to
protect Luther and to disseminate his ideas. Luther's intention had been to
reform the Catholic Church, but conditions were ripe for things to change
much more radically. Luther's 'heretical' ideas became the basis for a whole
new Church in Europe, the Protestant Church, one that would take women's
reading and education seriously.

The importance of the relationship between printing and the rise of
Protestantism starts with a proliferation of pamphlets. Luther's protest against
the preaching of indulgences inspired literally thousands of poorly written

pamphlets to circulate throughout the Holy Roman Empire. This wave of ephemeral publications made Luther's name known all over Europe. One of his concerns, and he was by no means alone, was to make the Bible available in the vernacular. Arguments about Bible-reading during the Reformation took place within the context not of *the* Bible, but a whole host of bibles. The Greek Septuagint of the third and second centuries BC formed the basis for later Latin translations. The Old Testament canon was established by Rabbi Akiba ben Joseph in the second century AD. What is known as the 'Vulgate' is Saint Jerome's Latin translation of the late fourth century AD. During the Middle Ages, bibles were produced in a vast plethora of translations that literate women, however scant their broader education, could read, including Gothic, Slavic, Armenian, Old English, West Saxon, Anglo-Norman, French, Frisian, German, Irish, Netherlandish, Central Italian, Provençal, Spanish, Catalan, Polish, Welsh, Czech and Hungarian.[6] In 1530, even before Luther had finished his translation, pastors in Zurich had printed a German Bible. Clerics in Antwerp published a Dutch Bible in 1526 and in 1532 Antonio Brucioli's Bible appeared in Italian. Pierre-Robert Olivétan's French Bible was published in 1535, and Miles Coverdale's English Bible was printed the same year.

With the advent of print, and in particular the new pamphlet format, there was increased awareness among growing groups of men and women readers of what was, in effect, a fundamental and no doubt to many disconcerting *instability* as to what the Bible really said. The humanists, and Erasmus most famously, rejoiced in this not as worrying choice, but as an historical fact encouraging an awareness of a long and important interpretive tradition. It was a woman reader of Erasmus, Margaret Roper, the erudite daughter of the martyred Thomas More, who was so struck by one of his central works that she undertook a translation. Erasmus's *Precatio dominica in septem portiones distribute* was published anonymously in 1525 as *A Devout Treatise upon the Paternoster*. It was dedicated to Margaret's cousin, Frances Staverton, described in Richard Hyrde's introduction as 'the studious and virtuous young maid Frances S'. Hyrde was a scholar and translator closely associated with the More family, and in his introduction he argued for the importance of women's intellectual education. Among other things, the *Treatise* questioned the simplistic idea of the 'authority' of the Bible and revealed it as a complex and sometimes contradictory body of writings.[7] It may well be that it was this aspect of Erasmus's work that had struck Margaret most forcibly when she read it in Latin, prompting her translation. Erasmus was one of a number of respected scholars who spoke out about the importance of making the Bible available to all, particularly women: 'I wish that even the weakest woman should read the

Gospel – should read the Epistles of Paul. And I wish that these were translated into all the languages so that they might be read and understood, not only by Scots and Irishmen, but also by Turks and Saracens [Muslims]'.[8] 'Even the weakest woman' is a telling phrase, hinting that some women constituted the most disenfranchised of all readers.

What is most striking is that the publishing revolution, once initiated, was so successfully sustained. When Luther died in 1546, his German Bible had gone through more than 400 full or partial reprintings. Demand was strong and women readers, able for the first time to reflect on the Bible in their own language and at leisure, found passages that stimulated thoughts about models of womanhood. Some of these women became powerful forces in the Reformation, in turn inspiring women to read widely, and radically to reconsider their identity and position in society. The domino effect was dramatic.

The availability of the Bible in the vernacular also inspired a new desire to assert national, local or individual religious identity. In the sixteenth century, all religious groups realised the need to have access to printing. In Poland and Hungary it was the Anti-Trinitarians; in Bohemia, the Utraquists; in Moravia it was the United Brethren. There was, naturally, heated scholarly debate about the capacity of the vernacular languages properly to communicate the sacred. Luther's respect for spoken language runs in parallel with his profound respect for all people, whether educated or not. Movingly, he writes: 'You must ask the woman in her house, the children in the streets, the common man in the market, and look at their mouths, how they speak and translate that way; then they'll understand and see that you're speaking to them in German'.[9] Luther begins with the women and children and the need to understand their language, before considering the ways in which the Bible can be made accessible to them. Like Erasmus, Luther was deeply committed to enfranchising women as readers of the Bible.

It is important to stress that there were bibles and bibles – and a plethora of bible commentaries. Women's individual humanity and equality were written in and out. In Coverdale's English Bible of 1539, like the Geneva Bible in 1560, Paul's Letters to the Corinthians were unexpurgated, and included the crucial lines: 'Nevertheless, neither is the man without the woman, neither the woman without the man, in the LORDE. For as the woman is of the man, even so commeth the man also by the woman, but all of God' (1 Corinthians 11.11). Many women readers would have been struck by this explicit statement of reciprocal equality between the sexes. Thomas Bentley, on the other hand, in the introduction to his *Monument of Matrones* (1582), a 1,600-page collection of prayers and meditations written by, for or relating to women, ignored these verses altogether. The Bible was often highly selectively quoted to assert women's subservience to men, and not only by Bentley. St Paul, quoted in part ('women should be submissive to their husbands'), was often the authority in this.

The reaction of the Church to the debates of the Reformation, and the effects of this on women's reading of both religious and secular works, were marked. The Church sought to reaffirm the importance of tradition and the authority of the clergy at a time of deep questioning and arguments for the sole importance of Scripture as the one rule of faith: the laity – and all women – were thus relegated to the position of passive listeners. But when King James I of England took to the throne, he was of the same view as the Puritan Dr John Rainolds who argued 'that there be a new translation of the Bible because those which were allowed in the reign of Henry VIII and Edward VI were corrupt and not answerable to the truth of the original'.[10] And this English version of the Bible would be read by very large numbers of women.

The Council of Trent (which met at Trent, now Trento in northern Italy) decreed on 8 April 1546 that the Roman Catholic Church was to respect the 'unwritten traditions' that 'have come down to us, transmitted as it were from hand to hand', as well as Scripture. The Council underlined the distinct roles of clergy and laity, denying the importance of direct access to the sacred texts for the latter. The laity's role was to listen to the teachings of the priests. Official censorship came in 1599 with the publication of the *Index auctorum et librorum prohibitorum* (*Index of Prohibited Books*) under the direction of Pope Paul IV. It was the first of forty-two editions. Its aim was to help the censors decide which publications to authorise and which to prohibit. In January 1562 the Council of Trent discussed the *Index* and schisms emerged. For many it was seen as excessively restrictive and a commission was appointed to draft a new version. The new *Tridentine Index* was approved by Pope Pius IV and published in Rome in 1564. It was the most authoritative guide so far issued by the Church and formed the basis of all subsequent indexes. It included overt references to what the reading of Scripture was and was not to be: 'no-one, relying on his own skill, shall – in matters of faith, and of morals … wresting the sacred Scripture to his own senses, presume to interpret the said sacred Scripture contrary to that sense which holy mother Church – whose it is to judge of the true sense and interpretation of the Holy Scriptures – hath held and doth hold; or even contrary to the unanimous consent of the Fathers'.[11] As women were all but excluded from positions of authority within the 'holy mother Church', this ban was of profound significance. It was motivated by a desire to control interpretation and it had the effect of excluding women from that highly influential activity.

There were many, both Catholic and Protestant, who objected to this line. In England attempts to control authority were directed towards an authoritative edition of the Bible, the King James version. The Dean of Westminster and the Regius Professors (those appointed by the Crown) of Hebrew in the Universities of Oxford and Cambridge were to draw up a list of scholars to undertake the task. Hugh Broughton, a notable but somewhat unpopular Hebrew scholar, sent various suggestions to the king, unsolicited. What Broughton daringly recommended, in order that the new translation be as technically accurate as the original, was that artisans be consulted about all manner of specialist terms: 'as embroiderers for Aaron's ephod, geometricians, carpenters, and masons about the Temple of Solomon and Ezekiel's tree'.[12] The language, in short, was to be one that ordinary men and women would immediately understand. It was a visionary and remarkable suggestion. Equally astute – and telling – was his recommendation that a very large number of people work on different sections, and that a small team then ensure overall coherence in terms of vocabulary and style.

Of course there was much to plunder from William Tyndale's Bible, cannibalised in successive editions. He had set out his principles of translation in a brief note, justifying his work: 'Because I had perceived by experience how that it was impossible to establish the lay-people in any truth, except the scriptures were plainly laid before their eyes in their mother tongue, that they might see the process, order, and meaning of the text'.[13] He used a language that was simple and unpretentious. He also introduced new words and compounds into the English language: 'Passover', 'peace-maker', 'long-suffering', and most importantly, 'beautiful'.[14] Tyndale was condemned as a heretic by Henry VIII. He was subsequently strangled and then burnt at the stake in the Low Countries in 1536.

The six teams of translators working on the King James version – two in London, Oxford and Cambridge respectively – were careful to retain much of Tyndale's inspired work. Although their concern was for that elusive idea of 'authenticity', their poetic inclinations are visible in their own 'Preface to the Reader': 'Translation it is that openeth the window, to let in the light; that breaketh the shell, that we may eat the kernel; that putteth aside the curtain, that we may look into the most holy place; that removeth the cover of the well, that we may come by the water'.[15]

Just as the Catholic Church sought to control the publication of books, so too did the English Crown. Henry VIII had decreed in 1538 that the Privy Council vet all books prior to publication, and this was upheld by Edward VI, and then by Elizabeth. Mary Tudor, herself a devout Catholic, had violently suppressed Protestant writing and reading. The result of these periods of varying degrees of censorship was that illegal presses sprang up in London, Presbyterian propaganda from Scotland found its way south, and Dutch Protestant publications flooded the English market.

The differences that the debates of the Reformation were to make for women are indissolubly bound up with Luther and his followers' emphasis on the importance of developing a private unmediated relationship with God, based on the reading of the Scriptures. These debates point to the widespread awareness of the power of writing and the relationship between printing and propaganda. Crudely speaking, the conflicting views of different religious groups promoting competing religious ideologies mirrored the polarised ideologies of certain men and women. Censorship was imposed by those in power to promote their own position and attempt to silence others, and women's position as readers and writers was under constant scrutiny. By the same token the debates of the Reformation and Counter-Reformation, made widely known through the spread of pamphlets, brought debates about women's intellectual involvement to a wider audience than ever before. And these arguments often blurred with the 'woman question'.

Court circles constituted a particularly privileged social space for women to read their work or have it read. Katherine Parr (1512–48), Queen of England, was one of the most courageous. Her *Lamentations of a Sinner* (published in 1547) is one of only three known Protestant confessions of faith by a woman published before the Civil War; the others are Margery Kempe's *Book of Margery Kempe* (c. 1433–38), discussed in the previous chapter, and Anne Askew's *Examinations* (1545–46).[16] Parr's position is the least extreme and, not surprisingly perhaps, encourages a personal development of faith through scriptural reading while seeking not to undermine or destabilise the status quo. Askew, on the other hand, had little time for the authority of the Church.

Parr's own education had been directed by Juan Luis Vives, the remarkable humanist and educational reformer. His *De institutione foeminae Christianae* had been commissioned by Catherine of Aragon, who no doubt made very clear the kind of book she wanted for her daughter Mary, later Mary Tudor. However, programmes for royal and aristocratic learning and behaviour quickly filtered down through the social classes. Vives' book was something of a bestseller, already in its ninth edition by 1592. His influence is particularly visible in Katherine's early sway over the king, Henry VIII, when she became queen in 1543. She was particularly concerned for the preservation of books, and successfully dissuaded Henry from plundering the university libraries of Oxford and Cambridge. Her commitment to reading is equally discernable in her establishment of a group of humanist reformers at court, some of whom became the tutors of Prince Edward and Princess Elizabeth, thereby ensuring that some of her educational vision rubbed off on the next generation.

Katherine also gathered together friends and religious women for readings of the new English Bible. But Henry became increasingly restive with their discussions about Church reform and, sensing this, his like-minded conservative supporters at court determined to have Katherine's close friend Anne Askew accused of treason, which they hoped would have the effect of incriminating Katherine herself. The queen's rooms were searched for material, especially unorthodox books. Askew was repeatedly interrogated, tortured and finally executed. Carried to her death in a chair as she was no longer able to walk, she was burnt at the stake at Smithfield, London, on 16 July 1546 when she was just twenty-five. Those who witnessed her execution, including Lady Jane Grey, were astonished by her bravery and reported that she remained silent until the flames reached her chest. When Katherine heard of Askew's fate – and very aware of what had befallen Henry's earlier wives – she submitted publicly to her husband's authority.

30 A volume of devotional tracts owned – and annotated – by Katherine Parr.

At some point during this crisis, however, Katherine wrote her *Lamentations* and it circulated at court in manuscript form. It was published shortly after Henry's death in January 1547. Katherine describes her Protestant conversion in a voice that is both personal and generalised. She avoids the sensational and writes measuredly and with emotional control. Her style reflects her wide reading, and the wisdom she had gained from her experience of the political complexities and intrigues at court. Her tone is always conciliatory, and avoids anything that might have stirred up either fear or indignation. It is the work of a woman of remarkable insight and astuteness.

Katherine positions herself between two extremes in a way that encourages the reader to see her argument as one of tolerant compromise, rather than as a call for significant reform. There is none of the principled defiance of Askew's voice. Katherine criticises the narrow holier-than-thou advocates of the extreme Protestant and self-denying kind, and she also rejects the conservative Catholic position that considered any discussion of the Bible in English to be heretical. But all this comes after her account of her confession and repentance. The form of the *Lamentations* has something of the satisfying sense of completion of the Psalms. Katherine's publication was highly influential. At its centre is the key Reformation commitment to the primacy of the individual's engagement with Scripture, as constituting the core essence of Christian life. Here was the Queen of England exhorting all, and particularly women, by example, to read and to regard that reading as the basis of the Christian faith. That is not to say that she encouraged a disregard for the Church's writings; she herself drew on aspects of Bishop John Fisher's work, for instance.[17]

Anne Askew had been protected by Katherine when she came to London to seek divorce, having left her husband's house because of her Protestant convictions.[18] Her case was founded on the contention that her husband had no claim on her because of his 'unbelief'; the courts rejected this. Anne stayed on in London, however, and participated, perhaps even led, a group of Protestant reformers made up in part of renegade clergy. By the mid-1540s conservatives in government were encouraged by the ageing king's resistance to take action. Anne was spied upon by government informers and was arrested in March 1545. She was questioned extensively about her religious views and her beliefs. Both her examinations (1545 and 1546) were published. One area that received particular attention was the question of transubstantiation, the physical transformation of the bread and wine of the communion service into the body and blood of Christ. Anne's *First Examination* records this inquisition. In June the Bishop of London, Edmund Bonner, prepared a statement of faith that she was forced to sign. She submitted, but only after having made certain small but significant alterations, which infuriated her prosecutors; they were not used to women like Askew standing up for their beliefs.

The real interest of Anne's writing lies in two distinct but interrelated areas and both are concerned with how language is read and understood. Anne argued for the freedom of individual faith, yet her inquisitors, in line with Henry's self-declared supremacy in the Church, regarded her religious dissent as a matter of heresy. There were plenty of trials for heresy, often carried out with scant respect for due process, and which resulted in execution. Those who questioned Anne were more concerned to restate certain conservative positions than to hear Anne's own views. The Protestants rejected liturgical practices that involved the display and worship of the Sacrament, for example, and what emerges in Anne's *Examination* is an equation of such displays with displays of 'his majesty's honour'. The rejection of the one implied a rejection of the other. Anne was brought to trial a second time on charges of heresy in June 1545. Whereas previously she had been questioned mainly by clerics, this time she was in the hands of two of Henry's most ruthless government ministers. Their torture became gradually more vicious as Anne continued to resist all forms of coercion. Even on the rack Anne maintained her silence.

The nature of metaphor frequently lay at the heart of examinations for heresy. Henry VIII's break with Rome did not involve a break with Catholic doctrine. In fact in 1539 this position was reinforced by the Act of the Six Articles which decreed severe penalties for denying the doctrine of transubstantiation. When Anne Askew was tried, she handled the question of metaphor with great skill and economy. If the communion bread is indeed the body of Christ, she suggests, then why are other biblical metaphors not understood literally also? 'Ye may not here (sayd I) take Christe for the materyall thynge that he is syngnfyed by. For than ye wyll make hym a very dore, a vyne, a lampe, and a stone, cleane conttarye to the hollye Ghostes meanynge'.[19]

Anne's writings perpetuated her memory and inspired the women reformers who suffered similar fates during the Marian persecutions (1553–58). During Henry's reign only a handful of the influential and outspoken reformers were women. In the second wave of persecutions, under Mary, more than sixty of the 300 or so burnt at the stake were women. Some were humble. For instance, during the reigns of Henry VIII and Edward VI, the daughter of a rope-maker, Joan Waste of Derby, craved access to the Bible in English, but was blind.[20] She saved up over a period of many years, bought a New Testament and paid people to read it aloud to her. She persisted in the reign of the Catholic Mary Tudor, which led to her arrest and burning at the stake.

The relationships between male martyrs and their educated female sustainers were of particular importance.[21] These committed women readers had a decisive influence on the development of English Protestantism. The preacher Heinrich Bullinger, most famously, had great influence over Lady Jane Grey, with whom he exchanged numerous letters. Grey was only one of a remarkable number of women who kept up intensive correspondence with reformist clerics.[22] Many became intimately involved in these debates and their ideas fed more or less directly into the influential writings of the Protestant reformers. To take but three, Luther, Calvin and John Knox (a German, a Frenchman and a Scot respectively) all corresponded extensively with well-read women, whose knowledge of letters and tracts exerted significant influence on the reformers' positions.

The tone of much of the correspondence between women and the Protestant reformers and martyrs is often self-denigrating, but this was something of a smoke-screen, and a necessary precaution at the time. In one letter Lady Jane Grey typically asked Bullinger 'to excuse the more than feminine boldness of me who, girlish and unlearned as I am, presume to write to a man who is the father of learning'.[23] Yet Grey's academic talents were noted early on. She was sent to live with the widowed Katherine Parr in 1547 and benefited from the many intellectual opportunities provided by the court circle. Katherine encouraged her to read the evangelical Protestant writers who had inspired her. A little later Grey was given instruction in the classics by the able John Aylmer. She corresponded with Bullinger, one of the most influential theologians of the Reformation, translated his book on marriage into Greek and exchanged queries about the proper translation of Hebrew.

Grey's death, aged sixteen, made a deep impression on English society. And in the nineteenth century there was a remarkable renaissance of interest in her. Paul Delaroche's painting, *The Execution of Lady Jane Grey* (1833), kindled her gentle saintly image, appropriate for the edification of Victorian girls. In reality Jane had developed into a keenly intelligent and forceful young woman, using expressions in her writing which tell of her religious fervour nourished by wide reading. She cast one believer whose theology she deplored as a 'deformed imp of Satan', and another an 'unashamed paramour of AntiChrist'. Jane was the sacrificial victim of the politics of the moment. Her execution in February 1554 was a result of her father's involvement in Wyatt's rebellion against Queen Mary, but the later sentimental Romantic representation of her belies her intellectual and religious zeal, which had more than a little edge to it. She had received a remarkable humanist education and became one of the most learned women of her day.

31 Paul Delaroche, *The Execution of Lady Jane Grey*, 1833.

Today she is remembered as a political victim and as a Protestant martyr, rather than as a particularly erudite and intellectually bold woman of the Reformation.

During Mary's reign a significant number of Protestant women provided refuge for fugitive Protestants. Thomas Rose, the leader of a risky underground Protestant congregation in London, was sheltered by Lady Elizabeth Fane for over two years. Wealthy women like Fane, and others like Anne Warcup and Joan Wilkinson, sent substantial financial support to imprisoned Protestants. And even less well-off women provided prisoners with what they could afford. The conditions of life in Tudor jails were brutal and without this support many would have died. These women were also willing to use bribes to ensure that prisoners received visitors, books and letters.

These relationships went beyond one-way charity. Many of the women supporters were sustained by the martyrs' writings, often written in direct response to theological concerns raised by themselves. Joyce Hales, a great friend of John Bradford, corresponded with him at length and this led him to write two treatises, 'The Defence of Election' and 'The Restoration of All Things'. His work, 'The Hurt of Hearing Mass' was written in response to Lady Fane's concerns about Catholic liturgical practices. He also shared his views with her about the primacy of the Pope.[24] Still more intimate is the comfort given by Bradford to Mary Marlar whom Foxe described as 'a good nurse unto him, and his very goode frende'. Mary was about to give birth and Bradford wrote a devotional piece for her on the passion of Christ hoping that it might provide comfort to her during the pains of childbirth and 'make the bitter waters more pleasant'.[25] Another martyr, John Philpot, offered to send Lady Fane a copy of his examinations as soon as he had finished writing them. Occasionally women provided both material and spiritual sustenance. John Careless included a note to Elizabeth Bernher in a letter to her husband: 'Elizabethe . . . I have sent you here a simple letter unsealed by cause you shoulde see it. Looke what is amys [amiss] in it I praye you mende itt and thether as it shulde goo I praye you sende it.'[26] Careless clearly considered Elizabeth the best judge of the worth of his letter, inviting her not only to read it, but to make any changes she thought fit to improve it and to decide how best it should be disseminated. The exceptional nature of relations between women sustainers and Marian martyrs was based, first and foremost, on men's recognition of highly intelligent and discerning women readers who also had intellectual and theological integrity.

Yet there are striking inconsistencies among the Protestants too. The most famous Protestant misogynist is surely John Knox. The title of his book, *First Blast of the Trumpet against the Monstrous Regiment* [or *Rule*] *of Women* (1558) says it all. For all his suspicion and condemnation of women at a general level, his direct relations with women run counter to his virulent polemics. He kept up an intense correspondence with his mother-in-law, Elizabeth Bowes, an educated woman of some social standing, during the years 1551–53. It is not known at what point he married her daughter, Marjorie. Many of these letters demonstrate Bowes' wide reading and keen scholarly discrimination, and Knox was deeply struck by Elizabeth's religious anxieties, writing: 'I have sene her (not for a starte, but in long continuance) powre furth teares, and sende to God dolorous complaints after than ever I heard man or woman in my life'.[27] Elizabeth's spiritual torment was heartfelt and Knox was moved to do all he could to find convincing biblical arguments to assuage her misery. Elizabeth's informed tenacity in questioning the validity of Knox's arguments impressed him deeply. She longed for the comforts of the Mass as an easy fix for salvation, while accepting Protestant arguments against idolatry. Knox had to work hard to find reasoning based on his intimate knowledge of Scripture, to answer her difficult questions about salvation and predestination. Knox was not known for his patience, but in his correspondence with Elizabeth he clearly felt sufficiently impressed to make an exception.

Other Protestant women showed greater confidence and were more interested in questioning the arguments of Knox and others in relation to the subject of men and women's equality. In the 'Epistle to the Reader' in her *The French History* (1589), Anne Dowriche begins by justifying her enterprise in relation to St Paul's First Letter to the Corinthians (14:26), including a paraphrase:

> Amongst many excellent precepts which St Paul gave unto the church, this is to be considered: let all things be done unto edifying. . . . That my only purpose in collecting and framing this work was to edify, comfort, and stir up the godly minds unto care, watchfulness, zeal, and ferventness in the cause of God's truth, you shall easily perceive by the choosing and ordering of these singular examples which hereafter ensue.[28]

What is striking is that Anne and her readers will also have been fully aware of Paul's more famous injunction against women speaking in public: 'Let your women keep silence in the churches: for it is not permitted unto them to speak, but to be under obedience' (1 Corinthians 14:34). Although some regard this as a post-Pauline addition, the two propositions seem to counter one another and parallel two contradictory views: male authorities barred women from exercising their intellectual or prophetic gifts, while at the same time theologians encouraged women's spiritual growth for 'self-edification', if not the edification of others. Anne appealed to this and, as a rider, argued for women's right to read and interpret Scripture guided by individual conscience. Still more boldly, she sees this as consistent with the right publicly to defend, and even to die for, Reformation doctrine. As the work develops, one senses Anne's excitement, involved in a worthy but also a risky enterprise. The content of Dowriche's *History* is heady and her style forthright: accounts of French Protestant suffering and persecution during the Wars of Religion.

Not dissimilar in spirit is *Jane Anger her Protection for Women*, published in 1589, which may or may not have been written by the eponymous Anger. The chances are that it was; and even if 'Jane Anger' was simply the pseudonym of a male author, the publication had a profound influence on a very large number of women readers. It was written in response to the male chauvinist work, *Boke his Surfeyt in Love*, which is now lost. The opening letter is addressed 'To the Gentlewomen of England' and the second, which is rather more combative in tone, is addressed simply 'To all Women in General'.[29] The work takes the form of those *controversia* or disputations popular at the time. The form is loose, made up of a compilation of allusions, sayings and proverbs, and the style is direct: 'At the end of men's faire promises there is a Laberinth, the . . . miles ends are marked with these trees, Follie, Vice, Mischiefe, Lust, Deceite, and Pride. These to deceive you will be clothed in the raiementes of Fancie, Vertue, Modestie, Love, Truemeaning and Handsomeness'.[30] Men are metaphorically described as snakes, eels and storm clouds. Cuckold's horns, she explains, are the gods' invention to protect men's foreheads from serious injury if they trip while pursuing women. But there are more earnest and straightforward statements too which speak of her desire to foster in women a conviction of their own intellectual and moral worth.[31] Still more fundamental and intriguing is her call for the need to 'question that now which hath ever been questionless'.[32] This is typical of the Reformation's sceptical force more generally: a realisation that much that has been read in a particular way, and promulgated as 'accepted truth', needs to be examined. And this encompasses far more than merely theology or the Church. Anger points to notions of both the 'objective' and the 'natural' and explores the degree to which these may simply be a matter of a male rather than a female point of view. Anger exposes double standards and the degree to which language embeds a view of the world that is by no means unbiased in terms of women and men. Anger was one of the most astute and controversial women readers and writers of her time. She, like others, was working within a Reformation tradition that, in essence, was a time of profound and widespread questioning.

Other women approached similar questions more obliquely. Most famously, Marguerite de Navarre wrote her own collection of tales (the *Heptameron*, published posthumously in 1558) to challenge the misogynist view of women presented by Boccaccio in the *Decameron* (c. 1350). The stories that make up Boccaccio's collection are supposedly addressed to women readers. Seven of his ten storytellers are also women. Despite this, most take the male characters' point of view and many tell of the apparent wrongdoings of women and the punishments then meted out to them. The seventh tale stands out in its lengthy descriptions of the cruelty to which a widow is subjected. She has kept a scholar waiting in the snow and he takes his revenge by abandoning her naked. The details of her gradual bodily degradation are graphic and exaggerated.[33] Navarre's stories are narrated by five gentlemen and five lady travellers who find themselves stranded in an abbey. As in Boccaccio's work, the telling of tales is proposed as an edifying way of passing the time, but in the *Heptameron*, the storytelling is followed by conversations that quickly become

32 Marguerite de Navarre, engraving by John Hinchcliff, 1864.

verbal battles between the sexes. Most of the stories are about love, amorous conquests and the nature of women's virtue, and include frank descriptions of adultery, rape and war. The framing of the stories obscures Navarre's own point of view but the reader is exposed to different approaches to key questions about how men and women live and how they might live. The double standards of courtly society in early modern France are exposed. In the utopian mountain setting of the *Heptameron* there are no hierarchies. Their banter is play and 'where games are concerned everybody is an equal'. More oblique are warnings made by the women storytellers and their characters against the 'devil who appears as half angel'; he is 'the most dangerous of the lot, because he's so good at transforming himself into an angel of light'. Within the *Heptameron*, it is clerics and other men of professional standing who are presented as half angels. The *Heptameron* is a complex work but its author clearly shared the view of one of the characters, Osille: 'Neither man nor woman is favoured in the work of God', she asserts, adding that St Paul 'commends himself to those women who have laboured with him in the Gospel'.[34]

The range of works published in the sixteenth century broadened. Many were intimately bound up with the debates of the Reformation and Counter-Reformation and many concerned the 'battle of the sexes'. But in the sixteenth century manuals of various sorts also began to be published in large numbers. These early versions of the 'how-to' format covered an astonishing range of skills. Noblemen could read about how to improve their hunting, including specialised treatises on catching birds and fish. The young nobleman, or not-so-noble-man, could refine his fencing skills or learn to box. There were accounting books for businessmen, books on all manner of craftsmen's practices, surveying manuals for estate managers, and books on winemaking for both the householder and the professional vintner. One of the bestsellers of the period was a manual that explained how to make a sundial in your own garden. No doubt this publication was one of the very first of a genre of book which takes up a significant amount of space in today's bookshops: variously described as home, DIY, interior decoration and gardening.

There were manuals aimed specifically at women readers too. Cookery books are already, in the sixteenth century, best-selling and, although not explicitly written for women, it is a reasonable assumption that they would constitute the readership, given the division of roles outlined in *Xenophon's Treatise of Householde*, translated by Gentian Hervet in 1532. Elsewhere women were encouraged to concern themselves with the preparation of meals. One of the earliest guides is entitled simply, *This is the boke of cookery* (1500), and many others followed; *A propre new booke of cookery* (1545) went into four editions, with much of it taken up by the preparation and cooking of meat and fish. Eucharius Roesslin's *The byrth of mankynde newly translated out of Laten into Englysshe. In which is entered of all suche thynges the which chaunce to women in their labor, and all suche infyrmitees whiche happen unto the infants after they be delivered. And also at the latter ende or in the thyrde or last boke is entreated of the conception of mankynde, and howe many ways it may be letted or furtheryd* (1540), is most likely the first book on childbirth in English. There were thirteen editions, proving, at a time of high infant and maternal mortality, its lasting relevance. The second edition makes explicit what is only implicit in the first, namely that it is 'otherwyse named the womans booke'. Most unusual for its time is the guidance for looking after babies, including advice to nurses about the swaddling of infants, which is quite contrary to modern hospital practice. It cautions against wrapping babies in a foetal position and quite tightly, as in the womb, so that they feel secure and content; rather, nurses are advised that the baby's limbs must be 'ryghte and strayght', otherwise the baby will not grow 'strayght and upryght'. Less alarming are the books on sewing and embroidery. One of the earliest and fullest was *A neawe treatys: as concernynge the excellency of the needle worcke Spanisshe stitche and weavynge in the frame . . . the whiche is difficyll: nat only for craftmen but also for gentlewemen*, published in Antwerp around 1530. These books also serve as a vivid reminder of just how much of daily life, for both women and men of different classes, involved the hands.

Devotional works taught piety and spirituality, but some also encouraged intellectual curiosity. Comically extravagant the titles of these sixteenth-century books may be, yet they often tell you all you need to know. Around 1549, Robert Wyer, a London printer, published a little quarto entitled, *Here is a necessary treatyse for all maner of persons to reade, and hath to name, the maydens crosse rewe*. A 'crosse rewe' (or 'cross row') meant a book arranged alphabetically. Its principal audience was 'maidens'. Here, from A to Z, and rhyming, is an essential guide to right living. Under 'K', women are advised to 'Knowe thy neyghboure well and certaynely'; under 'N', 'Nothynge to man is better than pacyence'.

One of the most influential treatises of the period was Juan Luis Vives' extravagantly entitled *A very frutefull and pleasant boke called the instruction of a Christen women, made first in Laten, and dedicated unto the queens good grace, by the right famous clerke mayster Lewes Vives, and turned out of Latin into Englysshe by Richard Hyrd. Which boke who so redeth diligently shal have knowledge of many thynges, wherin he shal take great pleasure, and specially women shall take great commodyte and frute towarde thencreance of virtue and good manners.*

Vives' abiding concern was to stress the three key female virtues: silence, piety and obedience. Arranged to provide necessary guidance from childhood to widowhood, Vives emphasises the need for moral instruction, knowledge of household crafts, and medical know-how. The fifth chapter is entitled 'What bookes to be read, and what not,' and recommends certain classical, devotional and inspirational works, but warns against the corrupting influence of romances such as *Amadis of Gaul*. This was a Spanish novel, a tale of knights-errant from the fourteenth century which became widely known in the sixteenth. In England and Germany it was mostly read in its French translation. Vives' work was first published in Antwerp in Latin in 1523 and was later translated into several European languages. The first three editions (probably two in 1529, and one in 1531) include a preface by Richard Hyrde, one of the first Englishmen to express his supportive views on women's education. However, one of the most far-reaching and categorical prohibitions in Vives' work is against women teaching:

30 The Inſtruction of

home. And to his Diſciple *Timothy* hee writeth on this wyſe : Lette a woman learne in licence with all ſubiection. But I giue no licenſe to a woman to bee a teacher, nor to haue authority of the man but to bee in ſilence. For *Adam* was the firſt made, and after *Eue*, and *Adam* was not betrayed, the Woman was betrayed into the breache of the Commaundement. Therefoze becauſe a Woman is a frayle thinge, and of weake diſcretion, and that maye lightlye bee deceyued : which thing oure firſte mother *Eue* ſheweth, whome the Diuell caught with a light argument. Therefoze a woman ſhoulde not teache, leaſte when ſhee hath taken a falſe opinion and beleefe of anye thing, ſhee ſpzeade it into the hearers, by the authozitye of maſterſhippe, and lightlye bzing other into the ſame erroure, foz the learners commonlie doe after the Teacher with good will.

What

a Chriſtian Woman. **31**

What bookes be to be
read, and what not.

The fifth Chapter.

Saint *Hierome* writing vnto *Leta* of the teaching of *Paula*, commaundeth thus: Let her learne to heare nothing, noz ſpeake but it that appertaineth vnto the feare of God, Noz there is no doubt, but he will counſaile the ſame of reading. There is an vſe now a dayes wozſe then among the Pagans, that Bookes written in our mothers tongues that be made but foz idle men and Women to reade, haue none other matter but of Warre and loue: of the which bookes I thinke it ſhall not neede to giue any pzecepts. If I ſpeake vnto Chziſtian folks, what neede I to tell what a miſcheefe is towarde when ſtrawe and dzy wood is caſt into the fire? Dea but theſe be written (ſay they) foz idle folke, as though idleneſſe were not a vice great enough of it ſelfe, without firebzandes be put vnto it, wherewith the fire maye catch a man all

33 Jean Luis Vives' *A very frutefull and pleasant boke called the instruction of a Christen women…*, 1529.

because a woman is a frail thing, and of weak discretion, and that may lightly be deceived: which thing our first mother Eve sheweth, whom the devil caught with a light argument. Therefore a woman should not teach, lest when she has taken a false opinion and belief of anything, she spread it unto the hearers, by the authority of mastership and lightly bring others into the same error, for the learners commonly do after their teacher with good will[.][35]

Baldassare Castiglione's *The courtier of Count Castilio divided into four bookes. Very necessary and profitable for yonge gentilmen and gentilwomen abiding in court, palaice, or place, done in Englyshe by Thomas Hoby,* published in London in 1561 in four editions, was written very much for the wealthier classes and is much less prescriptive. Originally published in Italian in the early sixteenth century it emphasises the importance of learning. The third book discusses the qualities to be cultivated in a gentlewoman including good conversation and wit, 'For many virtues of the minde I recken be as necessary for a woman, as for a man'. Castiglione outlines the need, in his chapter 'Of the

Chief Conditions and Qualityes in a Waytyng Gentlywoman', 'to be well born and of a good house', and to be 'learned'. A not dissimilar Italian work aimed at a middle-class audience of women is Gian Michele Bruto's *La Institutione di una Fanciulla Nata Nobilmente*, translated by Thomas Salter in 1579 as *Mirrhor of Modestie*. It is more conservative, holding up traditional values of female virtue: piety, humility and chastity. Those areas intimately associated with self-awareness, self-expression and a critical intellectual approach – including poetry, philosophy and rhetoric – are firmly discouraged. Romantic fiction and plays were proscribed in no uncertain terms.

Needless to say, practical treatises on marriage elaborated upon the distinct roles of women and men. Heinrich Bullinger, the Swiss reformer, was author of *The Christen state of matrimony, moost necessary and profitable for all of them, that intend to live quietly and godlye in the Christen state of holy wedlocke newly set forth in Englyshe* (1541), translated by Miles Coverdale. It was enormously popular and went into eight editions. Although one of the first rules states the almost universally recognised necessity that 'The husband is the heade of the Wyfe', Coverdale's translation also stresses the need for husband and wife to be friends, as well as lovers, and the rewards of caring for each other particularly at the outset of marriage.

Women and men were repeatedly preached to about the duties of wedlock. Joannes Oecolampidius's *A sermon . . . to young men and maydens* (c. 1548) warned both 'yong wemen and maydes' in equal measure against 'wanton and incontynent' behaviour and inappropriate dress. Books on marriage, principally of a practical kind, sometimes proposed new and (for the times) more subversive models of relations between a man and a woman. *Economicus*, the dialogue on household management by the ancient Greek polymath Xenophon, was translated into English in 1532 by Thomas Lupset as *Treatise of Householde*. It is even-handed in its own way. It is more 'honestie' for a woman to keep her house, and for the man to apply his mind to 'such things as muste be done abrode'. Women should not 'walke aboute', and men should not 'abyde sluggynge at home'.

Dedicated to Queen Elizabeth herself, Edmund Tilney's *A brief and pleasant discourse of duties in marriage, called the flower of friendship* was published in 1568. Through one of the female voices in the book, Tilney sets out the fundamental need for a wife to be under the authority of her husband: 'God commaundeth it, and we are bounde so to doe'; and again, 'The man both by reason, and law, hath soveraigntie over his wife'. Tilney's discourse rehearses arguments for different balances of authority and also explores Xenophon's idea that women assume authority in the home, and men outside it. This he rejects.

Elizabeth's own fears for social instability also emerge in the debate about free access to literature in the vernacular. Her concerns that ordinary women might recognise that Scripture needed to be interpreted, rather than simply conveying truths, appear obliquely in her writings: 'Every merchant must have his schoolmaster and nightly conventicles [religious gatherings], expounding scripture and catechising their servants and maids, in so much as I have heard how some maids have not sticked to control learned readers and say "such a man taught otherwise in our house."'[36] It is fascinating to know that women belonging to the least privileged groups were sometimes aware that writings could be interpreted in different ways. Elizabeth herself, however, was sustained by her own reading of Scripture and was one of a number of Renaissance women (Teresa of Avila above all) who referred metaphorically to reading material as 'food', emphasising its profoundly nourishing role. In her copy of the Epistles of St Paul, in August 1576, or perhaps a little later, she wrote: 'I walk many times into the pleasant fields of the Holy Scriptures, where I pluck up the good green herbs of sentences, eat them by reading, chew them up by musing, and lay them up at length in the high seat of memory . . . so I may the less perceive the bitterness of this miserable life.'[37]

The bulk of what most sixteenth-century women read told them how to be good wives, mothers or nuns, what to read and how. By and large the power of the press, amid women's growing literacy, manifests itself as a force of repression. Most books, however different their format, upheld the idea that women were inferior, physically, intellectually, morally and spiritually. There was, however, another genre that encouraged women to see themselves differently. In fictional works, chivalric romances and tales of courtly love, the presentation of feminine ideals encouraged a different discussion of the 'woman question'.

It was a woman, Margaret Tyler, who translated Diego Ortúñez de Calahorra's *The mirrour of princely deedes and knighthood . . . now newly translated out of Spanish into our vulgar English Tongue*, published in London in 1578. Tyler had served in the household of Thomas Howard, Duke of Norfolk. Given that she was not aristocratic, and most likely a servant, Tyler's accomplishment was remarkable. Her translation was in the vanguard, making a major Continental romance available in English. Tyler displays a measured approach, and a degree of calculated disingenuousness in her prefatory 'Epistle to the Reader', which purports to address both men and women, but one suspects that providing robust inspiration to her own sex was her primary concern. Here for the first time a woman affirms the intellectual equality of early modern women readers with their male counterparts. In a canny move Tyler defends her translation of a Spanish romance on the grounds that religion is better avoided because it is potentially dangerous and immodest for women to dabble in it. But her subject was, of course, bound to rouse controversy. Sixteenth-century Continental romantic fiction was routinely and bluntly denounced as immoral. English Protestants were suspicious of its Catholicity, while Renaissance humanists objected to stories in which love affairs occur outside marriage. Vives, a guarded but nevertheless major advocate of women's classical education, forbad the reading of courtly love stories. Nevertheless the genre grew steadily in popularity, not least because of women readers' interest in it. Indeed three of the most important sixteenth-century works of this kind were expressly dedicated to women: John Lyly's *Euphues* (1579), Philip Sidney's *Arcadia* (*c.* 1580) and, most famously, Edmund Spenser's *Faerie Queene* (1590).

Margaret Tyler appealed to an apparent contradiction in her prefatory epistle: if men habitually dedicate books to women, then women should surely be able to read these works without reproach. Her epistle is straightforward in its claim to equal rights as a woman reader and writer. She defends her choice of Ortúñez for two reasons: the author's moral integrity and creative originality, and the novel's subject, courtly love, which exercises the imagination and in relation to which first-hand experience is no more necessary for the woman reader than the man. She argues that intelligent and thorough reading is a necessary and sufficient preparation for a careful translation. This leads on to her most bold and unequivocal claim for the equality of men and women in relation to both reading and writing: 'My persuasion hath been thus, that it is all one for a woman to pen a story as for a man to address his story to a woman.' In a concluding flourish she adds that all she is doing is offering 'entertainment to a stranger'.[38]

Tyler was clearly well educated but we can only speculate as to how she knew Spanish sufficiently well to undertake her translation. Knowledge of Spanish was a rare accomplishment for the time. But Tyler's independent spirit and intelligence does invite comparison with another apparently relatively modest woman writer, Isabella Whitney. Her poetic letters and poems written for family and friends provide useful clues as to her background. It is probable that she was from a large family, that she had two younger sisters in service to whom she offers advice, and that she was free to write poetry, because she was unmarried or widowed. She portrays her own social position as being neither aristocratic nor lowly. Through misfortunes of various kinds, she finds time unexpectedly on her hands. She describes her position in one of her verses:

This Harvest tyme, I Harvestlesse,
and servicelesse also:

And subject unto sicknesse, that
abrode I could not go,
Had leasure good, (though learninglackt)
some study to apply:
To reade such Bookes, whereby I thought
my selfe to edyfye.[39]

Whitney's humble background sets her aside from other women writers of the period who were mostly associated with court circles. The majority of their writings were pious and earnest translations. Whitney's poetry, on the other hand, is mischievously ambiguous and her light tone suggests that her exaggerated laments may be wholly imagined, even mocking parodies of the genre. Her work has been likened to the 'native plain style' poetry of the likes of Gascoigne, whose mock 'Last Will and Testament of Dan Bartholomew of Bath' may have been written in imitation of Whitney.

The first of Whitney's two miscellanies is *Copy of a Letter* (1566–67) and it exists in only one manuscript, in the Bodleian Library, Oxford. The book contains four lighthearted love complaints, two voiced by women and two by men. In her dedication Whitney makes a good deal of her lack of originality: 'though they [her writings] be of anothers, yet considering they be of *my owne* gathering and making up: *respect my labour* and regard my good will.' Whitney presents herself then as a reader-harvester who arranges a selection of the ideas she has derived from others in a new way. Indeed her writing shows that she was a shrewd reader of anything and everything new on the London literary scene. There are echoes of Turberville's translation of Ovid's *Heroides* which was published the same year as her *Copy of a Letter*. She had also clearly read and drawn on Gower's *Confessio Amantis* and Chaucer's *Legend of Good Women*. But it is Hugh Plat's Senecan prose writing that is her principal source of influence. *A Sweet Nosegay*, the second miscellany of 1573, is in many ways a rewriting of Plat's more grandly entitled *Floures of Philosophie* (1572).

What Whitney offers is moral advice and verse on friendship, the lending and borrowing of money, the inconstancies of youth, and social honour. Her depictions of love and friendship are richly suggestive of a new sense of equality and reciprocity between men and women. And there were plenty of other comparable women poets and writers who were read and appreciated on the Continent: Catherine des Roches, Pernette du Guillet, Tullia d'Aragona, Mary Wroth, Gaspara Stampa, Louise Labé and Veronica Franco to name but a few.

There is also a formal – and in some ways distinctively feminine – originality in Whitney's work. The poems are preceded by a dedication, an author's address and commendatory verse. After the poems there are letters from Whitney to family members, and prose and verse epistles. This assemblage of different types of writing reflects the variety of reading material to which women had access at that time. And there is a suggestion that each form can provide insights into life, whether it be a formal poem or an intimate letter between sisters. Equally feminine are the things presented as desirable. In conventional Tudor poetry by male authors it is the lover's body that tantalisingly eludes the poet's grasp – he glimpses hands, lips, eyes. But in Whitney's writing it is the homely material comforts of books – along with cloaks, food and mints – for which she longs.[40]

Margaret Tyler and Isabella Whitney and others were unusual in their bold responses to reading. Most women of the period who were moved by their reading to write, confined their writing to socially acceptable 'feminine' genres. This included religious materials, along with advice to children, and translation of 'acceptable' works, which would not include Continental romances such as that of Ortúñez. A very small number of women, like Anne Dowriche, wrote first and foremost for small literate coteries of women readers, including Aemilia Lanyer. Her verse-meditation on the Passion, *Salve Deus Rex Judaeorum* (*Hail, God, King of the Jews*), published in 1611, is both religious and political in its expressions of regret for women's universal experience of misogyny and repression. It included separate dedications to no less than eleven different women. Like many of her contemporaries Lanyer found great solace in being able to read the Bible in a group with other women. The socially acceptable practice of group Bible-reading became an opportunity to discuss central episodes of biblical, and thus Western, history, in ways that were different from the male divines. These re-readings allowed the women to conceive of new possibilities for female identity. In Christ's 'feminine' qualities of love, nurturing and his passive tolerance of suffering, Lanyer found a recognisably female model, but one that did not go hand-in-hand with ideas of inferiority or blind submission to authority. But Lanyer's approach, in verse rather than prose, is somewhat oblique; Renaissance women had to work within a culturally specific language, and one that was considered to be acceptable.

The concerns of some women readers and writers on the Continent were sometimes refreshingly different. Perhaps the most celebrated example is the passionate and brave Louise Labé (*c.* 1524–66) of Lyon. During her lifetime the city rivalled Paris as a centre of books and learning. Louise was beautiful, energetic and thoroughly able in many areas. She could read discriminatingly and converse wittily, she could write, draw, ride, play the lute and sing, and wield various weapons with daunting expertise. At the age of sixteen she fell in love with a knight and rode off to fight alongside him at the Siege of Perpignan. Some years later she settled down with a rope-maker, as women who have run away with knights do from time to time. She had grown out of her earlier and numerous pursuits and reading became her sole passion. She established the foremost literary salon in Lyon and built up a remarkable library containing works not just in French, but also in Latin, Italian and Spanish. She remains well known as a poet, but should also be remembered for her astute insights into the nature of reading itself, perceptions which are articulated again with full force hundreds of years later by Proust in his *Remembrance of Things Past*, a work both about his life and an exposition of the re-creative power of memory. Labé wrote:

> The past gives us more pleasure and is of more service than the present; but the delight of what we once felt is dimly lost, never to return, and its memory is as distressing as the events themselves were then delectable. The other voluptuous senses are so strong that whatever memory returns to us it cannot restore our previous disposition, and however strong the images we impress in our minds, we still know that they are but shadows of the past misusing us and deceiving us. But when we happen to put our thoughts in writing, how easily, later on, does our mind race through an infinity of events, incessantly alive, so that when a long time afterwards we take up those written pages we can return to the same place and to the same disposition in which we once found ourselves.[41]

There is a simplicity in Labé's style which allows the reader to refashion her words into an expression of personal experience. Sixteenth-century women readers were seduced by her work and she has continued to be resurrected in translations by many other writers since; one of her somewhat unlikely later translators was the German Romantic poet Rainer Maria Rilke.[42] Labé's poetry is open to a different kind of engagement with the reader because its style is less complex and dense than other more florid work of the period. Perhaps for the poet herself this allowed the authentic experience to be relived, and triggered a new creative act: an unadorned sonnet was a faint reminder of the past that could be more fully reinvented in the present. Other readers, equally, are provided with a taking-off point, one that will necessarily connect with the individual's real, as opposed to imaginative, experience. For all the devotional works, manuals, conduct and cookery books flooding the growing markets, this was the kind of writing with which some women wanted to engage.

Elsewhere, romances that had flourished orally were gradually committed to paper for recitation and reading by elite minorities. Despite clerics' frequent denouncement of romances as malign worldly distractions from more substantive or moral works, fantastic fictions became increasingly popular. Romances were published in various formats and anthologies emerged, particularly in Antwerp, Seville, Saragossa and Barcelona. In Spain these generally appeared in two forms: as collections of several tens or even hundreds of poems in a single work, and as individual texts printed on one sheet in quarto format. This meant that new editions borrowed from each other and were simultaneously fed by surviving oral traditions. The printed form that won out comprised a single or a half-sheet, in quarto format, folded into a booklet of four or eight pages. Ambulant merchants and blind pedlars sold these throughout Spain.

34 *Le Colporteur* (*The Pedlar*) hawking his wares in this seventeenth-century painting.

The English sixteenth-century broadside ballads were a similar publishing phenomenon. These could be religious or secular and were sold by itinerant pedlars. They were extremely popular: roughly 3,000 were published during the sixteenth century. In France the bookseller-publishers had made a similar move, introducing the 'Bibliothèque bleue' in the late sixteenth century. These booklets were twenty-four pages in octavo or duodecimo format, 'double books' of twenty-four pages in quarto format, and 'histories' that could be anything between thirty-two and seventy-two pages. The material was both religious and secular, often recycled material from other genres. In London, readers distinguished between 'penny godliness' and 'penny merriment'. The Bibliothèque bleue offered stories of chivalry, fairy tales, 'wicked' stories (*gueuserie*: literally 'roguery') and how-to books. Alongside these publications, the printers also continued to produce saints' lives, almanacs and devotional works of various kinds. There were also *occasionnels*, news-sheets that reported on military campaigns; those that were published about the war with the Turks were part of a large-scale press campaign in Germany and Central Europe. And pamphlets popular with women readers announced astonishing events – miracles, monsters and natural catastrophes. All these forms of relatively cheap reading material would become increasingly available and at the same time less fanciful and more sophisticated over the next century. Women were becoming more important as readers in terms of the economics of publishing. Some, mostly men but also women, would try to put the brakes on. Others, mostly men, stood to make a great deal of money by encouraging the trends.

CHAPTER 6

――――•⁄•⁄•――――

Competing for Attention

IN 1615, an opportunistic fencing teacher, Joseph Swetnam, published a swingeing attack on women, *The Arraignment of Lewd, Idle, Froward, and Unconstant Women; or the vanity of them, Choose you Whether. With a Commendation of Wise, Virtuous, and Honest Women*. It was a misleading title, as there is virtually nothing by way of 'commendation' in this aggressive publication; there is however much virulent criticism in his miscellany of stories of naughty women, their depravities, and their scandalous behaviour, sometimes attributable to the influence of reading romances. Swetnam, as narrator, poses as a jaded traveller amusing himself by stringing together exaggerated tales of female wickedness. He recycles popular material from ballads, proverbial lore and well-known tavern stories, with many examples of women's dangerous sexuality and their surreptitious strategies for dominating the household. 'The lion being bitten with hunger, the bear being robbed of her young ones, the viper being trod on, all these are nothing so terrible as the fury of a woman. . . . A buck may be enclosed in a park, a bridle rules a horse, a wolf may be tied, a tiger may be tamed, but a froward woman will never be tamed', he counsels.[1] A little later he warns:

> For women have a thousand ways to entice thee, and ten thousand ways to deceive thee, and such fools as are suitors unto them, some they keep in hand with promises, and some they feed with flattery, and some they delay with dalliance, and some they please with kisses. They lay out the folds of their hair to entangle men into their love, betwixt their breasts is the vale of destruction, and in their beds is hell, sorrow and repentance. Eagles eat not men till they are dead, but women devour them alive[.][2]

Swetnam had rightly identified a lucrative market, and he sold well to hungry readers who consumed the author – whilst he was still alive. By 1634 his *Arraignment* was in its tenth edition. Women readers were likely to find this book not only offensive, but somewhat ludicrous in its exaggerated assessment of women. Some women readers, dismayed by what they read, took up their pens.

The period is also one in which prominent women book collectors feature. Frances Egerton (*née* Stanley), Countess of Bridgewater (1583–1636), was a keen bibliophile and one of the first to own printed plays by Shakespeare. Frances Wolfreston (1607–76/7) was typical of a particular class of woman reader. She left her books to one of her sons, Standford, and most of them remained at Statfold Hall, unbound and uncut, until they were sold at Sotheby & Wilkinson on 24 May 1856. The auction catalogue, *The Remains of a Library Partly Collected During the Reign of King James the First*, lists more than 400 titles published before Wolfreston's death, including some of Shakespeare's plays. They 'represent the leisure reading of a literate lady in her country house', with some history and theology, and a considerable number of titles (nearly half) being what we would now class as 'English literature'.[3]

The seventeenth century was a time of change in relation to publishing and this sparked lively debates amid different waves of formal and informal censorship in Europe and further afield. And where publishers had a freer hand they were quick to see the commercial benefits of entering into controversial publishing wars, sometimes between men and women writers. These often centred on arguments about the merits and demerits of women authors and women's reading. It was now possible for women to make a living through authorship, though very few had the courage to do so. Women authors continued to make more or less generous gestures towards men's superiority, while also recognising that their act of authorship was more than a symbolic sign of profound social change. In Dorothy Leigh's 'mother's legacy' (a kind of writing which became increasingly popular during the century), she provides her sons with advice about choosing a wife, for example, and describes how best to make a contribution to the Christian community. She ensures that she gives men more than their due by ascribing to them 'the first and chief place'. But she goes on to describe her writing as an act of 'boldness . . . so unusual among us [women]'. In addition she suggests that female authorship will change 'the usual order of women'.

Developments in printing and binding made books cheaper to produce and the continuing rise of literacy brought new readerships and new products, including printed ballads and broadsides (cheap single-sheet publications). Tracts about women's lives and women's education were especially popular with women readers. Some men, however, and indeed some women, considered these inappropriate reading material, which in turn inspired counter-publications that renewed debates about the 'woman question'. Romances written largely for women started to appear overseas, usually in translation, further increasing some people's anxieties about an unharnessed publishing industry that was becoming difficult to control. Diverse coteries of women – family groups, intellectual nuns, *salonnières* or Chinese women's poetry groups – now read more widely.

Some women readers were sufficiently outraged by Swetnam to fight back. Ester Sowernam (a 'sour' version of Swet['sweet']-nam), produced her counter-attack in 1617, less than two years after Swetnam's publication.[4] The title-page is an elaborate pseudonymous riddle. 'Ester' refers to the Esther of

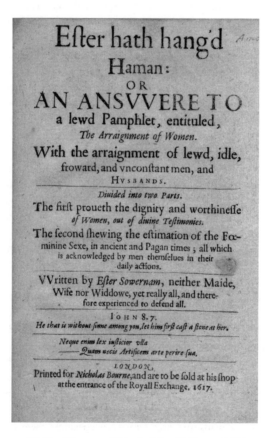

35 The title-page of *Ester hath hang'd Haman*, 1617.

the eponymous biblical book, which narrates how she is chosen from the harem to be queen. Behind the shadow of the virtuous woman author, this choice of name suggests, is the former prostitute. The riddle challenges and denies the description of women as either maid, widow or wife – or loose: the authoritative 'queen' retains the shadow of the fallen woman.

Sowernam's Ester is a teasing contribution to the *querelle des femmes* and plays a clever game with Swetnam. Her attentive reading of the Bible shows through everywhere. She ignores passages that uphold male superiority and concentrates attention on biblical women's strength and virtue. In her third chapter she describes the contributions of sixteen Old Testament women, some anonymous, who did more than their male counterparts to save the people. In the next chapter she celebrates women of the New Testament, Roman goddesses and European queens, including Elizabeth I and Mary Queen of Scots. Her strategy is, on the one hand, to display her wide reading, and on the other, to show up Swetnam's scholarly shortcomings. She exposes his plagiarisms, weak logic, unrefined style and poor grammar. Swetnam had attributed to God himself the notion that women were 'necessary evils', revealing, Sowernam insinuated, his limited reading. She also knew her Euripides and points out Swetnam's ignorance of the pagan author. Sowernam's work is a brilliant reply to 'all the objections which our adversaries hath vomited out against woman'.[5] And its success was inextricably bound up with the wide reading that she was able to draw on and which gave her writing impressive authority.

Rachel Speght was only nineteen when she fought back. She also wrote her pamphlet *A Muzzle for Melastomus* (meaning 'black-mouth', or slanderer) in 1617. In a similar spirit she entitles the last section of her work 'Certain Queries to the Baiter of Women'. She was the first Englishwoman to identify herself, by name, as a polemicist and critic of contemporary claims about the sexes. Speght also published a volume of poetry, *Mortalities Memorandum with a Dreame Prefixed* (1621), a Christian reflection on death and a spirited defence of the education of women. She was born in London in 1597 and was the daughter of a Calvinist minister. Her writings reveal that she was well educated in rhetoric and logic, and widely read in the classics and Christian material.

In her reply to Swetnam, Speght begins by asking for the protection of enlightened upper-class women readers and argues that not to respond to Swetnam would be silently to condone his ridiculous views, and equally, further to encourage this kind of publication. In her preface she makes two direct attacks. Firstly, she accuses him of illiteracy in filling what she calls his 'mingle mangle' arguments with grammatical howlers and errors of logic.[6] Secondly, she accuses him of blasphemy on two counts: degrading God's creation, woman, and twisting scripture to suit his own arguments. Two discussions follow.[7] In the first, she addresses the four biblical passages used by Swetnam to argue for women's inferiority. In the second she demonstrates her astute reading of Aristotle and makes a case for women based on causality.

Speght accepts Eve's relative weakness but argues that this makes her less culpable than Adam. She puts forward an imaginative argument about Solomon's claim that he cannot find a good woman in a thousand: it is a reference, she argues, to his own state of affairs, namely his harem of 700 wives and 300 concubines. Paul, she contends, was probably married judging by his use of pronouns. The exegesis is rigorous and logical. When Speght turns to her Aristotelian argument in defence of women she appeals to biblical examples of men and women who may be unequal in terms of strength and even mental capacity, but 'equal in dignity, both temporally and eternally'. Her final discussion is of the 'miraculous bond' of marriage. It is 'a merri-age, and this worlds Paradise, where there is mutuall love'.

Speght's later 'Epistle Dedicatory' from *Mortality's Memorandum* was written in direct response to vituperative male pamphlet-writers who had responded to her *Memorandum* in curious ways; they criticised its defence of women, yet also contended that it must have been penned by a male ghost writer, as it could not possibly have been written by a woman.[8] As writing became more common among women, this allegation became a source of deep frustration and outrage for women writers. Some claimed that Speght's clergyman father must have written the *Memorandum*, but she vigorously defended it as her own work. In addition she makes clear that it was written in response to her mother's death, and is something of a *memento mori*. She also dedicated it to her godmother, clearly indicating that she saw herself belonging to an intimate network of women readers. Speght defends and promotes women's right, even their obligation, to read and learn freely in order to encourage personal growth and wisdom in the service of society. There is a certain Calvinist dreariness to Speght's writing and it belongs firmly within the straight-laced Reformation tradition. Yet her example was a remarkable one. It was daring and unusual for women to write publicly and very rare for a learned, middle-class, unmarried young woman, outraged by her reading, to publish in her own name, openly attacking a male author.

Also in 1617, the pseudonymous Constantia Munda ('Pure Constancy') published *The Worming of a Mad Dog*.[9] Her indignation at Swetnam shows through strongly and her thrusts and parries are forceful. Her wide reading is everywhere put to use. The reader is dazzled by her deft quotations from

Greek, Latin, French, Italian and English authors. In her preface she thanks her mother for her extensive liberal education. It is necessity, Munda argues, that compels her to speak out despite contemporary conventions: 'feminine modesty hath confined our rarest and ripest wits to silence'.[10]

Pamphlet wars became increasingly popular and a change in the size of books was both a response, and further encouragement, to this and other new publishing trends. Most books until around 1600 were large and impressive tomes: folios and quartos at least twice the size of most modern books. Then the octavo and duodecimo formats came in, both roughly the size of modern paperbacks. Although the grand volumes attracted wealthy buyers and sold at high prices, they involved lots of expensive paper and were complicated and costly to bind. The sudden move to smaller formats towards the middle of the century, in France as elsewhere, was in part a response to something of a publishing crisis, when booksellers had to suspend the publication of expensive large formats; they now shared a market with a growing number of pirated editions, which had narrow page margins and small fonts, and largely served a less wealthy public.

In England, pirated books needed to be cheap and easy to conceal from those on the lookout for seditious material. Censorship had continued under Charles I, was abolished briefly in 1640, but was re-established by the Presbyterian and Puritan majority in the House of Commons in 1643, to ensure control of their Catholic or royalist adversaries. The number of sanctioned printing houses dropped to only twenty, but pirated editions continued to find their way onto the market. Authorised and unauthorised publications fought for sales. Throughout Europe publishers were soon aware of the much larger market for smaller, cheaper books. And as the print runs grew, so the price fell to the point where books were within the financial grasp of a growing reading public among the new middle class: merchants, shopkeepers, investors, distributors, and in many cases their wives too. Clandestine publishing was on the rise and the small books that were produced were also attractive to women readers who could conceal forbidden fruits more easily.

In England, the rise of the grammar schools also created a new textbook market. Edmund Coote's *Englishe Scholemaster*, written for both men and women, was published in 1596 with the idea of ensuring that teachers sufficiently understood the English language to teach well. Almost a century and a half before the appearance of Samuel Johnson's famous English dictionary, Robert Cawdrey published his *Table Alphabeticall* (1604), with a subtitle that indicated it had been 'gathered for the benefit and helpe of ladies, gentlewomen, or any other unskilfull persons'. For girls, titles like *The Virgin's A.B.C* (1630) appeared, subtitled 'an alphabet of virtuous admonitions for a chaste, modest and well-governed maid'. Authors vied for sales in a new and growing market for educational books, broadly defined.

Whereas the aristocracy and the clergy had hitherto been the driving forces in the book trade, now a new readership clamoured for new titles. Mercantile women's taste for ballads and, a little later, novels, proved a powerful and much contested force in the marketplace. For large numbers of readers, printed ballads and broadsides were the most important reading matter. Samuel Pepys had his collection bound into ten volumes, gathered in the seventeenth century. He drew on a collection by John Selden (1584–1654). Selden was conscious of the importance of ballads: 'Though some make slight of libels, yet you may see by them how the wind sits. As take a straw, and throw it up into the air; you shall see by that which way the wind is, which you shall not by casting up a stone. More solid things do not show the complexion of the times so well as ballads and libels.' Libels often consisted of single sheets (or 'broadsides') and did not necessarily convey the contemporary idea of a false or malicious piece of writing.[11] By far the most important printed media in the seventeenth century were printed ballads and broadsides. These were the first means of mass written communication. In England and France this dominance only came to an end with the rise of the chapbook in the later seventeenth century. These were small booklets, an extension of broadsides, containing folk tales (often with a moral), historical stories, abridged chivalrous romances, ballads, nursery rhymes and other short stories likely to appeal to children.

Pepys' collection of ballads is divided into themes: 'Devotion and Morality; History True and Fabulous; Tragedy *vizt* Murders, Executions, Judgements of God &c; State and Times; Love Pleasant; Love Unfortunate; Marriage, Cuckoldry &c; the Sea, Love, Gallantry and Actions; Drinking and Good Fellowship; Humour, Frollicks &c mixt.' These categories are broadly representative of the material that Pepys considered a crucial source for understanding ordinary people of the time and of both sexes. But there was a particular story, told in myriad ballads, which was of enormous appeal to women. Over 100 extant printed ballads tell versions of a tale in which a young woman escapes from her father and his authority through an amorous entanglement, then disguises herself as a soldier or sailor, encounters trials of love and bravery, and is rewarded with a happy ending, often a marriage.[12] These ballads were so commercially successful in part because they promoted an idea of physically strong women who were involved in the action, often warfare. They also exemplify a contemporary fascination with disguise and masquerading. These were stories that women wanted to read, and in large numbers, and they appealed to the moment. The decline in this particular story being told in printed ballads coincides with the fashion of women being promoted as delicate, passive and in need of male protection.

Around the same time England's municipal or 'circulating' libraries opened to the urban literate, both men and women. And institutions, beyond universities and schools for men and boys, began to establish their own libraries. Hospitals recognised the usefulness of providing reading material for patients, both for their distraction and for their improvement. Hospital libraries were founded at Greenwich (Holy Trinity Hospital, 1614), Guildford (Hospital of the Blessed Trinity, 1619), Westminster (Emanuel Hospital, *c.* 1619) and Farringdon (Scots Hospital of King Charles II, 1665). Likewise in Ireland, the Royal Hospital of King Charles II was founded in Dublin in 1665, and in Edinburgh, the Merchant Maiden Hospital in 1695. This last hospital school was founded for the education and protection of the daughters of impoverished merchant burgesses of Edinburgh.

By the mid-seventeenth century roughly half of the households in England owned their own books. This was very much ahead of patterns on the Continent. In France, Louis XIV successfully limited the number of printers and in 1667 handed the power to enforce book controls and exercise censorship to the Police Lieutenant. In Germany, the Thirty Years' War (1618–48) led to an economic downturn and during the 1630s the number of titles listed in book-fair catalogues was roughly a third of what it had been in 1619. The statistics for England, however, point to the significant increase in literacy levels among girls and women during the century.

Innovations in the education of girls were also taking place in France. Throughout the country convents were founded to educate girls. There were new congregations of nuns dedicated to teaching wealthier girls – and charging for their services – with a clear focus on the catechism. In the cities charity schools were set up to teach the poor, embarking on programmes of basic education for boys and girls. The mission of one school, in the Les Halles district of Paris, was typical of the new educational zeal:

> The instruction and education of poor little girls early in life is one of the principal good works that Christians can accomplish and provide and one of the greatest missions and most necessary works of charity that they can perform for the salvation of souls.[13]

All manner of publications fuelled discussion of the effects of this new enfranchisement of girls into the educational system. The French dramatist Molière's three plays, *Les précieuses ridicules* (*The Pretentious Young Ladies*, 1659), *L'École des femmes* (*The School for Wives*, 1662) and *Les femmes savantes*

(The Learned Ladies, 1672), tapped into contemporary debates about the silliness or seriousness of educated women. Gradually the view that women's silliness was less innate but rather a matter of lack of proper education gained ground.

Influential, larger-than-life figures like Mme de Sévigné repeatedly returned to the question of the education of girls. She herself had been fortunate enough to have been orphaned at an early age and received a far from conventional education from relatives in Paris. In one of her typically conversational letters (later published) – in this instance one of many to her daughter about her granddaughter, Pauline – she assumes an innate discretion in the girl-reader:

> For Pauline, who devours books, I would rather see her gobble up bad ones than not like to read at all. Novels, comedies, the Voitures, the Sarasins – none of them lasts long. Has she tried Lucian? ... Later she must read history. If you have to hold her nose to make her swallow it, I feel for her. If she doesn't like beautiful works of piety, it's too bad, because we know only too well that even those without piety find them charming. ... I wouldn't want her for a moment to stick her little nose into Montaigne or Charron or other writers of that ilk. It's very early for her. At her age true morality is what one learns in good conversation, in myth, and in examples of history.[14]

Voiture and Sarasin both wrote 'society verse', which was witty and polished and aimed at a sophisticated audience. De Sévigné was recommending verses that are flippant or mildly ironic. Trivial subjects are treated in an intimate, subjective way. Others at the time might have feared that such reading would encourage a girl to be facetious and sarcastic. The Greek satirist Lucian is also a curious choice. A brilliantly entertaining writer, he invented the comic dialogue as a vehicle for satire. These expose the pretensions of pompous philosophers and describe the daily lives of Greek courtesans. De Sévigné's perspective on what girls should and should not read is wonderfully relaxed. She believed what many others doubted – and continue to doubt: that inexperienced girls would not be moved to behave like fictional characters or assume the tone of the authors they read. Her conviction was that establishing a facility in and love of reading were fundamental to encouraging the reading of more intellectually nourishing books later on. Pauline was a lucky reader and her grandmother was highly unusual.

For all the establishment of schools of one sort or another for girls, and for all the titles of books clearly aimed at women, what do we know of women's literacy during this period? Estimating the numbers of girls attending the various convents and schools across the century, and the success of their education in terms of their reading ability, is not easy. The most reliable source for ascertaining literacy is probably the depositions made by witnesses before the ecclesiastical courts. People of all classes were called upon to provide evidence and their name, age, sex, address, place of birth, marital status and social or occupational status is recorded, along with their signature or 'mark'. Studies of over 5,000 depositions in the Diocese of Norwich and London between 1580 and 1700 demonstrate certain trends, likely to be roughly typical of England as a whole. Between 1580 and 1640 women's illiteracy ran at some 95 per cent in East Anglia; by the second half of the century the figure had fallen to roughly 82 per cent. In London, the figure for the earlier period is comparable; roughly 90 per cent of women were illiterate. But during the Stuart period the rate dropped dramatically. In the last decade of the century around half the female population of London could sign their names, as compared to only 20 per cent in the provinces. Women readers in London could buy ballads and broadsides inexpensively and although their literate counterparts in the provinces could sometimes pick these up from itinerant pedlars, their numbers were significantly smaller. Women's reading in the period was first and foremost an urban phenomenon.

As the century progressed, literate women were encouraged to read accounts of exemplary women's lives and to emulate them. *The Holy Life of Mrs Elizabeth Walker*, published in 1690, was prepared by her widower, the Revd Anthony Walker, but is very largely composed of her own writings:

> God was pleased to give her strength to go out her full time of eleven children, six sons and five daughters, besides some untimely and abortive births. . . . Her work and business was to improve their intellectuals; to season their tender hearts with a due sense of religion. . . . To promote and forward this, she taught them to read as soon as they could pronounce their letters, yea, before they could speak plain; and sowed the seed of early pious knowledge in their tender minds, by a plain familiar catechism. . . . When they could read tolerably well, she caused them to get by heart choice sentences of Scripture, then whole psalms, and chapters[.][15]

The Walker household is something of a study in miniature of the new schools that had started to spring up.

Up until 1640 most publications aimed at the female market were tedious practical guides of one sort or another, written by men. Women authors were very scarce and in the area of home and family, almost exclusively a woman's area of interest, there is only one important title by a woman, *The Countess of Lincoln's Nursery* (1622). Written by Elizabeth Clinton, Countess of Lincoln, it was her only publication, short, and remained in its first edition. But it is an unusual advice manual, which treats in intimate terms woman's duty, both religious and maternal, to breastfeed her own children, even if she is a member of the upper classes.

Literate women teachers, often nuns, still constituted an important group of women readers; so too, more surprisingly, did midwives. The second and all later editions of the enormously popular *The Birth of Mankind: otherwise named, the Woman's Book* were published in the name of the physician, Thomas Raynald. In the prologue, which is addressed to 'women readers', the author explains that his purpose is to familiarise women with their anatomies, the process of conception, and the business of childbirth and nursing. In the second edition Raynald added that the book would be useful to upper-class women when they attended births, and for guiding midwives through deliveries. But what were midwives' responses to reading these sorts of works?

In 1634 Peter Chamberlen, who had been appointed court physician in 1632, proposed that London midwives should be required to attend his lectures. The midwives, however, argued that the anatomy books already available to them 'would direct them better than his lectures'. The perceived threat to their profession triggered a politically-charged publication. Midwife Jane Sharp brought out a manual which, while making much of the need for practical experience – and, ironically, stressing to the reader the need for experience over reading – included essential information about female anatomy. Women did not need or intend men to be involved in the process of childbirth. The treatise, *The Midwives Book; or, The Whole Art of Midwifery Discovered* was published in 1671. By 1725 four editions had appeared. It was addressed to the mother, father and midwife and was divided into sections sequentially treating the stages from conception to birth and postnatal care. Sharp is particularly critical of the use of male midwives, and would seem to have been writing in response to the likes of Chamberlen whom she regarded as making inroads into her profession and interfering with midwives' practice.

At the time midwives were not required to sign their names in order to obtain a licence from the Bishop of London. A slightly different system was in place for those who applied to the Archbishop of Canterbury and there are records bearing senior midwives' signatures. It is not much to go on, but in London, at least, it seems likely that many midwives were literate, their occupation already professionalised, and protected by their confidence in their own practices – and feisty colleagues like Sharp.

Equally practical were gardening books written for women. These saw a significant rise during the seventeenth century. John Gerard's famous *Herball* (1597) was enormously successful. William Lawson's *The Country Housewifes*

Garden (1617) was the first gardening book explicitly written for women and explained 'herbes of common use'. It also includes a delightful set of designs for the arrangement of garden plots, an alphabetical list of herbs and vegetables and an illustrated guide to bees and beehives. It was incorporated in a later volume entitled *A Way to Get Wealth* (1637), the work of a woman printer.[16] In France, *Le jardinier François* was published in 1651 and begins: 'An Epistle to the Ladies. Mesdames, I do not have to make a panegyric here on the beauty, the utility and necessity of gardens. They speak enough for themselves to be judged.'[17] And women were familiar with sixteenth-century verses like Thomas Tusser's which begins, 'Wife unto thy garden and set me a plot . . .' and ends, 'Those, having other things plentiful then/ Thou winnest the heart of the laboring men'. Orchards and the cultivation of fruit had always been and continued to be the preserve of men. But women were expected to

36 A woman reading Gerard's *Herball* of 1597.

take vegetable and flower gardening seriously, and having knowledge of plants was part of a woman's broad domestic training.

One exceptional woman who concerned herself seriously with women's education beyond practical knowledge, was Lucrezia Marinella, from Utrecht.[18] She was a poet, intellectual and, remarkably, even a theologian. Her treatise *On the Nobility and Excellence of Women and the Defects and Vices of Men* came out in three editions in 1600, 1601 and 1621. She also wrote a Latin treatise, *Dissertation logica*, generally translated as *Whether a Christian Woman Should Be Educated* (1632). She had been taught, at her father's instigation, all the learned languages (particularly the biblical languages), philosophy, science and maths. Marinella staunchly recommended this curriculum for all women. She had read and been much impressed by Vives' *Instruction of a Christen women*, and although she maintained his line on the importance of women reading and understanding Scripture, she advocated a broader educational range than he had. One of her notable admirers was the Leiden theologian André Rivet (1595–1650) with whom she established a significant correspondence. He also introduced her to two other important women intellectuals of the day, Princess Elizabeth of the Rhenish Palatinate and Marie Le Jars de Gournay.

Correspondence between a man and a woman who were not related was unusual in this period. The subject of much of the letters between Marinella and Rivet – their reading and views on women's education and status – was still more exceptional. To mitigate social criticism, they assumed the personae of father and daughter in their letters. A similar literary disguise is employed by de Gournay and her 'father figure', the famous French philosopher Michel de Montaigne, with whom she enjoyed a close intellectual friendship. After Montaigne's death, his widow and daughter passed his essays to her to edit. Women like de Gournay wanted to read widely, but they also wanted to discuss their reading with the luminaries of the day. Determined not to be prevented by potential public disapproval, they found scholars in whom they were interested and cast themselves as metaphorical 'daughters'. But these women were unusual and far from numerous.

Towards the end of the century something more like a formal theory of women's education was beginning to emerge. François Fénelon's *De l'éducation des filles* (1687) was devoted solely to the question of girls' education. Claude Fleury, author of the immensely successful *Histoire ecclésiastique* (*Ecclesiastical History*), published in twenty volumes in 1691 and the first of its kind, considered the matter in the thirty-sixth chapter of his lengthy *Traité du choix et de la méthode des études* (*The History, Choice and Method of Studies*). Fleury advocated a curriculum including reading, writing, home economics and basic arithmetic, pharmacology and law. More than this would be pure pretension but, as he stated, 'it would be still better than if they spent their leisure time reading novels, gambling or talking of skirts and ribbons'.[19]

Other writers had been cashing in on women's interest in just such things for some time. Interest in women's fashion was growing. Wenceslaus Hollar's *Ornatus muliebris Anglicanus, or, The severall habits of English women from the nobilitie to the country woman* (1640) was probably the first printed fashion book. Hollar was an artist and the publication included a set of plates of women's costumes. Hugh Plat's *Delightes for Ladies* was published around the turn of the century and contained beauty tips, recipes for cosmetics and suggestions for making the home more attractive and comfortable – the fore-runner to the numerous titles which today come under the general heading of 'women's magazines', sold in their millions virtually worldwide. Plat's volume, or its design, had been carefully conceived to appeal to feminine taste, being pocket-sized with attractive decorative borders. In it is advice on how 'to adorne their persons, tables, closets, and distillatories: with beauties, banquets, perfumes & waters'. A few years later, in 1616, *A Treatise Against Paintng* [sic] *and Tincturing of Men and Women* condemned the use of make-up, vividly describing 'paintings laied one upon another, in such sort: that a man might easily cut off a curd or cheese cake from either of their cheeks'. Needless to say, publishers were aware of the commercial advantages of courting controversy in any area likely to generate a series of best-selling titles.

By the end of the century, Rachel Speght's restrained, moralising tone has been replaced by the fresh and vigorous style of many women writers. Mary Astell's *A Serious Proposal to the Ladies* (1694) also argues in favour of women's education, based on wide reading, but it is much livelier than Speght's publication. 'How can you be content to be in the World like Tulips in a Garden, to make a fine show and be good for nothing', she declares.[20] Early on she addresses her women readers: 'This is a matter infinitely more worthy your debates than what colours are most agreeable, or what's the dress becomes you best.'[21] Her chosen images adjust a notion of the female self as *seen* to *seeing*, with all the verb's range, encompassing the idea of 'seeing' as awareness or knowledge. 'Your glass', Mary continues, referring of course to a mirror, 'will not do you half so much service as a serious reflection on your own minds. . . . No solicitude in the adornation of yourselves is discommended, provided you amply care about that which is really your *self*'.

She is writing against a background of women's permanent dissatisfaction with the self as seen and judged by men and male-dominated customs and standards. Mary questions these, and appeals to women's capacity for content-ment: 'Do not neglect that particle of divinity within you, which must survive, and may (if you please) be happy and perfect, when its unsuitable and much inferior companion is mouldering in the dust'. She brings in notions of immortality, arguing that women should think about the shape of their lives, and how they will be viewed at death: 'Remember, I pray you, the famous women of former ages, the Orindas [pseudonym of the poet Katherine Philips] and the more modern heroines, and blush to think how much is now, and will hereafter be said of them, when you your selves . . . must be buried in silence and forgetfulness!'[22] In short, women must recognise that they are free to be themselves, to read, to learn, and to take responsibility for their own lives and contributions.

Astell's convictions rest on two beliefs: women's inferiority is a matter of nurture not nature, and that nurture, consisting of an inadequate education, is exacerbated by the aggravating influences of what quickly becomes 'Custom' personified:

Ignorance and a narrow education lay the foundation of vice, and imitation and custom rear it up. Custom, that merciless torrent that carries all before it, and which indeed can be stemmed by none but such as have a great deal of prudence and a rooted virtue. For 'tis but decorous that she who is not capable of giving better rules, should follow those she sees before her, lest she only change the instance and retain absurdity. 'Twould puzzle a considerate person for all that sin and folly that is in the world . . . did not Custom help to solve the difficulty. . . . 'Tis Custom, therefore, that Tyrant Custom, which is the grand motive to all those irrational choices which we daily see made in the world, so very contrary to our present interest and pleasure, as well as to our future.[23]

Astell's solution to all the woes of women's lives was 'to erect a monastery, or if you will . . . we will call it a religious retirement'[24] – which may well strike the modern woman reader as somewhat disappointing. But rather like the former women's colleges of Oxford and Cambridge, and their counterparts elsewhere in Europe and the New World, which are by and large now only notionally religious foundations, Astell's community of women 'shall have a double aspect'. On the one hand it would offer refuge, 'a retreat from the world for those who desire that advantage', and on the other, 'an institution and previous discipline, to fit us to do the greatest good in it [the world]'. Astell sums this up with greater clarity and force a little later, where she explains that the 'double aspect' has 'one great end': 'To expel that cloud of ignorance which Custom has involved us in, to furnish our minds with a stock of solid and useful knowledge, that the souls of women may no longer be the only unadorned and neglected things.'[25] Women, in short, may want women's communities in which to read, and read critically.

Astell may have been writing with a female readership in mind but she was also writing for all influential members of society in the hope that women would begin to receive a good education. Her *Serious Proposal* argues in part against those writers who continued to insist on women's preoccupation with no more than the domestic. Titles like William Gouge's blunt *Of Domesticall Duties* (1622), for example, regularly appeared. Women might enjoy a certain domestic authority in the running of the household but, make no mistake, the ultimate 'superioritie' lay firmly with the husband. Gouge considered women's place to be squarely within the home, or in Astell's terms, they were to be 'Tulips in the Garden'. Gouge's book sold well and went into three editions.

A good many men hoped that women could develop into something more interesting than a living ornament, while a good many women advocated the pretty horticultural model. One of the most famous titles by an Englishwoman of the period was Elizabeth Joceline's *Mothers Legacie to her Unborn Child*.[26] It was the most widely reproduced work of any Renaissance woman, being reissued eleven times between 1622 and 1674, translated into Dutch in 1699, and reprinted throughout the eighteenth and nineteenth centuries. Its popularity lay, in part, in the feared and not uncommon tragedy that was its inspiration: the death of a mother during or shortly after childbirth. It is beautifully written and Thomas Goad, almost certainly a family friend, provided a preface in which he celebrated Joceline's wide reading and scholarship. He comments on her prodigious memory and her wide reading of theology, history, and classical and modern languages.

All this was no doubt intended in part as a defence of Joceline in anticipation of male criticism of a woman assuming the role of moral teacher. But in many ways Joceline's views were in line with the predominant attitudes of the period. She echoes many contemporary preachers' doubts about the ability of learning alone – as opposed to that inspired by divine grace – to instil ethical virtue. While Joceline's desires for a daughter's upbringing may be conventional for the time, the imagery that she uses conveys a strong sense of her belief in the cultivation of an intelligent and individual feminine integrity, as opposed to intellectual pretentiousness:

I desire her bringing up may be reading the Bible, as my sisters do, good housewifery, writing and good works; other learning a woman needs not. Though I admire it in those whom God has blessed with discretion, yet I desire not much in my own, having seen sometimes women have greater portions of learning than wisdom, which is of no better use to them than a mainsail to a flyboat, which runs it under water. But where learning and wisdom meet in a virtuous disposed woman, she is the fittest closet for all goodness. She is like a well-balanced ship that may bear all her sail.

Like Astell, Joceline underplays the importance of physical appearance and instead emphasises inner qualities: 'O make choice not so much for her complexion as for her mild and honest disposition.'

Rachel Speght's somewhat adolescent indignation, Astell's wittier defence of the need for women to be broadly educated so as to participate more effectively outside the 'Garden', and Joceline's affectionate and measured views on the appropriate upbringing of a daughter, are representative of three quite different women's voices, each addressing other women first and foremost.

Male authors were also aware of the growing market for books for women readers.[27] Authors like John Lyly and Robert Greene specifically catered for a feminine readership. Nashe sarcastically called Greene 'the Homer of women', and his works were, it seems, read by women of all classes. Sir Thomas Overbury, in his work *Characters*, describes 'A Chambermaid': 'She reads Greenes works over and over, but is so carried away with the *Mirror of Knighthood*, she is many times resolv'd to runne out of her selfe, and become a lady errant.'[28] Thomas Powell, in his work *Tom of all Trades, Or The Plaine Pathway to Preferment* (1631), makes it clear that women of the lowlier classes are becoming keen readers of romance, a fact that he clearly regretted:

In stead of Song and Musicke, let them learne Cookery and Laundrie. And in stead of reading Sir *Philip Sidney's Arcadia* [sic], let them read the ground of good huswifery. I like not a female Poetess at any hand. Let greater personages glory their skill in musicke, the posture of their bodies, their knowledge in languages, the greatnesse and freedome of their spirits, and their arts in arraigning of mens affections at their flattering faces: This is not the way to breed a private Gentlemans Daughter.[29]

Authors and translators, on the other hand, openly appealed specifically to women readers. In L.A.'s *The Seuenth Booke of the Myrrour of Knighthood* (1598), the translator claims that he has tested his story out and 'directed the Historie as it were particularly to one or more Ladies or Gentlewomen'. And the title-page of *The Ninth part of the Mirrour of Knighthood* (1601) appeals to 'the high cheualrie of the gallant Ladyes'. William Webster's romance, *The Most Pleasant And Delightful Historie of Curran, a Prince of Danske, and the fayre Princesse Argentile* (1617), in its preface, 'To The Faire Reader, Or The

Fayrer Sex', claims that the work is solely for women readers. When new editions of previously published works came out, titles were sometimes changed to indicate that they would appeal particularly to women. John Kennedy's collection of verses, *The Historie of Calanthrop and Lucilla* (1626), for example, was retitled *The Ladies Delight, or: The English Gentlewomans History of Calanthrop and Lucilla*, in its second edition of 1631.

The number of remarkable women readers rose during the seventeenth century, and they were a motley lot. We know about their reading largely from their own writings. The intellectual areas that were gaining momentum at the time were no longer theology or literature, but science and philosophy, fields which were, once again, relatively closed to women because of their exclusion from the universities. Science did reach out to some women: Sir Christopher Wren asked his brother-in-law to teach his daughter mathematics, and his own sister's expertise in medicine – which was largely self-taught using medical publications – was both famous and commemorated on her tomb.

A good deal of women's reading went on within a closed family network. Many fathers encouraged and respected their wives' and daughters' literary interests. The seventeenth century saw the invention of manuscript 'miscellanies'. In England, these were produced in the universities, in the Inns of Court and also taverns: all places barred to women. But women were readers, owners and later contributors to university miscellanies. Elizabeth Wellden provided material for a miscellany compiled by several members of her family in the 1630s at Christ Church, Oxford. More remarkable still are the two song verses provided by Elizabeth Clarke for a dubiously licentious collection of jests and poems compiled at Brasenose College, Oxford, in 1595. Women had also contributed to miscellanies collected at court, although the term 'miscellany' only comes into use in the seventeenth century. It was within the context of the family, however, that women compiled their own miscellanies. Favourite pieces from their reading were selected and copied into miscellanies which were then lent to other members of the family. Ann Bowyer clearly enjoyed the poems of Raleigh, Churchyard and Donne. She and her siblings copied them into her miscellany which also includes handwriting exercises, moral sayings and playful palindromes; Ann writes, 'weomenkind ar man's woe', followed by 'o man wee weomen ar kind'.[30]

One of the most interesting of these compendia is Elizabeth Lyttelton's.[31] It is a small quarto, measuring approximately twenty centimetres by sixteen centimetres – about the size of a modern paperback, although somewhat squarer. It is bound in brown calf leather, indicating its practical use. Elizabeth was not the volume's first owner, but substantially added to the sermon notes it mostly contained. Mary Browne, Elizabeth's sister, was clearly also a reader of the volume and she signed both the front and back flyleaves. It seems that the miscellany was compiled by Elizabeth during two distinct periods. The earlier entries are mostly religious poems, passages from the classics translated into English, and extracts from her father's writings. He was a doctor who was passionate about books and reading and greatly encouraged Elizabeth's literary interests. She also evidently read to him. In letters to her brother, Edward, who studied medicine at Cambridge, their father often describes his and Elizabeth's reading: 'Wee lately read the seidg of Vien by Solyman', he writes in one, and in another describes how 'Your sister Betty hath read unto mee Mr Ricauts historie of the 3 last Turkish emperours'.

The best record of their reading actually appears in her miscellany, where there is a list copied out and entitled 'The books which my daughter Elizabeth hath read unto me at nights'. The titles of twenty-eight works are given, and in addition 'some hundreds of sermons' and 'Many Other Books, Treatises, discourses of severall kinds, which may amount unto halfe the books in folio, which are before set down'. What Elizabeth and her father read in the evenings included numerous accounts of the histories of Turkey, India, China, America and Italy, and travel writings about these same countries. The history of Great Britain, Queen Elizabeth and King James also interested them and informed their reading. Foxe's *Actes and Monuments* is also included on the list along with a number of classical writers including Plutarch and Suetonius.

Lyttelton read widely like many of her contemporaries. Here and there women were prompted by their reading to write, but by and large society still frowned upon women taking up the pen. Some women, therefore, carefully covered their tracks; they wanted to have their say but they were motivated neither by a desire for publicity nor for financial gain. In 1690 a work was published anonymously in Amsterdam, entitled *Opuscula philosophica quibus continetur, principia philosophiae & retentissimae ac philosophia vulgaris refutata quibus juncture sunt C.C. problemata de revolutione animarum humanorum*. The second of the three *opuscala* was published in an English edition in 1692, as *The Principles of the Most Ancient and Modern Philosophy: Concerning God, Christ and the Creature; that is, concerning Spirit and Matter in General*. Although Leibniz owned a copy of what he knew to be Anne, Viscountess Conway's work, it was a hundred years or so before it was appreciated that she was its author, and another 150 years before her influential involvement with Henry More and the Cambridge Platonists was recognised. This is far from surprising given that 'woman' and 'philosopher' were considered more or less polar opposites. Conway sets out her own system of metaphysics but she does this very much in dialogue with other philosophers, so we know much of what she had read. She provides a critique of her own teacher's metaphysics – that is, Henry More's – but also those of Descartes, Hobbes and Spinoza. Henry More is quoted as having claimed that he 'scarce ever met with any Person, Man or Woman, of better Natural parts than Lady Conway'.

Modern philosophers struggle with Conway for a number of reasons. Firstly, the 'original' Latin publication was in fact the translation of some of Conway's notebooks written in English, and clearly intended only to guide her own thinking. The subsequent English edition was therefore a translation of a translation, and may have been edited in the process, not to mention the fact that the work itself was incomplete and published a decade or so after her death. Add in the seriousness with which Conway treats mysticism and the kabbalah (a school of thought concerned with the mystical aspect of Judaism), and her overambitious desire to find common ground between Islam, Judaism and various forms of Christianity, and one easily sees why her work cannot, and should not, be read in the same way as that of most of her male contemporaries. Her letters suggest a different approach, one that (naturally) situates her outside the narrower disciplines of the university system, but nevertheless undertaking original enquiry. They show her reading vociferously, and then asking the trained philosophers within universities the crucial questions. Her letters to More, for example, encourage him to enter into debate with the writings of George Keith, with whose work she is clearly familiar. Some of the ideas put forward by Conway in her publications were themselves taken up by Keith; Conway's doctor and friend Francis Mercury Van Helmont's writing also shows clear echoes of Conway's thinking. Conway was a figure not unlike Leibniz, a collaborative, questing philosopher, rather than an outstanding metaphysician. Like Leibniz, Conway was clearly at ease with open debate which she equally enjoyed with her half-brother, John Finch, also an amateur philosopher.

Anne Conway's family background was prosperous and well connected, but complex. Deaths and remarriages brought siblings, half-siblings, and a number of family properties, both rural and in Kensington, London, where she was brought up. Anne's own father died before she was born and Anne was left largely in control of her own upbringing, along with her siblings and then half-siblings from her mother's second marriage, in addition to those of her father's previous marriage. She found herself one of a large heterogeneous family and while the boys were packed off to public school, it was her half-brother John's tutor at Cambridge who became her teacher by correspondence. But even before this, as her letters to her father-in-law demonstrate, she had read extraordinarily widely, including both well-known and obscure authors: Lucan, the Roman poet of the first century AD; Famiano Strada, a little-known Jesuit author; Guido Bentivoglio, an Italian ruler and political theorist; Dioscorides; Ramus; Copernicus; Athanasius Kircher, a better-known Jesuit scholar; Tommaso Campanella, a contemporary Italian philosopher, theologian and poet; and Descartes. Her own family, and the family into which she married, were both bibliophilic. Her father left his substantial library not to his sons, but to his children. Anne's intellectual abilities were recognised by her father-in-law, but rather than complimenting her on her ability to convey original ideas in lucid prose he observed, in one of his many letters to her, 'you write like a man'.[32]

Should the writings of the serious women writers of Counter-Reformation Catholicism be read as 'philosophy'? After all, many of the great moralists of the seventeenth century were women: Mme de Sablé, a Jansenist very much involved with the nuns at Port-Royal, in Paris; Mlle de la Vallière, a mystical Carmelite who became known as Soeur Louise de la Miséricorde; and Mme Deshoulières, a materialist inspired by Pierre Gassendi, the French philosopher, priest, scientist, astronomer and mathematician. These women were concerned above all with notions of vice and virtue and approached ethical questions in their own way. Whether or not their work is regarded as 'philosophy' in many ways misses the point. What matters is the fact that a not insignificant number of women read philosophy seriously and were willing to enter this area of intellectual debate on their own terms – and a large number of men were interested in entering into dialogue with them.

Intellectual women were often the butt of jokes and some seventeenth-century women perhaps took their reading more than a little too seriously. One such was Marie Guyart, who was born in Tours in 1599.[33] The small textile town had been caught up in the Wars of Religion: for a time, the Protestants had been in control, and the churches emptied of their graven images. Marie grew up as the Catholics were looking to reassert their control. The religious extremism of the time became her own, fed by her passion for reading.

Her father was a baker, although a distant relative on her mother's side was an abbess. Her parents resisted Marie's vocation to the novitiate and at the age of seventeen she married a local silk-maker. Unusually for a woman at the time, she kept autobiographical notebooks, hence we know that at the time of her marriage she ceased reading the 'vain' books of her youth and turned exclusively to books of piety including the French psalms. At eighteen a son was born, Claude, and at nineteen her husband died. Marie determined not to remarry, writing in a letter to Claude, 'Though I loved your father very much and was at first sensitive to his loss, still, seeing that I was free, my soul melted in thankfulness that I no longer had anyone but God in my heart, and could use my solitude to think of him and raise you to be his servant'. She dressed, she tells us, 'ridiculously' to ward off suitors and went in for serious bodily mortification. She found herself a spiritual director and was advised to read François de Sales's *Introduction à la vie devotée*. First Dom François, then Dom Raymond de Saint Bernard approved, if not encouraged, her self-mortification with nettles, iron chains and a bed of boards. But she was also encouraged to read, introducing her to a book culture that was highly unusual for a Catholic tradeswoman. She read saints' lives like Teresa of Avila's, the Scriptures, and the mystical writings supposedly by Saint Dionysus the Areopagite.

In the light of modern psychology, or at least its popular versions, it is not surprising that the combination of self-harm – she notes in her diary that her self-inflicted wounds, the blood stemmed by haircloth so as to increase the pain, must be kept secret from the world, 'otherwise I would be considered a madwoman' – and the religious enthusiasm inspired by her reading, should have produced visions. Her physical resilience was remarkable, and so too, more surprisingly, was her psychological strength. One might have supposed that she would have died young and be remembered by some as a saintly figure. But her story becomes increasingly extraordinary. She entered the Ursulines, in Tours, and not much later became involved in teaching the novitiates of the convent. Her reading, and writing, continued. She familiarised herself with the Catechism of Trent and the writings of Cardinal Bellarmine. Her calling to the riskiest of all ventures apparently came to her in another vision in which she found herself walking hand in hand with a laywoman through an inspiring and grandiose landscape of high mountains and misty valleys. Her vocation was to the poor souls in need in faraway lands.

So it was that she found herself in the little community of Ursulines on the Quebec promontory high above the St Lawrence River. The sisters lived in an encampment surrounded by a cedar stockade and suffered fires and threats of attack by the indigenous Iroquois. Needless to say, Marie was the first Mother Superior. But for all the apparent madness of Marie's mission, she instituted a pragmatic and humane approach. The Ursulines, she insisted, should first learn the Amerindian languages: Huron, Algonquin, Montagnais and Iroquois. Some of the girls arriving at the convent were brought by the Jesuit priests whose flying missions took them into the hinterland, aided by snowshoes in winter and canoes in summer. Some girls came to the community of their own accord, or were delivered by their parents, particularly from those groups whose lives had been destroyed by Iroquois attacks. But by the 1660s the Iroquois were also sending their daughters to the 'saintes filles'. A school was established at this point, educating both French girls, the daughters of the colonists, and the 'filles sauvages' alongside each other. The school still exists today.

When Marie died she left a curious body of writing including notices for the *Jesuit Relations* (published reports that documented the Jesuit missions in New France), obituaries for the Ursuline sisters who had died in the house in Quebec, and letters to sisters in Europe and certain devout lay people who took a great interest in her venture. She also left manuscripts in Algonquian and Iroquoian that she had used in her teaching. Her autobiography, completed in 1654, was written for her son Claude and niece Marie Buisson, who had entered the Ursulines at Tours. Fortunately her son recognised just how remarkable his mother's life had been, and edited the autobiography alongside extensive commentaries, allowing us insight into the successive and distinct instalments of 'Marie de l'Incarnation's' unusual life, spurred on by her own drive and the early influence of very particular reading.

Marie's letters were read by nuns back home, and her obituaries were no doubt read by women readers. Women's unwillingness to seek publication, not to mention the difficulties of finding a publisher, meant, however, that what women read was mostly written by men. Much of what women had access to, throughout the seventeenth century, remained forms of 'advice' – spiritual, practical, domestic and familial. Access to the Bible in vernacular languages was perhaps the most significant reading material and increasing numbers of women, from a range of social classes, read and considered its wisdom. Some were intrigued and disturbed by its contradictions, particularly those bound up with questions as to the nature and worth of 'woman' and what this might mean for the way in which women lived. This in turn had the effect of soliciting responses by those few women who dared to write. In this way, women were bound into a dialogue that predetermined the areas about which they then wrote.

Nevertheless, as women began to enter into the world of publishing, women readers did read books by other women – within the privileged coteries of the urban upper classes, to begin with, but gradually also the new middle classes of Europe, which gained access to literary works, novels in particular. The relatively few women writers during the period had internalised the idea of their writing as, to use an anachronistic notion, an act of transgression. But for all their apologies, they did write and publish, and usually for contemporary women readers.

There is a wonderful comic irony in expressions like Anne Bradstreet's 'I am obnoxious to each carping tongue/ who says my hand a needle better fits'.[34] Bradstreet was born and brought up in seventeenth-century England before relocating across the Atlantic; she is known as the earliest published poet of North America. She was an accomplished writer of verse history and adapted her favourite classical authors. She also wrote a brief spiritual autobiography (almost a mother's legacy) and various meditations. She is best remembered, however, for her personal lyrics. Bradstreet was one of a number of women writers who read Elizabeth I's writings decades after her death. For example, Lady Diana Primrose's poem, 'A Chain of Pearl. Or a Memorial of the peerless graces, and Heroic Virtues of Queen Elizabeth of Glorious Memory', eulogised the earlier queen, herself an author. This was a cunning move.

Elizabeth herself had been given an exceptional education and was rigorously schooled so as to be fluent in numerous languages, including Latin, Greek, French and Italian. She allegedly once claimed to a visiting ambassador that she knew many languages better than her mother tongue. She also studied theology, history, philosophy, rhetoric – and sewing. She was deemed an earnest child and was considered to have inherited the best from both her parents, namely firmness and a high intelligence. Her tutor Roger Ascham had great respect for her thoroughness and excellent memory, claiming – tellingly – that she had a man's intellect.

At a time when women were in many ways discouraged from authorship, women writers could allude to the former monarch and author as an exemplar. Bradstreet's 'In Honour of that High and Mighty Princess Queen Elizabeth of Happy Memory' also celebrates the former monarch's exceptionally wide reading and scholarship. By appealing to Elizabeth, both Primrose and Bradstreet demonstrated their objections to the customs of the day and found a way to present their own political commentaries. They also revealed an awareness of the importance of women's writing as a way of ensuring a connectedness with women across time. They both flourished some considerable time after Elizabeth's death and the implication is that other women will read their poetry long after their own demises. The idea of writing as much for their contemporaries as well as for future women readers became increasingly important in this period.

Nevertheless, women authors were not welcome on the public stage. Their writing was often described as public prostitution, as in Richard Lovelace's poem 'On Sanazar's Being Honoured with Six Hundred Duckets': 'Now as her self a Poem she doth dresse,/ And curls a Line as she would do a tresse,/ Powders a Sonnet as she does her hair,/ Then prostitutes them both to publick Aire'. Rochester similarly declared, 'Whore is scarce a more reproachful name,/ Than poetess'. For all the atmosphere of general reproach, keen women readers of women authors proliferated nevertheless. Some were exceptional in their determination to be recognised as serious and discriminating readers too.

Lucy Hutchinson (*née* Apsley) was born in 1620 in the Tower of London. Her father was Sir Allen Apsley, Lieutenant of the Tower. She was given a good education in 'languages, music, dancing, writing and needlework'.[35] Lucy confesses that she was 'averse from all but my book' from childhood, uninterested in music and dancing and far outperforming her brothers in Latin. In her teens she started to write poetry and songs which were much admired by her friends. She wrote a modestly entitled 'autobiographical fragment' at some point in the middle of the century. In it she reveals a good deal about the differences between attitudes to boys' and girls' interest in reading: 'By the time I was four years old', Lucy writes, 'I read English perfectly . . . my genius was quite averse from all but my book, and that I was so eager of, that my mother, thinking it prejudic'd my health, would moderate me in it; yet this rather animated me than kept me back, and every moment I could steal from my play I would employ in any book I could find, when my own were locked up from me.' Lucy's father encouraged her, but 'my mother would have been contented if I had not so wholly addicted myself as to neglect my other qualities: as for music and dancing I profited very little in them, and would never practice my lute or harpsichords but when my masters were with me; and as for my needle, I absolutely hated it.' Yet Lucy claims that for all her bookish pleasures and the 'serious discourses being frequent at my father's table and in my mother's drawing room', her purpose was clear: 'I was convinc'd that the knowledge of God was the most excellent study, and accordingly applied myself to it, and to practice as I was taught'. It is difficult to know how seriously to take her conclusion.

Margaret Cavendish was bolder still. She read and wrote for her own and her husband's pleasure, and he enthusiastically encouraged her writing. Her works (poems, plays, speeches, biography, autobiography and speculative science) were published in expensive folio volumes by two women printers, and were intended primarily for presentation rather than sale. In 1656 Margaret published her *True Relation of my Birth and Breeding*, an autobiographical fragment not unlike Lucy Hutchinson's. In it, she excuses, not without some pride, her aberrant womanhood, 'being addicted from my childhood . . . to write with the pen than to work with the needle'.

Her alleged intention in writing about herself, hedged about by the conventional gestures of modesty, is to ensure her own posterity, within the historical record: 'I intend this piece . . . to tell the truth, lest after-ages should mistake, in not knowing I was daughter to one Master [John] Lucas of St. John's . . . second wife to the Marquis of Newcastle; for my Lord having had two wives, I might easily have been mistaken, especially if I should die and my Lord marry again.' Margaret supposedly writes her autobiography because of fears

37 Frontispiece of a 1671 edition of *The World's Olio*, showing Margaret
Cavendish in her closet.

of a kind of absolute identity-erasure, one bound up with the marriage laws
and naming conventions of her time. She is self-deprecating, as custom
expected; 'He [her husband] creates himself with his pen, writing what his wit
dictates to him, but I pass my time rather with scribbling than writing, with
words than wit'.

Nevertheless Margaret explains that it is only by writing that she can clarify
her thoughts: 'when some of those thoughts are set out in words, they give the
rest more liberty to place themselves in a more methodical order, marching
more regularly with my pen on the ground of white paper'. Her appeal to her
readers is still more direct and she proposes an extravagant comparison: 'I
hope that my readers will not think me vain for writing my life, since there

have been many that have done the like, as Caesar, Ovid, and many more, both men and women, and I know no reason I may not do it as well as they.' Interestingly she is unable, or unwilling, to cite any autobiographical work by a woman. She goes on to anticipate criticism, and it is here that she voices her desire to be identifiable as an individual, despite her marital status and the anonymity that comes with it. 'Verily I believe some censuring readers will scornfully say, why hath this Lady writ her own life? Since none cares to know whose daughter she was or whose wife she is, or how she was bred, or what humour or disposition she was of'. Cavendish's preoccupation with her putative readers and their likely responses to her writings are typical of women writers of the period.

A decade later she published *The New Blazing World* (1666), her own 'serious proposal', to pick up on Astell's title, and a good bit more attractive and daring than Astell's work. Again Margaret is highly conscious of her readership and prefaces her work with a note 'To the Reader':

> I am not content to live a melancholy life in my own world; I cannot call it a poor world, if poverty be only want of gold, silver and jewels; for there is more gold in it than all the chemists ever did. ... As for the rocks of diamonds, I wish with all my soul they might be shared amongst my noble female friends. ... I am ... as ambitious as ever any of my sex was, is, or can be; which makes, that though I cannot be Henry the Fifth or Charles the Second, yet I endeavour to be *Margaret the First*.

How so, her readers in the seventeenth century asked, and still ask today? 'Although I have neither power, time or occasion to conquer the world as Alexander and Caesar did; yet rather than be mistress of one, since Fortune and Fates would give me none, I have made a world of my own: for which nobody, I hope, will blame me, since it is in every one's power to do the like.'

Margaret Cavendish felt moved to provide both a lengthy preface and an 'Epilogue to the Reader', in which she declared, 'By this poetical description, you may perceive, that my ambition is not only to be Empress, but Authoress of a whole world'. Her sense of triumph has given her 'more delight and glory, than ever Alexander or Caesar ... in conquering this terrestrial world'. She then appeals to her readers and suggests that they have two simple choices: 'if any should like the world I have made, and be willing to be my subjects, they may imagine themselves such, and they are such, I mean in their minds, fancies or imaginations'. On the other hand, should they feel unmoved to join Margaret in her 'blazing world', they have another option: 'they may create worlds of their own, and govern themselves as they please'. Cavendish was encouraging an extraordinary emancipation of women's imaginations. Reading is, by implication, a radical way to understand and reinvent your life and the society around you. Through reading, new 'blazing worlds' may come into being, worlds in which women have greater freedoms, both in terms of their free movement, but even more crucially their psychological and imaginative liberties. Reading can set women free.

One of Margaret's many women readers was Dorothy Osborne. In a letter to her husband Sir William Temple she wrote: 'let me aske you if you have seen a book of Poems newly come out, made by my Lady New Castle. For God sake if you meet with it send it to mee, they say tis ten times more Extravagant than her dresse. Sure the poore woman is a little distracted, she could never bee soe ridiculous else as to venture at writeing book's and in verse too. If I should not sleep this fortnight I should not come to that.'[36] However critical Dorothy may be, she was still eager, like many other women, to read Margaret's latest publication. Cavendish was nicknamed 'Mad Mags' and attracted much criticism for her forthright views and for daring to go into print. Everything about Margaret's writing points us forward to the growing number of women writers, writing the kinds of works other women wanted to read. She appeals to the heroes of the classical world, those warring men whose triumphs have made them immortal. Other women were aware of ancient precedents of a more useful sort: classical women writers.

In her introduction to her *Poems* of around 1685, Anne Finch, Countess of Winchilsea, trots out the useful sort of disingenuous lines: 'Alas! A woman that attempts the pen,/ Such an intruder on the rights of men,/ Such a presumptuous creature is esteemed,/ The fault can by no virtue be redeemed'. But there can only be delicious irony in her verses, as what we read brings us into direct contact with a most attractive 'presumptuous creature'. The poem continues, encapsulating what women of the seventeenth century were up against in terms of 'Custom':

> Good breeding, fashion, dancing, dressing, play,
> Are the accomplishments we should desire;
> To write, or read, or think, or enquire,
> Would cloud our beauty, and exhaust our time,
> And interrupt the conquests of our prime;
> While the dull manage of a servile house
> Is held by some our utmost art and use.

But not by Anne, who appeals to the past:

Sure, 'twas not ever thus, nor are we told
Fables, of women that excelled of old;
To whom, by the diffusive hand of heaven,
Some share of wit and poetry was given. . . .
How we are fallen! Fallen by mistaken rules,
And Education's, more than Nature's fools;
Debarred from all improvements of the mind,
And to dull, expected and designed, . . .
So strong the opposition faction still appears,
The hopes of thrive can ne'er outweigh the fears.

Of course the fearless Anne is busily contradicting herself, to the reader's delight, and enters her 'blazing world' as a 'friend':

Conscious of wants, still with contracted wing,
To some few friends, and to thy sorrows sing.
For groves of laurel thou wert never meant:
Be dark enough thy shades, and be thou there content.

But the 'groves of laurel', and the 'whole worlds' available to authoresses would continue to attract women writers, mindful of their 'few friends' and potential 'subjects', particularly women readers. The 'woman question' and the battle of the sexes would continue to be earnestly debated, but some women, like Lucy Hutchinson, Margaret Cavendish and Anne Finch, simply wanted to get on with the business of writing books for women readers. These writers were poets and essayists. Soon the novel would become the most important kind of book – both for women writers, and growing numbers of happy women readers.

In Europe, among the most interesting reading material available to women was in translation. English editions were produced in considerable numbers for English women. In the preface to his translation of Ovid's *Epistles* (1636), Wye Saltonstall appeals to both sexes: 'Ladies and Gentlemen, since this book of Ovids, which most Gentlemen could reade before in Latine, is for your sakes come forth in English'. Other translators were less tactful about women's more limited linguistic knowledge: 'I have caused these little bookes to bee published in our vulgar English, custome excusing the most of your sexe from the knowledge of the learned tongues', said one; 'we must always remember that what we write here, is for women and not philosophers', cautioned another.[37] Novels also began to appear in translation, encouraging a certain internationalism among the reading circles of Europe. Cervantes's pastoral romance, *La Galatea* (1585); the first part of *Don Quixote* (1605), often considered the first European novel; Quevedo's picaresque *Don Pablo* (1626); Grimmelshausen's *Simplizissimus* (1669); Bunyan's *Pilgrim's Progress* (1660–72); Mme de Scudéry's ten-volume *Artamène, ou le Grand Cyrus* (1649–53) and *Clélie* (1654–60); Honoré d'Urfé's *L'Astrée* (1607–28): all these crossed national boundaries and were translated and retranslated.

One of the most celebrated women writers of the period was also a translator from both Latin and French. Aphra Behn (1640–89) was to have enormous influence over contemporary women readers. She was a prolific dramatist and one of the first professional female authors in England. Much of the criticism levelled against her – and it rarely abated – was a function of her political views which were in many respects liberal, while at the same time curiously pro-monarchist. She was often accused of bawdiness, a feature of drama of the period but unbecoming in a woman playwright. She stood up to her detractors with considerable *sang-froid* and even accused those women who added their voices to male objections of feigning a more refined feminine sensibility than they actually possessed.[38]

Her life was eventful. She was born near Canterbury in 1640, and may well have spent some of her early life in Dutch Guiana. She married Johan Behn, a merchant of Dutch or German parentage, in 1664, but the marriage seems not to have lasted. She worked as a spy for the English in 1666 and it was her imprisonment for debt that led her to write for a living. Behn wrote a series of successful plays. The first, *The Forc'd Marriage*, was staged in 1671. *The Rover* (1681), which was her most successful, was produced in two parts and included in its cast the famous Nell Gwyn, Charles II's mistress. Behn also drew on the tradition of the Italian *commedia dell'arte* for *The Emperor of the Moon* (1687), an important forerunner of the modern-day pantomime.

Behn's novel *Oroonoko* (1688) tells the story of an enslaved African prince and it is now widely regarded as a foundation stone of the English novel. Behn was highly esteemed by many of her contemporaries and regarded as something of a celebrity. She was admired by many for the financial independence she gained as a function of her writing. She was loved – but also ridiculed – for advocating equality between the sexes. She herself was a passionate reader and described 'That perfect tranquility of life, which is nowhere to be found but in retreat, a faithful friend and a good library'. Behn's name remains familiar today not least because of the recognition Virginia Woolf famously claimed she deserved: 'All women together ought to let flowers fall upon the tomb of Aphra Behn, which is, most scandalously but rather appropriately, in Westminster Abbey, for it was she who earned them the right to speak their minds. It is she – shady and amorous as she was – who makes it not quite fantastic for me to say to you tonight: Earn five hundred a year by your wits.'[39]

The narrator of *Oroonoko* is in many ways a fictionalised Behn. This brings a certain vividness to the writing and establishes an intimate connection with the reader. The more recent debate about whether or not Aphra Behn really travelled to Suriname and whether *Oroonoko* should be read as a real travel account shows how convincing the narrator is. What is also distinctive is Behn's use of her narrator to voice ideological reservations. Although she does not openly criticise slavery, her indictments of bureaucracy, politics and male dominance are convincing. It is difficult to differentiate between the narrator and Behn, except by comparison with her biography. Her life was unusually eventful and she benefited from the relaxed atmosphere of the Restoration. One major change was the inclusion of actresses on the stage. Behn had the support of an informal coterie of women friends and readers of her work in manuscript. In this way she tested out her writing on a group of trusted women readers and made appropriate adjustments, on the basis of their responses, before going into print. This intimate relationship between writer and readers gave women like Behn the confidence that women readers, and perhaps men, might appreciate her work.

This was also the case for Behn's two most important women-author contemporaries, Anne Finch and Orinda (Katherine Philips). A good deal of what women wrote in response to their reading remained unpublished in manuscript form and was read largely by an inner circle often made up exclusively of other women. This was true of men too, but the prejudice against going into print and entering the commercial world of publishing remained stronger in relation to women.

On the Continent the informal coteries that women readers and writers enjoyed had been transformed into the relative formality of the *salon*. To refer to the French *salon* of the seventeenth century is, of course, an anachronism, as the word enters the French language with its specialised meaning only in the eighteenth century. But the phenomenon of women and men congregating to read and discuss their reading begins in earnest a century before the word comes into usage. Seventeenth-century *salons* were in many ways the successors to earlier court circles, and developed in palaces, piazzas and private residences. Some of the tiny minority of women who enjoyed this contact with a wider world through participation in *salon* society, would go on to write highly influential works, which could be read by those who enjoyed no such privilege.

The first *salons* emerged in France at the beginning of the seventeenth century and proliferated as the middle class grew in the second half of the century. The Parisian women's *salons* were places where widows and women whose husbands tended to be of liberal persuasion could meet for conversation. Two of the most famous literary *salons* in Paris were the Hôtel de Rambouillet, established in 1607 by Catherine de Vivonne, marquise de Rambouillet and, in 1652, the rival *salon* of Madeleine de Scudéry, a former *habituée* of the Hôtel de Rambouillet.

The reading of the vast novels that were beginning to be published was particularly popular. Honoré d'Urfé's *L'Astrée* was read avidly by women and men, and the ideals of romantic love, with set rules and rituals of conduct, were assimilated into the milieu of the *salon*. *L'Astrée*, a pastoral novel, was published between 1607 and 1627; a posthumous final volume appeared in 1628. It is probably the single most influential work of seventeenth-century French literature, and immensely long: forty tales, spread over sixty books. It was popular throughout Europe, being widely translated and read at every royal court. The plot twists and turns but it centres on the love of a shepherd and shepherdess in the fifth century. The main characters are Astrée (named after Astraea, immortalised in Ovid's *Metamorphoses*) and her lover Céladon. The couple undergoes numerous trials, mostly because of the malign political

38 Abraham Bosse, *Conversation de dames en l'absence de leurs maris: le dîner*, seventeenth century.

intrigues of the other characters. There are endless digressions that are not strictly related to the main plot but which make vivid the world in which the hero and heroine live. The sheer scope and astonishing variety of the novel lent it to *salon* discussions of myriad types.

Mme de Rambouillet reigned supreme over her *salon* for many years. Half-French and half-Italian, she had been well educated like her mother before her. Henri IV's court lacked sophistication, and her *salon* rivalled the king's. The décor of the *salons* was stagey, to say the least, and encouraged somewhat exaggeratedly refined behaviour. Despite – or perhaps because of – the theatrical setting, women were more prepared to express their own views, and some of these were remarkable. Take Mlle de Scudéry's famous assertion: 'One married in order to hate. Hence a true lover must never speak of marriage, because to be a lover is to want to be loved, and to be a husband is to want to be hated.' Women involved in the *salon* movement grew in confidence as readers and writers. Mmes de Lafayette, Scudéry and Sévigné's novels were born from their experience of the wit, clever conversation and observation of human behaviour within the *salon* milieu, and in turn further encouraged women to write.

Women across Europe were reading novels and works in translation as well as in foreign languages when they had the education. During the so-called Golden Age of Spanish literature, the works of María de Zayas y Sotomayor (1590–1661), and particularly her female characters, enlighten the reader to the unfortunate lives of most contemporary Spanish women. Among her many admirers were the celebrated writers Lope de Vega, who dedicated some of his verses to her, and Alonso de Castillo Solórzano, who called her the 'Sibila de Madrid' ('Sibyl of Madrid'). De Zayas's background was aristocratic and she had received an exceptionally good education. She was particularly enamoured of Italian writing and her most well-read works, *Novelas Amorosas y ejemplares* (*Amorous and Exemplary Novels*), published in 1637, and *Desengaños Amorosos* (*Disenchantments of Love*), published in 1647, are directly influenced by Boccaccio, so much so that they are referred to as the 'Spanish Decameron'. (She was equally influenced by Miguel de Cervantes's *Novelas ejemplares* [*Exemplary Novels*] which were also written in the style of the Italian *novella*, exemplified by Bocaccio, allowing for stories within stories.) In these two works the character Lisis invites a group of friends to her home to distract her and encourage her recovery from illness. Each of her friends tells a story about a particularly striking life experience. Each evening two stories are narrated and this goes on for five nights. The majority of the stories tell of events in which women have been deceived, or treated brutally, even abused. On the basis of these experiences they denounce their vulnerable position in society: 'Why vain legislators of the world, do you tie our hands so that we cannot take vengeance? Because of your mistaken ideas about us, you render us powerless and deny us access to pen and sword. Isn't our soul the same as a man's soul?' Later Lisis's husband listens to her laments. He is incensed by her endless complaints and 'began to beat her with his hands, so much so that the white pearls of her teeth, bathed in the blood shed by his angry hand, quickly took on the form of red coral'.[40] De Zayas was immensely popular during the seventeenth and eighteenth centuries, and it was only in the nineteenth that her writing was censured for its alleged vulgarity. Using the idea of storytelling within a story in many ways mimicked the reality of *salon* conversation.

Reading within these coteries was very distinctive. It was not simply a matter of a group, as elsewhere and throughout the history of reading, sharing favourite authors and discussing them, but something much more dramatic and bound by certain conventions. Intimate insight is provided by the way some of these groups used pseudonyms. The study of pen-names is itself a seventeenth-century phenomenon. Vincent Placcius was working on his monumental *Theatrum Anonymorum et Pseudonymoron* in the last quarter of the century (published in Germany in 1708) and Adrien Baillet published his *Auteurs deguisez* in 1690. These works attempted to 'unmask' the pseudonymous author. The assumption was that the use of pseudonyms was a deliberate disguise, the intention being either to protect the author or to hide fraudulent practices.

The Parisian *précieuses*, the circle clustered around Mme de Rambouillet and closely associated with Honoré d'Urfé's famous *L'Astrée*, went in for the same games. So too did coteries in England, like the group associated with Katherine Philips, whose close friend Cotterel translated one of the 'Rambouillet' authors, La Calprenède. Gauthier de Costes, seigneur de la Calprenède (1609/10–63) was a French novelist and dramatist. In 1650 he was made gentleman-in-ordinary of the royal household. He was the author of several popular heroic romances. Members of these circles themselves assumed pseudonyms and the line between life and fiction blurred. Rather like the use of the mask, those within the society knew the identity of the face concealed, but a charade could be enacted. The use of a pseudonym, like the mask, encouraged 'play' and rather than creating a barrier between the reader and the author, actually functioned as a means of breaking down the divide between real life and the fictional worlds of the novels associated with these coteries.

The sudden rise in diary-keeping at around the same time is a not wholly dissimilar social innovation; it was another form of social networking, but in its seriousness, far removed from the pleasures of the *salon*. At work here was a new sense of individual personal identity. And the fact that diary-keeping also ran in families and that diaries were lent to relatives and friends to read, reveals a new sense of group-belonging. In England and, later, America, diary-keeping was bound up with the Puritan ideology of individual responsibility for salvation. The Winthrop and Isham families wrote diaries spanning three generations.

The Winthrop family tradition began in 1594 when Adam Winthrop, an auditor at Trinity College, Cambridge, began his diary. His son John, later governor of Massachusetts, began his in 1606. This record-keeping allowed the wider family a direct insight into the lives of their relatives, and was particularly interesting for female relatives who, by and large, circulated less in the world. The diaries also served to establish a strong sense of family identity. Some accounts from John's journal of 1630–49 must have made chilling reading, particularly to women relatives back home: '13 April 1645: Mr. [Edward] Hopkins, the governor of Hartford upon Connecticut, came to Boston, and brought his wife with him (a godly young woman and of special parts) who was fallen into a sad infirmity, the loss of her understanding and reason, which has been growing upon her divers years'. We know very little about Mrs Hopkins, aside from this record of Winthrop's. She was not alone in finding the narrow, isolated and earnest Puritanism of New England too much to bear. Reasonably enough, she turned first to reading, and then to writing, presumably for solace. But this eminently sensible survival strategy was, according to Winthrop, the cause of her 'loss of reason and understanding', which had come about:

> by occasion of her giving herself wholly to reading and writing, and had written many books. Her husband, being very loving and tender of her, was loathe to grieve her; but he saw his error, when it was too late. For if she had attended to household affairs, and such things as belong to women, and had not gone out of her way and calling to meddle in such things as are proper for men, whose minds are stronger, etc., she had kept her wits, and might have improved them usefully and honourably in the place God had sent her.[41]

Mr Hopkins' ultimate decision was to hand over his wife to his brother in Boston, 'a merchant, to try what means might be had here for her. But no help could be had'. If only Mrs Hopkins had been born into the Parisian *salonnière* society of the mid-seventeenth century she would surely have 'kept her wits'. Winthrop's diagnosis is a bleak reminder of what was prescribed for women's lives in seventeenth-century New England. And the general pattern would remain remarkably static for a long time to come. Mrs Peabody's 'foreign library', which was both a circulating library and a bookstore, would eventually breathe some refreshing air into Boston, but not until the middle of the nineteenth century.

Elizabeth Isham initiated the Isham diary dynasty in 1609. Sir John Isham's travel diary begins in 1626 and Thomas Isham started his account, written in Latin, in 1671 when he was aged seventeen. It is likely that Elizabeth was either the mother or grandmother of John, and John most likely Thomas's uncle. The family seat was at Lamport Hall in Northamptonshire. These family diaries circulated amongst relatives, and their readers learned of the trials of their relatives' lives and their spiritual journeys.

More earnest coteries of women's reading groups than the *salons* were also established in France during the period. Françoise d'Aubigné, marquise de Maintenon (1635–1719), was the second wife of Louis XIV, but her marriage to the king was never officially announced or admitted. In June 1652, Françoise, having lost her mother and living in reduced circumstances, agreed to marry the celebrated burlesque poet Paul Scarron, who was severely disabled. She looked after him with great dedication and they gathered a group of celebrated writers around them. The marquise had been well educated in Latin, and she spoke both Italian and Spanish. She was a close friend of Mme de Sévigné, Mme de La Fayette and Mme de Montespan. The more illustrious sometimes condescendingly referred to her as 'la charmante malheureuse' ('the charming unfortunate').

Mme de Maintenon's greatest enthusiasm was for education. She brought up women members of her family, her nieces the comtesse de Caylus and the duchesse de Noailles, and looked after the education of the princess of Savoy (the future duchesss of Burgundy), aware that she might one day be queen of France. The first school that she founded was for fifty young girls at Rueil, in 1682, overseen by an Ursuline nun, Mme Brinon. The school grew and grew and in 1686 moved to Saint-Cyr, to the magnificent Baroque buildings designed by Jules Hardouin-Mansart. The house at Saint-Cyr was called the Institut de Saint-Louis and educated some 200 girls. Admission was selective: the pupils had to prove both poverty, and four degrees of nobility on their father's side.

Mme de Maintenon's vision was original. As the king's confessor, La Chaise, wrote: 'The object of Saint-Cyr is not to multiply convents, which increase rapidly enough of their own accord, but to give the State well-educated women; there are plenty of good nuns, but insufficient numbers of good mothers of families. The young ladies will be educated more suitably by persons living in the world.' Mme de Maintenon drew up the charter for the institution in great detail. The girls were divided into four classes, relative to their ages. The youngest concentrated on reading, writing, grammar and the catechism. At the age of eleven, history, geography and mythology were added. In the third class (up to the age of sixteen) they also learned drawing and dancing. In their final two years they were introduced to ethics and manual crafts. Racine was commissioned to write tragedies for the pupils at Saint-Cyr, due to Mme de Maintenon's conviction that moral behaviour was best learned if acted out. At some point before or just after her husband's death in 1715, she moved permanently to Saint-Cyr and received many visitors.

During the same period, on the other side of the world, there were more examples of serious women readers and advocates of women's education. In seventeenth-century China many Ming women were celebrated readers. Unlike their male counterparts they were reading not to pass civil service exams, nor were they reading merely to pass the time. They read for edification and often with an obsessiveness that bordered on fanaticism. One work that was particularly popular was a tribute to love by the great late Ming playwright Tang Xianzu, *The Peony Pavilion*. Its heroine, Du Liniang, became the

39 Julie Philipaut's painting of 1819 shows Racine reading his tragedy *Athalie* to Louis XIV and Mme de Maintenon.

alter ego for generations of young women. The collating, copying, lending and borrowing of the play went on with fervour and there were stories of the fatal consequences of such addictive reading. These tales became so widespread that a superstition arose, reminiscent of Winthrop's account of poor Mrs Hopkins in New England, linking women's reading with untimely death. This did not stop Qing women but allowed for a curious new notion of reading as the ultimate transcendental act, bringing salvation alongside the danger of death.

Much of the detail about women's reading in this period emerges from the story of three women's passion for the play in *The Peony Pavilion: Commentary Edition by Wu Wushan's Three Wives*, sometimes known as *The Three Wives' Commentary*, published by their widower in 1694. The work is comprised of essentially biographical accounts of the women's intense experience of reading *The Peony Pavilion*. Chen Tong collated and corrected different versions of it, intent on establishing a correct version. She was then given an authentic copy by her sister-in-law. She worked on a commentary and fell ill as a result of lack of sleep, such was her obsession. Her mother then decided to save her daughter by burning her books, but her wet nurse managed to salvage the first volume of *The Peony Pavilion*. All this was too late and Chen died on the eve of her marriage to Wu Wushan. The second wife, Tan, committed Chen's commentary to memory and wrote her own. In 1675 she died and Wu married Qian Yi. She too was an obsessive reader and read the commentaries of her 'sisters'. It was Qian who persuaded her husband to publish the play with their commentaries and she sold her jewellery to finance the printing. It came out in 1694 and included afterwords from members of the women's poetry club in Hangzhou.

In the early years of the seventeenth century in Japan women's reading was the subject of anxious debate as commercial booksellers in Kyoto started to publish the corpus of earlier fiction at affordable prices.[42] Classics of the Heian period, particularly *Genji monogatari* and *Ise monogatari*, and other works in the courtly female poetic tradition, were deemed inappropriate. But by the end of the century both works had been published in numerous editions and arguments for their damaging influence on women readers subsided.

These works had been deemed 'difficult' and up until this point a teacher would have guided readers. But as publishing commercialised, digests and condensed versions of these classics were published and these facilitated private reading. It was the simultaneous availability of these works combined with their new accessibility to women readers, who were able to engage with them alone and without guidance, which seems to have aroused concerns.

Hayashi Razau (1583–1657) published a guide to reading and warned against the *monogatari*, writing that 'they contain the language of sycophantic laughter and false wit and lack the means to instruct or reprove'. This is because they were 'written by women and girls'. Nagata Zensai (1597–1664) was even more explicit in his criticisms: 'all educate their daughters with Genji monogatari and Ise monogatari. This is doubtless because they want them to compose waka [poetry]. What possible benefit can there be in women composing waka? People simply want to accustom women to lewd behaviour'. There were some women, however, who argued in favour of allowing girls to read the *monogatari*. Nonaka En (1660–1725), a doctor, wrote a guide to female behaviour for a friend who was about to marry. She criticised women who were concerned above all with their looks and recommended reading as the best way to learn valuable moral lessons. Among the works she recommended was the *Genji*.

The iconographic record is equally mixed. In the second half of the seventeenth century Japanese advice books for women were often illustrated with images of women surrounded by books, implying the desirability of reading. On the other hand, in many *shunga* scenes (of erotic love), the floor is often strewn with books implying that some reading at least leads inevitably to sex.

In late fifteenth-century Italy, when printing was transforming the availability of reading material, women were advised against reading secular literature. In sixteenth-century England, the criticism voiced by Roger Ascham of *Morte d'Arthur* or Thomas Salter's condemnation of Greek and Latin literature a little later were all similar responses to the sudden rise in the amount of reading material women might have to hand. Ascham wrote of 'the fowlest adoulteries by subtlest shiftes' and Salter of the 'filthie love' and 'abhominable fornications' in ancient literature. Attitudes to women's reading in seventeenth-century Japan bear close comparison.

Admiration for women who read and wrote coexisted with anxieties about their effects in many different cultures. And this would be the pattern wherever publishing industries developed. The liveliness of debates about women and books would increase as literacy among women continued to rise. At the same time, more women were prepared to make the transition from writing in manuscript for limited circulation, to writing and translating for print. And often they sought a readership made up principally of women. It would be the successors to novels like *L'Astrée* and *Oroonoko* that would excite the most heated arguments. In eighteenth-century Europe, but also further afield, the novel became the site of fierce battles as its content broadened and gradually replaced conduct books. One of the most extreme reactions to these changes

40 A book, itself depicting a *shunga* scene, has been cast aside in this erotic print by Okumura Masanobu, *Sweets from a Temple*.

was the appearance of supposedly 'scientific' proofs of the dangers women faced if they read. These tracts would in part replace the conjecture, polemic and superstition that infused the discussions of women's education and reading during the seventeenth century. But as women's reading became intertwined with leisure and social advancement, it became a still more contested activity and the subject of continuing and intriguing debates.

CHAPTER 7

---ᴏ∕∕ᴏ---

Answering Back

Iɴ 1748, Samuel Richardson, one of the most popular authors of the day, received an anonymous letter from one of his women readers. This was not an unusual event. In fact, as his novels rolled off the presses in edition after edition, he invited his readers to tell him what they thought of them. He solicited material for his prefaces from his readers as well as, most interestingly of all, original letters which he could use more or less verbatim in his epistolary novels. Many of his readers, mostly women, eagerly complied. The letter he received in 1748 had been prompted by one reader's concern 'for the virtuous in distress'. She was reading Richardson's *Clarissa* and feared that the author was about to subject his heroine to 'a fatal catastrophe'. She begged him to spare Clarissa from 'rapes, ruin, and destruction'. If he did not comply with her request, she hoped that he would 'meet with applause only from envious old maids, surly bachelors, and tyrannical parents'. She thought fit to explain that she was a sensible woman reader and not 'a giddy girl of sixteen'. If he took her for a 'fool' in writing to him in this way, she didn't 'care a straw'.[1] In this instance at least, Richardson took no notice and plotted his heroine's miserable end. Thus began one of the most affectionate, intriguing and extensive correspondences between a male author and a woman reader. She was Lady Bradshaigh, a voracious reader and not atypical of a particular class of women.

In many ways the most radical changes in women's reading in the eighteenth century took place in England where the morality of the novel – especially 'just' endings – was increasingly debated. It was there that the ascendancy of the novel first occurred, followed by France and Germany, and then the rest of Europe. By the turn of the century the newly independent United States of America opened up as a rapidly growing and particular

41 Auguste Bernard d'Agesci, *Lady Reading the Letters of Heloïse and Abelard*, c. 1780.

market. Literacy rates in some areas of the United States were more impressive than anywhere else in the world. In the decade between 1787 and 1797, 84 per cent of New Englanders and 77 per cent of Virginians signed their wills: a crude measure of literacy, of course, but significantly higher than anywhere else.[2] But for the time being, in most parts of the New World, women had access to a much more limited range of books than their European counterparts.

What women in Europe read, however, was not bound by national borders. The eighteenth century also saw a significant rise in the quantity and length of translations. Many were undertaken by women readers who came across works that particularly impressed them and which they wanted to make available to other women compatriots. A typical example of a woman writer's enormous influence and popularity with readers, much-read in translation, was the aristocratic but later impoverished Mme de Genlis. She was largely self-educated and like many women of the period both a great reader herself and keenly interested in the education and the promotion of women's reading and pedagogy more broadly. She was much struck (not wholly favourably) by her reading of Rousseau's famous educational novel in five books, *Émile: or, On Education*, published in 1762. One of the volumes focused specifically on the education of a girl, Sophie. According to Rousseau the education of young women was to be geared exclusively to men's happiness:

> Thus the entire education of women must be relative to men. To please men, to be useful to them, to be loved and honoured by them, to raise them when they are young, care for them when they are grown-up, to console them, to make their lives agreeable and gentle – these are the duties of women in all times and this is what they must be taught from childhood.[3]

Rousseau did believe that women should read to 'cultivate their minds' but, again, for the purposes of pleasing their husbands and his social circle. Women's conversation would thus be 'pleasing but not brilliant, and thorough but not deep. . . . When people talk to her they always seem to find what she says attractive'.[4]

Rousseau claimed that his theories were based on the directions of 'Nature' and it was this emphasis that led, no sooner were his books published, to their banning in both Paris and Geneva. They became European bestsellers all the same and no doubt in part because of Rousseau's ideological extremism. At the time of the French Revolution *Émile* served as one of the inspirations for what became a new national educational system. During the second half of the eighteenth century (1751–96) it appeared in no less than sixty-one English editions, probably making it the most read book in England, after the sceptical philosopher Voltaire. Mme de Genlis was both shocked and impressed by it and her reading inspired her to write her own educational treatise, *Adèle et Théodore*, in 1782. Tellingly, the girl's name is ahead of the boy's in her title. Its popularity in England almost eclipsed the reception given to Rousseau and Voltaire. Genlis objected to Rousseau's libertinism, particularly his claim that original sin does not exist, which she saw as a direct threat to Christian principles. But she also objected to Rousseau's prescriptions for only limited female education. This runs through *Adèle* and is expressed fully and explicitly in the third volume of her *Veillées du Château* (1784). This work was her most successful to date. The initial print-run of 7,000 copies sold out in eight days. It was quickly translated into numerous foreign languages with at least sixty printings in France, Britain, America, Germany, Spain and Italy.[5] What Genlis had to say about women's education and the ways in which men have controlled it was a direct attack on Rousseau:

> When men condescend, which is very seldom, to employ themselves a little on our education, they wish to give us vague notions, consequently often false, superficial knowledge, and frivolous talents. ... A man of letters, whose daughter gives evidence of wit and love of poetry, may be induced to cultivate these talents, but what will be her father's first care? Why, to rob the young scholar of that confidence that inspires fortitude, and that ambition which surmounts difficulties. He prescribes bounds to her efforts and commands her not to go beyond them. ... [He] traces a narrow circle round his young pupil over which she is forbidden to step. If she has the genius of Corneille or Racine, she is constantly told to write nothing but novels, pastorals and sonnets.[6]

Genlis was admired for her relative conservatism but also for the novelty of her educational method and for her equal concern for the education of girls and boys. One of her most imaginative innovations was to make the reading – or the acting out, while reading – of short morality plays an integral part of education. She believed that this instilled the right values and was also an excellent way of honing literacy skills. A similar method had been practised in Mme de Maintenon's school for impoverished young gentlewomen at Saint-Cyr. But nobody in the eighteenth century before Genlis had written new morality plays adapted to the needs of a young lady's polite education.[7] Her *Théâtre à l'usage des jeunes personnes* (1779–80) was successful as it was seen to be particularly suited to the education of young girls. The famous Mrs Elizabeth Montagu (1718–1800), social reformer, patron of the arts, hostess, writer and founder member of the Bluestockings, recommended it to her nieces. It was celebrated in the *Critical Review*, when first translated in 1781 (as *Theatre of Education*), and described as 'peculiarly serviceable to young women, whom they were principally calculated to instruct'.

Maria Edgeworth read *Adèle et Théodore* as soon as it was available and immediately began an English translation, but another translator published ahead of her. Other women readers were equally struck. Jane Austen refers to it approvingly in *Emma*, and Mary Wollstonecraft studied it carefully while writing her *A Vindication of the Rights of Woman* (1792). But when Genlis arrived in England in 1791 in the wake of the French Revolution, the British public discovered that she was not altogether the rare case of a morally upright Continental woman writer she had been taken for: she had separated from her husband in 1782 and two of her daughters were most likely illegitimate. This was at a time when the apparent morality of an author's life was often seen as a prerequisite for authoring moral works, and Genlis lost the admiration of many of her friends and readers including the Romantic poets and Frances Burney. But the sales of her books remained strong all the same.

England's pre-eminence in the eighteenth-century publishing world, particularly in relation to women readers, was a function of the relative economic and political stability symbolised by the Glorious Revolution of 1688, followed by an earlier Industrial Revolution than elsewhere in Europe. In London, the number of printing presses rose from approximately seventy in 1724, to over 124 in 1785. From 1688 on, the growing influence of Protestant mercantile interests brought significant social change: political power shifted from the aristocracy to include the landed and middle classes. And these middle classes steadily gained cultural influence, particularly in relation to publishing. With this came dramatic changes to the position of the woman reader. 'Leisured' wives and educated daughters became crucial evidence of social advancement and success. And reading and leisure became intimately associated. Fathers, husbands and brothers encouraged women's reading with a new urgency but many of them sought to control what was read.

Publishers were quick to see a niche market for advice manuals and conduct books and for the inclusion of guides of one sort or another in magazines – all principally for a female readership. Among other things these promoted a new ideal domestic woman. She was gentle, virtuous and untainted by the world of manual labour and, more importantly, public affairs and business. Upper- and particularly middle-class Englishwomen began to read more widely and much of what they read encouraged them back into the private sphere of the family. Periodicals provided an abundant source of domestic ideology, persuading women that their true vocation lay with home and family, while the public world of opinion, work and politics was reserved for men. Magazines for women appeared all over Europe. Among the most dogmatic was *La Pensadora Gaditana* (1763–64), in effect the first Spanish newspaper exclusively for women. It was published by Beatriz Cienfuegos, although some believe that to be a pseudonym employed by a savvy priest. The fifty-two 'essays' came out weekly and promoted a moral agenda within male-dominated social structures typical of the values of the Antiguo Régimen. Some of this material did, however, emphasise women's innate moral qualities, and it demonstrates a decline in the earlier preoccupation with unrestrained female sexuality. The eighteenth century did not see a dramatic break with the portrayal of the ideal woman in advice books, manuals and magazines, but rather depicted women's position with a new force and realism.

The new-found confidence of many eighteenth-century women readers naturally prompted reactions. Figures like the Earl of Shaftesbury (1671–1713), statesman, politician, philosopher and highly influential writer, sounded dire warnings. He had been tutored by the philosopher John Locke and is remembered above all for his letters to his illegitimate son, published a year after Shaftesbury's death, most of which are concerned with his son's and other young men's education. But he also campaigned vigorously against the modern novel and feared for its effects on women readers. In his work, *Soliloquy, or Advice to an Author* (1710), he criticised contemporary writers as rakish in their attempts to seduce their readers, particularly women, likening their works to 'poisonous fungi, edifying mushrooms, fancy clothes and fancy fictions'.

In France a number of substantial works had been published in the seventeenth century on the theory of the novel. Georges de Scudéry's preface to *Ibrahim* (1641) and Pierre Daniel Huet's *Traité de l'origine des romans* (1670) are original and scholarly. But during the eighteenth century, despite the meteoric rise in popularity and the concomitant commercial success of the novel, much less work of a theoretical kind appeared. There were only a handful of short prefaces or the odd preliminary 'Advice to the Reader', generally rehearsing the same old arguments for or against the usefulness and moral influence of the novel. Two writers, however, made their more developed views known.

L'Abbé Jacquin's line was typical of that of the Church. He published his *Entretiens sur les romans et l'application des talents, ouvrage moral et critique* in Paris in 1755. The abbé, with little stylistic flourish, is concerned above all for the maintenance of order (that is, of the Régime) and particularly women's place within it. The structure he adopted in his work is not without cunning. His *Entretiens* are dialogues and he successfully persuades his female interlocutor, at the outset a convinced advocate of the novel, to see things his way.

Romantic love, in his view, is quite simply corrupting. Novels detract from more appropriate religious reading. Finally, and most tellingly, the novel primarily concerns women, and so gives them undue attention, if not (by implication) power, thus undermining a social order based on marriage, the family and class structure, in all of which the man must have absolute authority over the woman.

A counter-argument put forward by Nicolas Lenglet-Dufresnoy (1674–1755) was more refreshing. He was worldly, a French diplomat, historian and writer, and his works are numerous and various. His independence of mind and brave opposition to the royal censors under Louis XV resulted in five periods of imprisonment in the Bastille, in the citadel in Strasbourg, and in Vincennes. His tone is often mordant and he made many enemies. *On the Use of Novels* (1734) was as provocative as many of his earlier works. With brilliant irony he contrasts the spurious authority of history with the humility of the novel and its 'ennobling' powers. Stories of love, he claimed, central to the novel as a genre, could only be morally instructive. On a rather different and not altogether convincing tack, he cautions that depriving the people, particularly women, of this sort of material would only drive the novel into a murky and dangerous underground. Finally, he argues for the importance of the novel in terms of the educational enfranchisement of women. This last point was his most contentious.

It was not only literary figures who entered the debate about women and reading. Numerous 'scientific' treatises detailed the alleged physiological effects of the activity. These inventive medical works were taken very seriously. Pierre-François Tissot was the author of a number of such engaging tomes including *On Onanism: Dissertation on the Maladies Produced by Masturbation* (1760) and *Nymphomania, or A Treatise on Uterine Frenzy* (1771). He frequently warns of the risks to health that reading can have on women. He describes the case of a 'woman who suffers convulsions after a few hours of reading' and of a girl of ten who 'read when she should have been running about, and who at twenty is a vapourish woman and does not nurse well'. The 'cure' to the medical problems allegedly caused by reading was, needless to say, preventing or limiting access to novels – and marriage. That all this was part of a barely disguised conspiracy to harness women's sexuality, and thus maintain the social order, seems as good an explanation as any.

Paradoxically, these and other attempts to control eighteenth-century women readers had the effect of creating a culture in which women were much more self-conscious about the power of their reading. Many were aware that they were crucial pawns in the game of social mobility, and a highly lucrative market for the rapidly industrialising publishing industry. Publishers continued to bring out numerous practical books on cookery, gardening, sewing and so on. But they also sought to satisfy the growing desire for women to self-educate, publishing histories and scientific, theological and philosophical works, some specifically written for women and sometimes by women.

Known as the 'Historian in Petticoats', Catharine Macaulay was Britain's first woman historian, and she was ridiculed by some and highly admired by others. She was a voracious reader. Like many other women of her background and era she educated herself thanks to the free access she had to her father's extensive library. She became a passionate reader of histories of the Roman Empire and mapped what she read about the decline of Rome onto the changing domestic social and political scene. She had also been struck, but not wholly convinced, by David Hume's popular six-volume *History of England*, published between 1754 and 1762. During the eighteenth century it came out in some fifty editions, and by 1900 almost 200 editions had been published. Macaulay's ideas did not altogether square with Hume's conservative bent. So she embarked on her own work, and the opening volume of her *History of England* appeared in 1763.

This bluestocking's commitments, unlike the majority of those of her (mostly conservative) colleagues, alarmed both Tories and Whigs. She called for the abolition of hereditary titles, the redistribution of land, and changes in the laws of inheritance. Members of Parliament should take their responsibilities to their constituencies much more seriously (and Parliament should therefore sit for shorter periods). Electoral reform was necessary in the interests of greater democracy and honesty. The voting system, she argued, should be modernised to enfranchise more people. Finally, she implied that the continuing expansion of the British Empire would encourage an insatiable lust for luxury items which would have a thoroughly uncivilising and pernicious effect on society, encouraging greed and selfishness. She was also a staunch advocate of copyright laws to protect authors' rights.

Macaulay had developed these views through careful reading of the myriad pamphlets circulated during and after the Civil War. She was in turn much read by contemporary women readers and was an inspiration to other aspiring women historians. She remained widely popular despite attracting personal hostility first by marrying a man much older than herself, and then a man much younger. She was something of an enigma to her many intellectual friends, both women and men.

Macaulay was as passionate about women's education as she was about history. She knew Locke's famous treatise, *Some Thoughts Concerning Education* (1693), and that of his French Catholic contemporary François Fénelon, *De l'éducation des filles* (1687). She had also read Rousseau's *Émile*

42 Robert Edge Pine's portrait of Catharine Macaulay. To indicate her republican sentiments and commitment to democracy, she is dressed as a Roman matron and wears the purple sash of an elected Roman senator. The letter in her hand refers to her friend and patron Revd Thomas Wilson, who probably commissioned the portrait.

and de Genlis's works on women's education including her educational plays. These informed her *Letters on Education* (1790) which is exceptional in including a chapter on women's potential contribution to landscape design. When Macaulay read Burke's *Reflections on the Revolution in France* that same year and took exception to it, she immediately set to work on a pamphlet, *Observations on the Reflections of the Rt. Hon. Edmund Burke, on the Revolution in France*, which was published just before her death in 1791.

Elizabeth Carter was an equally serious and critical reader. She was strongly encouraged in her education by her clergyman father and learnt several modern languages, Latin, Greek, Hebrew and Arabic. She wrote some poetry but her major contribution was as a translator of works that she thought should be made accessible to English women readers, most importantly Francesco Algarotti's *Il newtonianismo per le dame* (*Newtonianism for Women*, 1737). Despite its earnest and somewhat misleading title, it was a book she much admired and her translation became an eighteenth-century bestseller. It was a crucially important work and one of the main publications through which Newtonian ideas reached the general public in Europe.[8] But it is not the dry anti-religious scientific treatise that the reader might expect. The book is in fact a lively and lighthearted dialogue between a *chevalier* (cavalier or knight) and a marchioness (la marchesa di E***).

Through their delightful conversation, even banter, past theories of the nature of matter and light are sketched out and then dismissed as unsubstantiated. The setting is an Italian villa near Lake Garda and this location allows for the clever experimental use of dining rooms with mirrors, picture galleries, gardens and fountains to stage the spectacle of Newtonian optical science. By the end, the marchioness has to agree that Newton is right and not just about light, but almost everything else embraced by his philosophy. Algarotti allows for an extrapolation of experimental science into the realms of metaphysics, morals and politics; it was the only work of popular Newtonianism to be placed on the Catholic *Index* (1739). Carter had been well aware of the radical importance of the Italian work, disguised within a genteel rococo conversation. Hers was the first translation and others in English, French, German and Dutch followed. Carter had proved herself to be one of the most discriminating women readers of the eighteenth century. It was by no means unusual for translators to provide titles for their works that were unlike the original; that Carter translated Allgarotti's as closely as possible indicated her belief that women, above all, should read the work.

Like Catharine Macaulay, Elizabeth Carter was also passionate about women's education and knew both Locke's and Fénelon's treatises. She was struck by her reading and dared both to question the differences between men and women, and to call for change. She was a friend and editor of Samuel Johnson, sometimes working on his periodical *The Rambler*, as well as of a number of notable women intellectuals of the day, including Hannah More and Hester Chapone. These women were all voracious readers and often advocated a fresh approach to the books they came across. There was much to delight in, as well to learn from, and their less 'establishment' educations liberated them from the narrow approach of some more highly trained male scholars.

These women read, enjoyed and admired Shakespeare and wrote about his poetry and plays with an uninhibited enthusiasm. Publishers were aware of the need for books about him to meet the growing demand for introductions to his works. Both Elizabeth Montagu, in *An Essay on the Writings and Genius of Shakespeare* (1769), and Elizabeth Griffith, in *The Morality of Shakespeare's Drama Illustrated* (1775), demonstrated their wide reading. Both believed that his writings were much more immediately accessible than others had suggested. Montagu loved Shakespeare's facility in creating easily recognisable characters.

This was something that she felt Samuel Johnson had singularly failed to highlight in his *Preface to Shakespeare* (1765). And Griffith claimed that his 'anatomy of the human heart was delineated from *nature*, not from *metaphysics*; referring immediately to our intuitive sense and not wandering with the schoolmen'.[9] Writers like Montagu and Griffith warned against the stifling pretension and selectivity of some commentaries penned by male writers and encouraged readers, particularly women, to read and enjoy the poet and playwright in an open and direct way.

Walking through the print and book *quartiers* of Paris today, or the equivalent areas in other cities, the eye is likely to be drawn to dismembered eighteenth-century scientific publications. They might be colourful, highly detailed illustrations of different species of sea urchin, or different designs for the rigging of tall ships, or an architectural survey of one of Europe's great medieval cathedrals, or a horticultural work illustrating the exact place to prune the branches of a quince tree, or one of the vast numbers of maps produced during the period. Occasionally, but increasingly rarely, one sees the real thing: propped open on a book stand, the work in its entirety, as it would have seduced the eighteenth-century reader. The rise of autodidacts, women and men, in the period meant that publishers were eager to meet the demand for scientific works, broadly defined. There are magnificent examples of botanical and entomological works by women. Two of the most notable and well-read botanists were Elizabeth Blackwell and Priscilla Bell Wakefield. Blackwell's *A Curious Herbal* (1737–39) with drawings taken 'from real life', and Wakefield's *An Introduction to Botany* (1796) contributed new perspectives and techniques to the historical tradition of botanical illustration and writing. Wakefield went on to be an innovative landscape gardener, including industrial elements – mills and even awe-inspiring gunpowder factories – in her picturesque schemes. These women were important initiators of a feminine 'green' tradition.[10] Their publications and other similar expensive tomes were for an elite market and both public and private libraries.

This was another new aspect of the world of books in the eighteenth century: books were not only bought to be read, but also to be integrated into the growing number of private libraries. Book-collecting was an activity that only the wealthy could take seriously. The new encyclopaedias and dictionaries which we so associate with the Enlightenment were within reach of only a small minority, although the growing number of public and university libraries bought copies. And many public libraries were open to women, often providing a separate reading room. The eighteenth century gave birth to the bibliophile and they were by no means all men. Most wealthy women bought their own books. The poet Elizabeth Thomas, who haunted the bookshops around Great Russell Street in London, had built up a library of some 500 books which, on account of poverty, she was forced to sell with enormous regret. Women readers like those in the Blue Stockings Society in Britain, the *bas bleus* in France, and their imitators on both sides of the English Channel, bought and read serious works of this kind. These women read for hours a day and many were inspired to take up their pens. They were an elite minority.

During the first half of the eighteenth century, women's reading was dominated by conduct literature in numerous forms: sermons, devotional writings, family letters, poetry, chapbooks and instruction manuals proffering advice on customs and manners, spiritual guidance and practical guidelines on the running of the household and the upbringing of children. Most of these were aimed at women of the middle and upper-middle classes, although chapbooks – small booklets containing ballads, fables and moral tales for adults and children – were within the buying power of increasing numbers of the working classes.

The titles of instruction manuals alone suggest the extraordinarily varied nature of what was on offer. Daniel Defoe's *Some Considerations upon Streetwalks with a Proposal for lessening the present Number of them* (1726) argued that women's sexuality must remain under male authority. Alongside other advice he suggests that older women should not marry younger husbands as the latter will inevitably weary of them, gratifying their desires at the expense of the virtue of younger women who would then be forced into prostitution. Defoe's most popular conduct book, *The Family Instructor* (1715), teaches correct social behaviour within the family. In a series of dialogues, proper conduct between husbands and wives, parents and children, masters (and mistresses) and servants, are all delineated. What is advocated is dismally conventional. His *On the Education of Women* (1724), on the other hand, vociferously argues for women's pedagogy. Some of the inconsistencies in Defoe's recommendations to women must have dizzied many contemporary woman readers.

How women should behave was the subject of other more covert forms of conduct literature. An anonymous 'physician' published *The Pleasures of Conjugal Love Explained: In an Essay Concerning Human Generation* in 1740. The author argues against the prevalent view that women were 'hotter' because of an excess of blood; his line is that women's amatory desires are a function of the 'inconstancy of their imagination'.[11] It is easy to see why many view took such a dim view of the growing fashion for reading romantic novels. Men continued to be advised either explicitly or implicitly to keep their women firmly under control.

One of the most widely read advice manuals was George Savile's *The Lady's New Year Gift: or, Advice to a Daughter* (1688). It came out in more than fourteen editions during the eighteenth century. He encourages daughters to submit to paternal authority, and warns first and foremost against amatory love: 'The Mind will have no rest whilst it is possessed by a darling Passion'.

Some men, however, were more progressive. The women addressed in John Gregory's *A Father's Legacy to his Daughters* (1774) are 'companions and equals'. He advises the cultivation of 'sensibility', that ubiquitous and protean eighteenth-century virtue: 'Without an unusual share of natural sensibility, a very peculiar good fortune, a woman in this country has very little probability of marrying for love.' His daughters must have been moved, on reading their father's advice, that what he wished for them were marriages based on mutual affection and respect. More conventionally, he described how women were designed to 'soften' men's hearts and 'polish' their 'manners' and the husband's role was to protect their wives.

The advice offered by women to women was equally various. In her two-volume *Strictures on the Modern System of Female Education* (1799) the conservative evangelical philanthropist Hannah More firmly warned women to conform. Learning, for More, was inextricably bound up with faith and good works. Above all she encouraged women to live discreetly: 'If a young lady has that discretion and modesty without which all knowledge is little worth, she will never make an ostentatious parade of it, because she will rather be intent on acquiring more than on displaying what she has'. At the other end of the spectrum Mary Wollstonecraft, in *Thoughts on the Education of Daughters: with Reflections on Female Conduct, in the More Important Duties of Life* (1788), while conceding that women are at risk of excessive emotionalism, explained this tendency as a function of a lack of intellectual work and access to other pursuits enjoyed by men. The proposed remedy was a decent education akin to that given to the opposite sex.

For all their historical interest, these conduct books make dry, if occasionally comic, reading. But during the course of the century the subject matter of these didactic tomes gradually found its way into the novel and often into novels in epistolary form. At the same time the conduct book went into decline. Defoe came to the novel late, but the behaviour of the fictional heroines of his *Moll Flanders* and *Roxana* intrigued and inspired women readers of his day, and thereafter. Virginia Woolf was one of vast numbers of admiring women readers and devoted a chapter to him in *The Common Reader* of 1919.

Samuel Richardson had set out to write a conduct book but saw that his material could instead be dramatised in the form of a novel: *Pamela*, one of the great publishing phenomena of the century. Two other very successful epistolary novels followed: *Clarissa: Or the History of a Young Lady* (1748) and *The History of Sir Charles Grandison* (1753). Richardson attracted many women admirers, and he was well aware that they made up the bulk of his readership. In a reply to his most loyal lady correspondent, Lady Bradshaigh, Richardson acknowledged, 'My acquaintance lies chiefly among the ladies; I care not who knows it'. A hundred years later his popularity with women readers still drew the scorn of male authors; William Makepeace Thackeray blasted Richardson's novels as 'sentimental twaddle', and claimed their author was dependent on the inspiration of inferior social contacts – his readers being 'old maids and dowagers'. But the letters sent by women to Richardson, and the epistolary exchanges that followed, became crucially important market research.

Richardson was allegedly alarmed by some women readers' responses to his work. In 1755 he published *A Collection of the Moral and Instructive Sentiments* to counteract those who 'misread' his novels. His aim in *Pamela*, and a little later in *Clarissa*, had been 'properly [to] mingle Instruction with Entertainment, so as to make the latter seemingly the View, while the former is really the End'. He extracted what he considered to be the essential instruction in his three novels and arranged it alphabetically as an accessible conduct book. In a letter to an admiring woman reader he described the contents as 'the pith and marrow of nineteen volumes'.[12] Under 'A' he listed abstract and concrete terms worthy of comment: 'Adversity', 'Affliction', 'Advice and caution to women', 'Air and Manners', 'Address', 'Anger' and so on. The preface was written by an Oxford scholar, Dr Benjamin Kennicot, who describes the misreading of Richardson's epistolary novels (which he calls his 'Letters'):

> Such is the great plan, such the benevolent scheme, of these collections . . . which have already been translated into several foreign languages. . . . But as the *narrative* part of those Letters was only meant as a vehicle for the *instructive*, no wonder that many readers, who are desirous of fixing in their minds those maxims which deserve notice distinct from the story that first introduced them, should have often wished and pressed to see them separate from the chain of engaging incidents that will sometimes steal the most fixed attention from its pursuits of serious truths.

Needless to say Richardson's *Collection* sold poorly. His readers had delighted in his vivid descriptions of characters caught up in difficult lives and outcomes left hanging in the balance until the very close of the novels. These dramatic stories were open to interpretation – and far more entertaining than his pre-eminently dull *Collection*.

Richardson exchanged numerous letters with contemporary women writers including Sarah Fielding, Jane Collier, Elizabeth Carter and Hester Chapone. But by far the most important of Richardson's woman reader-critics was Lady Bradshaigh. She was from a landed family whose fortunes had fallen and then risen again and she was in many ways typical of his female audience. She held a dim view of intellectual women, not uncharacteristic of her class. Her voluminous correspondence with the novelist was circulated by Richardson in manuscript form among those close to him, and he considered publishing it, describing one section of it as 'the best Commentary that cd. be written on the History of Clarissa'.[13]

Lady Bradshaigh's earliest letters to him, in 1748, were anonymous. In breathy prose she described her reading experience of *Clarissa* thus far:

> Had you seen me, I surely would have moved your pity. When alone, in agonies would I lay down the Book, take it up again, walk about the room, let fall a flood of tears, wipe my eyes, read again, perhaps not three lines, throw away the book, crying out, excuse me, good Mr Richardson, I cannot go on; it is your fault – you have done more than I can bear; [I] threw myself upon my couch[.][14]

This intimate and playful relationship between an author and a woman reader was far from uncommon. Alexander Pope corresponded with many of his women readers who were remarkably open in their enthusiasms or reservations about his work, particularly his portrayal of women. Henry Fielding's sister, Sarah, herself a novelist, was her brother's most important reader; she may well have also contributed to some of his writing. For over twenty years Jonathan Swift regarded Esther Johnson, 'Stella', as 'his most valuable friend'. Between 1710 and 1713 he wrote a famous series of letters to her, later published as *The Journal to Stella* in Sheridan's edition of 1784. Swift constantly asks her view of his latest writings. From his time to our own there has been speculation that the two were secretly married, since their relationship seemed as inexplicable then as now. In myriad ways, women readers exerted considerable and direct influence over what men wrote. They were not the passive, impressionable readers that some have cast them as.

Lady Bradshaigh did not always get her way with Richardson but she provides a crucial window into the mind and soul of one keen woman reader. If we take her account of her regular periods of swooning at face value,

43 Richardson (far left, wearing his usual morning dress) reads *Sir Charles Grandison* to a group of friends in the grotto of his house at North End, 1751. The original drawing was by the poet Susanna Highmore (reading, bottom right). Also present is the writer Hester Chapone (seated by the stairs, listening attentively).

reading *Clarissa* – which is a massive novel – must have been a slow process. In fact, reading the novel and writing her innumerable letters to its author must have been the principal activity of her waking hours for weeks and months. Richardson was pleased with the novel's effects on her and many like her, described by later commentators as an arousal bearing every possible parallel to erotic subordination and sublimation. Richardson advised the distraught Lady Bradshaigh that she consider her 'susceptibility' not a weakness, but rather 'Humanity, and see how your Sentences will run': her reading, carefully directed by the author, would bring rewards to her own writing.

Richardson and Lady Bradshaigh went on to exchange numerous letters while he was penning *Sir Charles Grandison* and the author openly acknowledged his debt to her; the novel's success was 'owing to you . . . more than to any one Person besides'.[15] Nearing the end of his life he asked for Lady Bradshaigh's copies of *Pamela* and *Clarissa*, which she had heavily annotated, so that he could be guided by her reactions in preparing new editions. Her first edition of *Clarissa* was a presentation copy signed by Richardson and she filled the margins with her reactions as she read; to these are added

Richardson's own responses to them, and hers then to his. Bradshaigh emerges as a contrary reader but Richardson's third edition shows that he was persuaded by many of her criticisms. Her corrections, particularly regarding aristocratic language and customs, were readily accepted. But Bradshaigh's insistence that the novel should have a happy ending and that Clarissa marry Lovelace was bluntly refused. Bradshaigh's scribbles suggest that Clarissa could live contentedly as a single mother, raising her brother James's son. This woman reader believed that the dishonoured woman could – and should – be allowed a good life. Richardson, however, did take some heed of Bradshaigh's reading and altered the character of Lovelace to emphasise his not negligible shortcomings.

Most women of the period, those of the growing middle class, left far less extensive records of their often wide reading. Even where there are letters describing books and reading, they give the impression of conforming to the conventions of the age; the experience of reading this book or that is described as the reader-writer feels it *ought* to be described. But Eliza Haywood may be a further example of another type of eighteenth-century woman reader. Had Haywood's circumstances been different, she too would have left little for us to go on. But largely by force of financial necessity she became a professional writer, a role still widely despised at the time. She was prolific and her writing was often a reaction to – or directly fed by – her reading.

Haywood was certainly of relatively humble origin but little is known about her life, and her own fragmentary accounts are often contradictory or misleading. She was born the daughter of a London shopkeeper around 1690 and most likely married around 1710. She seems to have left her husband at some point between 1715 and 1720. What we know for sure is that she took the London publishing scene by storm in 1720 with her attention-grabbing book *Love in Excess; or the Fatal Enquiry*. It is a complicated, fast-paced love story complete with kidnappings and clever servants trying to advance their mistresses' amorous interests. Most tellingly, as a morality tale it is ambiguous: the two women who have fallen in love with the hero, D'Elmont, both end up dead – Ciamara, who has an erotic appetite and is obviously the 'bad' woman, and Violetta, the chaste 'good' woman. Within five years the novel was already in its sixth edition, and Haywood had also clocked up more than twenty other works, mostly fiction, by and large published in several editions. Some of her works were parodies, based on her reading – of men. And male authors played the same game. The original title of Daniel Defoe's famous *Roxana* (1724) was *The Fortunate Mistress*, a direct inversion of the title of a novel by Haywood, published the previous year, *The Unfortunate Mistress*. Defoe's title is, of course, ironic. In the event the full title of Defoe's work was *Roxana: The*

Fortunate Mistress Or, a History of the Life and Vast Variety of Fortunes of Mademoiselle de Beleau, Afterwards Called the Countess de Wintselsheim in Germany, Being the Person Known by the Name of the Lady Roxana in the Time of Charles II.

Pope was direct in his dismissal of Haywood's *Memoirs of a Certain Island Adjacent to the Kingdom of Utopia* (1725) and *The Court of Caramania* (1727), both being 'most scandalous books'. Like many, he objected to plots in which love intrigues threatened the social status quo while the endings remained unconcluded in terms of 'just, moral' outcomes. In Haywood's *Memoirs* she had criticised Martha Blount, one of Pope's closest friends. He responded directly in his famous *Dunciad* (1728):

> See in the circle next, Eliza plac'd;
> Two babes of love close clinging to her waist;
> Fair as before her works she stands confess'd,
> In flow'rs and pearls by bounteous Kirkall dress'd.[16]

The 'babes of love' were long considered a reference to Haywood's alleged illegitimate children. There is no evidence for this in her biography, slim though it is. It is more likely that it refers to rival pairs of publishers battling for Haywood, first Edmund Curll and William Chetwood in 1728, then Samuel Chapman in 1729, and John Osborne from 1741–43.[17] There is an engraving of Haywood wearing pearls, and Pope suggests that she is the 'prize' to be awarded to the winning publisher in a urinating competition. Pope was mocking the success of 'tear-jerkers' and alluding to Jonathan Swift's *Gulliver's Travels* where the hero puts out a fire caused by a maid who has fallen asleep – while reading – in the same manner.

Haywood and Pope were both highly popular with women readers, although Pope attracted the 'Ladies'. He believed that women should be able to read the great works of classical literature and clearly had them in mind when he published his translation of the *Iliad*. Pope may have considered that women's role was subordinate to men's, but he believed passionately in the need for women to receive a better and broader education. Many women considered 'Pope as their poet'.[18] More than any other eighteenth-century writer, he moved women to respond in print to their reading of him. So we know that they read him and reacted differently – in opposition, in support, touched or entertained, imitative or hostile. Lady Mary Wortley Montagu, Mary Leapor, Mary Deverell, Charlotte Lennox, Lady Sophia Burrell, all read and then rewrote Pope. Haywood alienated the Tories, but had notable Whigs on her side. Sir Richard Steele, Irish writer and politician, and co-founder, with Joseph Addison, of the *Tatler* and then the *Spectator*, was a supporter. While writing popular novels, Haywood also wrote for periodicals and produced conduct books. *The Female Spectator* (four volumes, 1744–46), a monthly periodical, was written in answer to the *Spectator*. In it, Haywood assumed four personae (Mira, Euphrosine, Widow of Quality and The Female Spectator) and took up various positions on questions of contemporary interest, including marriage, the raising of children, education, conduct and women's reading. It was the first periodical written for women by a woman and perhaps Haywood's most significant contribution to women's reading. The eighteenth-century book market was rapidly commercialising and Haywood, like many of her male writer friends, particularly those from less-than-aristocratic backgrounds and not supported by a patron, needed to be shrewd about the reading market.

In the late spring of 1741, a not atypical publishing race was on. Readers – women first and foremost – waited with excited anticipation. Two novels were about to appear, one by Haywood and the other by James Parry. Both were responses to reading Samuel Richardson's then best-selling and now classic novel, *Pamela*, subtitled *Virtue Rewarded. In a Series of Familiar Letters from a beautiful Young Damsel, to her Parents.* On 26 May 1741, an advertisement was published for Parry's forthcoming novel, *Memoirs of the Life of Mr James Parry . . . being the Anti-Pamela of Monmouthshire.* Less than three weeks later a further advertisement appeared, this time for the same book but now titled *Anti-Pamela: Or Memoirs of Mr James Parry.* But before Parry's book was available to readers, Eliza Haywood, having snatched the most commercially attractive part of his proposed title, pipped him at the post and published her *Anti-Pamela.* An advertisement appeared in the *London Evening-Post* (23–25 June 1741):

This Day is publish'd,
(Price 2s. stitch'd, 2s. 6d. bound)

ANTI-PAMELA; or, Feign'd Innocence detected: In a Series of Syrena's Adventures. A Narrative which has really its Foundation in Truth and Nature; and at the same time that it entertains, by a vast variety of surprising Incidents, warns against a partial Credulity, by showing the Mischiefs that frequently arise from a too sudden Admiration.

Publish'd as a necessary Caution to all young Gentlemen. Printed for J.Huggonson, in Sword and Huckler Court, over-against the eleven days Crown Tavern on Ludgate-Hill.

Parry's novel appeared on 27 June with a further amended title: *The True Anti-Pamela: or, Memoirs of Mr James Parry*. Henry Fielding also published his *An Apology for the Life of Mrs. Shamela Andrews* in the same year.

Women readers of Richardson's original *Pamela* wrote to him in their thousands and responses were laudatory, subtle, crude, familiar or vituperative. The novel has its sensational scenes involving ladies' stockings and undressing, and its heroine is in many ways revolutionary. It had captured the imagination of its readers for all manner of contradictory reasons, and kicked up one of the great literary storms of the century, and beyond. Pamela, a young and attractive servant girl – the 'beautiful young damsel' of Richardson's subtitle – inspires the passionate love of her master, one Mr B.; while egging him on, she resists his attempts to strip her of her honour – on a number of occasions succeeding almost literally by only a hair's breadth – and successfully manipulates him into marriage. The plot can be summed up in a sentence, and it has numerous literary precedents; both Edmund Spenser's Una and John Milton's Lady come to mind. What caused the furore was not the 'Feign'd Innocence detected' but the heroine's status-bending rewarded.

Richardson's *Pamela*, as the subtitle indicates, is an epistolary novel that allows for alternative interpretations. When Pamela's frustrated would-be seducer calls her 'artful baggage', or describes what he sees as her 'lucky Knack at falling into Fits, when she pleases', the reader can sympathise with his sense that she is manipulating him; or the reader may side with the novel's clever but vulnerable heroine. These ambiguities added to the novel's *succès de scandale*. Elsewhere Richardson claimed that his approach to fiction was more straightforward: 'When a *guilty Character* is introduced it should in the Conclusion appear to be signally punished or distressed, that others may be deterred from the Pursuits of those Follies, or Mistakes, which have been the Occasion of its Misfortunes.' And contrariwise, '*Virtue* or *Innocence*' must not be 'permitted to suffer; but . . . a *Prospect* at least should be opened, either *here* or *hereafter*, for its Reward.' Women authors, he claimed – and Eliza Haywood must surely be one of those he had in mind – 'like the *fallen Angels*, having lost their own innocence, seem, as one would think by their Writings, to make it their Study to corrupt the Minds of others, and render them as depraved, as miserable, and as lost as themselves.' Many women readers of *Pamela* considered his heroine a lamentable, wholly self-interested wheeler-dealer.

What Haywood scorned in *Pamela* was the heroine's hypocrisy, together with its improbable dénouement, in which the servant girl ends up marrying a wealthy, highly eligible country squire. Throughout, Pamela is endangered by other characters and reacts unpredictably. She is everywhere the hopeless victim, incapable of taking any independent action. In many ways, although her tricks can be a delight, she is one of the most infuriating heroines in fiction.

Haywood indicated in her title that she was writing for 'young Gentlemen'. There is reason to doubt her sincerity; she certainly attracted large numbers of women readers at home and abroad. In 1743 French and Dutch translations were published; a German edition came out in 1743–44, and a second in 1746. *Anti-Pamela* was as controversial as the original, but for more obvious reasons. Haywood transforms the passive and unbelievable Pamela into the feisty, unpleasant and wholly convincing Syrena Tricksy who, needless to say, controls the narrative throughout. Unlike Pamela she is not sexually attracted to her would-be suitors and her only concern in seeking a husband is to gain wealth, and with it, power. Syrena is serially seduced, and then abandoned. It is a book with a clear moral: the dangers of sexual license.

Despite Haywood's appeal that the novel serve as a warning to men, there is plenty of evidence that she was also concerned about the potentially corrupting powers of *Pamela* (and numerous other novels) if read by women of a similarly lowly status as the novel's heroine. Might not more and more servants attempt to seduce men of a higher class, using sexual favours as a way of ensnaring them in socially inappropriate marriages? Would it ever work in real life, or would the servant girls simply suffer moral humiliation, and the loss of their employment, like Ms Tricksy? At the very end of *Anti-Pamela* the heroine (or anti-heroine) is 'sent under the Conduct of an old Servant of one of her kinsmen to *Wales*', presumably implying a lonely rural backwater where Syrena will see no more of 'society'.

The subtitle of *Anti-Pamela* emphasised its 'Foundation in Truth and Nature' and in one of many subsequent publications which demonstrate that Haywood's reading, and no doubt re-reading, of Richardson's *Pamela* was still an obsessive force behind her own writing, she considered the vulnerability of maids. Two years after the publication of *Anti-Pamela*, she wrote a treatise for the growing number of literate servants, *A Present for a Servant-Maid* (1743). This advice book has a number of interesting entries on areas of life and their dangers that relate directly to *Anti-Pamela*. One of the heroine's misdemeanours comes under the heading, 'Telling the Affairs of the Family', in other words giving away the household's secrets. Then there is a warning against superstition, particularly 'Listening to Fortune-tellers', again one of Ms Tricksy's weaknesses. Haywood counsels against 'Giving pert or saucy answers', which her fictional character does with considerable quick-wittedness. Loyalty meant not 'Hearing any Thing said against your Master or Mistress'. 'Giving your Opinion too freely' was also proscribed; finally, and most tellingly, giving in to 'Temptations from your Master', and 'Apeing the Fashion'. Much of

Pamela's successful social climbing is achieved by way of dress. Women readers were aware of this.

The 'Pamela Controversy' was also known as the 'Pamela Vogue'. Spin-offs appeared: prints, mugs, fans, even playing cards, all with a *Pamela* theme. Questions of fashion, appearance, subterfuge and insincerity, and how outward signs relate to 'real' class, are all central to the furore Richardson's novel created and Haywood's further fuelled. *Pamela* was a novel that everyone was reading, 'misreading' or pretending to read and the book itself became a fashion accessory. The writer and critic Anna Barbauld noted, 'at Ranelagh . . . it was usual for ladies to hold up the volumes of Pamela to one another, to shew they had got the book everyone was talking of'. Ranelagh Gardens were public pleasure gardens in Chelsea, London, complete with rotunda (since demolished). Like the less fashionable Vauxhall Gardens, it was a popular place of entertainment, with outdoor music.

The many other clones of the original *Pamela* and *Anti-Pamela* were clearly written to propel their authors onto a very roomy bandwagon. The publishing scene had developed, and was rapidly internationalising. Manufacturing industries were making all manner of new products, including cheap books within the buying power of many, particularly in the cities. At the same time, in the growing urban areas, clothes became quite as potentially threatening to the status quo as books, whereas in rural areas throughout Europe and beyond, until well into the nineteenth century, the peasantry wore traditional dress, or comparable 'uniform'. In relation to what women were wearing, Daniel Defoe, who always felt he had his finger on the pulse, remarked in his essay *Every-Body's Business, is No-Body's Business* (1725):

> Our Servant Wenches are so puff'd up with pride, now a Days, that they never think they go fine enough: It is a hard Matter to know the Mistress from the Maid by their Dress, nay very often the Maid shall be the finer of the two.

The airs assumed by maids are largely accounted for by their reading. What should be read and what should be worn were becoming confused. Women were dressing so as to look like fictional characters and the images they saw in magazines. Appropriate dress and appropriate reading became two connected subjects of debate. Sometimes they were almost conflated; an article in the *London Magazine* of March 1737 argued, 'Dress should be properly adapted for the Person, as in Writing, the Style must be suited to the subject'. Deviation from these strictures was deemed by many to be subversive.

Numerous Continental authors took their turns at rewriting *Pamela*. There were Italian versions, and a play, *Nanine* (1743), by none other than Voltaire – a middle-class Richardson transformed into a gentlemanly 'bagatelle', as the author himself described it. The most dramatic *Pamela* on the Continent was a French play: François de Neufchâteau's *Pamela*, which opened at the Comédie-Française on 1 August 1793 in the midst of a volatile political climate. France seemed ready for a reaction to the excesses of the Revolution. The play was closely modelled on an English translation of Carlo Goldoni's Italian comedy, *Pamela Nubile* (1750), itself based, of course, on Richardson's novel. In Neufchâteau's play, Pamela turns out to have been a gentlewoman in disguise. It was hugely successful, but when the Committee on Public Safety, which was only just managing to fulfil its title, got wind of the fact that the heroine, rewarded at the end of the play by a glorious marriage, was in fact aristocratic and not a humble servant girl after all, the National Convention decided to throw both the playwright and all the actors in prison. The Comédie-Française was closed for the first time in its history. This is a striking reminder of just how politically sensitive the arts were in the eighteenth century. And women's growing participation in middle-class culture as readers, theatregoers and writers, had the potential to be particularly politically inflammatory. With more leisure time than their male counterparts, women were the major market for cultural products and for the novel most contentiously.

Richardson's *Clarissa*, and its many imitations and radical rewritings, was one of the publishing phenomena of the century. And all this fed and enlivened the debate about the affective power of women's reading. Lady Bradshaigh, for all the no-doubt light self-parody, was only one of many women readers who took to their couches to rest, such was the devastating effect of their reading. Does it make Denis Diderot's claims for women's incapacity to distinguish fiction from reality any more plausible? Many women readers, Diderot claimed, considered Richardson's characters to be real, whether alive or dead, living, or having lived, in England's capital. Diderot recounts the following: 'One day a woman of taste and unusual sensibility, wholly preoccupied by the story of Grandison which she had just read, said to one of her friends about to leave for London, "I would be grateful if you would visit, on my behalf, Miss Emilie, Mr. Belfort and above all Miss Howe, if she is still alive." '[19]

One woman reader who thought about all these questions and contested contemporary views was Anna Barbauld. She is in many ways typical of the growing group of middle-class educated women readers. Her father was a Presbyterian minister and headmaster of a dissenting school for boys in

Kibworth Harcourt in Leicestershire. She was a poet and admired by the English Romantics, most notably William and Dorothy Wordsworth and Samuel Taylor Coleridge. She was also a children's writer and essayist. She took a keen interest in politics and was a staunch advocate of the novel, unapologetically championing its importance for women readers.

At the end of the century she and Walter Scott were both considering major publishing projects in the form of multiple-volume works which would offer readers an edited selection of novels, each prefaced by a biographical sketch of the author. The idea was to offer 'tasters' of major novels so as to guide the growing number of readers, especially, in Barbauld's case, women readers. Collections of poetry, drama and essays had been published before and these had been very successful, but as yet there had been no comparable anthology of the novel. They were deemed important in part because they contributed to the growing sense of national consciousness and identity, important features of the eighteenth century at home and further afield in the British Empire. Barbauld's reputation at the time was high, both as a poet, but still more so as the editor of Richardson's *Correspondence . . . biographical* in six volumes (1804). She was approached by publishers and signed a contract ahead of Scott. The result was her monumental but largely forgotten fifty-volume *The British Novelists*, published in 1810 – the first collected introduction to the British novel.

To propose Barbauld as an exemplary eighteenth-century woman reader on the basis of her vast work raises certain intriguing questions; in particular, to what extent were her own reading preferences actually represented in it? Her publisher was naturally seeking substantial sales to the newly literate body of readers keen for pointers as to where to begin with the rapidly increasing number of available novels. And her publisher was unlikely to accede to the inclusion of novels that might be deemed scandalous. Fortunately Barbauld wrote an extensive introduction to her work setting out her criteria for inclusion and exclusion, and deftly asserting her own likes and dislikes irrespective of what is actually represented in her volumes. This, combined with her choices, reveals one eighteenth-century woman's understanding of the social and political significance of the novel and, more particularly, why she thought the novel of particular importance to women readers as an educational tool, broadly defined.

So who is in and who is out? Barbauld's selection is heavily weighted in favour of the novel post-1755. Of the twenty-nine novels included, only seven are from the first half of the century or earlier. Her introductory essay, 'On the Origin and Progress of Novel-Writing', pays due regard to three women novelists: Aphra Behn, Eliza Haywood and Delarivier Manley. The last, born in

1663 on Jersey in the Channel Islands, achieved considerable notoriety with her satirical romances about contemporary political scandals. Her *Secret Memoirs . . . of Several Persons of Quality* (1709) sought to expose the private lives and vices of Whig ministers, and after its publication she was arrested for libel. Barbauld's praise of Manley was a bold move. But in her introduction Barbauld gives pride of place to Defoe, Richardson and Fielding. Her publisher no doubt approved of this but there is sincerity in her admiration consistent with her project as seen in the round. Barbauld highly rated their preference for realism over the marvellous, the formal unity they achieved, and the affective powers of their writing. However, this apparent preference for the well-known male authors of the day is balanced by her actual selection. Charlotte Lennox's *Female Quixote* (1752), her version of Cervantes's famous story, is given significant space, and Barbauld's twenty-three other choices demonstrate an extraordinarily heterodox and unconventional view of the novel. She includes a substantial amount written by women at a time when the status of women authors remained much debated: Frances Brooke's *History of Lady Julia Mandeville* (1763), Frances Burney's *Evelina* (1778) and *Cecilia* (1782), Ann Radcliffe's *Romance of the Forest* (1791) and *Mysteries of Udolpho* (1794), and Maria Edgeworth's *Belinda* (1891) and *Modern Griselda* (1805).

Barbauld carefully justifies her selection and explains that she has chosen 'the most approved novels from the first regular productions of the kind to the present time'. She has also striven to provide 'variety in manner'.[20] But she is also explicit about the publisher's commercial interests: 'some regard it has been thought proper to pay to the taste and preference of the public, as was but reasonable in an undertaking in which their preference was to indemnify those who are at the expense and risk of the publication'.[21] There are some curious omissions. In her introduction she could not be more flattering about Amelia Opie's novels, yet not a single one is included; 'Copyright', she explains, 'was not to be intruded on'. On the other hand, John Hawkesworth's now largely forgotten *Almoran and Hamlet* (1761) is the chosen representative of Oriental fiction, despite Barbauld describing the style as 'turgid'. Barbauld also succeeds in alerting her readers to books we assume she would have liked to include had it not been for the publisher's objections. *Vathek* was held by Barbauld to be 'the only modern composition which has seized the genuine spirit of the Arabian tales'.[22]

Vathek (alternatively titled *Vathek, an Arabian Tale* or *The History of the Caliph Vathek*) was written by William Beckford in French, translated into English in 1786 and published anonymously as *An Arabian Tale, From an Unpublished Manuscript*, claiming to be a direct translation of an Arabic work.

The novel tells of Caliph Vathek who renounces his Islamic faith and sets out to gain supernatural powers by engaging in licentious activities with his mother. But Vathek fails and ends up in hell, controlled by a demon, Eblis, and is forced forever to wander, robbed of speech. Barbauld warmly recommends the book to her readers. Her publisher no doubt considered the work unsuitable for a family audience and feared bad publicity, but Barbauld refused to remain silent about the books she herself had clearly enjoyed and esteemed.

What is also striking is the political stance of so many of the writers included. Here the rational tradition of dissent dominates. Many of the authors Barbauld chooses were known for their support of progressive causes: the American War of Independence, the abolition of the slave trade, the French Revolution (at least in its early stages), and opposition to the Seditious Meetings Act of 1795 (also known as the 'gagging' act). Barbauld is equally radical in her position on women authors – and her defence of women novelists. While 'many paltry books' are published every year, 'it may safely be affirmed that we have more good writers in this walk, living at the present time . . . than at any time since . . . Richardson and Fielding'. Furthermore, she argues that 'a great proportion' is made up of 'ladies'. These, she claims, have strengthened the novel: 'Surely it will not be said that either taste or morals have been the losers by their taking the pen in hand. The names of d'Arblay, Edgeworth, Inchbald, Radcliffe, and a number more will vindicate this assertion'.[23]

Barbauld is at her most original and bold when treating the modern woman reader. Unlike the vast majority of well-read people in the period, she refutes the notion that women readers are vulnerable to the contemporary novel because the form has become less conspicuously fictive. She argues that the novel, even in its most realistic incarnations, remains unequivocally fictional. And she is broad in her definition of it, embracing Gothic and Oriental novels as well as novels of manners. She describes the delights of reading fiction: 'it is pleasant to the mind to sport in the boundless regions of possibility; to find relief from the sameness of every-day occurrences by expatiating amidst brighter skies and fairer fields'.[24] This was surely the experience of very large numbers of women readers of the period. This unadulterated pleasure is benign because Barbauld's idea of the reader is of one ever alert to the novelist's pen as magic wand. And the intentions of the novelist's magic are equally always before her envisioned reader, no doubt a version of herself. She uses the character of Henry Fielding's Tom Jones to illustrate her point: 'He [the reader] has no doubt but that, in spite of his irregularities and distresses, his history will come to an agreeable termination. He has no doubt that his parents will be discovered in due time'. And why does the reader make these assumptions? 'Not from the real tendencies of things,' Barbauld claims, 'but from what he [the reader] has discovered of the author's intentions'.[25] Readers, whether men or women – she makes no distinction – enjoy the novel but they are also self-aware.

Barbauld also argues for readers' consciousness of the novel's political dimension. Novels show us how societies work but may also suggest how things might be made better. They 'take a tincture from the learning and politics of the time, and are made use of successfully to attack or recommend the prevailing systems of the day'.[26] She proffers a daring example. The French Revolution was inspired not only by political theorists but by writers like Marmontel, who was immensely popular in England, Germany and the United States, and who produced novels which displayed a 'sentiment of toleration, a spirit of free enquiry, and a desire for equal laws and good government across Europe'. The excesses of that period of French history were a breach of 'justice and moderation', but Marmontel's writings stand as important and significant contributions to a better and fairer Europe all the same. This was a bold position to assume. But it underlines her conviction, shared by many, that the novel should have 'some serious end . . . in view'.[27]

44 Richard Samuel, detail from *Portraits in the Characters of the Muses in the Temple of Apollo*, 1778. Barbauld is standing behind the artist Angelica Kauffmann, gesturing with her left hand.

Barbauld's fall from grace was not long in coming and it is representative of the fate of many intelligent women readers of the period who dared to make their views known. Equally telling is the fact that it was a (mere) poem, 'Eighteen Hundred and Eleven', that did for her. Britain had been at war almost continuously with France since 1793 and the country was in a dire state. In her poem Barbauld criticised Britain's involvement in the Napoleonic Wars and predicted that America would soon rise as a global power at the expense of British interests. The predominantly acerbic criticism she excited was a deep shock and she published nothing further in her lifetime. And Scott would soon publish his ten-volume series, *Ballantyne's Novelist's Library* (1821–24), eclipsing Barbauld's monumental work. Women writers are scantily represented by Scott; only Ann Radcliffe and Clara Reeve, the latter almost forgotten today, are included. At the same time a crucial record of one woman's reading disappeared from view.

Barbauld had many friends and supporters (at least until relatively late in life) and was loosely associated with the London Bluestockings, but she largely worked independently. Many women readers of the period were part of more or less formal societies and were both supported and to some degree protected by their numbers. Among these coteries were the famous Bluestockings, who organised conversation evenings with a view to stimulating interesting discussion. Lady Montagu made her house in London's Mayfair the centre of intellectual society, regularly inviting learned women and entertaining political figures like the Conservative Lord Lyttelton, Horace Walpole, who was also notable as an art historian, antiquarian and man of letters, and the writer Samuel Johnson. Hand in hand with the group's intellectual ambitiousness went more than a little ambivalence about the novel. Montagu would ask her sister to send her the latest publications while at the same time expressing a degree of disdain. In a typical letter she remarks, 'I see in the newspapers the names of many novels. I do not doubt, but that the greater part of them are trash, lumber, &c. &c.; however, they will serve to kill idle time.'[28] She was particularly circumspect about women novelists who made a living by the pen. Her argument was that they would be tempted to 'fall into the notions that are most acceptable to the present taste' – in other words, to pander to the majority of their readers, mostly women, many of whom had, in Montagu's view, little education and therefore lacked discrimination.

Other women readers expressed different anxieties about their reading and what others knew of it. Hester Thrale Piozzi, as she has come to be known, was born into a very comfortably-off landowning family in Wales in 1741. She married the rich brewer Henry Thrale in 1763 and they had a large family.

The marriage was unhappy, but they lived in London and Hester entered society, relishing friendships with well-known writers of the day, including Samuel Johnson, James Boswell, Oliver Goldsmith and the aspiring young novelist Fanny Burney. Her husband died in 1781 and three years later she married Gabriel Mario Piozzi, an Italian music teacher. Johnson disapproved – he may himself have been in love with her – and the marriage caused a split between them, with only a partial reconciliation shortly before his death. Burney too thought that Hester had married below her class and the friendship cooled.

Hester Piozzi was a compulsive reader and she had no inhibitions about jotting in the margins of her books, but she kept her habit secret for many years, presumably out of a sense of shame; in 1790 she wrote in her diary, 'I have a Trick of writing in the Margins of my books, it is not a good Trick, but one longs to say something'.[29] Forms of self-censorship are difficult to identify but eighteenth-century women readers still had complicated and sometimes guilty feelings about their reading, and more particularly the freedom they should exercise in relation to the interpretation of a book. Hester should not have felt so intimidated. She was widely read. She knew French, Spanish, Italian and Latin and later picked up some Greek and Hebrew. Samuel Johnson advised her and her first husband on their library. She wrote poetry, travelogues and a memoir of Johnson together with an edition of her correspondence with him. But it was not until much later in life that she 'came out' as a perpetrator of marginalia. It may be that her earlier unease about 'talking' in her books was assuaged by her status as a published author and for this reason she no longer felt she had to hide her 'Trick'.

The jottings in the margins of Hester's own books and those she annotated to give to members of her circle, display her 'chatting' privately with her books and 'chatting' for the benefit of her friends. When she read memoirs that included character judgements of those known to her, she noted her agreement or expressed reservations. For example, she read and heavily annotated Sir William Forbes's *Account of the Life and Writings of James Beattie ... Including Many of his Original Letters* while she prepared her own *Anecdotes of Samuel Johnson*. Forbes's account includes commentaries on many of Hester's own acquaintances including, of course, Boswell. Beattie thought well of Boswell, but Piozzi wrote her own astute comment in the margin: 'I am not convinced of any such Thing. Boswell meant to gain Attention; whether by giving Pain or Pleasure he car'd *not*. Like the Children Rousseau tells of who speak and act all from y[e] Motive of Pourvu qu'on s'occupe d'eux [As long as they attend to us].'[30] The battle of the Boswell biographies – Boswell's and Piozzi's – was a popular subject for contemporary satirists and cartoonists.

Peter Pindar wrote a book about their rivalry, *Bozzy and Piozzi*, which includes a Hogarth engraving depicting them arguing vociferously. Boswell rhetorically asks, 'Who, mad'ning with an anecdotic itch/ Declar'd that Johnson call'd his mother, b–tch?' In Piozzi's *Anecdotes of Samuel Johnson* she quotes Johnson as saying, 'I did not respect my own mother, though I loved her: and one day when in anger she called me a puppy, I asked her if she knew what they called a puppy's mother'.

Piozzi developed into an unusually free-spirited reader with both access to a large library and, in later life at least, the confidence to respond freely to her reading. She was by no means alone. Piozzi's trajectory from inhibited to forthright reader was typical of the general pattern of women readers in the eighteenth century. Some of them, like Piozzi, then became writers.

One of the most celebrated was Charlotte Lennox. Her best-known novel was an answer to Cervantes's *Don Quixote*. *The Female Quixote: or, The Adventures of Arabella* was first published in 1752, and then reprinted and packaged in a series of great novels in 1783, 1799 and 1810. It was equally successful on the Continent, being translated into German in 1754, into French in 1773 and again in 1801, and into Spanish in 1808. Lennox was

45 William Hogarth's eighteenth-century etching depicts Hester Piozzi, Samuel Richardson and James Boswell squabbling.

herself a great reader and women's reading is very much woven into the fabric of her novel. Her heroine, Arabella, expects life to conform to the world of seventeenth-century French fiction: La Calprenède's *Cassandra*, *Cleopatra* and *Pharamond*, and Mlle de Scudéry's *Clélie* and *Artamène, ou le Grand Cyrus*, novels that Lennox had obviously read carefully and critically.

Arabella is the daughter of a marquis who has been alienated from court and forced to retire to the country with his wife. Soon after their arrival in the provinces Arabella is born and a few days later her mother dies. Away from society, and deprived of the crucial influence of a mother, tutors are nevertheless summoned from London to educate the girl in languages, and to teach her music and dancing. Needless to say she develops into an utterly charming and accomplished young lady. However, with too much idle time on her hands and access to her father's extensive library, a corrupting influence begins to take hold of Arabella. She has had free access to a 'great Store of Romances, and, what was still more unfortunate, not in the original *French*, but very bad Translations'.[31] Passages where Arabella recites large chunks of the novels that have led her astray are interspersed throughout the book. Thankfully, Lucy, Arabella's maid, is a wholesome realist and finds her mistress's expectation that she should assimilate the behaviour and conventions of the characters of Arabella's much-loved novels amusing, and utterly absurd. All this comes with considerable comic effect. When Lucy is instructed that under no circumstance must she accept bribes for carrying letters – an occurrence that, to her regret, she has never met with – she nevertheless succumbs without difficulty when the situation arises. Much of the burlesque humour is provided by the ever down-to-earth and quick-witted Lucy.

The novel's hero is the aristocratic Sir Charles Glanville. His rival is the rakish and ridiculous Sir George Bellmour who, like Arabella, reads romances voraciously. Lennox provides a double for Arabella too, in Sir George's sister, the unserious and flirtatious Charlotte. While Arabella initially prefers Sir George, in the end a learned cleric succeeds in helping her to distinguish reality from fantasy, and Arabella marries the patient and loyal Sir Charles. He enters the novel early, naturally falling passionately in love with Arabella, and considering her a woman not only of beauty, but also of wit and learning. But he is expected by Arabella to conform to her heroic ideal, which he singularly fails to do:

> For Heaven's sake, Cousin, replied Arabella, laughing, how have you spent your Time; and to what studies have you devoted all your Hours, that you could find none to spare for the Perusal of Books from which all useful

Knowledge may be drawn; which give us the most shining Examples of Generosity, Courage, Virtue, and Love; which regulate our Actions, form our Manners, and inspire us with a noble Desire of emulating those great, heroic, and virtuous Actions which made those Persons so glorious in their Age, and so worthy of Imitation in ours?

Sir Charles is of course at a loss. Arabella duly lends him the requisite reading material and the long-suffering hero struggles to read and digest numerous lengthy tomes. He ends up cursing the authors whose endless pages have filled the head of the woman he loves – a woman he considers essentially the most accomplished in the world – with such utter silliness. There is humour, but also moments of pathos. Arabella is deluded to the point where she is filled with very real fears. Her imagination is taken up 'with the most extravagant Expectations, she was alarmed by every trifling Incident, and kept in a continual state of Anxiety by a Vicissitude of Hopes, Fears, Wishes and Disappointments'. There is a morbid tragicomedy in Arabella's expectation that Sir Charles, when struck down by illness, be prepared to give up his life for her; 'If he loves me not well enough to die for me, he certainly loves me but little; and I am less obliged to him.' Luckily, he recovers.

Lennox was a professional writer, and making a living was tough. She undertook a great deal of translation work, as this was one way of assuring a reasonably steady income, and she wrote novels, plays and versions of numerous other authors' works, both English and Continental. She never apologised for receiving payment for her work; unlike Lady Montagu, who declared that women who wrote for a living were corrupted, she had no choice. The grand lady of letters was, in a sense, quite right, but it may well be that Lennox was 'corrupted' less directly by the competitive literary market-place, than by her friends' advice as to how best to win popularity in it. The wares that they encouraged her to produce were less exciting than the more daring kinds of books that she might otherwise have penned. Men like Johnson, Fielding and Richardson, all of whom were keen to encourage, guide and support young women writers, had their own ideas about women's fiction which may to a greater or lesser degree have inhibited those women they promoted. Both Johnson and Richardson had read and advised Lennox on her *Female Quixote*. Johnson recommended against a third volume, which Lennox thought necessary to bring about a convincing conclusion. She followed his advice, and thus the novel ends abruptly and unconvincingly. Arabella is 'cured' of her romantic visions – by religion. Anna Barbauld, who as well as being a critic and poet was herself a writer of utopian novels, rightly described the two-volume work as:

Rather spun out too much, and not very well wound up. The grave moral-
izing of a clergyman is not the means by which the heroine should have been
cured of her reveries. She should have been recovered by the sense of ridicule, by falling into some absurd mistake, or by finding herself on the brink
of becoming the prey of some romantic footman, like the ladies in Molière's
Précieuses Ridicules, the ridicule of which has pretty much the same
bearing.[32]

The novel may end conventionally but there are other aspects of it that
reveal Lennox's critical reading of Cervantes's romance. In both works the
characters that surround the quixotic protagonists sometimes confuse fiction
and reality. But in *The Female Quixote* some interesting role reversals take
place. When the characters act out Arabella's imagined fictional scenarios at
her bidding, the men behave in a more 'womanly' manner; they are passive,
obedient and devoted, and Lennox allows them only a single love for their
entire life. Arabella, when she casts herself as heroine, displays certain typically masculine traits; it is she who speaks and controls, and those around her,
including the men, fall into line. The conservative reader of Lennox's novel
may have been comforted by the silliness of Arabella's ways and her subsequent acquiescence. Other readers will have been aware that this is not the
only story in the novel.

Lennox's first works, *Harriet Stuart* (1750) and *Shakespeare Illustrated*
(1755), are rather different. The latter presents daring criticism of many of
Shakespeare's women characters; the former is innovative in terms of its
experimental nature. And Harriet is a very different heroine from Arabella:
intelligent, quick-witted, seductively charming, and above all highly independent. She is unwilling to be compromised by the attitudes of her family,
friends, wider society – or her husband. Lennox's readers, especially women,
assumed that the novel was highly autobiographical, although this was
scarcely the case. However, shrewd as ever, Lennox encouraged this reading,
even inventing fictitious episodes in her own life so as further to encourage an
autobiographical interpretation. Some readers remained circumspect; Bishop
Warburton wrote in a letter, 'Nothing is more public than her writings,
nothing more concealed than her person'. Questions still linger over who
Lennox really was, and what kinds of writing she might have produced had it
not been for the constraints of the contemporary publishing world.

At the heart of this complex of reading and writing novels, were the
questions that Haywood made implicit in the title of her *Anti-Pamela* and
Lennox in her very different *Female Quixote*: the relations between writing
and 'truth to life'. Diderot cleverly pinpointed the capacity of Richardson's

writings, however unintentionally, to leave the reader free to interpret his fictions in a way that made them *true – for them*. Furthermore, Diderot claimed that this made Richardson's (and by implication his own) fictions truer than history, as the truth of novels pertained to both the wider picture and the minutiae of human experience: gesture, expression, even the colour of a flower. Readers of Richardson, Diderot claimed, were able, on the basis of his *plastic* writing, to shape the blood and bones of what became, in effect, their own 'real life' characters. And there is plenty of historical evidence to prove Diderot right, particularly in the letters from Richardson's women readers.

Eighteenth-century women readers engaged with reading in new ways. Rather than reading and re-reading a limited number of books, they started to read more, and more widely. The Enlightenment's emphasis on reason also encouraged more critical reading, and journals and magazines (often barely distinguishable) fed debates about the meaning and relative significance of newly published books. Women's magazines, in particular, would soon become enormously significant cultural forces. *The Lady's Magazine: or Entertaining Companion for the Fair Sex* dominated the market for half a century (1770–1820) and reached almost every middle-class family in Britain. It was also available at circulating libraries (for a small fee), and even coffee-houses. Rather than reproducing unattainable conduct-book ideals, it addressed the woman reader as a player in the economy of books and magazines – and all manner of consumer products coming on the market.[33]

Not unlike today's women's magazines, *The Lady's Magazine* provided a medley of different material: advice columns (in the form of 'The Matron', one of the first agony aunts), gossip pages, theatre and book reviews, serialised fiction, sheet music, articles on fashion (including dress and embroidery patterns) and cookery. Vastly improved transport networks, which in turn provided an efficient postal service, meant that the magazine could be swiftly despatched beyond England, to Scotland, Ireland and America.

This was by no means the first women's magazine, but it was infinitely more successful than its predecessors. It was innovative in publishing a good deal of material by women for women. It was also heterodox in its approach. Unlike all previous magazines, it offered a plethora of material that the reader could make of as she thought fit. Often the same issue would advocate contra-dictory views: a piece on reformed 'rakes' making the best husbands, along-side another warning 'a rake is always a rake', and so on. Fashion articles detailing the latest trends would be published together with ironic articles. Satire was a keystone: models of ludicrous 'effeminacy' were printed alongside pieces advocating more or less the same. All in all it was the magazine's

46 'A Moral Tale', *The Lady's Magazine*, 1776.

freewheeling ethical and political positions that kept its readers coming back for more. There was something for everyone. But above all it provided a forum in which women were encouraged to participate both as readers – and writers.

In March 1789 yet another new series appeared, intriguingly entitled *The Index*. The idea was to create a collaborative 'very great book of the world' to which readers were encouraged to contribute. Women were invited to enjoy all manner of fictional material, but also to consider their own reading by way of satirical material on women readers and 'misreaders', and to contribute to a debate on print culture more generally. Implicit in the broad and heterogeneous make-up of the magazine was a sophisticated female readership, one in which discrimination – whether for books or, in the 1789 edition, 'the newest

Parisian fashions' – was to be encouraged. Readers had never before been given so many steers. And these changes were true of women readers of varied backgrounds, many of whom wrote to the writers and magazine editors of the day in response to what they had made of their reading.

Many of the women with whom Richardson corresponded were relatively untutored and without intellectual pretensions or aspirations, and many were from clerical families. One untrained provincial reader was Jane Johnson (1706–59). She was a great letter-writer and, fortunately, her voluminous correspondence survived the fate of no doubt countless other women readers of her background and time.[34] During this period the postal service vastly expanded and letter-writing became central to the lives not just of the elite but of almost everyone who could write, even with limited proficiency. In fact letter-writing became a crucial way of honing literacy skills which were then passed on to the next generation through family networks of letter-readers.

Jane Johnson's father had been a 'menial estate servant' but he managed to buy land in Warwickshire which was later sold. Jane married Woolsey Johnson, a Cambridge graduate, in 1735. They lived in the small market town of Olney in the northern corner of Buckinghamshire, some fifty miles from London where Woolsey was a vicar. Jane was devout and an avid reader who sought to answer typical questions about how to live – and not to live – through her extensive reading. In the margin of her favourite thriller, the eight-volume *Letters Writ by a Turkish Spy* (fictional letters purporting to have been written by an Ottoman spy in Louis XIV's court), she copied out the phrase, 'This Western World lies drown'd in Wickedness', and then noted in the margin, 'This is the exact picture of Great Britain at this present time Anno Domi 1755. Pray God Grant my sons may escape the contagion, & live Virtuous in a nation flowing with . . . wicked practices. Amen'.[35] The book is supposedly based on real letters and allows the reader to follow the adventures of its Muslim hero as he encounters the hypocrisy of Europe and its religions.

Jane was no scholar of the classical languages and so she tackled the great volumes of history and literature by reading translations and more popular works. Johnson left a record of the core of her reading: 'The Books that are to be Read by All that would be Eloquent, Polite, Genteel & agreeable; Wise in this world, & Happy in the next; are the Bible, Homer, Milton, the Guardians, Spectators and Tatlers. These should be Read over & over again, & short Extracts Learn'd by Heart . . . these are the only Books necessary to be read for improvement, all others only for Diversion. Whoever follows this rule will think justly, & write and talk eloquently'. Jane was a great copier of facts and sayings that she harvested from all manner of books. She was typical in reading for moral and general instruction but she was also quite open about reading for entertainment. In her letters she quotes from her core library, but also from Juvenal's satires and *Plutarch's Lives,* citing Aristotle, Plato, Demosthenes and Theophrastus. Like many of her contemporaries, including Samuel Richardson, she knew the classics through translations and modernisations. Among her more lighthearted favourites are the *Arabian Nights' Entertainments* and Aesop's famous *Fables.* Her letters to women friends and those she received from them are dominated by accounts of the pleasures of current reading and excitement about what will be read next.

Her letters also include little poems, and those to her children include simple stories, usually with a moral end. We see her developing both more sophisticated literacy skills, and literary abilities. This relationship between reading, letter-writing and literature was equally visible among women on the Continent. And for some French women, the line between letter-writing and the writing of epistolary novels blurs. Well-known letter-writers include Mme de Graffigny, Mme de Charrière, Mme d'Epinay, Mme Roland and Mme de Châtelet. Letters allowed women to discuss controversial questions – prompted by their wide reading – about what it meant to be a woman living in France at the time, politics, science and, of course, religion. But for both de Graffigny and de Charrière, letter-writing was crucial to their own writing. Just as Richardson had exploited his readers' responses to his works when they were still hot off the press, so these two women tested out their plots in discussions in their correspondence with friends. Mme de Châtelet depended equally heavily on her friends while experimenting in scientific writing.

Correspondence between women grew in importance throughout the eighteenth century in England and France and also in Germany, Italy, Spain, Russia and America. And the subject of the letters was often women's reading, the pleasures of which are frequently described, moving seamlessly from accounts of reading to personal memoir or political history, from advice to confession or *billet-doux.*

These disembodied networks of exchange make an interesting counterpoint to the social networks of women actually gathered together, whether Bluestockings or participants in other kinds of women's *salons.* Claims that the eighteenth-century French *salon* was the epitome of the intellectual women's reading group are exaggerated. The women who frequented them certainly encouraged writers to produce books more to their liking, refining language and, consequently, manners. After the instabilities of the Fronde years, a period of civil war in the mid-eighteenth century, most *salonnières* expected writers to uphold political stability in the form of the monarchy. All this had the effect of encouraging writers to produce books in which right living was more a matter of social convention than considered morality. Many influential men participated in the *salon* culture, dominating conversation while women entertained. Some of the most interesting writers of the time, Diderot and d'Holbach, to name but two, were considered too dangerous to be admitted.

Most problematic were the slippery conventions that underpinned *salon* conversation. What mattered was to find the *juste milieu*, to avoid controversy, and to interact in a measured, conciliatory way. *Honnêteté*, an almost untranslatable notion, embraced most of the mores of the social group including naturalness (whatever that may be), modesty and propriety, and opposed, above all, the alleged pretentiousness of the *femme savante* ('learned woman'). The novelist Henri Beyle, better known by his pseudonym Stendhal, was not too wide of the mark when he outlined, with typical exaggeration, the topics of *salon* discussion: 'One could talk freely about anything whatever, provided one did not talk about God, or the priests, or the king, or the men of power, or the artists protected by the court, or any part of the establishment . . . or anything which involves the use of free speech'. It was clearly important to be seen to have a copy of this book or that, and the limits on free discussion were many. Conversations about reading under the strict contraints of the *salon* must have seemed more like a linguistic game than an open exchange of ideas about interesting books. By and large the *salon* upheld conservative literary prejudices.

The Spanish *tertulia* were a comparable social phenomenon. Women like Josefa de Zúñiga y Castro, Countess of Lemos, presided over a group called the Academia del Buen Gusto (Academy of Good Taste), one of the most famous Spanish *salons*. Others flourished thanks to the Duchess of Alba and the Countess-Duchess of Benavente. More cosmopolitan *salons* also existed. Mme de Staël's, at Coppet in Switzerland, drew an international coterie of writers, many exiled abroad in the wake of the French Revolution. Other writers, like Mme de Charrière, were also writing from beyond France's borders, and she reflected and wrote, mostly novels and essays, throughout the pre-Revolutionary, Revolutionary and post-Revolutionary period. There is a vast correspondence between de Charrière and James Boswell who highly valued her readings of his works. Her concerns were often associated with religious doubt, but she also read and wrote extensively on the upbringing and education of girls. Like their counterparts within France – Mmes Tencin, de Graffigny, Riccoboni and de Genlis – women in exile were not only avid readers of the novel, but also contributed significantly to its direction, often in more radical ways.

Elsewhere, in Germany for instance, women were encouraged into the world of learning as part of an attempt by the emerging professional classes to create a national culture *à la française*. The term *belles-lettres* came into the German language and clearly signified something different from *Literatur*. In part, of course, it referred to French literature, often in translation, but it also points to the growing audience for books likely to appeal specifically to women. Figures like Christiane Mariane von Ziegler (who provided libretti for Bach), Anna Helena Volckmann, Sidonia Hedwig Zäunemann and Luise Gottsched, read English and French women novelists and wrote against the dominant social order, modelling their writing on 'feminine' French works. Polish-born Gottsched was considered one of Europe's leading intellectual women during her lifetime. She wrote several popular comedies, and translated the *Spectator* (nine volumes, 1739–43), Alexander Pope's *The Rape of the Lock* (1744) and other English and French works. What she chose to translate were works she had enjoyed and admired and which she felt would be important particularly to the escalating numbers of women readers in Germany.

There were also social groups of women readers, as elsewhere in Europe. Margaretha Susanna von Kuntsch was a member of an important literary circle in Altenburg. Three generations of women readers (and some men) were associated with her home there and German variations of the *querelle des femmes* enlivened discussions. Two of her male friends, Jakob Thomä and Johann Sauerbrey, wrote important works encouraging women's proper education. Kuntsch, who used the poetic pseudonym Sylvie, was a poet but hesitated to go into print. When she did, she prefaced her work with the lines: 'Here Sylvie wrote her poet's work/ And dedicated it to none other than her loved ones/ who were true to her: The world is full of danger/ and whoever writes for many/ opens herself to ridicule.'[36] There were plenty of German men of the Enlightenment who frowned on women writers and tried to control or at least direct the reading habits of women close to them. Goethe, whose work was widely admired by women readers in Germany and in translation, wrote while still a student to his sister Cornelia who had been much struck by Richardson's *Sir Charles Grandison*: 'You foolish woman with your Grandison. . . . You must read no more romances. . . . I absolutely forbid it.' Instead Goethe proposed that he would choose extracts from worthy tomes and 'teach her how to read'. This would be 'better . . . for her than twenty novels'.

Despite various attempts to counter women's determination to read freely, by the end of the eighteenth century women were reading everywhere and reading more. One German visitor penned an astonished account of the state of things in Paris:

> Everyone in Paris is reading. ... Everyone, but women in particular, is carrying a book around in their pocket. People read while riding in carriages or taking walks; they read at the theatre in the interval, in cafés, even when bathing. Women, children, journeymen and apprentices read in shops. On Sundays people read while seated at the front of their houses; lackeys read on their back seats, coachmen up on their boxes, and soldiers keeping guard.[37]

With the steady rise of literacy, eighteenth-century women readers were naturally more various than their predecessors. And as the number of novels flooding the market in the last couple of decades of the century rose, so attitudes to it became increasingly polarised. Snobbery among both men and women readers became blatant. In a letter to her friend Catherine Talbot, the earnest Elizabeth Carter wrote, 'Indeed it would be a *pure perte* ['pure loss' (of time)] to spend my time in reading novels . . .; for most of them are so perfectly like the gossiping of the Misses in a country town, that it is only making a few visits, and one may have it all original and fresh'. Reading and class were increasingly associated. Talbot was as straight-laced as Carter. She responded to her reading of Homer's *Odyssey* by writing an essay on 'The Danger of Indulgence of the Imagination'.

The most verbose commentator on the insidious changes in women's reading habits was the moralist Hannah More. Looking back over the changes of the eighteenth century she wrote:

> Sentiment in the present age is the varnish of virtue to conceal the deformity of vice; and it is not uncommon for the same persons to make a jest of religion, to break through the most solemn ties and engagements, to practice every act of latent fraud and open seduction, and yet to value themselves on speaking and writing sentimentally. But this refined jargon, which has infected letters and tainted morals, is chiefly admired and adopted by young Ladies of a certain turn, who read *sentimental* books, with *sentimental* letters, and contract *sentimental* friendships.[38]

Similarly, in 1771, looking back on the changes in servant women's behaviour over the preceding decades, a Viennese author wrote with more than a hint of condescension: 'They also play the part of sentimental souls, demand the right to *belles-lettres*, read comedies, novels and poems conscientiously, and learn entire scenes, passages or verses off by heart, and even argue about the sorrows of young Werther.'[39]

What many commentators remarked on, even conflated, was the emergence of *new* reading classes: those among the 'lower orders', and women. It is clear in the language employed that the emergence of these new groups was perceived as a threat to the status quo. The 'reading habit' is often conjured up as 'a bug', a disease that is so poorly controlled as to lead to an 'epidemic'. James Harris, in his *Hermes* of 1751, recommended those with 'liberal leisure' read the ancient Greek writer Xenophon and avoid 'the meaner productions of the French and English Press . . . that fungous growth of Novels and Pamphlets'.[40]

Metaphors about books being good or bad for the body were widespread. Writing to Elizabeth Montagu, one of the greatest women readers of the age, Elizabeth Carter remarks in a letter of 26 October 1759:

> I have not read the History of the Penitents, except a little extract, with which I was greatly pleased. It is much to be wished indeed that the general fashion of novel reading did not render such antidotes very necessary. Various kinds of antidotes perhaps are necessary to the various kinds of poison imbibed in the study of these wretched books, by which the understanding, the taste, and the heart are equally in danger of being vitiated.[41]

Grander women frequently expressed their contempt for a good many 'popular' novels and implied that fiction was by definition misleading. In letters of the period the 'novel' is opposed to 'history', or 'fiction' to 'truth': 'the historical sketch you sent me turns out to be no more than a novel'; 'would you have me write novels like the Countess of D. . .? and is it not better to tell you a plain truth . . .?'[42] However suspicious some women were of the novel, or claimed to be, it would soon establish itself as the most important genre for women readers and writers. And it was the advent of women entering the publishing world in more significant numbers that changed both the novel, and women's responses to it as a genre. The likes of Eliza Haywood brought about a fundamental change. The novel, she insisted, and she was one of many, must be 'true to life' and true to women's lives as well as men's; many novels by men failed, women claimed, in this fundamental respect.

Whether to be distracted, or to enjoy serious intellectual engagement, women in this period became wholly absorbed in their reading. Anne Bristow, second wife of Francis, First Earl of Effingham, according to an article in the *Scots Magazine*, died in November 1774 'of a shock caused by her clothes taking fire as she was reading in her rooms at Hampton Court'.[43] Very much like today's TV soap operas, women waited impatiently for serialisations of novels to appear: 'We have just finished part of a novel entitled L'Honnête Homme, or the Man of Honour,' opined Mary Delany; 'it is a fine character, but we have left the hero of the story *in so forlorn a condition* that we repent having read it, as we don't hear when the rest will be published'.[44]

Women's reading in the eighteenth century was a subject of almost universal and often extravagant excitement. In part this was a matter of its relation to leisure and social advancement. Enlightenment values further encouraged serious women's reading. And as always reading could threaten the present state of affairs. But one woman reader had a remarkable work written for her that was sober, reasoned, affectionate and prophetic. At the end of the turbulent eighteenth century in France, and shortly before his death, the marquis de Condorcet (1743–94) wrote 'Advice To My Daughter' with only one woman reader in mind. His wife had taken their young daughter to the country for safety in the wake of the Revolution, and Condorcet, deeply attached to his only child, penned five or so pages to her, divided into five sections. Whatever the wider moves afoot in society, and however uncertain the times, Condorcet provides advice on the need for independence, much of which may seem useful to young women – and indeed men – today. He begins affectionately: 'My child, if as a baby you were sometimes comforted by my loving care, and if your heart preserves the memory of those moments, I hope you will place your trust in this advice, which is prompted by my love for you, and that it will help you to find happiness.' He outlines how nothing in the world is certain and that independence is fundamental. His advice is to 'become accustomed to working, so that you are self-sufficient. . . . Though you may become poor, you will never become dependent on others'. Choose, he suggests, something 'which does not occupy the hands alone, but engages the mind'. Secondly, he advises how to use the time remaining after the day's work is done: 'People whose minds are active . . . need to be stimulated by new ideas and impressions.' But he cautions against company as the sole solution:

> If you cannot exist alone, . . . you will find that you are necessarily subject to their tastes and desires. . . . Nothing, therefore, is more vital to your happiness than ensuring that you have some means, entirely dependent on you alone, for filling your spare time, keeping boredom at bay, assuaging your fears and distracting you from painful thoughts. You can only do this . . . by exercising the mind. Ensure that you do so while you are still young.

Again he insists, 'If you do not attain some degree of perfection in these skills, if you do not shape, stretch and strengthen your mind by methodical study, these abilities will be of no use to you; fatigue and disgust at your own mediocrity will soon outweigh your pleasure'.

Economic independence, and attaining a level of education (by methodical study), he placed at the beginning of his 'Advice'. The Women's Liberation Movement of the 1960s placed precisely this emphasis on freedom from dependence – on men. In the sixteenth or seventeenth centuries, an aristocrat like Condorcet might have recommended, in the absence of an appropriate marriage, entering the cloister. But what he advises is first and foremost the training and exercise of the mind through reading.

Particularly in the last quarter of the century, in part in the wake of the French Revolution, the 'woman question' was increasingly debated by philosophers and writers in Europe, many of whom argued for the irrationality of current laws and educational practices and sexual double standards. Many were men: Montesquieu, Voltaire, Diderot, Defoe, Locke, Hume and Condorcet emerged as leading proponents of women's rights. Of course Olympe de Gouges, Mary Wollstonecraft and the Prussian dignitary Theodore Gottlieb von Hippel, in his *Sur l'amélioration du sort de la femme au point de vue de droit de cité* (*On the Improvement of the Plight of Women in Terms of Citizenship*, 1790) had all argued for greater equality in matters educational, economic and even political; their outraged opponents solicited prominent German philosophers, Johann Fichte and Georg Hegel, most famously, to counter their arguments. But even Wollstonecraft's *Thoughts on the Education of Daughters: with Reflections on Female Conduct, in the more important Duties of Life* (1788) stops short of Condorcet's recommendations to his daughter.

Wollstonecraft's title, with its emphasis on the appropriate fulfilment of 'Duty', falls short of the marquis' recommendation for a way of life that allows for full economic independence, allied to the necessary education to read, think and reflect in any remaining leisure time, for the sake of finding happiness, or at least contentment. At one point in her *Thoughts on the Education of Daughters*, Wollstonecraft seems to be moving in a similar direction: 'In a comfortable situation, a cultivated mind is necessary to render a woman contented', she declares. But she is not contemplating the dullness which might result from an idle life: 'A sensible, delicate woman, who by some strange accident or mistake, is joined to a fool or a brute, must be wretched beyond all names of wretchedness, if her views are confined to the present scene. Of what importance, then, is intellectual improvement, when our comfort here, and happiness hereafter, depends on it.' Here, education is presented rather as something of an insurance policy in a worst-case scenario. Wollstonecraft unappealingly emphasises the importance of religion, dogmatically asserted: 'Principles of religion should be fixed, and the mind not let to fluctuate'.

The publication of Mary Wollstonecraft's *Vindication of the Rights of Woman* (1792) was for a long time upheld as a glorious early feminist triumph, providing women with an explanation of how and why they had become the inferiors of men and what they might do to remedy the situation. But this is an exaggeration. Only a few thousand copies of the work were printed during the 100 years after first publication, a figure usually surpassed by novelists and poets like Sir Walter Scott and Lord Byron on the first day of publication. But Wollstonecraft's work would be rediscovered later and then become highly influential.

Lafayette's *Déclaration des droits de l'Homme et du Citoyen* was essentially modern political theory that argued for equality in law, for all citizens, including those at that time excluded: children, criminals, the insane and women. It was widely read by women and men in France and abroad, particularly in America, a country in which both Lafayette and Condorcet took immense interest. Lafayette's was a bold and broad vision; Condorcet's 'Advice' to his daughter is the intimate, personalised version of it. But their ideas would only begin to be more widely held in the nineteenth century, when reading had spread still further. In many parts of the world women readers as well as a burgeoning number of celebrated women writers would soon be as important in the publishing marketplace as men.

CHAPTER 8

Books of Their Own

THE nineteenth century was in many ways a golden age for reading, and for women's reading in particular. Eighteenth-century trends continued to accelerate. The printing and publishing industries expanded, responding to new markets at home and overseas, and meeting the demand from rising numbers of the literate for affordable reading material. Industrialisation brought other changes which were to have a profound effect on reading habits. Gaslights meant that workers, including a growing number of women, were able to read more comfortably than by candlelight in the evenings after a twelve-hour shift in the increasing numbers of factories. Better postal services made it easier to order books and magazines and to correspond about one's reading with family and friends who did not live locally.

These material changes were accompanied by wide-ranging debates about what women (now often bracketed with children and the working classes) should be encouraged to read, or discouraged – even prevented – from reading. One of the most striking phenomena of the nineteenth century was the pervasive anxiety, whether undisguised or more subtly expressed by both men and women, about the access these newly literate groups had to varied reading material. And the growing number of titles written by women was often treated with singular suspicion.

This situation was hitherto unknown and seemingly uncontrollable. The three great revolutions – the American, the French and the Industrial – were all deemed, for better or worse, to have been fuelled by more widespread reading. In their wake, many saw allegedly subversive material as further fanning the flames of change whether social, economic or political. Crucially, all these were deemed to be sure to bring radical changes in terms of how men and women would live alongside one another in national as well as marital

47 *How to Make a Chatelaine a Real Blessing to Mothers.* A 'chatelaine' was a set of small chains attached to a woman's belt designed for keys – not to harness children while reading.

and familial contexts. Women, it was thought, would be tempted to neglect their duties, seduced by engrossing books.

Not all images of the period of women reading were comic. Among the vast and varied range are paintings designed, among other things, to discourage women from reading, particularly novels. In Antoine Wiertz's *The Reader of Novels* of 1853, a naked woman lies on her back, her shoulders supported by a large cushion, with a book held above her head. Beside her are a number of other books. The mirror ensures that little of her body escapes the viewer's gaze. What you do not immediately see, in the shadows at the left-hand edge of the painting, is a small face, and a hand stretching out, gently pushing another book towards the reader. As you examine the face more carefully you see a tiny sharp little horn above his forehead. So here we have the Devil himself, or one of his minions, tempting the woman reader with a supply of popular fiction. The woman is alone, in her own space, with curtains ensuring that she is reading in secret – the implication being that if women are given this kind of privacy in the home, no good will come of it. Women's reading, the novel and sexuality are intimately related. There may even be a

48 Antoine Wiertz, *The Reader of Novels*, 1853.

suggestion that a woman who has a good supply of fiction may be sexually self-sufficient.

Antoine Wiertz (1806–65) was an artist of uneven quality who nevertheless contrived, with the financial assistance of the Belgian government, to build himself a studio in the shape of a Greek temple. His oeuvre embodies the transition from Romanticism to Symbolism. He was fascinated by the macabre and his work now provides amusing insights into contemporary attitudes. The devil attending *The Reader of Novels* speeds the woman on her way to perdition with the mildly erotic novels of Wiertz's contemporary, Alexandre Dumas, famous above all for his novel *The Three Musketeers*.

By the nineteenth century, women's reading of the novel brings the debate on women readers to a climax. Not only do women writers begin to become serious contributors, often writing mainly for women readers; women readers also become the major consumers of fiction. Publications more or less overtly committed to promoting women's reading and education also started to appear. The *Cornhill Magazine* in England was one of the most successful 'family' magazines, also known as 'shilling monthlies', in the mid-nineteenth century.[1] Like other similar publications it included serialised fiction by writers, women and men, including George Eliot, Elizabeth Gaskell and Anthony Trollope, and was affordable for the lower middle class while also appealing to the more affluent. It was conceived primarily as a magazine for women. Other literary reviews at the time tended to be dismissive both of women readers and the contemporary novel. The *Saturday Review* was typical of the literary magazines of the day marketed for the male reader. In an article published in 1857, a reviewer wrote: 'It would be hard to mention a single modern English novelist of eminence who has written either as an artist or a philosopher. They mostly write either in the spirit of pamphleteers, or of tradesmen whose chief object is to sell their goods'. The *Review* was particularly hostile to the *Cornhill Magazine* in part no doubt because some of its authors, including John Ruskin, had switched allegiance to the new publication.

The image of the woman reader promoted by the *Cornhill Magazine* was as a better wife and mother, and a more useful member of society than her less well-read counterpart. William Makepeace Thackeray, the magazine's editor from 1860–62, described its mission in an elegantly indirect fashion: 'There are points on which agreement is impossible, and on these we need not touch. At our social table we shall suppose the ladies and children present.' At the same time he advocated a mixed reading regimen: 'Novels are sweets. All people with healthy appetites love them – almost all women; – a vast number of clever, hard-headed men. . . . Judges, bishops, chancellors, mathematicians are notorious novel-readers; as well as young boys and sweet girls, and their kind, tender mothers.' To ensure a balanced diet he also recommended 'roast', by which he meant factual material to be consumed alongside fiction. And the two were sometimes carefully juxtaposed in a single issue of the magazine. Lord Lufton and Lucy Roberts, characters in Anthony Trollope's *Framley Parsonage*, appeared as examplars in a non-fictional piece on 'Falling in Love'.[2]

Some of the fictional characters in the serialised novels that appeared in the *Cornhill Magazine* were also exemplary educated women: George Eliot's Romola (from the novel of the same name) is both intelligent and educated and devoted to her scholar-father; Elizabeth Gaskell's Cousin Phillis studies Greek and Latin, losing in love but finding consolation in her self-education.

The pre-eminent example is the much-loved Lucy of Trollope's *Framley Parsonage* who is not particularly physically attractive, but is intelligent and bookish and finally wins the man she loves through a combination of patient perseverance and a willingness to help others.

Peculiar circumstances made it easier for the *Cornhill Magazine* to defend its position in relation to women's independence and education. The middle of the nineteenth century saw a rise in the number of older single women. Various factors contributed to this state of affairs but the primary explanation was that middle-class men had started to postpone marriage until their careers were established and their finances on a stable footing. The situation was much discussed, and the essayist and philanthropist W.R. Greg coined the infelicitous term 'redundant women' to designate this growing and problematic group. Clearly they needed to be able to earn their own living and the *Cornhill Magazine* promoted educational and professional possibilities for them. This coincided with the opening of various women's colleges such as Queen's (1848), Bedford (1849), the North London Collegiate School (1850) and the Cheltenham Ladies' College (1853).

Whereas women had previously been able to enter principally only the teaching, writing and acting professions, other opportunities opened in the second half of the century including the medical profession (as both nurses and doctors). There were women scientists as well as women government officials. The *Cornhill Magazine* had helped to shape attitudes and bring about new openings for women's education, and in November 1864, in an article entitled 'Middle-Class Education in England – Girls', Harriet Martineau, who is often described as the first British woman journalist, was explicit in her arguments for the same government funding to be provided for the education of girls and boys: 'there must be tens of thousands of middle-class women dependent on their own industry: and it can hardly be doubtful, even to the most reluctant eyes, that the workers ought to be properly trained to the business of their lives'.[3] But her recommendations in terms of curricula went beyond the necessities of a professional training. She argued that Greek and Latin should be taught to girls, and even claimed that they had a superior natural facility for language learning.

The protofeminism of the *Cornhill Magazine* was tempered by references to the merits of being married to a well-read wife, and the economic benefits to the nation of an educated female workforce at a time of growing international competition. Comparisons were drawn with France and America and the importance of educated women in those economies. In terms of sexual politics, however, the editorial policy remained a parody of the Victorian. Thackeray rejected material by Trollope and George Meredith on the grounds that women readers would be offended. He also turned down Elizabeth Barrett Browning's poem 'Lord Walter's Wife' because it included 'an account of unlawful passion felt by a man for a woman' that would lead to 'an outcry' from the magazine's readers. Browning responded forcefully to the rejection: 'I am deeply convinced that the corruption of our society requires not shut doors and windows, but light and air – and that it is exactly because pure and prosperous women choose to ignore vice, that miserable women suffer wrong by it everywhere'.[4] The arguments taken up by the *Cornhill Magazine*'s authors, both of fiction and factual articles, were typical of more forward-looking contributors to the debate about women's education elsewhere. But fears of changes to the status quo if women were educated and entered the professions – thus threatening the proper fulfilment of their traditional roles and duties, particularly those associated with class – led some individuals and institutions to assume reactionary ideological positions.

The Church, particularly in France, and the medical profession pronounced dire warnings about the consequences of women's widespread access to books and made extravagant claims about the deleterious effects this was having, both on the nation and individuals. The Catholic Church in France mounted an earnest campaign between 1817–30 against what were known as *mauvais livres* (bad books). Voltaire and Rousseau topped the list of the most dangerous, but soon other philosophical publications, novels and indeed all literary works were deemed subversive to Church and State. Some senior clergy criticised these moves and regarded them as an extreme form of anti-intellectual intolerance; the Bishop of Avignon described some of the book-burners as 'cossacks of fanaticism'.[5] But whenever republicanism loomed, the Church would fret over reading material; it held heated discussions with the Republic about school textbooks up until the outbreak of the First World War.[6] These debates made a deep impression on French women, and mothers erred on the side of caution when it came to their daughters' reading.

These battles, whether public or private, conjured an atmosphere in which reading a novel, above all, was by no means universally accepted as a suitable way for a girl or woman to pass her leisure time. Novels were already popular across France, Germany and Italy, but their growing ubiquity was accompanied by discussions, tracts and exchanges of pamphlets all arguing for or against women's access to them, replicating the debates of the *Cornhill Magazine*.

Within the medical profession some physicians continued to express peculiar fears about the effects of reading on women's behaviour and general well-being. The widely-held assumption was that there were fundamental physiological and psychological differences between men and women, and that women's heightened sensibilities made them prone to hysteria and madness. Both these conditions might be induced by excessive and inappropriate reading, particularly of novels.

Robert Carter, a London doctor, counselled on the management of hysteria. Reading, he advised, 'will only be found advantageous under peculiar circumstances. Silent reading encourages reverie; and reading aloud, unless it is particularly well done, is a nuisance to everybody within hearing, while the matter read is at least as likely to be injurious as beneficial'. The professional charged with monitoring the patient should, he advised, watch attentively to see the effects of the patient's reading on mood. If this was not 'satisfactory', attempts should be made to distract the patient from their reading: 'This may be done by obtaining a book upon some practical subject; such, for instance, as bee keeping'.[7] One can imagine the scene: a woman is excitedly reading the climax of a novel only to have the book removed and substituted with a specialist tome on apiary. Surely this would provoke something like a hysterical response in many women readers, regardless of their alleged mental instability.

Some members of the British intelligentsia shared similar convictions. W.R. Greg wrote repeatedly of the dangerous influence of novels on women. His 'most special and preëminent concern' was for the 'correctness of women's feelings and the justice of their estimates'. 'Correctness' and 'justice' according to whose opinion, one might ask? In one of numerous articles, published in the *National Review*, he claimed: 'Novels constitute a principal part of the reading of women, who are always impressionable, in whom at all times the emotional element is more awake and more powerful than the critical, whose feelings are more easily aroused and whose estimates are more easily influenced than ours'.[8]

Some incurably romantic men believed that women's reading of poetry would fashion them into the kind of creatures they ought to be. Charles Fletcher Dole, a Unitarian minister, explained what women of the 'new world' would be like: 'The old world thought of woman as a creature provided for man. . . . The poets and prophets are teaching the world to think of woman as divine and infinite being. . . . Let every woman *pray* to be that which Wordsworth and Lowell saw in their visions, let every man *expect* this noble type of woman, and *the demand shall produce the supply*'.[9] That Dole has recourse to the language of economics is telling: by the mid-nineteenth century, publishing had become a significant sector in the US economy. Some women, however, were far from attracted to this male fantasy. Their reading was not aimed at achieving a metamorphosis into a no-doubt unattainable poetic ideal.

While some men promoted women's reading of the poets, some women were among the most vociferous critics of women reading novels. Many of the women who were notable and highly influential social reformers of the day argued passionately for women's universal education, while supporting the view that the reading of novels should be discouraged, or even prevented. There was a new self-consciousness about the socio-economic and political ramifications of reading – how literacy could change women's lives for the better – which manifested itself in reading programmes promoted by women and new kinds of writings by women authors; these, broadly speaking, were religious and conservative. At the same time, some appealed to a women's literary tradition which had hitherto gone unnoticed. The influence of women's writing on women readers was identified as a key part of 'women's history', itself a new concept.

Elizabeth Fry, of what would become the great Quaker chocolate business empire, was one of a growing group of influential women social reformers and activists, with a particular commitment to the improving powers of appropriate reading for women of all social classes. In *Memoir of the Life of Elizabeth Fry* (1848), she asserts: 'Among the vast changes of the last century, there was no change greater than that which took place in the education of women.'[10] She recognised this shift not in politically-driven educational programmes, but in the homes of the people of England reading magazines and journals:

> Many, as they sipped their coffee, with the *Spectator* of the morning in their hand, were awakened to the consciousness of a higher destiny for women, than the labour of the tapestry frame, or pursuits of an entirely frivolous nature. A taste for reading became more or less general. The heavy wisdom of Johnson, the wit of Swift, the satire of Pope, the pathos of Gray, and the close painting of Goldsmith, found among women not only those who could enjoy, but who could appreciate their different excellencies.

Fry rightly identified magazines as the crucial new influence which often introduced readers to some of the major writers of the day, as well as earlier respected authors. Women writers of the eighteenth century, according to Fry, had also made important contributions, working as an informal collective: 'Mrs. Montague, Mrs. Carter, Mrs. Chapone, with a group of gifted friends and associates, proved to the world the possibility of high literary attainments existing with every feminine grace and virtue.'

Fry was also an inspiration to many other women who were persuaded by her social vision. Significant numbers became involved in the business of raising money and providing reading matter for the 'underprivileged'. They ensured that prisons, hospitals and even some industrial complexes made books available, and above all to women. Fry also inspired Miss Elizabeth Lang Grindrod and Miss McLarene, spinsters of determination and courage. Their primary concern was for the transported prisoners forced to leave their country for their country's good. They committed themselves to providing for both the prisoners' education on the voyage and their reading needs in the penal settlements. In 1818, Elizabeth Fry had turned her attention to the appalling conditions on convict ships and in particular for the welfare of women convicts while in transit. Most of the women who were forcibly deported were illiterate and many – alcoholics, prostitutes and thieves – would have had little choice but to continue to live in the same way upon arrival in Australia. Fry and her supporters believed that the four months of the voyage offered a unique opportunity to transform these women's lives and self-understanding through education. Her work became institutionalised in the form of the Convict Ship Committee, a branch of the British Ladies' Society for Promoting the Reformation of Female Prisoners. Many of the women involved helped financially from afar, but Misses Grindrod and McLarene travelled with the convicts aboard the *Garland Grove* and ran an onboard school for the women and children. Their 'report' for Elizabeth Fry records that the library contained volumes on travel, history, religion and serious poetry, but no 'novels, plays, or other improper books'.[11] Almost all the women on the ship were successfully taught to read, the next task being to ensure there was sufficient appropriate reading material in the penal settlements to continue the good work.

It is tempting to dismiss Fry as an idealist with a somewhat authoritarian desire to impose her vision on anonymous others – that is, women criminals and mostly women of the working classes. But she visited and talked with women in workhouses and prisons and was, it was widely recognised, a good listener. In portraits of the time she appears to be matronly and earnest, but she made things happen and was respected. In 1818 she was invited to address Parliament about her concerns for reforms in women's prisons. She had visited more than a hundred convict ships and regularly visited women in Newgate Prison and read to them. It is true that she was one of many educated women who considered that novels, in the hands of less-educated women, might not be improving, but to bring about what she saw as the most urgent reforms she also had to be realistic about what was attainable in the climate of the day.

In Fry's outline of women's literary history she cited only English women writers. In the wake of foreign revolutions, foreign writers were identified as a pernicious influence on English society:

Like all other changes in society, the opposite extreme was reached, before the right and reasonable was discovered. Infidelity was making slow, though sure advances upon the Continent. Rousseau and Voltaire were but types of

49 Elizabeth Fry reading to the women in Newgate Prison, 1816.

the state of feeling and principles in France. The effects gradually extended to our own country, and England has to blush for the perversion of female talent, the evil influence of which, was only counteracted by shewing as a beacon light, to warn others from shipwreck. Science and philosophy, so called, advanced and flourished, but by their side flourished also the Upas tree [a fatally toxic species] of infidelity, poisoning with its noxious breath the flowers and the fruits, otherwise so pleasant to the eye, and so good for the use of man. The writings of Hannah More, were well calculated to enlighten and improve her sex; she spoke as woman alone can speak to women; but she was then only rising into celebrity, and as an author little known.[12]

Hannah More was writing in part to counter what she, like Fry, perceived as a wave of dangerous and subversive political writing, some of it home-grown. In 1791, Thomas Paine, the radical propagandist and voice of the working classes, had published *The Rights of Man*, a forceful defence of the French Revolution. It sold somewhere in the region of a million copies. As Fry made clear, More set out to provide edifying reading for 'her sex': salutary literature which upheld both Church and Nation. Her 'Cheap Repository Tracts' sold for either a halfpenny, or a penny and a half, per copy. Interestingly, we know that one of her humble readers, Henrietta Harrison, who made no literary contribution of her own, did not read More's *Practical Piety* (1821) right through but selected chapters which were of personal relevance. Between 1828 and 1845 she re-read those that she found most instructive or comforting. The chapter on 'True and False Zeal' she read four times and the chapter entitled 'Cultivation of a Devotional Spirit' no less than seven times.[13] Extensive reading had not altogether replaced intensive reading for less privileged women, but titles like More's, aimed specifically at women readers, were widely available and affordable.

Towards the middle of the century there was general acceptance of the usefulness of women's literacy. Novels, particularly by women, remained contentious, but women's literacy was now generally seen as a good thing. Many considered that a new workforce including educated women was important for wealth-creation and the strength of the nation. This awareness was first visible in England. Mounting international economic competition encouraged the growing enfranchisement of women into office work. When Catherine Napier's *Women's Rights and Duties Considered with Relation to her Influence on Society and on Her Own Condition. By a Woman* was published anonymously in 1840, reviewers were explicit in their admiration. One commented:

This is a well-written and valuable book, on one of the most important subjects that can engage the citizens of a free state. . . . Once upon a time, it was the fashion to sneer when female education was mentioned. . . . Their education was confined within the narrowest limits, and their characters received an impress of frivolity which we have no warrant for supposing that nature intended they should bear. It was impossible that society should not suffer from the backward state of mental cultivation in which half its members were kept, and the injustice done to women in cramping their intellects and narrowing the sphere for exerting them produced the consequences that were to be expected in the erroneous training of the men.[14]

The reviewer goes on to remark on the tangible benefits already visible as a function of educating women: 'It is observable that the increase of our national strength and greatness has kept pace with the diffusion of sounder opinions on the rights of women, and the duties which the character of their minds and the station they fill in the scale of being fit them for discharging.'

Some women readers did not agree that the novel as a genre should be written off. Instead they set out to provide readers with something more nourishing than the Continental novels which were often seen as potentially morally and politically subversive, if not irreligious. Women who found Continental fiction mildly shocking included highly intelligent and well-read readers. Jane Austen often read within her family and on one occasion Mme de Genlis's sentimental novel, *Alphonsine*, was their chosen book. The heroine errs after the non-consummation of her marriage and has an illegitimate daughter. She is forced underground – quite literally – and spends years in the darkness with her child, doing all she can to bring her up to be educated and morally upright. Austen wrote of the novel: 'We were disgusted in twenty pages as, independent of a bad translation, it has indelicacies which disgrace a pen hitherto so pure; and we changed it for [Charlotte Lennox's] the *Female Quixote* which now makes our evening amusement, to me a very high one'.[15]

There were plenty of successful women novelists critical of the 'indelicacies' of foreign fiction by women, and concerned instead to encourage a useful life and service to others, using the novel as the vehicle. Some of these writers attracted admirers ranging from bishops and statesmen to vast numbers of the Great British Public. Two of the most celebrated were Marie Corelli and Mrs Humphry Ward. And it is not altogether a coincidence that they were both women. For all manner of tedious social reasons, Victorian women were deemed to 'speak from the heart' in a way which would have been frowned upon in a man.

It would be an understatement to describe Ward and Corelli's novels as dated. Yet at the same time they displayed something new: they read in part as psychological sketches which dispensed with some of the repressive circumlocution – and stuffiness – of Victorian writing conventions. Corelli was wonderfully straightforward about her method, and implicit in it was the key to her extraordinary popular success. In 1886 she published her first novel, *A Romance of Two Worlds*, which she described in these terms:

I attribute my good fortune to the simple fact that *I have always tried to write straight from my own heart to the heart of others*. . . . 'A Romance of Two Worlds' . . . was the simply worded narration of a singular psychical experience, and included certain theories on religion which I, personally speaking, accept and believe. . . . Once published, the career of the 'Romance' became singular, and totally apart from that of any other so-called 'novel'. It only received four reviews, all brief and distinctly unfavourable. . . . Ignored by the press, it attracted the public. Letters concerning it and its theories began to pour in from strangers in all parts of the United Kingdom.[16]

Among her extensive readership were thousands upon thousands of so-called ordinary readers. But many of her admirers were as establishment as could be:

the Prince of Wales, the deans of Gloucester and Westminster, the renowned preacher Father Ignatius (known as a 'prophet in his generation'). Queen Victoria herself was a devoted admirer, as was Alfred Lord Tennyson. Corelli's women readers came from diverse social backgrounds. The Duchess of Sutherland wrote in a letter to a friend, 'I have dinner on a tray [and], in between mouthfuls of fried sole and partridge, read [Ruskin's] Sesame and Lilies [1865] and [Corelli's] Barabbas by turn.'[17] The best-selling American poetess and writer Ella Wheeler Wilcox was one of Corelli's most celebrated women supporters; her best-known work was *Poems of Passion* and her most enduring poem was 'Solitude', which contains the famous lines, 'Laugh, and the world laughs with you; Weep, and you weep alone'. The critics were dismissive of both women writers.

Some readers were similarly critical. The novelist Margaret Oliphant thought Corelli's novels were derivative, explaining in a letter: 'I suppose there was no man who had a greater command of the public in his day [than Bulwer Lytton]. To be sure, one might say the same of Miss Marie Corelli, who, by the way in the only book of hers I can read, seems to be founded upon Bulwer.'[18] Gladstone's well-read daughter Mary, and her husband the Revd Harry Drew, read Corelli's novel *Vendetta* together in 1887. She commented in a letter, 'goodish plot but rather rot'. More highbrow critics lampooned Corelli and expressed their aversion for the melodrama of her writing. She was also criticised for recurring themes throughout her books which attempted to reconcile Christianity with Eastern ideas of reincarnation, out-of-body projection and other mystical topics.

But Corelli's novels were widely considered safe reading for women and older girls; so too were those by the more earnest Mrs Humphry Ward. Mary Augusta Ward began her career as a writer of articles for *Macmillan's Magazine*, also writing a children's novel, *Milly and Olly*, published in 1881. There followed a number of novels for adults, especially women, which were religious and upheld conservative Victorian values. Like Corelli's readership, Ward was read by women of every social class. She made a deep impression on Hannah Mitchell, a farm labourer's daughter:

> One of them [some guests in the area] asked me if I was fond of reading and told me that she herself wrote books and was staying in the neighbourhood hoping to include the dale in her next book. Many years afterwards I read *The History of David Grieve* and at once remembered our visitor. Comparing dates I realised it was Mrs Humphry Ward, seeking the atmosphere of the wild valley she described so well.

But not all her readers were enthusiastic. Gertrude Bell, the writer and traveller, wrote of the same novel:

I am longing to hear what you think of D.G. [*David Grieve*]. I read the first volume this morning – oh! how dull it is, how dull! how full of unnecessary detail, how flatlessly and pointlessly written! I like some of the childhood scenes, though I thought them nearly all in a measure spoilt by too great length and by that absolute want of humour which is characteristic of her. And why all that foolish ghost episode that leads to nothing, and why all those useless illnesses and deaths, and why all those long stories of the birth and parentage of each character? Then the Manchester part is awfully feeble and uninteresting – no I cannot think it will catch on even with the B.P. [British Public]. And all written with such effort and such painstaking – that's the pity of it. I'm bound to say however that I think the English is very slipshod.[19]

Ward's books were very popular in Britain, however, and positively best-selling in the United States. According to the *New York Times*, her novel *Lady Rose's Daughter* outsold any other in the United States during 1903; the same was true of *The Marriage of William Ashe* published two years later.

Ward's most successful work in Britain was her religious novel *à thèse*, *Robert Elsmere*, published in 1888, which quickly sold more than a million (authorised) copies; like so many bestsellers of the day, sales of the unauthorised pirated editions probably matched or surpassed those of legitimate editions. The story tells of an early Victorian clergyman whose faith begins to be shaken by his reading of German philosophy, particularly the Rationalists Friedrich Wilhelm Joseph Schelling and David Strauss. But it is also the story of the emotional conflict that arises between the young pastor Elsmere and his wife, whose dogmatic, unquestioning faith and narrow orthodoxy brings their mutual love to an impossible impasse. Elsmere resists both atheism and Roman Catholicism and instead is drawn to 'constructive liberalism' (which Ward had read of in the works of Thomas Hill Green), which stressed good works, especially among the disadvantaged and uneducated. Ward was also influenced by her uncle, Matthew Arnold, and his vision in both his poetry and essays. Although she was hugely popular she did met with criticism. Oscar Wilde quipped that her novel was 'simply *Literature and Dogma* [by Arnold] with the literature left out'.

Many of Ward's other works attracted the admiration of notable women readers. The social reformer Beatrice Webb wrote enthusiastically to her in September 1896 about her novel, *Sir George Tressady*:

the story is very touching and you have an indescribable power of making your readers sympathise with all your characters, even with Letty and her unlovely mother-in-law. Of course, as a strict utilitarian, I am inclined to estimate the book more in its character of treatise than as a novel. From this point of view it is the most useful piece of work that has been done for many a long day. You have managed to give the arguments for and against factory legislation with admirable lucidity and picturesqueness – in a way that will make them comprehensible to the ordinary person without any technical knowledge.[20]

Ward practised what she preached and helped to establish an organisation promoting education among the poor. She also worked as a teacher in the settlements she founded in London, first at Marchmont Hall, in Marchmont St, and later in Tavistock Place, Bloomsbury. Her declared aim was what she termed 'equalisation' in society. But for all her commitment to equality, she had little sympathy for the Suffragettes. In fact she went on to become one of the founders of the Women's National Anti-Suffrage League in 1908, and chaired its Literary Committee. Its remit was to warn readers of material which supported – explicitly or implicitly – women's suffrage, and to promote writings which convincingly shored up the status quo. Ward, like Fry and her followers, was not alone in her commitment to censoring nineteenth-century women's reading, and this took different and sometimes comical forms.

Some went along with the prevalent idea that women's minds and decorum could all too easily be corrupted by inappropriate reading. Henrietta Bowdler was the spinster sister of the more famous Thomas Bowdler who until relatively recently received full credit – or blame – for the expurgation of Shakespeare's plays which Henrietta had actually undertaken. *The Family Shakespeare* was first published anonymously in 1807, containing twenty-four of the plays. The idea behind it was explained in the preface. The editor, readers were told, had 'endeavoured to remove every thing that could give just offense to the religious or virtuous mind'. In 1818, Longman, Hurst & Co. of London published *The Family Shakespeare, in Ten Volumes; in which nothing is added to the original text; but those words and expressions are omitted which cannot with propriety be read aloud in a family*, this time naming Dr Thomas Bowdler as the sole editor. By the 1820s more people were reading and looking for material that could be read within the family. Interest in *The Family Shakespeare* rose steadily.

It was fuelled by differences of critical opinion expressed in the two most important reviews of the day, *Blackwood's Magazine* and the *Edinburgh Review*. While there had been a number of negative reviews when the first edition came out, there were more when the second edition was published. In

February 1821, *Blackwood's* disparaged the new edition, describing it as 'that piece of prudery in pasteboard', and going on to take a stand against all forms of expurgation. Characteristically, if *Blackwood's* condemned a publication, the *Edinburgh Review* would come out in favour of it. This time they referred to *The Family Shakespeare* as a 'very meritorious publication', claiming that it made 'other editions of Shakespeare . . . obsolete'. The wars between reviewers of *The Family Shakespeare* brought it to the attention of a very wide public and sales consequently soared. By 1850, eleven editions had been printed, testifying to its huge commercial success.

Each play was preceded by an introduction that summarises and justifies the changes made to the text. Most of the alterations and excisions were to references of a sexual nature. In *Romeo and Juliet*, for example, Mercutio's line, 'the bawdy hand of the dial is now upon the prick of noon' (Act II, Scene iv), is replaced by the line, 'the hand of the dial is now upon the point of noon'; Juliet's 'Spread thy close curtain, love performing night' (Act III, Scene ii), becomes 'and come civil night'. Some lines were deemed best omitted altogether. Iago's line in *Othello*, 'Even now, now, very now, an old black ram/ Is tupping your white ewe. Arise, arise!' (Act I, Scene i), was excised in its entirety. The verb 'to tup' describes the act of a ram inseminating a ewe.

Although the first *Family Shakespeare* was published anonymously, many assumed that Thomas Bowdler was its editor, and brother and sister did nothing to disabuse their readers. It protected Henrietta from public knowledge that she, an unmarried woman of some social standing, knew enough – particularly about sexual improprieties – successfully to have edited Shakespeare. But the verb ('to bowdlerise') that resulted from the Bowdler enterprise is as much Henrietta's legacy as her more famous brother's. In one sense Henrietta is an example of a 'secret' woman reader. Many nineteenth-century women readers had access to a wide range of material, but some exhibited different kinds of inhibition about their reading and sometimes sought forms of concealment of one kind or another.

At the same time women's own accounts of their attitudes to their reading proliferated. Some were bold and open about their responses, particularly in letters and diaries. Much of the mannered conformism expressed by women readers in the eighteenth century fell away and women began to express more confident, individualistic and sophisticated accounts of what they had read. Some women were of course writer-readers and Jane Austen's family, for example, spent a good deal of time in shared reading. Jane was often wonderfully forthright in her responses: 'Ought I to be very much pleased with *Marmion* [by Sir Walter Scott]? – as yet I am not. – James [Jane's eldest brother] reads it aloud in the Even^g'.[21]

New classes of women readers also emerged and some expressed their views with refreshing directness. Harriet Martineau was born in 1802 into a middle-class family. She was an ardent campaigner for the abolition of slavery and the rights of women, and friend of a remarkable group of writers and thinkers of the day including John Stuart Mill, George Eliot, Edward George Bulwer-Lytton, Elizabeth Barrett Browning, Thomas Carlyle, Florence Nightingale and Charlotte Brontë. She railed against the submissive position in which women were so often obliged to live – and worse still, to think. She wrote contemptuously of the conventions that dictated the reading habits of a woman: 'She was expected to sit in her parlour with her sewing, listen to a book read aloud, and hold herself ready for [female] callers. When the caller came conversation often turned naturally on the book just laid down, which must therefore be very carefully chosen lest the shocked visitor should carry to the house where she paid her next call an account of the deplorable laxity shown by the family she had left.'[22] Reading aloud was still highly popular and, of course, could also be a form of family censorship.

Later in her life Martineau reflected on how her attitudes to reading had changed with age: 'I could not now read "Lalla Rookh" through before break-fast, as I did when it appeared. I cannot read new novels . . . while I can read with more pleasure than ever the old favourites, – Miss Austen's and Scott's. My pleasure in Voyages and Travels is almost an insanity'.[23] Women readers like Martineau had become highly self-conscious in terms of their reading and its significance in their lives. Life's stages are recognised as marked by particular books which were read in distinctive ways – in a rush of excitement – or re-read. And different kinds of books are understood as more or less appropriate to the different ages of a woman's life. For Martineau, contemporary fiction would seem to have become less important to her as an older reader, and been replaced by the re-reading of 'old favourites' and by travel writing.

Like Martineau, Lady Louisa Stuart was aware that her responses to reading and re-reading were conditioned by considerations outside herself. Stuart was one of many women readers who corresponded with Sir Walter Scott, one of the most successful writers of the age. In one letter, Stuart reveals her sophisticated understanding of the affective power of the novel, and how that power was intimately bound up with the emotional culture of the moment:

One evening a book was wanted to be read aloud, and what you said of Mackenzie made the company choose *The Man of Feeling* though some apprehended it would prove too affecting. However, we began, I, who was the reader had not seen it for several years, the rest did not know it at all.

I am afraid I perceived a sad change in it, or myself – which was worse; and the effect altogether failed. Nobody cried, and at some of the passages, the touches I used to think so exquisite – Oh Dear! They laughed. ... Yet I remember so well its first publication, my mother and sisters crying over it, dwelling upon it with rapture! And when I read it, as I was a girl of fourteen not yet versed in sentiment, I had a secret dread I should not cry enough to gain the credit of proper sensibility.

She continues:

The circumstance has led me to reflect on the alterations of taste produced by time. What we call the taste of the Age, in books as in anything else, naturally influences more or less those who belong to that Age, who converse with the world and are swayed by each other's opinions. ... In my youth Rousseau's *Nouvelle Heloïse* was the book that all mothers prohibited and all daughters longed to read: therefore, somehow or other they did read, and were not the better for it if they had a grain of romance in their composition. Well! I know a young person of very strong feelings – one of 'imagination all compact', all eagerness and enthusiasm. She lately told me that she had been trying to read the *Nouvelle Heloïse*, but it tired and disgusted her, so she threw it by unfinished. I was heartily glad to hear it; but, I own, a good deal surprised, for if she, the same she, had lived fifty years ago, she would have been intoxicated and bewildered and cried her eyes out.[24]

These insights, among many, helped Scott to ensure that he satisfied his important female readership, attending very much to 'the taste of the Age'. But Lady Louisa's description also exposes how women's anxieties about responding with appropriate 'sensibility' began to be replaced by a more straightforward and relaxed attitude. Gradually what might be called a more natural response to reading supplanted the need to be seen to respond as female friends or family expected. In addition, as the number of available titles rose, women no longer felt compelled to be seen to be reading the book of the moment.

Jane Carlyle's openly confessional attitude to the experience of reading fiction is also distinctively nineteenth-century. She belonged, broadly speaking, to the middle class and was unhappily married to Thomas Carlyle. She wrote 'The simple Story of my own first Love' in 1852. It was a somewhat pathetic attempt to make sense of her life. But her vast correspondence and her journal give better insight into her remarkable spirit. Books were her greatest solace and she described reading borrowed novels quite openly as 'like having an illicit affair'.[25] Perhaps she felt that the shared experience of reading the same novel – of holding the same physical object in her hands – created an intimate relationship between the novel's owner and herself; and all the more so if the fictional work was about forbidden love.

Increasing numbers of middle-class and working women began openly to describe their pleasure in reading fiction, the usefulness of all manner of manuals (on cookery and gardening, for instance), and a new sense of solidarity with women elsewhere in the world and from the past. This idea of connectedness with other women – across space and time – was life-changing for many. Olive Schreiner's autobiographical novel, *The Story of an African Farm*, for example, tells the story of a spirited young woman, Lyndall, living on an isolated ostrich farm, who struggles to take control of her own fate. It was published in England in 1883 and it sold well both in Britain and America, the author being hailed by the editor of *The Pall Mall Gazette* as 'the only woman of genius South Africa has produced'. Schreiner's book was read by a large and varied readership, including the writer, feminist and pacifist Vera Brittain, famous above all for her autobiographical *Testament of Youth* (1933). In it, Brittain acknowledged the deep impression Schreiner's novel had made on her in her childhood: 'I spent a good many troubled, speculative, exciting hours with the little volume clasped in my hands.'[26] It was widely read among all classes. In her memoirs, Mary Brown – to whom Schreiner dedicated her *Story* – described a Lancashire working woman telling her, 'I read parts of it over and over'; when asked which parts they were, she replied, 'About yon poor lass [Lyndall]. . . . I think there is a hundred of women what feels like that but can't speak it, but she could speak what we feel'.[27] The frankness of the Lancashire woman's account of her sense of identification with the novel's brave but disadvantaged heroine combines with an acute understanding of the way in which reading puts us in touch with experiences and feelings that we may not, ourselves, be able to articulate.

Women writing to friends often commented with approval if one of their maids took an interest in reading. Elizabeth Barrett (later Barrett Browning) wrote delightedly to her friend and fellow writer, Mary Russell Mitford, in 1841 to tell her of her maid's pleasure in reading Mitford's novels: '[Crow] is an excellent young woman – intelligent bright-tempered & feeling-hearted, – more to me than a mere servant; since her heart works more than her hand in all she does for me! And her delight in your Village [*Our Village*] I gave her to read, was as true a thing as ever was that of readers of higher degree. She says to me that if we go to Reading, she means to visit the Village, and will know every house in it just as if it were an old place to her!' In a letter to a friend, the journalist Helena Swanwick discussed the inadequacies of a string of domestic servants whom she had employed in the 1890s, adding: 'The best I had in those years was a young Welshwoman, who read the novels of Meredith ... and enjoyed them.'[28] George Meredith, Victorian novelist and poet, far ahead of his time, regarded women as wholly the equals of men.

Women in rural areas took a similar delight in reading and expressed their enjoyment with the same lack of inhibition. The daughter of an artisan in the Vaucluse in southern France, born at the turn of the century, described her own and other women's reading and how it differed from men's. Unlike the male members of her family who read the political and sporting sections of newspapers, she and her women friends would extract the serials of novels: 'I would cut out and re-bind the instalments from the paper. We'd pass them among the women. On Saturday night the men would go off to the café and the women would come to play cards at our place. Most importantly, we'd swap our instalments, things like *Rocambole* and *La porteuse de pain*.'[29] Pierre Alexis Ponson du Terrail's Rocambole was an adventurer and his exploits eventually filled six large volumes. The novels represent an important moment of transition from the Gothic novel to modern heroic fiction. Indeed, the word *rocambolesque* came into the French language (and others) to define any kind of fantastic adventure.

Serial publications of this kind were becoming increasingly sensitive to reader satisfaction as the numbers of sales of a particular issue were carefully monitored by the publishers. Sales dropped dramatically when the orphan-adventurer Rocambole failed to transform more rapidly into the do-gooding hero readers had expected. Ponson du Terrail was forced rapidly to reissue the number having re-created his hero to his readership's liking. This kind of flexibility to market demand was, of course, a source of anxiety to those who saw the primary function of reading as 'improving'. Xavier de Montrépin's *La porteuse de pain* (*The [Female] Bread-carrier*) came out in 1884 and also proved immensely popular. It is another adventure story and tells of a young widowed heroine wrongfully accused of killing her employer and burning down his factory where she worked. She is sentenced to life imprisonment. Twenty years later she escapes, assumes a new identity and sets out determined to find the real culprit. These two novels, read by the women of the Vaucluse, are typical of the stories that proved so popular to the newly literate in those parts of the world where reading was rapidly gaining ground. The Vaucluse women, like vast numbers of women readers elsewhere in the world, most likely never owned a book but created their own homespun copies and lent and borrowed among themselves, creating a tight-knit reading group.

Increasingly, more loosely-knit reading groups appeared, based on the new ease of corresponding with readers in other parts of the country and overseas.

People started to travel abroad more often, and the growing number of translations meant that there was more reading across national borders too. Of course there were purists like the writer Chateaubriand who doubted whether it was possible to translate a literary work from one language to another: 'In a living literature, no-one is a competent judge except of those works in his own language. You believe in vain that you possess instinctively a foreign idiom, someone else's breastmilk. ... The more intimate, individual, national the talent, the more its mysteries elude the mind that is not a *compatriot* to this talent. ... Style is not cosmopolitan like thought: it has a native land, a sky, a sun all of its own.'[30] On the whole, women had a somewhat different attitude believing, more or less consciously, that there was a woman's language in novels by women which transcended national tongues.

While Fry railed against the woeful influence of Voltaire and Rousseau in England, some French women recognised the originality of English women writers and the potential they had to sell to French readers, women above all. Yet while French-speaking women read and admired British novelists they also showed a certain lack of respect and restraint in translation. The Swiss writer Isabelle de Montolieu, for example, in her 'Translator's Preface' to *Raison et Sensibilité, ou Deux Manières d'Aimer* (Austen's *Sense and Sensibility*), admits to having followed '[her own] custom' and 'made some small changes' that she considered necessary. She, or her publisher, also indicated to the reader that the novel had been 'liberally' translated from the English. Publishing in 1815, de Montolieu is highly conscious of contemporary national differences: 'Perhaps it is not yet the moment to offer reading material which so little calls to mind all the disturbances delivered up to us [the French Revolution], and which doesn't even offer the least political allusion.' But the translator is clear about the changes in the novel form which this book represents: 'English novelists no longer lead their readers in underground passages, in hideaways, in castles with double walls ... their current novels enter too much into the circle of real life.' The 'hideaways' in this novel are metaphorical: they are women's hearts and minds. As *Sense and Sensibility* was published anonymously, de Montolieu claims that she has no idea who its author was, but adds, 'there is no doubt that she could only be a woman; a man would not have known how to capture these nuances, develop these feelings, penetrate the heart of woman with so much detail and truth. There are *hiding-places* of which men are unaware, however able they may be, of which only a woman knows the secret.'[31]

De Montolieu encouraged her readers to consider the merits of a new kind of English writing, one that had shaken itself free of the excesses and exaggerations of the Gothic tradition. On the other hand, Elizabeth Barrett

Browning, writing from Italy to her friend Mary Russell Mitford in 1847, expressed her pleasure in French authors: 'At Pisa, Robert read to me while I was ill [after a miscarriage], & partly by being read to & partly by reading I got through a good deal of amusing French book-work, & among the rest, two volumes of Bernard's new ["]Gentilhomme Campagnard." Rather dull I thought it, but clever of course – dull for Bernard. Then we read "Le Speronare" by Dumas – a delightful book of travels.' However, Elizabeth bemoaned the state of her host nation's literature. She and her husband had been lent a copy of *Niccolò dei Lapi* by an Italian professor who called on them while they were 'reading, sighing, yawning' over the book; 'he [the professor] called it "excellent, très beau," one of the very best romances, upon which, of course, dear Robert could not bear to offend his literary and national susceptibilities by a doubt even. I, not being so humane, thought that any suffering reader would be justified (under the rack-wheel) in crying out against such a book, as the dullest, heaviest, stupidest, lengthiest.' Elizabeth goes on to decry the library: 'the catalogue . . . offers a most melancholy insight into the actual literature of Italy. Translations, translations, translations from third and fourth and fifth rate French and English writers, chiefly French; the roots of thought, here in Italy, seem dead in the ground. It is well that they have great memories – nothing else lives.' In another letter to Miss Mitford, she again complains of the dearth of any decent books: 'What is purely Italian is, as far as we have read, purely dull and conventional. There is no breath nor pulse in the Italian genius. Mrs Jameson writes to us from Florence that in politics and philosophy the people are getting alive – which may be, for aught we know to the contrary, the poetry and imagination leave them room enough by immense vacancies.'[32]

Elizabeth was also typical of many women readers of the period in her impatience to read works about which she had heard. In a characteristic exchange with Mitford, she wrote: 'You have not read all Tennyson's poems – neither have I – but did you see his "mermaid" at the end of Leigh Hunt's paper on mermaids in the New Monthly Magazine? . . . I am very anxious to read something besides – having seen in Saunders & Ottley's catalogue of new publications – *A new novel by Miss Mitford*. How long are people to stand on tiptoe waiting for it?'[33]

Mary Russell Mitford was born in 1787 in Alresford, Hampshire, and boarded at the St Quintins' school in Chelsea (the successor to the Abbey School in Reading where Jane Austen had been a pupil).[34] She was a particularly gifted linguist and became a lifelong enthusiast of French literature. She returned home in 1802 and continued to read widely, particularly novels and drama and in her late teens started to publish poetry. Her father's extravagances led to the ruin of the family's finances and it was Samuel Taylor Coleridge who advised her to write historical tragedies with a view to making enough money to support her parents. She enjoyed much success and became something of a name. Mitford kept up a voluminous correspondence with her many literary, musical and artistic friends and acquaintances, including William Harness, Thomas Noon Talfourd, Henry Chorley, Harriet Martineau, John Ruskin and, most importantly, Elizabeth Barrett, whom she first met in 1836 and with whom she shared a devotion to French books.

Mitford also wrote stories for the *Lady's Magazine* in the early 1820s, one of an ever-rising number of publications aimed at the rapidly growing market for women's reading. Sales of the magazine increased dramatically as a result of her contributions, which were collected in the first volume of *Our Village: Sketches of Rural Character and Scenery* (1824). This sold well and a second edition appeared only four months later, with further volumes following. *Our Village* was, Mitford claimed, 'an attempt to delineate country scenery and country manners, as they exist in a small village in the south of England'. Harriet Martineau called it 'graphic description'. Some reviewers criticised Mitford's treatment of humble rural scenes, which were deemed unsuitable for ladies; most readers found her writing refreshingly true to their own experiences. *Our Village* established Mitford as an author, an acceptance that came more easily as a woman author of country sketches than as a tragic dramatist, an area of publishing still dominated by men.

Mitford's broad social canvas attracted readers from all classes both in England and America, and primarily women. At the end of her life she published *Recollections of a Literary Life* (1852), versions of pieces published in the *Lady's Companion* in 1850–51 or based on earlier letters. This was 'an attempt to make others relish a few favourite writers as heartily as I have relished them myself'.[35] She included extracts from a wide range of British and American literature along with reminiscences and observations of local life. Mitford was one of a growing number of keen women readers who came to writing out of financial necessity and who staunchly promoted women's reading. Writings like Mitford's appealed both to urban women and the growing numbers of women readers in the countryside.

By the middle of the nineteenth century, working women across Northern Europe, America, Australia and Japan were becoming committed readers of idealised accounts like Mitford's, and above all novels, mostly as a function of the rise of affordable newspapers and magazines that published fiction in serial form. While there was growing awareness of national literary differences, there was also concern that increasingly powerful and international commercial pressures were driving a wedge between reading material that was more accessible and more immediately satisfying, and that which took more time and reflection.

In 1848, the shrewd news-vendor businessman William Henry Smith (he of W.H. Smith fame) bought the rights to set up book and newspaper stands in the railway stations across England, aware that train-travel offered a new captive market: large numbers of people constrained to hours of leisure. Similar initiatives were later undertaken in railway stations elsewhere in Europe and America. Reading during railway journeys and while waiting to board a train required material that was longer than a periodical instalment, but shorter than, say, a Trollope novel. Ten years into his new venture Mr Smith introduced 'yellow-backs', cheap shilling novels. George Routledge soon introduced a rival 'Railway Library' series. It was the Bulwer Lyttons and Harrison Ainsworths that profited, as their work was immediately accessible, and the novelists better known now, the Anthony Trollopes and George Eliots, were little affected.

50 Edouard Manet, *The Railway*, 1872–73. The little girl is presumably looking at a train that is belching out steam while the woman has looked up from her reading.

Sir Walter Scott was explicit in his judgement of the likes of Lytton: 'There is, I am sorry to say, a slang tone or morality which is immoral.' It was Lytton who discovered 'uplift', that device that makes acceptable a character or event that one's animal instincts urge one to enjoy, but which one's 'civilised' self would normally take exception to. It is the key to popular entertainment whether in fiction, film or today's real-time strategy games. In the nineteenth century, uplift was often used to distract the reader from the idealisation of a criminal or, seemingly, to excuse a woman's immorality. This was the 'slang tone of morality' Scott so lamented. Q.D. Leavis, in her seminal study *Fiction and the Reading Public* (1939), seemed to concur. She claimed that Lytton's 'lowering of the level of appeal' made him 'the first of modern best-sellers'. She went further:

> His pseudo-philosophic nonsense and preposterous rhetoric carry with them a debasing of the novelist's currency. But they were taken seriously by the reading public. . . . To make a useful generalization: best-sellers before Lytton are at worst dull, but ever since they have almost always been vulgar. The direction Lytton gave to popular fiction caused it to set its face away from literature. . . . [It became] voluptuous day-dream instead of the dispassionate narration of the complicated plot.[36]

During the course of the nineteenth century there was a growing awareness that the novel had begun to divide. Two large and distinct reading publics emerged, one more educated, one less so. Dickens discovered the 'laughter or tears' formula, one that continues to account for large numbers of blockbuster films, alongside those that incite nothing but sheer terror or black eroticism. Dickens's method suppresses the intellectual response in favour of arousing tears directly from the heart, as it were. Of course the reader is aware of Dickens's tricks and can cut them off at source. Dickens is at one with his humble readers, whereas the eighteenth-century writer was at one with a more educated group. This results in a childlike quality to Dickens's writings which contrasts with a perspective, discretion and desire for balance in the eighteenth-century novel, broadly speaking. His novels also distinguish themselves from more difficult nineteenth-century novels written for a narrower audience.

This division was exacerbated by a complex set of causes and effects working on each other. Chambermaids had become an increasingly significant group of women readers in a rapidly urbanising world with a growing middle class. Three constraints bore on their reading habits: what was available on the market, what was affordable, and time. The last had the most direct effect on what was produced. The chambermaid, unlike the women and men of the middle class, could only read for relatively short periods, between fulfilling her work and, sometimes, family duties. Periodical publication synchronised with the lifestyle of chambermaids and their class counterparts in other occupations. This in turn put pressure on certain novelists to think less about the total effect of their novel, and more about the immediate impact of its parts. The cumulative effects of the novel had to be subordinated to more sporadic reward. The novelists who adapted to meet the needs of this 'penny-in-the-slot' novel – writers like Charles Reade, Wilkie Collins and, most famously, Dickens – were despised by those novelists who were unwilling to abandon the novel 'proper': one that allowed for a subtler accumulation of complex structural and stylistic elements, and the use of irony, for example, rather than mere comfort or entertainment. Trollope, Thackeray and above all George Eliot, belong in the second group. This categorisation is of course crude and both Dickens's *David Copperfield* and *Great Expectations* arguably bridge the divide.

The rise of the periodical press was closely allied to the more populist kinds of novels. The British publisher Edward Lloyd set up rotary presses (used by the *Sunday Times*, founded in 1822) to publish serialised novels in the *Penny Sunday Times* and *People's Police Gazette*, publications largely aimed at the literate working class. Lloyd also hit lucky with a 'Penny Blood' series, launched in 1836, which told, in sensational tones, of the lives of rogues, thieves and bandits. It was to counter this kind of 'sleaze' – no doubt highly attractive to children – that religious groups produced alternative publications. Fifty years later, the Religious Tract Society founded two weeklies: *The Boy's Own Paper* and *The Girl's Own Paper*, which sold more than half a million copies each. The fact that the Religious Tract Society ran two publications in parallel (in addition to two 'annuals') demonstrates the degree to which it believed that boys and girls needed different kinds of edifying reading.

The first weekly number of *The Girl's Own Paper* appeared on 3 January 1880, priced at one penny. For this, the Victorian young lady received sixteen quarto three-column pages with numerous steel engravings. It contained the first serial parts of two long stories, a short story, three poems, an article on the 'Girlhood of Queen Victoria', a piece on 'Fashionable Costumes of Long Ago', articles on needlework and cookery, 'Useful Hints' (on health matters), and a competition which asked girls to write 'an essay on the life of any one famous English woman, born in the present century'. The magazine was published by the Leisure Hour Office of the Religious Tract Society, at 56 Paternoster Row, London, near St Paul's Cathedral.

By the end of the century there was widespread and unabashed awareness of what reading markets wanted – and what huge sums of money could be

51 This illustration, captioned 'Reading the Advertisements', illustrates an article entitled 'Advertising Swindles' in *The Girl's Own Paper*, 1887.

made by writers who got things right. Mrs Stoker, mother of the best-selling Abraham ('Bram') Stoker, read her son's *Dracula* on its first publication and wrote to her son: 'No book since *Frankenstein*, or indeed any other at all, has come near yours in originality and terror. . . . Poe is nowhere. . . . In its terrible excitement it should make you a widespread reputation, and much money, for you.'[37] On both counts this woman reader was correct.

Elsewhere in Europe similar opportunities were emerging. The publishing trade in France struggled during the 1830s and 1840s as books were still relatively expensive. But publishers like Louis Hachette in Paris were both aware of demand and shrewd about the marketing strategies that would keep them ahead of their rivals. Hachette invented new advertising and distribution strategies and targeted children and women readers. Women's desires to self-educate were satisfied by books like Mme de Saint-Ouen's *Petite Histoire de France* (1832), which sold well over a million copies.

In 1848 Gustav Havard won a risky publishing gamble. He brought out Prévost's *Manon Lescaut* in an attractive and heavily illustrated edition and priced it at just twenty centimes at a time when most workers earned between two and four francs a day. He had banked on vast sales if he priced the book at the right level. Chambermaids bought Prévost's romantic masterpiece in droves. By 1856 Havard had sold an astonishing 60 million books. The age of the large edition, cheap paperback had arrived. From now on the French book trade, like the English, was driven not by the tastes of a relatively small elite, but by what the wider public wanted.

In rural areas, however, specialist periodicals (for doctors, farmers and the like), administrative documents, school textbooks and reference works (including dictionaries) made up the bulk of what was read, and these largely by men. But while working women in the French countryside still had limited access to the novel other than in serialised form in newspapers, the French novel quickly travelled overseas and found captive women readers. Russian, Japanese and American women were the devoted readers of Victor Hugo, Émile Zola and, later, Jules Verne. In Germany the elite had read mostly French works, but German publishers were soon to respond to market opportunities in a country that was to industrialise more rapidly and fundamentally than France. Urbanisation was swift, standards of living rose sharply, education was introduced widely and efficiently and operated to high standards. The status of booksellers was high, further encouraging able men into a booming profession. Soon Berlin and Stuttgart were competing with Leipzig as centres of a revolutionised industry. Books were published in German, but also in many other languages for export to something more like a world market.

There were bookselling opportunities, however, which were much more open to other European publishers. In North America it was the dominant colonial powers – the British, French, Dutch and Spanish – who vied to sell books to the New World. From the East Coast mostly British pioneers moved west and the establishment of printing presses, particularly those dedicated to newspaper publishing, came early. Tennessee had a newspaper at the start of the eighteenth century (1701), Ohio by its close (1793). St Louis' first print shop was founded in 1808, and San Francisco's in 1848. By the end of the eighteenth century the novel was firmly planted on American soil and was women's preferred reading, with the English novel establishing something of a monopoly. But as the importance of literacy for economic, administrative and social progress (in short, nation-building) started to affect educational policies, so literacy rates rose and America's own literary production started to take off. Novels by men and women shaped the vision of a modern America and women's position in it was presented in different, sometimes opposing ways. Some of the patterns of European women's reading repeated themselves in America – but there were differences too.

52 Jane Stuart, *Interior Scene, c.* 1835. The woman has put down her own book to listen
to her child read aloud. To the right there are other books on the mantelpiece.

CHAPTER 9

—⟨∞⟩—

Nation-Building

R EADING – men's, women's and children's – lay very much at the heart of the American egalitarian vision. The United States Constitution, drafted in 1787, was far more than symbolic rhetoric. Nor was it simply a set of laws to be appealed to if need be. Benjamin Franklin (1706–90), one of the founding fathers of the nation, ensured that thousands of copies were produced and widely distributed. His intended readership was made up solely of white male property owners, and he was himself one of Philadelphia's leading publishers. Whatever the limits of his vision, and notwithstanding his self-interest, his commitment to literacy should not be underestimated: egalitarianism was to be founded on reading and access to written material. New methods of teaching literacy were devised and it was largely women who did the teaching. In schools, girls would, by and large, be educated alongside boys in the New America.

Women readers were fundamental to the new and rapidly growing society and well positioned to use, or abuse, their power. The potential for reading to be advantageously harnessed for the nation (or not) was recognised, and goes some way to explaining why black people were forbidden either to read or write. It is startling to recall that laws enforcing this were in place in the southern states until the abolishment of slavery in 1865. If it was discovered that a black person had learnt to read or write, punishments were severe, ranging from whipping to hanging. Despite these disincentives, clandestine activities which flew in the face of the prohibitions triumphed. One woman reader whose influence cannot be overstated, was the 'mistress' of the famous black abolitionist, writer and publisher, Frederick Douglass (c. 1817–95), who was born into slavery:

53 By the third quarter of the nineteenth century, mixed schools had opened in almost every corner of America. Winslow Homer's *The Country School*, 1871, depicts a class underway. The teacher is reading aloud and some children are reading along. A group of girls is working on its own, while the youngest children (on the right) are simply listening; the girl has her book on her lap, but the boy has put his to the side, rubbing his eyes, tired and strained by the task in hand.

The frequent hearing of my mistress reading the Bible aloud ... awakened my curiosity and respect for this *mystery* of reading, and roused in me the desire to learn. Up to this time I had known nothing whatsoever of this wonderful art, and my ignorance and inexperience of what it could do for me, as well as my confidence in my mistress, emboldened me to ask her to teach me to read. ... In an incredibly short time, by her kind assistance, I had mastered the alphabet and could spell words of three or four letters. ... My master forbade her from giving me any further instruction ... but the determination which he expressed to keep me in ignorance only rendered me all the more resolute to seek intelligence. In learning to read, therefore, I am not sure that I do not owe quite as much to the opposition of my master, as to the kindly assistance of my amiable mistress.[1]

Douglass's *Narrative of the Life of Frederick Douglass, An American Slave, Written by Himself* was first published in 1845. Slave narratives were popular in America and Britain. One of Douglass's readers went on to write *The*

54 A slave girl reading, 1876.

Bondwoman's Narrative by Hannah Crafts, A Fugitive Slave Recently Escaped from North Carolina.[2] The manuscript of this work came to light only in the twentieth century although the episodic nature of the narrative suggests that it was written for serial publication and may have been published in a magazine under a different name or title. Nothing is known about Hannah Crafts and the name could be a pseudonym. What is clear is that 'Hannah' was well read. The narrative of her life, which is filled with horror, violence and sexual exploitation, was clearly influenced by a number of earlier works including Douglass's autobiography but also various mid-nineteenth-century English classics by Charlotte and Emily Brontë and Charles Dickens. There are echoes of other American works including Harriet Beecher Stowe's *Uncle Tom's Cabin* (1852), and Williams Wells Brown's *The Escape, or a Leap for Freedom* (1858).

The general consensus is that the manuscript was written in the 1850s but two works that were published in the 1860s also bear some resemblance to Hannah's narrative: William Craft's *Running a Thousand Miles for Freedom: The Escape of William and Ellen Craft* (1860) and Harriet Jacobs' *Incidents in the Life of a Slave Girl Written by Herself* (1861). The authenticity of slave narratives is often questionable. White abolitionists have been suspected of ghosting narratives for slaves they knew or at least heavily editing their writings. But if 'Hannah' was a woman slave and her narrative her own, then it would demonstrate that some women slaves read widely and with considerable critical insight. There is certainly some evidence of literate women slaves including a remarkable photograph of a slave girl reading in Aiken, South Carolina, around 1856.

Black women were as keen to read as any other group. Founded in 1894, the Aurora Reading Club is the oldest African-American Women's Club in the United States still in existence. The intent of its six charter-members was to promote literacy at a time when all but the most basic education seemed an impossibility for black women.

The extraordinary success of reading programmes within the American educational system – under the umbrellas of both Church and State – accounts for American prowess in publishing terms. By 1850 the United States was producing 240 dailies with a circulation of 750,000. Just into the twentieth century this had soared to 2,340 with a circulation of 24 million each day. Dailies were by far and away America's most important reading matter and they had diversified to include a wide range of material – local, national, factional, fictional, religious, educational and escapist.

In the United States there was an early awareness of the importance of women's literacy, and a significant body of writing was published, targeted specifically at women readers, which encouraged participation in the formation of an idealised American community. A particular kind of conscientious domesticity, theories about education, missionary zeal and social work, were all written in. 'Domestic literacy narratives', as they have been unattractively but accurately termed, were often penned by women writers including many of the most popular of the day: Lydia Sigourney, Catharine Sedgwick, Frances Harper and Harriet Beecher Stowe. Readers considered their writing to be a contribution towards the common good. Scenes in their books mostly depict middle-class mothers teaching those in their care not simply to read, but also to write and talk about literature. Reading is presented above all as a source of shared knowledge and social improvement.

55 This reading scene from the time of the Civil War by Lilly Martin Spencer is entitled *The War Spirit at Home*. The children are playing at soldiers while their mother, holding a baby who may never have known its father, reads the latest news from the front.

By the beginning of the nineteenth century, most women read less advice literature and more novels than previous generations, though the novel was still viewed with suspicion by some. This attitude had been prevalent in the eighteenth century with claims that the novel was 'literary opium' and had pernicious effects on 'the Young of the fair sex'.[3] Some continued to warn against the novel in the nineteenth century, and they were not all men. Nancy Johns Turner Hall (1792–1850), the daughter of a Virginian Presbyterian preacher, wrote her recollections of her life in 1844 and blamed her reading of novels for her first rash and unsuccessful marriage. The relevant chapter was titled 'My first peep into novels, and its consequences. Heartrending disappointment'. Her father had a substantial library and, at a loose end one day, she was drawn to various novels: 'Unfortunately for me I now spied in a corner, where they seemed to have been placed merely to fill up a vacancy; about half a doz. Novels, such as Peregrine Pickle, Roderick Random, Gil Blas, and others. . . . While conscious of the sin, I opened & read them, one after another until all were perused . . . when I had read the last, I almost wept that there were no more to read.' She deeply regretted reading these novels and wondered at them having been available to her: 'Why my good and pious father suffered such vile books as these surely were to encumber his shelves, I *never could imagine*'. The novels inspired dreams of idealised love and such was her longing for life to be like fiction she was blind to the folly of marrying the man she did, aged sixteen. She advised her readers: 'in your proper sphere, try to render [this world] less miserable by acts of usefulness but *never* sit down supinely & fold your hands and dream yourself away into the regions of fancy until a new and fairy world arises under your creative hand. If you do; depend upon it you will reap your reward in disappointed hopes, & consequent misery.'[4]

In Boston, readers had access to European writing of a more thought-provoking kind. From 1840 to 1852 the visionary and spirited Elizabeth Palmer Peabody ran a bookstore and circulating Foreign Library, at 13 West Street, which she claimed 'contained no worthless books'. But like many bookshops and libraries it served as more than a place to buy or borrow books. It became something more like a *salon* for Boston's intellectual community, including the Transcendentalists, a dissenting group that emphasised individual intuition over the strictures of established religion. Peabody also published *The Dial*, a periodical for the dissemination of Transcendentalist thought. For many women readers, Peabody's Library was crucial to their intellectual development. Among them was the reformer and abolitionist of slavery, Margaret Fuller. Sophia Ripley, who with her husband and others had founded their utopian experiment in communal living at Brook Farm, also spent time at Peabody's establishment. Peabody gave them access to foreign authors, including Kant and Hegel, Goethe, Coleridge and Wordsworth, and the Swedish philosopher and scientist Swedenborg. She provided them with classical works too: Plato and the English Neo-Platonic writers, as well as Confucius and the sacred writings of the Vishnu Purana and the Bhagavad Gita.

Outside the privileged milieux of Boston, women readers enjoyed more popular works by women writers; their contribution sheds less expected light on the American woman reader in the nineteenth century. It was not until the middle of the century that America freed itself from significant dependency on British publishing, opening the way for popular American authors. During the early decades American publishers and printers competed to bring out popular English titles and American newspapers and magazines were designed very much along English lines. Writers like Thackeray, Dickens and Eliot were the bestsellers of the day. With the extension of the railways and a new sales infrastructure, America was ready to expand its own industry. Independent bookstores opened in every major city and town, and soon book-buying became a regular American habit. Readers now had choice and the books that sold were no longer simply what was available, but what readers really wanted. For the first time supply could directly meet demand.

It was in this new commercial climate that Sarah Payson Willis, because of her astute awareness of what American women wanted to read, was to succeed to an extraordinary degree. Her own life had not been easy, no easier than the average American woman, and she drew cleverly on her own experience of a 'rags to riches' life in her journalism and fiction. She fashioned an image of herself as one of the very first celebrity authors of America. She was born into a family of journalists in 1811. Both her grandfather and father had edited newspaper columns; the former had advanced the cause of patriotism during the Revolutionary War, the latter the fight against federalism. Her father then founded one of America's earliest religious newspapers, the *Boston Recorder*. But none of these were really profitable activities. Then Sarah's first husband died and she was divorced from her second, leaving her with three young children to look after and virtually no financial resources.

In the 1850s she started to write the kind of articles that she herself would want to read, mostly about the trials and injustices of poverty and women's heroic efforts to manage life whatever their circumstances. She also wrote somewhat sentimental pieces about the homeless children living on the streets of New York and the injustices of a society in which women's and children's lives were invariably more vulnerable that men's. But amid the pathos there is a sharp satirical wit and a softening irony. Willis was published, under the catchy pseudonym of Fanny Fern, in magazines like the *Mother's Assistant*, the *True Flag*, and the *Olive Branch*. It is clear from the title of her first book publication, a compendium of her previously published articles entitled *Fern Leaves from Fanny's Portfolio*, that she was already making a name for herself. *Fern Leaves* was an overnight success and sold more than 70,000 copies in the first year. Her autobiographical novel, *Ruth Hall* (1854), further boosted her celebrity status. Ruth, like Fanny, struggles as a writer to feed her family. She is successful not only in terms of finding a keen publisher, but equally in ensuring that her financial rewards are maximised. Ruth agrees to publication on condition that she receives stocks in a local bank. These turn out to be

56 A pen-and-ink drawing of Fanny Fern (Sara Willis Parton) by her daughter, Ellen Eldredge Parton.

worth some $10,000, a sum similar to Fanny's actual earnings, and by any measure far more than her grandfather or father had ever earned in their publishing endeavours.

Sarah Payson Willis came from a background that had given her insights into the world of journalism, publishing and public opinion. She had an astute sense of what moved and interested a large number of contemporary women readers and she knew how to pace her contributions so as to establish a loyal fan club. Other best-selling women authors of the period also give insights into what women in particular wanted to read. Hannah Adams, for instance, was another of the early American authors to make a living from writing. Her mother died when she was twelve and because she was a frail child her father kept her away from school but encouraged her appetite for reading: 'my first idea of Heaven was of a place where we should find our thirst for knowledge fully gratified', she wrote in her autobiography. Although in a quite different way, Adams' writings on comparative religion and history proved popular in their liberal approach.

An unexpected event also significantly boosted her reputation. Early in the century the Revd Jedidiah Morse involved her in a legal dispute: they were both writing histories of New England and Morse tried to persuade Adams to abandon her book. The cultural climate was still one in which a serious man of letters – and the cloth – considered himself to be superior to a woman writer. Although Adams was loath to engage in a legal battle she had many supporters who encouraged her not to give in and who financed the resolution of the dispute: Morse was required to apologise and pay legal damages – and Adams' reputation received a significant boost. Adams' readers were not exclusively men; she also had a very direct influence over women in the privileged social world. She was often invited to dinners and house parties, sometimes as a guest for weeks or even months on end. She was an excellent conversationalist and many who met her naturally went on to buy and read her books.

Among the working classes, however, reading continued to be seen by some employers and others with control over women's lives as a distraction from work and domesticity; others were supportive. Young women flooded to the New England mills for employment from the 1820s until the outbreak of the Civil War. As one mill girl noted in her memoirs some forty years later, 'we were as fond of good story-books as any that live in these days of over-flowing libraries.'[5] She recalled that the evening leisure hours were much enjoyed; 'the [boarding-house] dining-room was used as a sitting-room. ... [The mill girls] gathered around the tables, and sewed, and read, and wrote, and studied.' Some read for amusement, some for distraction, and some for self-improvement. Despite their small wages many girls bought books as well as borrowing from a variety of libraries and, of course, each other. Some mills had their own libraries, known as counting-house libraries, sometimes stocked by the owners of the factory, sometimes by the workers themselves. Middle-class women in New England encouraged working-class women in their reading endeavours and, in some cases, in their writing. Local periodicals were established to which some mill girls and women sent contributions. This literary atmosphere among nineteenth-century working class women had no counterpart elsewhere in the world. But it was not universally supported in New England; there were accusations of social pretension and, more seriously, some mill owners feared that their employees were distracted from their work.

Circulating libraries that lent and sold were important sources for a range of reading material. Sabbath School libraries were established to lend books that countered the 'evil influence' of the books offered by the circulating libraries, including European novels. Mill girls had to avoid being seen with 'radical' newspapers, as they would be instantly dismissed for the 'offence' and worse still blacklisted throughout New England. Lucy Larcom, who worked in the mills of New England from the age of eleven, noted that in most cases workers were 'strictly forbidden to have books at their work'.[6] Again, if found with a book they would lose their job and their names would be sent to other mill owners to ensure that they were unlikely to find alternative employment in the region.

While American literacy rates rose steadily throughout the nineteenth century, patterns of literacy in Europe were not uniform, and women's position as readers differed significantly. By the mid-nineteenth century a clear divide had opened up between rates of literacy in Northern, Protestant Europe (and parts of the Americas) and Southern (mostly Catholic) Europe. Earlier and more successful industrialisation, and with it education, roughly mapped onto Church affiliations. Sweden, with a literacy rate of some 90 per cent, led the league, followed by Scotland and Prussia (roughly 80 per cent). England and Wales were somewhere between 65 and 75 per cent literate, and France, 60 per cent. Further south, only 25 per cent of the Spanish population was enfranchised into the world of reading, in Italy only 20 per cent, and in Greece and the Balkans less than 20 per cent. Educational advances in Russia had been negligible and the country remained only 5 to 10 per cent literate. The great Russian works of the period, by Gogol, Lermontov, Pushkin, Turgenev and above all Tolstoy, had far more readers outside the country than within it.

From the late 1700s, accelerating in waves until the 1900s, Western colonialism exerted its educational forces on cultures that had relied hitherto solely on oral transmission. Gradually those colonised either adopted or adapted the Latin alphabet to create their own written script that met their own needs. A range of written indigenous languages also emerged: Africa's Vai, N'ko, Mende, Bamum and Osmanian scripts, for instance. On the other side of the world the Sikwayi (Sequoya) invented a Cherokee script, while in the Hudson Bay area, Cree emerged. There was also an Alaskan script, and various scripts in the Caroline Islands, the *rongorongo* script of Easter Island and many more. The invention of these writing systems facilitated more organised trading and those areas with a written language tended to engage more openly with missionaries than regions that continued to rely purely on the oral. Gradually a *littera franca* emerged using the Latin alphabet, as this was more accessible to outsiders and part of an international system. These were all practical languages and, for the time being, almost exclusively the preserve of men.

In Muslim Africa, however, the Arabic consonantal language, which had been the written language of tens of millions of people for several centuries, held its ground. But relatively little was actually read, and only by a tiny minority, apart, of course, from the Qur'an. According to Muslim religious law, the holy text was not to be altered, summarised or otherwise changed in any way. This, of course, made learning to read extremely difficult, in turn explaining the high levels of illiteracy in the Muslim world. It was only at the end of the nineteenth century that Islamic countries accepted the inevitability of printing, but acceptance, or limited acceptance, of women's literacy comes later. Some women's involvement in the scholarly culture was now a thing of the distant past.

In colonial Africa, south of the Sahara, British, French, Belgian and German colonisers introduced the Latin alphabet. Protestant missionaries encouraged the reading of Bibles which they had laboriously translated into African vernaculars, while Catholic missionaries taught their own mother tongues, French and Portuguese, in order that the colonised could read their Bibles. This meant that for those who had learnt the colonisers' language, other material in that language also became accessible, if available. But the Bible and the Qur'an were significantly more read than anything else.

A further overseas market was created by those oppressed communities who had left Europe for religious and political reasons. French book pedlars, mostly from Normandy and the Alps, travelled to South America to sell to émigrés. They created networks similar to those in Europe and mostly sold works of political and religious importance. Similar book networks served and organised by pedlars existed in Poland (mostly under Russian domination), Greece, and Armenia (under Turkish rule).

By the close of the nineteenth century Western reading habits had penetrated vast regions of the world. With Western-style reading came all manner of cultural baggage: genres, styles and ethos. Even China, with a centuries-old reading tradition of its own, was beginning to see its reading habits assimilated by Western ways. This touched the lives of a small number of men, rather than women. But women's private reading of poetry, in particular, did not die out. And there were occasional signs that some literate women were not altogether contented with the status quo, one in which fathers and husbands had total control over every aspect of girls' and women's lives. In Imperial China there had been a long tradition of courtesan poetry, celebrating romantic love, and by the eighteenth-century some women of the gentry were also writing. But the implied rise of women's literacy did not bring greater social freedoms; if anything, there was a backlash. However, a small number of works by women challenged this male domination. The *tanci* was a musical narrative accompanied by plucked lutes and often performed by two or three women. It was generally regarded as a specifically women's genre, and was relatively informal, less bound by convention than poetry, and with the capacity for more extensive storytelling. Some *tanci* implicitly questioned women's place in later Imperial Chinese society.

The Destiny After Rebirth was begun by Chen Duansheng (1751–?96) and finished by Liang Desheng (1771–1847) in the early nineteenth century. Chen Duansheng had two children. Her husband Fan, an official, was charged with corruption and sent into exile. She died in her forties, still awaiting his return. *The Destiny After Rebirth* tells a story that is both highly conventional and unusual: a man and three women are reincarnated with a view to finding perfect love as husband and wife – along with two concubines. In traditional fashion, all manner of obstacles have to be overcome as the story unfolds. Men Lijun, the heroine, assumes the identity of a man and proves extraordinarily successful, easily clearing the hurdles in the examination system, becoming prime minister and winning the emperor's complete confidence. From this position she is able to counter a number of forces (the details are complex) that stand in the way of the lovers achieving their amatory ambitions. The difficulty then becomes Lijun's unwillingness to expose herself as a mere woman, as she has become accustomed to her privileges and her considerable political influence. After further twists and turns in the plot, the emperor is persuaded to investigate Lijun's true gender. She is given a powerful wine to drink and falls unconscious. Her real identity is then revealed: the palace maids take off her shoes and inside them are the tiny red shoes of a woman with bound feet. Lijun is then given an impossible choice of punishment: either she must marry the emperor or lose her life. And here Chen Duansheng's *tanci* ended. Whether she was unable to find an appropriate denouement or whether her own death intervened, we will never know.

The story was finished by Liang Desheng, an able nineteenth-century woman writer. And the ending conforms to tradition: the emperor grants Lijun clemency and allows the predestined quartet – husband, wife and the two courtesans – to live as the ideal ménage that they have long sought. Liang Desheng's completed *Destiny After Rebirth* became the most celebrated and popular *tanci* of the Chinese tradition. Her forced and conventional ending was what nineteenth-century women readers wanted. Chen Duansheng, on the other hand, had tried to stir things up. Her heroine enjoys a man's education and the political career that outstanding academic success brings. And she is loath to give it all up and assume the role of a Confucian wife, a subordinate position in a foursome under the total authority of a husband. Literate women in eighteenth-century China, however small in number, imagined lives outside the strict patriarchal structures of their day. The example of *The Destiny of Rebirth* suggests that by the nineteenth century, long-standing conservative traditions had been reasserted. Women readers were comfortable with Liang Desheng's reactionary telling of her predecessor's potentially much more exciting and revolutionary story.

In many parts of the world, the nineteenth century, and particularly the second half of it, was the Golden Age of reading – especially of women's reading. The century saw the rise of the modern woman reader and she was a much more protean being than previous, though still the object of suspicion and fear. The nineteenth century also witnessed the birth of both the history and an amateurish sociology of women's reading. Articles with titles like 'What Girls Read', 'Do Our Girls Take an Interest in Literature? The Other Side of the Question' and 'The Novel-Reading Habit' proliferated.[7] The

57 Nineteenth-century advertisement for Niagara Gloss Starch.

debates were as varied as the woman reader herself. Sentimental images of girls and women quietly reading became increasingly popular, particularly within advertising. But it is the growing number of references to women readers in novels and the views voiced by women novelists which convey much of the complexity and intrigue of the story, and often provide the most beguiling commentary on the century's changes.

Jane, of Charlotte Brontë's *Jane Eyre* (1847), has been orphaned and has no-one to direct her reading. She delights in free access to her uncle's book-shelves although John Reed, her quick-tempered teenage cousin, does what he can to prevent her from reading them: 'You have no business to take our books . . . they *are* mine; all the house belongs to me, or will do in a few years. . . . Now, I'll teach you to rummage my book-shelves.' He hurls the book she has been reading towards her and Jane falls against the door, cutting her head. Books, she learns, represent wealth – and power.

The eponymous heroine of Flaubert's *Madame Bovary* (1856) is a reader who struggles hopelessly to make her life like that of a romantic novel, and deludes herself into believing that she is succeeding only to recognise her failure at the end of the novel when her debts, like the modern credit card phenomenon, become impossible ever to repay. She commits suicide. Emma Bovary's reading is, in a sense, the evil character of the novel, driving her further and further from the straight and narrow path of conformism, be that social, economic, religious, sexual, even erotic. Or is Emma herself culpable because of the influence she allows her reading to exert over her? Flaubert was taken to court for allegedly corrupting public morals in *Madame Bovary*. In part it was the woman reader of the novel who was on trial: had Emma never opened a work of romantic fiction, would she have behaved as she had and would tragedy then have been averted for her poor husband and child? Or had Austen's comic version of the woman reader confusing fiction and reality been transformed into a great tragic one?

The debate as to what constituted a 'sensible' woman reader as opposed to a 'silly' woman reader was equally bound up with the question of 'silly' women novelists, often the most successful of the day who, some argued, encouraged this kind of close identification. In her delightfully forthright way, George Eliot described, in an article in the *Westminster Review* (1856), 'Silly novels by Lady Novelists': 'a genus with many species, determined by a particular quality of silliness that predominates in them – the frothy, the prosy, the pious, or the pedantic. But it is a mixture of all these – a composite order of feminine fatuity, that produces the largest class of such novels, which we shall distinguish as the *mind-and-millinery* species.' Eliot would no doubt have had ˜e compassion for the 'silly' novelists had they been driven by economic necessity; but they are 'Ladies'. She concludes: 'In all labour there is profit; but ladies' silly novels, we imagine, are less the result of labour than of busy idleness.'[8] This kind of writing is not driven by financial need and furthermore it perpetuates the stereotypes and prejudices that shaped the 'silly Lady Novelists' in the first place. By implication Eliot suggests that novels of any worth should break out, should present a challenge, should hold up a mirror to reveal what is ignored or denied.

In Eliot's *Mill on the Floss* (1860), Maggie Tulliver craves reading that can inform her about life. Even as a child she hungers for books 'with more in them'. Books, she believes, can guide women's lives. Henry James's woman reader in *The Portrait of a Lady* (1881), Isabel, is almost the polar opposite of Eliot's. She is described, 'One wet afternoon,' as being 'seated alone with a book. To say she was occupied is to say that her solitude did not press upon her; for her love of knowledge had a fertilizing quality and her imagination was strong'. However, a little later in the novel, the narrator suggests that Isabel's enjoyment of reading may be more to do with imaginative escape than instruction. The room in which she reads is a 'mysterious apartment which lay beyond the library and which was called, traditionally, no-one knew why, the office.' Isabel reads widely: foreign novels in translation, poetry and Continental philosophy. As she has had little education and there is no-one to guide her in what she reads, the suggestion is that she is somewhat unanchored by it all. When Isabel later hears that she is to be going abroad, to England, she declares that it will be 'just like a novel'. We know, as readers, that she will be disappointed.

In Thomas Hardy's *Tess of the D'Urbervilles* (1891), the peasant girl Tess has been seduced and abandoned by a man of a higher class. She blames her mother for not allowing or encouraging her to read the kind of books that might have taught her how life often goes: 'Why didn't you tell me there was danger in menfolk? Why didn't you warn me? Ladies know what to fend hands against, because they read novels that tell them of these tricks; but I never had the chance o' learning in that way, and you did not help me!'

By the end of the century, in industrialised societies at least, there was growing consensus that what mattered now was that women be educated – in the interests of the nation. But it was also widely agreed that reading could be life-enhancing for the individual woman, as long as women read with 'appropriate discrimination' and stopped being 'silly'. Women were reading quite as extensively as men and had access to ever-increasing kinds of reading material. But perhaps the greatest change was women's growing confidence in their own individualism as readers. They no longer felt obliged to be seen to respond as they thought they ought. More and more they read what they wanted to read, and said what they thought. A letter written by Fanny Kemble, the famous English actress and author, to a school friend on 27 June 1835, sums up much of this. It lists 'the books just now lying on my table, all of which I have been reading lately':

Alfieri's 'Life', by himself, a curious and interesting work; Washington Irving's last book, 'A Tour on the Prairies', rather an ordinary book, upon a not ordinary subject, but not without sufficiently interesting matter in it too; Dr. Combe's 'Principles of Physiology'; and a volume of Marlowe's plays, containing 'Dr. Faustus'. I have just finished Hayward's Translation of Goethe's 'Faust', and wanted to see the old English treatment of the subject. I have read Marlowe's play with more curiosity than pleasure. This is, after all, but a small sample of what I read, but if you remember the complexion of my studies when I was a girl at Heath Farm and read Jeremy Taylor and Byron together, I can only say that they are still apt to be of the same hetero-geneous quality. But my brain is kept in a certain state of activity by them, and that, I suppose, is one of the desirable results of reading.[9]

It was Jane Austen, however, who had raised the question of the woman reader to a new level and with typical subtlety, at the very outset of the century, in *Northanger Abbey* (begun in 1798 and sold to a publisher in 1803). Her character, Catherine Morland, is a passionate reader of the Gothic novel. When she is invited to visit Northanger Abbey she expects it to be gloomy, mysterious and full of horrors. All this comes from her reading of Ann Radcliffe's novel *The Mysteries of Udolpho*. At one point while staying at Northanger, Catherine is excited to find 'an immense heavy chest!' and wonders, 'what can it hold? – Why should it be placed here? – Pushed back too, as if meant to be out of sight!' The reader's expectations mount with Catherine's, but we recognise how Austen has manipulated us when the trunk eventually turns out to contain nothing more than a laundry list, a written document that so beautifully symbolises domestic tedium. Austen is satirising the Gothic tradition but also implying that the confusion of fiction and reality is less alarming than comic. Implicitly, she encouraged women to read more intelligently, in the earnest hope that they might retain a proper sense of distinction between the complicated constructs of a fictional world, and reality. Jane Austen simply exposes the tremendous power of reading to bring delight and insight, and to quietly empower the reader.

Austen, more than any other author of the period, wrote what the most critical women readers wanted to read. For all her wit and measure, she provided a new truth to life in the novel, with all its horror, but conveyed without sensationalism. Lady Robert Kerr wrote to her soon after the publication of *Mansfield Park* (1814): 'You may be assured I read every line with the greatest interest & am more delighted with it than my humble pen can express. The excellent delineation of Character, sound sense, Elegant Language & the pure morality with which it abounds, makes it a most desirable as well as useful work, & reflects the highest honour &c. &c. Universally admired in Edinburgh, by all *wise ones*. – Indeed, I have not heard a single fault given to it.'[10] The poet and writer Catherine Hutton summed up the view of many women readers of the day in a letter to John Murray, one of Austen's publishers: 'I have been going through a course of novels by lady authors, beginning with Mrs Brooke [an eighteenth-century novelist] and ending with Miss Austen, who is my especial favourite.'

Many male readers, on the other hand, found this contrast between the control and lightness of touch of Austen's language, and the terrors of the human relationships her novels explore, deeply disconcerting. W.H. Auden,

58 *The Circulating Library* by Isaac Cruikshank, 1764–*c*. 1811.

looking back from the twentieth century with all the benefit of literary historical perspective, wrote in his 'Letter to Lord Byron':

> You could not shock her more than she shocks me;
> Beside her Joyce seems innocent as grass.
> It makes me most uncomfortable to see
> An English spinster of the middle class
> Describe the amorous effect of 'brass',
> Reveal so frankly and with such sobriety
> The economic basis of society.[11]

The rhymes take us to the heart of the matter: Austen's astute awareness of
contemporary events, wars abroad and domestic unrest at home, the Industrial
Revolution and the upheavals in English society which it brought in its wake,
and the weakening of stable value systems. All this brings fundamental social
change, in the relationship between 'class' and 'brass' ('money' as opposed to
'wealth') and the effects of this on the 'sobriety' or the stability of 'society'. By
way of contrast with Auden's male reading of Austen, Virginia Woolf, one of
the most astute modern women readers, suggested that 'of all great writers she
is the most difficult to catch in the act of greatness'.[12] Woolf did not mean that
Austen was difficult to read; rather, that Austen's readers were often unaware
of how the author had crafted her fiction so as to affect them as profoundly as
they recognised. Austen did not tell her readers how to read, nor did she tell
them how to live.

The nineteenth century witnessed an extraordinary growth in the
number of women writers and many proved especially popular with women
readers. Equally, women readers in many parts of the world had a good deal
more choice in what to read. By the end of the century the volume of material
on the market, particularly for those living in urban areas, was overwhelming.
In a common exchange of letters, one harassed reader wrote:

> You bid me tell you what I read; and, in obedience to your commands, I
> confess myself to be at present under a course of *historical physic*, which
> ought to have been administered to me in my youth, and for want of which
> I have grown up under many infirmities. . . . I am therefore labouring hard
> amongst the ruins of antiquity, tho' even amidst their profound recesses I
> sometimes have a little of the dust of *modern rubbish* thrown into my eyes.
> The truth is, in a town, it is very difficult to refrain from following the multi-
> tude in their pursuits of literature. One is so *baited* with new books that one
> is forced to take them up in self defence; for who would dare to drag forth a

huge musty volume of Roman antiquities, in preference to an elegant little epitome of modern biography?[13]

From now on in the industrialised world, women readers would be subject to increasingly powerful commercial forces trying to thrust reading material upon them, while in other parts of the world women continued to belong to an illiterate majority, or longed for access to more reading material than was available to them. For some, though, the twentieth century would bring fresh air.

—◦◦◦—

CHAPTER 10

The Modern Woman Reader

Time is a gift, but it can be a suspect one, especially in a culture that values frenzy. When I began this book, almost everyone I knew seemed to be busier than I was. I supported myself, contributed my share to the upkeep of the household, and engaged in all the useful wifely and motherly duties and pleasures. But I still had time left to read. . . . I had constructed a life in which I could be energetic but also lazy; I could rush, but I would never be rushed. It was a perfect situation for someone who loved to read[.][1]

THE modern world presents all manner of opportunities and hindrances to reading. But the journalist and critic Wendy Lesser, like scores of other twentieth- and twenty-first-century women, makes time for books. *Nothing Remains the Same: Rereading and Remembering* explores the extent to which we are what we read. It measures our awareness of how we have changed as a function of our experience of re-reading works that we remember well from earlier in life.

Some of the books that had delighted Lesser in childhood no longer worked their magic upon re-reading, like Kingsley Amis's *Lucky Jim*. Her attitude to the heroines of *Anna Karenina* and *Middlemarch* had also changed with age, and she found her sympathy had moved away from them to other characters in the novels. *Don Quixote*, on the other hand, which she had enjoyed at the age of eleven for its wit and pathos, retained its emotional force; forty years on, Lesser could now discern the power of Cervantes's voice, his capacity to address his reader directly and somehow timelessly across the four centuries that separate him from the modern reader. Lesser makes little of his misogyny, no doubt accepting it as a seventeenth-century view now happily superseded; in contrast, Charlotte Lennox, seeing the male prejudices of Cervantes's novel continually being lived out around her, was moved to write her *Female Quixote*.

Lesser's musings on her readings and re-readings provide interesting insights into the works as well as allowing her readers to consider the question that really intrigues her: 'Do the books actually cause you to develop in a particular direction, or are they simply markers along an existing route? . . . The question piques and tantalizes but, like all questions about how we turned into who we turned into, it has no firm answer.' Whether or not Lesser's reading – or anyone's – actually is profoundly formative, it is certainly the case that her reading has helped her to understand herself, her life, how she has changed, and the modern world she lives in.

Other women's records of their reading tell us more about twentieth-century reading tastes and habits, although as always there are both characteristic and extreme examples. One of the latter is undoubtedly Louise Brown. In 2004 it was reported that the then ninety-one year old had borrowed an astonishing 25,000 books from her local library over a sixty-year period – and she had never had to pay a fine. She read quickly and for long periods and had almost exhausted the supply at the public library in Stranraer, south-west Scotland, having got through a minimum of six books a week since 1946. The quantity of books that Louise has read may be unusual, but her preferences are less so. In fact they are characteristic of large numbers of women's reading in the modern period. Louise reads romances, historical novels and war stories. 'I started reading when I was five,' she explains, 'and have never stopped. I like anything I can get my hands on. I also like Mills and Boon for light reading at night.'[2]

A couple of years before Louise began her life of reading, Hilary Spalding, a seventeen-year-old English clergyman's daughter, kept a diary for the year 1943. In it she recorded everything she read – more than a hundred titles. There are some classics, including Shakespeare's *Antony and Cleopatra*, Scott's *Guy Mannering* (the only book she read twice during the twelve-month period), Charlotte Brontë's *Jane Eyre* and the first volume of a nineteenth-century translation of Alexandre Dumas's *The Three Musketeers*. Not all her reading was fiction. Other titles include *The Ballet Lover's Notebook*, *How to Think* (a 1938 precursor of Alain de Botton's work of the same name), and a work on English dramaturgy entitled *The Amazing Theatre*, published in 1939. She also read some poetry, including Tennyson's *The Dream of Fair Women*, T.S. Eliot's *Little Gidding* (which had only recently been published) and a collection, *Sixty Poems*. Although there are few plays noted, she did read Sean O'Casey's *Juno and the Paycock*, a play set in the Dublin tenements during the Irish Civil War of the 1920s. A film version directed by Alfred Hitchcock came out in 1930, which may show that some of Spalding's reading was inspired by films she had seen. Also among the many novels in Spalding's diary was Margaret Mitchell's *Gone with the Wind* of 1936, made into a film three years later.

Most of Spalding's reading was of novels, including historical and romantic fiction, and many by contemporary women authors like Helen Waddell, Catherine Dodd, Margaret Irwin and Mary Webb. But she also read plenty of fiction by male authors, including thrillers like Hammond Innes' *Attack Alarm* (1931) and crime novels like Conan Doyle's *The Hound of the Baskervilles* (1902). There are some curiosities too. John Steinbeck's *The Moon is Down* (1942) is a propaganda novel and was commissioned by the Office of Strategic Services, a US intelligence agency founded during the Second World War – and the predecessor of the CIA. The story is concerned with the military occupation of a small town in an unnamed country somewhere in Northern Europe. The invading army is of an anonymous nation at war with both England and Russia. There are, of course, parallels with the German occupation of Norway. Steinbeck's novel was immediately banned in Nazi-occupied France, but was published illegally by a resistance group.

Separated by more than half a century, Brown, aged ninety-one and Spalding, aged seventeen, share not dissimilar reading tastes and both are avid readers, even if Brown's rate is almost twice that of the young Spalding's. Both read serious as well as lighter books and both are interested in history and war stories, as well as romantic fiction and classic novels. This mirrors the overall picture of keen women readers over the last hundred years or so.

The history of women's reading in the twentieth century is obviously more familiar than that of earlier periods. There is plenty of statistical information available on women's reading in the twentieth and twenty-first centuries and surveys and polls allow for overviews of women's literacy and illiteracy worldwide, giving insights into reading and gender differences. The story has to be told in a rather different mode, one that allows for the sheer numbers, huge variety and burgeoning types of reading material available. Many modern women choose what to read without constraints, and read widely and apparently without any inhibitions. Yet in some parts of the world religious texts – the Qur'an and the Bible pre-eminently – remain the most important and sometimes the exclusive reading material for the growing number of literate girls and women.

In the West, in the early decades of the twentieth century newspapers and periodicals continued to be more important reading matter to women than books. In fact, late nineteenth-century patterns of women's reading were, broadly speaking, maintained. What changed were the numbers of literate women in different parts of the world. By 1900, 90 per cent of the populations of the UK, France, Germany and the US were functionally literate, and educational initiatives at the turn of the century were to increase levels of literacy further. Political revolutions brought literacy in their wake. Under Stalin's long rule (1924–53), educational programmes across the Soviet Union became more widespread and organised; at the turn of the century less than a third of the population (and only 18 per cent of women) were literate but by the outbreak of the Second World War 87 per cent of the population (and 82 per cent of women) aged nine and above could read.[3] In China there was a comparable drive towards mass literacy after the Communist Party's victory in the Civil War in 1949. The idea that 'a talentless woman is virtuous' ('*nuzi wucai bianshi de*') had been celebrated as a traditional value until the late nineteenth century, so the promotion of reading in the mid-twentieth

59 A woman sits engrossed in the *Suffragette*, 1913.

century was particularly important for women, many of whom attended night schools and literacy classes. The number of illiterate women before the Revolution was estimated at some 90 per cent; in 2009, this had dropped to less than 10 per cent of those aged fifteen and above and less than 1 per cent of those aged between fifteen and twenty-four.[4]

Another reading revolution came in the form of the paperback. The nineteenth century had seen certain paperback innovations in the form of penny dreadfuls and dime novels. But their share of the market was nothing compared to the twentieth-century paperback. The decisive breakthrough was result of changes in sales channels and retailers. Pocket Books, launched in the US by Robert de Graff, broke the long tradition of bookstores' monopolies by signing contracts with four newspaper wholesalers who undertook to sell their books at news-stands and in shops, across a staggering 100,000 outlets. After just two years Pocket Books had sold 8.5 million copies and by the end of the '40s their sales had outstripped the total combined unit sales of all the bestsellers published in the US since 1880. Unsurprisingly, other paperback publishers soon adopted similar distribution policies. In the UK, Penguin Books transformed publishing in the 1930s through its cheap and well-made paperbacks sold on the high street, particularly in branches of Woolworth's; a buyer for the company was persuaded by his wife that the books would sell well to women visiting the chain.

Paperback originals (that is, new books not previously published in hardback) emerged in the late 1930s. Some new paperback genres catered for niche markets, including lesbian pulp novels which sold in large numbers – to women and men – from the middle of the century on. But not all mass-market paperbacks were escapist fiction. Some were surprisingly influential. *Mrs Miniver* by Jan Struther (the pen name of Joyce Maxtone Graham) was one of a stream of books written by women for a largely female readership about the day-to-day familial and domestic challenges faced by the people of Britain immediately before and during the Second World War.[5] The book, based on a collection of Struther's columns written for *The Times*, was first published in the UK in 1939 and in the US the following year. It was hugely successful, going through thirteen printings between July 1940 and October 1941, with an affordable hardback being issued in 1942 and a further paperback with six printings in its first five months. But these figures were not what prompted Winston Churchill to state that the book 'had done more for the Allies than a flotilla of battleships'; it was the novel's powerfully realistic descriptions of lives that American men and women could sympathise with, which President Roosevelt himself considered to have been a significant factor in terms of shifting public opinion in favour of US intervention in the

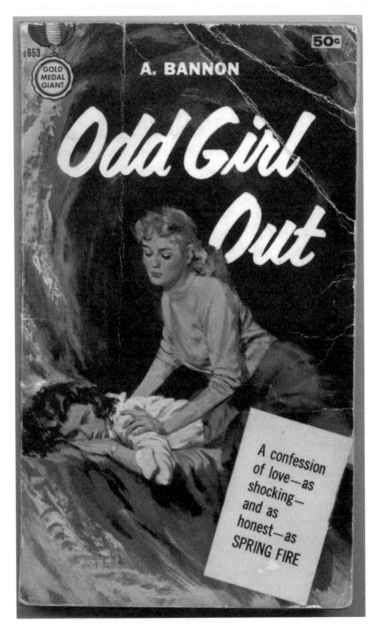

60 Cover of Ann Bannon's lesbian pulp fiction novel *Odd Girl Out*, 1957.

war. Mass-market paperbacks like *Mrs Miniver* could make a difference, it seems, to the course of history.

The novel demonstrates what powerful propaganda best-selling fiction could be. The film adaptation of *Mrs Miniver* was released in 1942 alongside reprints of the book, an early example of how books and films would increasingly feed off the other's success, sometimes reaching a fever pitch where very large numbers of people would see the same film and read the same book. The early fears of film's threat to reading proved to be false. In the first place, the phenomenon of the silent movie actually encouraged literacy because of the need to be able to read on-screen intertitles: short printed text filmed and edited into the action at various points. (The development of the soundtrack gradually made intertitles redundant but, interestingly, they continued to be used well into the 1930s to add narration, even after dialogue was provided by a soundtrack.) When 'talkies' came in, a large number of box office hits were film versions of books. And rather than making the reading of them redundant, the film adaptations boosted book profits to an extraordinary degree. Sales of Margaret Mitchell's *Gone with the Wind*, published in the summer of 1936 at the almost unprecedented price of three dollars, reached something close to a million by the end of the same year. But it was the adaptations for stage and screen, above all the 1939 film starring Vivien Leigh and Clark Gable, which boosted sales enormously. More recently, J.K. Rowling's *Harry Potter* series has enjoyed a similar success from its phenomenal film franchise.[6]

The advent of film, radio, television and the Internet was accompanied in each case by more or less extravagant prophecies about the detrimental knock-on effects the new media would have on reading. But in many ways, they have been a stimulus rather than a threat. Two of the longest-running radio programmes – *Woman's Hour* (1945) and *Book at Bedtime* (1949) – have had positive effects on the sales of books, often by women. *Woman's Hour* spoke directly to the woman reader in her domestic space. The first programme, presented by a man, went out at two o' clock in the afternoon – when women would have completed the morning's housework, washed up after lunch, and so would have a little time in hand before the children returned home from school. Early compelling topics included 'How to hang your husband's suit'. Other items were more topical, including 'Cooking with whale meat', at a time when rationing was still in force. From the very outset, variety was part of the programme's wide appeal, with slots filled by women talking about unusual experiences – 'I married a lion-tamer', for example. But reading, as a subject, gradually became more important and a large number of popular women authors were interviewed about their recent publications. Reading was, of course, the *raison d'être* of *Book at Bedtime*, enjoyed by a large audience of women and men.

The rise of television has almost certainly had a detrimental impact on the amount of time many people spend reading, but some broadcasts certainly encourage book-buying. Sales of many of the classics have been boosted by television adaptations, especially of Jane Austen's novels; the BBC's 1995 adaptation of *Pride and Prejudice* surpassed previous ratings and sent book sales rocketing in both the UK and Australia. It remains one of the best-loved books in literature, as the results of recent polls have shown; it has been ranked the third most re-read book in Britain, first in a poll of books that people in the British nation 'can't live without', the second most popular book in the UK in a BBC poll in 2003 and the most popular in 2007.[7] Nor is Austen's popularity limited to English-speaking countries. In 2004 an Indian adaptation, *Bride and Prejudice*, became a Bollywood box office hit; Lizzy Bennet became Lalita and made the actress Aishwarya Rai a worldwide name. We do not know what proportion of the audiences were women, but it would be uncharacteristic of Austen's readers generally if they were not substantially female.

Television programmes that promote reading have enormous influence on book sales. 'The Richard and Judy Book Club' was launched on *Richard & Judy* in 2004, and exerts great sway on British readers' reading. Their selection of Karen Joy Fowler's *The Jane Austen Book Club* (2005) – itself a story of the shifting relationships among five women and one man who meet to share their responses to reading – generated sales of £68 million. The sixteen books featured in the Richard and Judy Book Club Summer Reads promotions in 2004 sold close to 4 million copies according to Nielsen BookScan. Amanda Ross, who dreamt up the Book Club, chooses the books; this makes her an extraordinarily influential woman reader. In a similar vein, 'Oprah's Book Club', part of *The Oprah Winfrey Show* where host and audience discussed a new book each month, ran from 1996–2011. It was hugely popular and wielded the power to completely transform the fortunes of books by millions of sales. During its life, Oprah was one of the most powerful women readers on the planet.

These TV shows have provided the impetus for the founding of a staggering number of new reading groups. The Association of Book Group Readers and Leaders, an online service for book groups in America, recently estimated that there were some 500,000 book groups with between 1 and 5 million members in America in 2002, twice as many as in 1994, before Oprah's launch in the mass media. Precise gender statistics have not been established but there are far more all-women groups than all-men. It is a modern-day phenomenon, though not an entirely new one. In earlier periods the relative paucity of successful new publications meant that a community of women readers was often more or less automatic. In the mid-eighteenth century, one had to read (or more importantly, be seen to read) novels like Samuel Richardson's *Pamela* to be fashionable. In the nineteenth century the serialisation of novels in the major periodicals of the day created a similar community of readers. Although the number of published titles rose steeply in the mid-twentieth century, women still come together to share in their reading. Today there are women's reading groups all over the world meeting in bars and restaurants, at workplaces, in prisons and, of course, in readers' homes. They involve varying age-ranges and socioeconomic classes and some are urban, some suburban, some rural. Women's reading groups are now as varied as women readers.

Some are long established and exclusive. The New York reading group, Causeries du Lundi ('Monday Chats'), has been running almost without a break for 125 years. (The name comes from the French literary critic Charles Augustin Sainte-Beuve's series of topical columns published every Monday in the Paris press between 1849 and 1869.) The New York group was founded by the philanthropist Elizabeth Hamilton Cullum. An early member of the Causeries described Cullum's vision for it, which was 'to develop latent talent where it might exist, in women looked upon as mere society women'. Rather than reading published books and meeting to discuss them, the group is a forum for women to read out their own work. Early essays were on art, architecture and archaeology. Today many women read out accounts of foreign travels. Current members are not unlike their nineteenth-century precursors; they tend to be well-born and well-off, although most of them now work. And it remains highly exclusive; new recruits have to be introduced by current members and admission is based on the impression made at three probationary meetings. Then you are either approved – or not.[8]

Three thousand miles to the west, very different women meet in very different circumstances. On Orkney, in the Outer Hebrides of Scotland, a reading group attracts members from a fifteen-mile radius. Like many rural groups it is made up of both 'ferryloupers' (incomers) and Orcadians (established residents) which makes for a particular dynamic. For readers who feel cut off, reading groups are particularly important, hence their presence in prisons, secure psychiatric hospitals, and day centres for the blind. A notable reading group in Cornton Vale, a women's prison in Stirling, Scotland, met in 2001 for weekly contextual Bible study under the guidance of a new chaplain. Some of the women were Christians (both Protestant and Catholic), while

61 The Causeries du Lundi reading group in New York, 2005.

others clearly attended to enjoy distraction and the refreshments – no doubt like many participants in reading groups elsewhere. The women felt an immediate identification with Jesus's agony and sense of abandonment in Gethsemane. Reading of Jesus's arrest, one asked, 'how long did he get?' The women also read critically and many objected to Jesus's acceptance of his fate in Gethsemane, and were frustrated that he did not protest his innocence. The Cornton Vale group clearly helped its members to make a new kind of sense of their imprisonment. They often recognised their own experience in biblical stories and characters – Ruth and Naomi were of particular interest. But the complexities of theological study also threw up problems. The relationship between sin and suffering proved particularly sensitive for the group leader.[9] Some wanted to know just how much more they had to take by way of punishment for their wrongdoings – in terms of months and years – before they might feel a sense of redemption and find an end to their suffering.

Another unusual women's reading group is made up of a fellowship of Israeli women in Chicago who have been meeting for more than a decade, discussing Israeli authors in Hebrew so as to maintain contact with their language, culture and community. Another group in Abu Dhabi is international with members from England, Scotland, Ireland, the US, Canada, Australia, New Zealand, the Philippines, Germany and Syria. Discussion is in English, which is a challenge for the only Japanese participant. One member reported: 'Last week we "did" *Emma*, the subject matter of which seemed to be a bit nearer life in Syria than in modern England.' Clearly the multiculturalism of the group brings fresh insights.[10]

The differences between the reading material available or chosen by modern women as opposed to men vary enormously from one part of the world to another. But even in those areas where men and women have equal access, disparities remain surprisingly marked. Certain distinctions emerge in childhood. In those countries with high levels of literacy there has been growing awareness that boys trail behind girls in reading performance at all age levels and the gap widens by the end of the teenage years. This is not a new trend: girls have been outperforming boys in US Department of Education reading tests for more than thirty years. The literacy gender gap spans every racial and ethnic group and holds true regardless of income, disability or facility with spoken English. In every country in the world, females, on average, have a higher level of reading literacy than males. And the difference is significant in all countries except Israel and Peru.

Some educators believe that teachers fail to offer boys appropriate reading matter, arguing that boys are stimulated by different material than that preferred by girls.[11] A study of reading tastes conducted in a school in a southeastern US state showed differences that adhere to common gender stereotypes. The girls reported a stronger interest in romance, friendship and animal stories, adventure and historical fiction, while the boys preferred adventure stories and non-fiction, particularly sports and science.[12]

Reading choices among adult men and women also differ. A 2004 poll surveyed 800 British men and women about their reading preferences, particularly which novels they would say were 'watershed' books; that is, those that had sustained the reader 'through key moments of transition or crisis in their lives'. For women, *Jane Eyre* was the clear winner, followed by *Pride and Prejudice*. Other top titles included *Anna Karenina*, *Lord of the Rings*, *The Hitchhiker's Guide to the Galaxy*, *Catch-22*, *Gone with the Wind*, *Rebecca*, *Heart of Darkness* and *The Golden Notebook*. For men, favourite novels were essentially novels of ideas that explore, sometimes among other concerns, essentially intellectual questions in which alienation, fate, free will and angst are central, including Albert Camus' *L'Étranger* (translated as *The Outsider* or *The Stranger*), Gabriel García Márquez's *One Hundred Years of Solitude*, J.D. Salinger's *The Catcher in the Rye* and Kurt Vonnegut's *Slaughterhouse-Five*. Most interesting was the initial response of a large proportion of the men: there was some unease with the notion of a 'watershed novel' in and of itself, and many of the men participating in the survey were reluctant to consider their reading in relation to moments of transition or crisis in their lives. It could well be that men are simply less willing to talk about aspects of their experience that they consider private; or it could be that men read with quite different expectations as to the effects their reading may have on them.

Surveys of this sort can provide only relatively crude insights into the differences between men's and women's reading, but some of these were striking. The notion that a work of fiction could act as a 'mentor' was raised by some of the men but not by any of the women, whereas the idea that a novel took the reader on an emotional journey that found resolution in a way which mapped onto their own lives and life-crises mattered to many of the women, but not the men. Six male authors were among the women's top twenty but only one female author appeared in the men's, Harper Lee's *To Kill A Mockingbird*. Yet both women and men claimed that the gender of the author played no role in their reading choices.

Some still argue that, as has been the case for much of history, the publishing world continues to be controlled largely by men, disadvantaging women authors – and therefore also women readers who might want to read their work. Others are convinced that the market is highly competitive and consumer-led, the industry mixed in terms of the gender of commissioning editors and marketing personnel, and the men in publishing in any case unbigoted and unprejudiced. And it is certainly the case that many women have been exceptionally successful in publishing, commanding very considerable power as highly self-conscious women readers. Gail Rebuck is chair and chief executive of Random House UK, one of the leading trade book publishers. Texan-born Dame Marjorie Scardino is responsible for the remarkable upturn in the fortunes of the *Financial Times* and its parent company, Pearson PLC. Scardino is the first female chief executive of a FTSE 100 company and has headed up Pearson, which is also home to the Penguin publishing group and Pearson Education, for over a decade. Victoria Barnsley's publishing career has been equally stellar. At the age of thirty she founded Fourth Estate and is now HarperCollins's UK chief executive.

Women readers like these are shaping the future of reading for both women and men. But the fact that debates about the influence of women and men on reading continue to be lively and heated suggests that women's and men's reading is still a subject of widespread interest, and seen by many as some kind of mysterious litmus test of gender difference. These and associated questions about men's and women's reading have also been assimilated into academic debates within various disciplines. Feminist literary theory – an approach to the study of literature and textual analysis that foregrounds questions of gender and the power relations between the sexes – is now part and parcel of most literature degrees.

In many countries women became significant players within the arts subjects in universities after the Second World War – and much of what it is to be an academic is dependent, of course, on reading. Women historians have recovered and read material which has allowed for new accounts of women's history in many parts of the world. Other women have authored many literary critical studies since the 1950s, sometimes drawing on or influencing other disciplines, and leaving what is essentially a record of what and how a group of highly self-conscious women readers have read. Reading is a way to gain knowledge and it may be that certain kinds of literary material, with all its associated ambiguities and difficulties, provide privileged modes of understanding ourselves and the world.

Different perspectives on reading emerge most readily today from the burgeoning number of more or less developed accounts on the web. Readers' reviews and descriptions of reading pleasures on blogs and in chatrooms allow the modern reader to read about others' reactions and to communicate her thoughts as never before. For those who argue that the publishing industry remains biased in favour of male authors and male tastes, then free access to all manner of written material online puts some of the commissioning editors' power in the readers' hands.

Some of the most successful bloggers in recent years have been women whose work has appealed mostly to a female readership. 'La Petite Anglaise' attracted an ardent following of readers – mostly women – with her lively accounts of her life as a single woman and single mother in Paris: the joys and frustrations of bringing up her bilingual toddler, 'Tadpole', who issued from her relationship with 'Mr Frog'; her failed romance with a man she met online; and her problems with her job. When Catherine Sanderson took her former employers to a tribunal for unfair dismissal, and won, her blog became globally famous. She was offered a £450,000 two-book deal and subsequently published a memoir based on her blog and a romantic novel, *French Kissing*, which have both sold well – mostly to women. Sanderson was inspired by 'Belle de Jour', who it was later revealed is Dr Brooke Magnanti, a UK-based scientist and a former London call girl. Her blog was enormously popular, winning the *Guardian*'s blog of the year award in 2003 and developing into three books (the first two of which were top-ten hits in the UK hardback and paperback charts) and a television series. Magnanti and Sanderson are two of many women writers who have made the transition from web-based to conventional publishing, achieving considerable commercial success underpinned by a substantial and largely female readership.

It is difficult not to feel excited by the myriad new reading opportunities available in the digital age. But the story of the woman reader in the twentieth and twenty-first centuries is also one of continuing illiteracy for very large numbers of women, as well as sophisticated new forms of censorship. The differences between women's reading experiences in different parts of the world are more marked than ever.

UNESCO has estimated that by 2015 nearly 800 million adults in the world will still be illiterate, perhaps as much as a fifth of the total world population. And throughout the world, rates of literacy are lower for women than for men: two-thirds of the world's illiterate people are women. South Asia has the highest rates of illiteracy; there, almost 60 per cent of women are illiterate. In the Arab states more than half the female population is illiterate, and almost half the women of Sub-Saharan Africa cannot read. In East Asia and Oceania (excluding Japan, Australia and New Zealand), the statistic drops sharply to some 20 per cent. In Latin America and the Caribbean more than 10 per cent of women are illiterate. Even in the so-called 'developed' world, some 2 per cent of women cannot read, roughly twice the proportion of men.[13] By and large, in developing countries and countries dominated by poverty or oppressive regimes, it is women who feel most keenly the urgent necessity of literacy. The trends have been encouraging – global adult illiteracy more or less halved between 1970 and 2005 – but there is still a very long way to go.[14]

The acquisition of literacy is only the first basic step towards being a reader. The availability of things to read continues to vary greatly from one part of the world to another and censorship, both of printed publications and, increasingly, of web-based reading material, is by no means a thing of the past. Some supposedly democratic countries with constitutional guarantees of freedom of expression are imposing digital filters, as are some undemocratic countries. Despite there being considerable Internet censorship in China, there are 17 million bloggers – but very few of them dare discuss sensitive issues, still less openly criticise government policy. Among Chinese blog tools are filters that block allegedly 'subversive' word strings and the companies responsible for sites, whether national or foreign, are under considerable pressure from the authorities to screen content. Chinese censorship is primarily of material that could be deemed politically inflammatory, but the Internet has also been a place where women's rights are discussed. In 2010, in a court in Fuzhou, three people were sentenced to between one and two years in prison for posting material online to help a woman pressurise the authorities to reinvestigate her daughter's death; police had ruled that the woman had died during an abnormal pregnancy.[15]

The Iranian Constitution stipulates that 'publications and news media shall enjoy freedom of expression provided that what they publish does not violate Islamic principles or the Civil Code'.[16] The definition of 'Islamic principles' is, of course, a matter of debate. But the Iranian authorities have been particularly determined to prevent women from reading material of an allegedly sexually subversive nature.[17] This includes 'images of women in provocative attire', according to the ONI (OpenNet Initiative).[18] Women's online magazines have been subjected to particularly rigorous scrutiny. Most of these are fashion magazines, but many also include articles about women's lives and forms of discrimination against women. Some also cover stories about human rights and women's oppression. *Marie Claire*, for example, has a section called 'World News on Women' that focuses on women's experiences in various countries. These, by implication, are often critical of some governments' policies. The magazine is heavily filtered and was forbidden by at least one Iranian proxy server.[19] Other blocked sites include playgirl.com, cosmopolitan.com, glamour.com, harpersbazaar.com and vanityfair.com. In previous periods censorship could prevent widespread access to certain kinds of reading but total censorship must have been rare; it only takes one extant copy of a book to be copied and recopied for it to escape the censors and begin to circulate again. The filtering of a country's media, and the blocking of servers, on the other hand, is a new and almost unassailable form of censorship.

There is growing awareness of the need to expose and oppose these repressive and pervasive tactics. In the UK, the Index on Censorship has developed into one of the world's highest-profile organisations promoting free expression. Feminists Against Censorship (FAC) was set up in 1989 in response to the National Council of Civil Liberties' condemnation of pornography. It defends the free production and availability of sexual material and upholds the idea of individual sexual expression. And while pornography is still sold to a largely male readership – though it could be argued that it is more looked at than read – today's women are reading more sexually explicit and erotically stimulating fiction than even twenty or thirty years ago. The so-called 'bonk-busters' – the fiction of Jackie Collins, Danielle Steel and Jilly Cooper – were extraordinarily successful in the 1970s and 1980s, selling in vast quantities around the globe. More recently the trend has been towards 'harder' romantic fiction. Black Lace (an imprint of Virgin Books) published top-shelf reading. Their website described their wares: 'we produce the most cutting-edge fantasy fiction because we never underestimate female sexuality. . . . And our readers still expect narratives that are entertaining as well as arousing. . . . Black Lace continues to change and develop to keep pace with an increasingly sophisticated audience.' That audience wanted stories that explored the darker side of sex, while still delivering an engaging narrative. Other cultures would not countenance such books.

It was, of course, precisely this pleasure that men feared women enjoying when women started to gain wider access to books in the eighteenth century, and then still more so in the nineteenth – and novels in particular. Wiertz's naked woman reader wickedly devouring novels supplied by the devil beside her bed returns to mind. Reading always has been an intriguing private activity and one that, for large numbers of women over the last century, remained controlled because of its continuing association with sexual fantasy and the crossing of the line from the imagined to the enacted. Even in the swinging sixties in London, some surprisingly outdated views on women's reading emerged during the *Lady Chatterley* trial. At one point the chief prosecutor, Mervyn Griffith-Jones, asked if D.H. Lawrence's novel was the kind of book 'you would wish your wife or servant to read?'[20] Implicit in his question was the suggestion that reading can encourage transgressive behaviour – a notion that was debated in classical times, when Ovid argued that the 'chaste' woman reader's reading would not make her behave immorally. Moral responsibility, he implied, rested with the reader, not the writer. Ovid also doubted that his poetry had the power to move people to action as others claimed. Griffith-Jones clearly believed that immoral reading might encourage an immoral society.

Not all women readers advocate complete access to reading material, of course. Those in communities or societies dominated by fundamentalist ideologies are acutely aware of the power of reading and are concerned to prevent free access to books that might undermine their values. For instance, many American Christian mothers have called for the 'satanic' *Harry Potter* books to be banned, and censored in libraries. They have even organised public book burnings. Men's anxieties about what women read, and how, may have lessened or completely receded in many parts of the world. In these places it is often women readers, more than their male counterparts, who have become the militant censors of children's reading – both boys' and girls'.

In other parts of the world, however, in response to widespread censorship, informal women's educational fellowships have been set up often in dangerous circumstances and with ambitious objectives. A conscious desire to read across national boundaries lies behind one account of a very particular group. The 2003 bestseller *Reading Lolita in Tehran: A Memoir in Books* by the Iranian academic Azar Nafisi, provides intriguing and not uncontroversial insights. It is an account of the author's time teaching at the University of Tehran from 1979 during the Revolution (1978–81) until she was expelled in 1981 because of her refusal to wear the veil. The same year she was appointed to the Free Islamic University and Allameh Tabatabei University. She resigned fourteen years later. Her book club ran from 1995 to 1997, when she decided to leave the country.

The book is structured around accounts of the group's discussions of Western literature. The most controversial novel read by the club, which comprised seven women students and Nafisi, was Nabokov's *Lolita*, first

62 Two women reading *Lady Chatterley's Lover*, 1960. The woman on the left appears to have bought three copies.

published in Paris in 1955. It is notorious both for its curious narration – the unreliable account of the middle-aged Humbert Humbert – and for his obsession with a twelve-year old girl with whom he establishes sexual relations. Just as Humbert shapes Lolita into an obstinate girlish manipulator, the ayatollahs and Islamic fundamentalists project their own fantasies onto Iranian women.

But Nafisi shies away from any crude comparisons: 'we were *not* Lolita, the Ayatollah was *not* Humbert and this republic was *not* what Humbert called his princedom by the sea. Lolita was *not* a critique of the Islamic Republic, but it went against the grain of all totalitarian perspectives.'[21] Instead of merely mapping their own identities onto Lolita, Nafisi's women readers used the book as a peculiar new lens through which they could see their own lives in a startlingly new way.

Reading Lolita in Tehran was in many ways as controversial as *Lolita* itself. Professor Hamid Dabashi of the University of Columbia claimed that the book was grist to the mill of the Bush administration's attempts to legitimise attacks on Iran and Iraq. He also argued that Nafisi was attempting to win her students over to a Western, American vision of life. This kind of debate about the influence of 'foreign' reading has, of course, a long history; the ancient Romans worried about the influence of Greek culture, particularly what were seen as its feminising features. Nafisi vociferously denied the allegations made against her but the rumpus is ample evidence of the continuing political significance of some reading. And although global marketing strategies have led to vast print-runs of fewer Western titles sold in English and English translation throughout the world, which threatens to impose a cultural conformity and damage the capacity of local publishers to publish in local languages for local communities, books like *Reading Lolita in Tehran* remind us of the value of reading against the grain. Nafisi's primary aim, as any sensitive reader of her account will recognise, was to explore individual women readers' responses to books that are culturally distinct.

Some women's belief in their right to read and encourage others to read has led them to take great risks, like Nafisi. In Herat, Afghanistan, under the Taliban, girls and women were excluded from education. A fellowship of women writers who belonged to the Herat Literary Circle set up a group called the Sewing Circles of Herat as a cover for establishing schools for women. The Golden Needle Sewing School was founded in the mid-1990s. Christina Lamb, a journalist and writer, found out about it while visiting Afghanistan. It became central to a book she wrote about the country, *Sewing Circles of Herat: A Personal Voyage Through Afghanistan*, published in 2002. For five years women came to the school ostensibly to sew, but actually to read together. And most of their reading was made up of banned foreign titles:

> They would arrive in their burqas with their bags full of material and scissors. Underneath they would have notebooks and pens. And once they got inside, instead of learning to sew, they would actually be talking about Shakespeare and James Joyce, Dostoyevsky and their own writing. It was a

63 Two Iranian students reading a newspaper, 2000. This is the original photograph, cropped to hide the actual reading material, that was used on the jacket of Nafisi's *Reading Lolita in Tehran*. Insinuations of sex and the forbidden are still part and parcel of depicting women readers.

tremendous risk they were taking. If they had been caught, they would have been, at the very least, imprisoned and tortured. Maybe hanged.[22]

Children playing outside the school would act as lookouts and if they saw the religious police in the area would alert the women, giving them time to hide their books and take up their sewing.

This is an extreme but by no means unique example of the kinds of risks women have been willing to take for the sake of reading and for the opportunity to discuss their reading with others. These dangers were made much more immediate for me in the autumn of 2012. Malala Yousafzai was shot in the head by Taliban gunmen, returning home from school by bus. Some weeks later, she was flown to the UK and admitted to the Queen Elizabeth Hospital in Birmingham, only an hour or so from where I live. She was born in the Swat District of Pakistan in 1997 and became a well-known activist promoting education – particularly girls' – while a schoolgirl not yet in her teens. She began her famous blog in 2009. At times the Taliban had banned girls from attending school in the Swat Valley and when the Pakistani military moved into the area the second Battle of Swat took place. That summer the *New York Times* made a documentary about her life under the Taliban. She rose to world fame and is the youngest person ever to have been nominated for the Nobel Peace Prize.

A week or so after the attempt on her life, Gordon Brown, the former British prime minister and now UN Special Envoy for Global Education, started a petition with three aims in view. The first called on 'Pakistan to agree a plan to deliver education for every child'; the second for 'all countries to outlaw discrimination against girls,' and the third called on 'international organisations to ensure the world's 61 million out-of-school children are in education by the end of 2015'. The petition is called, 'I am Malala'.

This is an ambitious initiative and one which has already moved the goal of world literacy higher up global development agendas. And the Internet and e-readers can only make access to reading material increasingly available, inexpensive and private. The market for e-books is international, and reading on an e-reader relatively secret. The future of women's reading – like the future of the relations between women and men – looks as challenging, intriguing, contested and lively as its past.

—◦◦◦—

Endnotes

Introduction

1. Doris Lessing, *Index on Censorship*, vol. 28, no. 2 (Apr. 1999), pp. 158–9.
2. Anna Seward, letter to William Hayley, 17 Aug. 1789, in *Letters of Anna Seward: Written Between the Years 1784 and 1807*, ed. A. Constable, vol. 2, Edinburgh: Archibald Constable, 1811, p. 399.
3. P.F. Kornicki, 'Unsuitable Books for Women?: "Genji Monogatari" and "Ise Monogatari" in Late Seventeenth-Century Japan', *Monumenta Nipponica*, vol. 60, no. 2 (2005), pp. 147–93.
4. The successive versions of the *Index* are published in the Sherbrooke University edition, ed. J.M. De Bujanda, 10 vols, Quebec: Centre d'Études de la Renaissance, 1985–95.
5. For an excellent overview of censorship, see *The Oxford Companion to the Book*, ed. Michael F. Suarez and H.R. Woudhuysen, vol. 1, Oxford: OUP, 2010, pp. 596–8.
6. Alberto Manguel, *A History of Reading*, London: Flamingo, 1997, p. 270.
7. Randall Martin, ed., *Women Writers in Renaissance England: An Annotated Anthology*, 2nd edn, London: Longman, 2010, p. 91.
8. Steven Roger Fischer, *A History of Reading*, London: Reaktion Books, 2004, p. 273.
9. Alan Bennett, *The Uncommon Reader: A Novella*, New York: Farrar, Straus and Giroux, 2004.
10. Ibid., p. 11.
11. Ibid., pp. 21–2.
12. Ibid., pp. 30–1.
13. Hans-Georg Gadamer, *Philosophical Hermeneutics*, trans. David E. Linge, Berkeley, CA: U of California P, 1976, p. 57.
14. Georg Christoph Lichtenberg, *The Lichtenberg Reader*, trans. and ed. Franz H. Mautner and Henry Hatfield, Boston, NJ: The Beacon Press, 1959, 'Notebook E'; Ralph Waldo Emerson, *Society and Solitude: Twelve Chapters by Ralph Waldo Emerson*, ed. H.G. Callaway, New York: Edwin Mellen Press, 2008.
15. Quoted by Sandra Gilbert and Susan Gubar, *The Madwoman in the Attic: The Woman Writer and the Nineteenth-Century Literary Imagination*, New Haven and London: Yale UP, 1979, p. 30.
16. Jacques Olivier, *Alphabet de l'imperfection et malice des femmes . . . augmenté de plusieurs histoires . . .*, Rouen, France: J. Oursel, 1683.

17. Princess Elizabeth Asquith Bibesco, http://www.quotationspage.com (accessed Mar. 2011).
18. Jane Collier, *An Essay on the Art of Ingeniously Tormenting*, ed. Katharine A. Craik, Oxford: OUP, 2006, pp. 14–20, 49–59.
19. James Fordyce, *Sermons to Young Women*, 5th edn, 2 vols, London: D. Payne, 1766.
20. Richard Sheridan, *The Rivals*, ed. Tiffany Stern, London: A&C Black Publishers Ltd, 2004, p. 39.
21. Javier Marias introduces the marquise du Deffand in his witty and whimsical little book, *Written Lives*, trans. Margaret Jull Costa, Edinburgh: Canongate, 2007, pp. 92–9.
22. Ibid., pp. 22–7.
23. Betty Travitsky, ed., *The Paradise of Women: Writings by English Women of the Renaissance*, Westport, CT: Greenwood Press, 1981, pp. 52, 62.
24. For a recently published, well-illustrated introduction to images of women and books, see Christiane Inmann, *Forbidden Fruit: A History of Women and Books in Art*, New York: Prestel Books, 2009.
25. Marcel Proust, *In Search of Lost Time*, vol. 6, *Time Regained*, trans. Andreas Mayor and Terence Kilmartin, rev. D.J. Enright, London: Vintage Books, 2000, p. 273.
26. Jesse Lee Bennett, *What Books Can Do for You: A Sketch Map of the Frontiers of Knowledge, with Lists of Selected Books*, New York: George H. Doran Company, 1923, pp. vii, 43.

1 Primitives, Goddesses and Aristocrats

1. Michel Schmidt-Chevalier, 'Were the Cave Paintings in Southwest France Made by Women?', *Leonardo*, vol. 14, no. 4 (Autumn 1981), pp. 302–3.
2. Ibid., p. 302.
3. For summaries of research on the earliest writing systems see: Henri-Jean Martin, *The History and Power of Writing*, trans. Lydia G. Cochrane, Chicago, IL: U of Chicago P, 1994; and Steven Roger Fischer, *A History of Writing*, London: Reaktion Books, 2001.
4. P. Michalowski, 'Writing and Literacy in Early States: a Mesopotamianist Perspective', in D. Keller-Cohen, ed., *Literacy: Interdisciplinary Conversations*, Cresskill, NJ: Hampton Press, 1994, pp. 49–70.
5. See William Hallo and J.J.A. van Dijk, *The Exaltation of Inanna*, New Haven and London: Yale UP, 1968; and Betty de Shong Meador, *Princess, Priestess, Poet: The Sumerian Temple Hymns of Enheduanna*, Austin, TX: U of Texas P, 2009.
6. Meador, *Princess*, p. 182; Hallo and van Dijk, *Exaltation*, p. 57.
7. Betty de Shong Meador, *Lady of Largest Heart: Poems of the Sumerian High Priestess Enheduanna*, Austin, TX: U of Texas P, 2000.
8. *The Epic of Gilgamesh*, trans. Nancy K. Sandars, London: Penguin Books, 1972, p. 102.
9. Tzvi Abusch, 'The Development and Meaning of the Epic of Gilgamesh: An Interpretive Essay', *Journal of the American Oriental Society*, vol. 121, no. 4 (Oct.–Dec. 2001), pp. 614–22.
10. S.A. Meier, 'Women and Communication in the Ancient Near East', *Journal of the American Oriental Society*, vol. 111, no. 3 (1991), p. 542.
11. Karen Rhea Nemet-Nejat provides fascinating insights into women's lives and scribal activities in *Daily Life in Ancient Mesopotamia*, Westport, CT: Greenwood Press, 1998, pp. 150–1.
12. Quoted by Steven Roger Fischer, *A History of Reading*, London: Reaktion Books, 2004, p. 23, rephrasing Alberto Manguel, *A History of Reading*, London: Flamingo, 1997, p. 183.
13. Meier, 'Women and Communication', p. 542.
14. John Baines, 'Literacy and Ancient Egyptian Society', *Man* (New Series), vol. 18 (1983), pp. 572–9; L. Lesko, 'Literacy', in D. Redford ed., *The Oxford Encyclopedia of Ancient Egypt*, Oxford and New York: OUP, 2001, vol. 2, pp. 297–9.
15. Fischer, *History of Reading*, pp. 31–2.

16. Ibid., pp. 45–97.
17. An excellent account is provided by Rosalind Thomas, *Literacy and Orality in Ancient Greece*, New York: CUP, 1992. André Lardinois and Laura McClure, eds, *Making Silence Speak: Women's Voices in Greek Literature and Society*, Princeton, NJ: Princeton UP, 2011, is equally informative and devoted to women.
18. Quoted by Wesley Trimpi, 'The Definition and Practice of Literary Studies', *New Literary History*, vol. 2, no. 1, *A Symposium on Literary History* (Autumn 1970), pp. 187–92.
19. The two-volume collection of essays, *Re-Reading Sappho: Reception and Transmission*, ed. Ellen Greene, Berkeley and London: U of California P, 1996, provides vivid insights into Sappho, her literary legacy and the myths surrounding her.
20. Martin West, 'A New Sappho poem', *Times Literary Supplement*, 21 Jun. 2005, p. 8.
21. Christine de Pizan, *Le Livre de la Cité des Dames*, Paris: Stock, 1986; Christine De Pizan, *The Book of the City of Ladies*, trans. Rosalind Brown-Grant, London: Penguin Books, 2000.
22. Anne Carson, *If Not, Winter: Fragments of Sappho*, New York: Alfred A. Knopf, 2002.
23. Sappho's afterlife has been largely in the hands of men. A thorough scholarly study of Sappho's literary legacy is provided by Margaret Williamson in *Sappho's Immortal Daughters*, Cambridge, MA: Harvard UP, 1996.
24. Susan Gubar, 'Multiple Personality: The Sappho Companion edited and introduced by Margaret Reynolds', *The Women's Review of Books*, vol. 18, no. 12 (2001), pp. 13–14.
25. Judith Hallett, *Fathers and Daughters in Roman Society: Women and the Elite Family*, Princeton, NJ: Princeton UP, 1984.
26. Emily A. Hemelrijk, *Matrona Docta: Educated Women in the Roman Élite from Cornelia to Julia Domna*, London and New York: Routledge, 1999, p. 99.
27. A lively and accessible introduction to Ovid the man and his poetry is Sara Mack's *Ovid*, London and New Haven: Yale UP, 1988. See also Elaine Fantham, *Ovid's Metamorphoses*, Oxford: OUP, 2004.
28. Bruce Gibson, 'Ovid on Reading: Reading Ovid. Reception in Ovid Tristia II', *Journal of Roman Studies*, vol. 89 (1999), pp. 19–37.
29. Martial, *Select Epigrams*, ed. Lindsay Watson and Patricia Watson, Cambridge: CUP, 2003, pp. 12–13.
30. Quoted by Fischer, *History of Reading*, p. 45.
31. Susan Silberberg-Peirce, 'The Muse Restored: Images of Women in Roman Painting', *Women's Art Journal*, vol. 14, no. 2 (Autumn 1993–Winter 1994), pp. 28–36, p. 28.
32. *Quintilian: The Orator's Education*, Loeb Classical Library, 5 vols, ed. and trans. Donald A. Russell, Cambridge, MA and London: Harvard UP, 2001.
33. See Jennifer Hall, *Lucian's Satire*, New York: Arno Press, 1981.
34. Juvenal, Satire VI, ll. 451–4, *Juvenal and Persius*, Loeb Classical Library, trans. Susanna Morton Braund, Cambridge, MA: Harvard UP, 2004, p. 277.
35. For a fascinating account of the lives and status of prostitutes in the ancient world see Christopher A. Faraone and Laura K. McClure, eds, *Prostitutes and Courtesans in the Ancient World*, Madison, WI: U of Wisconsin P, 2006.
36. Anna McCullough, review of Emily Hemelrijk's *Matrona Docta*, *The Journal of Roman Studies*, vol. 97 (2007), pp. 285–6.
37. Hemelrijk, *Matrona Docta*, p. 122.
38. See T. Hägg, *The Novel in Antiquity*, Columbia and Princeton: UPs of California, 1991; R.L. Hunter, *A Study of Daphnis and Chloe*, Cambridge: CUP, 1983; and G. Anderson, *Eros Sophistes: Ancient Novelists at Play*, New York: OUP, 2000.
39. Brigitte Egger, 'The Role of Women in the Greek Novel: Woman as Heroine and Reader', in *Oxford Readings in the Greek Novel*, ed. Simon Swain, Oxford: OUP, 1999, pp. 108–36.
40. *Lucian*, Loeb Classical Library, trans. A.M. Harmon, Cambridge, MA: Harvard UP, 2006, vol. 4, p. 273.

41. *The Writings of Medieval Women: An Anthology*, trans. Marcel Thiebaux, London: Routledge, 1994, p. 52.

42. Gerontius, *The Life of Melania the Younger*, ed. and trans. Elizabeth A. Clark, New York and Toronto: Edwin Mellen, 1984, quoted by Fischer, *History of Reading*, p. 79. See also Anne Yarbrough, 'Christianization in the Fourth Century: The Example of Roman Women', *Church History*, vol. 45, no. 2 (Jun. 1976), pp. 149–65.

43. Quoted by Fischer, *History of Reading*, p. 91.

44. See J.J. Collins, 'Sibylline Oracles (Second Century BC–Seventh Century AD)', in James H. Charlesworth, ed., *The Old Testament Pseudepigrapha*, Garden City, NY: Doubleday, 1983, vol. 1, pp. 223–316.

45. Quoted by Fischer, *History of Reading*, p. 90.

46. *St Augustine's Confessions, with an English Translation, by William Watts, 1631*, 2 vols, Cambridge, MA and London: Harvard UP, 1989; see R.S. Pine-Coffin, *Saint Augustine: Confessions*, London: Penguin Books, 1961; also Donald G. Marshall, 'Making Letters Speak: Interpreter as Orator in Augustine's "De Doctrina Christiana"', *Religion and Literature*, vol. 24, no. 2 (Summer 1992), pp. 1–17.

2 Reading in the Not-So-Dark Ages

1. *A History of Women in the West*, vol. 2, *Silences of the Middle Ages*, ed. Christiane Klapisch-Zuber, Cambridge, MA: Belknap Press of Harvard UP, 1992.

2. Quoted by Alberto Manguel, *A History of Reading*, London: Flamingo, 1997, p. 97.

3. See the introduction to *Letters of Medieval Women*, ed. Anne Crawford, Stroud: Sutton Publishing, 2002.

4. Quoted by Manguel, *History of Reading*, p. 49.

5. Isidore of Seville, quoted by Malcolm Beckwith Parkes, *Pause and Effect: An Introduction to the History of Punctuation in the West*, Berkeley, CA: U of California P, 1993, p. 35.

6. Caesarius's *Vita*, written by contemporary admirers, is translated along with other important texts by William E. Klingshirn in *Caesarius of Arles: Life, Testament, Letters*, Liverpool: Liverpool UP, 1994. For what is essentially a biography, see William E. Klingshirn, *Caesarius of Arles: The Making of a Christian Community in Late Antique Gaul*, Cambridge: CUP, 1995; see also Julie Ann Smith, *Ordering Women's Lives: Penitentials and Nunnery Rules in the Early Medieval West*, Aldershot, Hampshire and Burlington, VT: Ashgate, 2001, pp. 201–4.

7. Klingshirn, trans., *Caesarius of Arles: Life, Testament, Letters*, p. 39.

8. *Sainted Women of the Dark Ages*, ed. Jo Ann McNamara, John E. Halborg and Gordon Whatley Durham, NC: Duke UP, 1992, p. 93.

9. Karen Cherewatuk and Ulrike Wiethaus, *Dear Sister: Medieval Women and the Epistolary Genre*, Philadelphia, PA: U of Pennsylvania P, 1993.

10. Baudonivia, *Vita*, in McNamara, Halborg and Whatley, eds, *Sainted Women*, p. 86.

11. Maeve B. Callan, 'St Darerca and Her Sister Scholars: Women and Education in Medieval Ireland', *Gender and History*, vol. 15 (Apr. 2003), pp. 32–49.

12. St Bridget of Sweden, *Revelationes*, autograph manuscript, Royal Library, Stockholm, Sweden, http://www.theeuropeanlibrary.org/exhibition/treasures/religions/ (accessed Jan. 2012).

13. Patricia Ranft, *Women in Western Intellectual Culture, 600–1500*, New York and Basingstoke: Palgrave Macmillan, 2002, p. 2.

14. Ibid., p. 196.

15. Bede, *The Ecclesiastical History of the English Church and People*, Oxford: OUP, 1996, ch. 22.

16. Ranft, *Women*, p. 3.

17. Ibid., p. 3.

18. Ibid., pp. 11–12.
19. See Dhuoda, *Liber Manualis*, translated as *Manuel pour mon fils*, ed. Pierre Riché, trans. Bernard de Vregille and Claude Mondézert, 2nd edn, Paris: Les Editions du Cerf, 1991, including an excellent introduction.
20. For a fascinating study of Hrotsvit's rewritings of Terence, see Katharina H. Wilson, *Hrotsvit of Gandersheim: The Ethics of Authorial Stance*, Leiden and New York: E.J. Brill, 1988.
21. Ibid., p. 79.
22. Ibid., p. 78.
23. Stephen L. Wailes, *Spirituality and Politics in the Works of Hrotsvit of Gandersheim*, Selinsgrove, PA: SU Press, 2006.
24. Rosamond McKitterick, 'Women in the Ottonian Church: An Iconographic Perspective', *Studies in Church History*, vol. 27 (1990), pp. 79–100.
25. Mohammad Akram Nadwi, *Al-Muhaddithat: The Women Scholars in Islam*, London and Oxford: Interface Publications, 2007.
26. Deng Xiaonan, 'Women in Turfan during the Sixth to Eighth Centuries: A Look at Their Activities Outside the Home', *Journal of Asian Studies*, vol. 58, no. 1 (Feb. 1999), pp. 85–103.

3 History, Mystery and Copying

1. Anna Komnene, *The Alexiad of Anna Comnena*, trans. E.R. Sewter, London: Penguin Books, 2009, p. 3.
2. Ibid., p. 3.
3. Ibid., p. 150
4. Ibid., p. 150.
5. Ibid., p. 150.
6. Judith Herrin, *Women in Purple: Rulers of Medieval Byzantium*, Princeton, NJ: Princeton UP, 2004.
7. *Byzantine Monastic Foundation Documents: A Complete Translation of the Surviving Founder's Typika and Testaments*, ed. John Thomas and Angela Constantinides Hero, Washington, DC: Dumbarton Oaks, 2000, p. 1564.
8. *Bibliotheca Hagiographica Graeca*, 2nd edn, Brussels: Société des Bollandistes, 1909.
9. Steven Roger Fischer, *A History of Reading*, London: Reaktion Books, 2004, pp. 170–1.
10. Samuel H. Cross, 'Mediaeval Russian Contacts with the West', *Speculum*, vol. 10, no. 2 (Apr. 1935), pp. 137–44.
11. Leo Wiener, *Anthology of Russian Literature from the Earliest Period to the Present Time*, 2 vols, New York and London: G.P. Putnam's Sons: 1902–3, vol. 1, pp. 51–6.
12. Ibid., p. 54.
13. Joan M. Ferrante, *To the Glory of Her Sex*, Bloomington, IN: Indiana UP, 1997, p. 186.
14. Hildegard, letter to Guibert of Gembloux, before 1177, in Karen Cherewatuk and Ulrike Wiethaus, *Dear Sister: Medieval Women and the Epistolary Genre*, Philadelphia, PA: U of Pennsylvania P, 1993, p. 49.
15. Patricia Ranft, *Women in Western Intellectual Culture, 600–1500*, New York and Basingstoke: Palgrave Macmillan, 2002, p. 55.
16. Ibid., p. 69.
17. *The Letters of Abelard and Heloise*, trans. Betty Radice, rev. M.T. Clanchy, London: Penguin Books, 2003.
18. Abelard, *Sicet Nom*, quoted in ibid., p. lxxxi.
19. Ranft, *Women*, p. 44.
20. Radice, trans., *Letters*, p. 68.
21. Quoted in Ranft, *Women*, p. 68.
22. Ibid., p. 49.

23. Ibid., p. 45.
24. Kelly Boyd, *Encyclopedia of Historians and Historical Writing*, 2 vols, London and Chicago: Fitzroy Dearborn Publishers, 1999; *Renaissance and Renewal in the Twelfth Century*, ed. Robert L. Benson, Giles Constable and Carol D. Lanham, Cambridge, MA: Harvard UP, 1982.
25. Frank Barlow, *The English Church 1066–1154: A History of the Anglo-Norman Church*, London: Longman, 1979, p. 229.
26. Nicholas Orme, 'The Culture of Children in Medieval England', *Past and Present*, vol. 148, no. 1 (Aug. 1995), p. 77.
27. This anecdote is cited by Carolyne Larrington in her indispensable book, *Women and Writing in Medieval Europe: A Sourcebook*, London: Routledge, 1995.
28. See http://plato.stanford.edu/entries/maimonides/ (accessed Jan. 2012) and Oliver Leaman, *An Introduction to Classical Islamic Philosophy*, Cambridge: CUP, 2002.
29. James E. Lindsay, *Daily Life in the Medieval Islamic World*, Greenwood, CT: Greenwood Press, 2005.
30. Ibid., p. 198.
31. Mohammad Akram Nadwi, *Al-Muhaddithat: The Women Scholars in Islam*, London and Oxford: Interface Publications, 2007.
32. Lois Beck and Guity Nashat, *Women in Iran from the Rise of Islam to 1800*, Champaign, IL: UI Press, 2003. The number of women scholars continued to rise. The fifteenth-century Islamic writer Al-Sakhawi devoted an entire volume of his twelve-volume biographical dictionary, *Daw al-lami*, to his teachers, providing details of 1,075 women scholars.
33. Eileen Power, *Medieval English Nunneries, c. 1275 to 1535*, Cambridge: CUP, 1922 (new edn, 2010).
34. Marie-Luise Ehrenschwendtner, 'A Library Collected by and for the Use of Nuns: St. Catherine's Convent, Nuremberg', in *Women and the Book: Assessing the Visual Evidence*, ed. Lesley Janette Smith and Jane H.M. Taylor, London: British Musuem Press, 2007, pp. 123–32.
35. Margaret Deanesly, 'Vernacular Books in England in the Fourteenth and Fifteenth Centuries', *The Modern Language Review*, vol. 15, no. 4 (Oct. 1920), pp. 349–58.
36. David N. Bell, *What Nuns Read: Books and Libraries in Medieval English Nunneries*, Kalamazoo, MI: Cistercian Publications, 1995.

4 Outside the Cloister

1. Steven Roger Fischer, *A History of Reading*, London: Reaktion Books, 2004, p. 165.
2. Carolyne Larrington, *Women and Writing in Medieval Europe: A Sourcebook*, London: Routledge, 1995, pp. 223–4.
3. Quoted in Albrecht Classen, *The Power of a Woman's Voice in Medieval and Early Modern Literatures*, Berlin and New York: Walter de Gruyter & Co., 2007, p. 125.
4. Joseph Bédier, 'Les lais de Marie de France', *Revue des Deux Mondes*, Paris, 15 Oct. 1891. Translation by R. Howard Bloch, *The Anonymous Marie de France*, Chicago and London: U of Chicago P, 2003, p. 24.
5. *The Lais of Marie de France*, trans. Glyn S. Burgess and Keith Busby, London: Penguin Books, 1999, p. 41.
6. Marcelle Thiébaux, ed. and trans., *The Writings of Medieval Women: An Anthology*, 2nd edn, New York: Garland Press, 1994, p. 279.
7. *Ancrene Wisse: Guide for Anchoresses*, trans. Hugh White, London: Penguin Books, 1993.
8. Bella Millett and Jocelyn Wogan-Browne, eds, *Medieval English Prose for Women: Selections from the Katherine Group and Ancrene Wisse*, Oxford: Clarendon Press, 1992.

9. Alberto Manguel, *A History of Reading*, London: Flamingo, 1997, p. 73.
10. Franco Mormando, 'Bernardino of Siena, "Great Defender" or "Merciless Betrayer" of Women?', *Italica*, vol. 75, no. 1 (Spring 1998), pp. 22–40.
11. Arnved Nedkvitne, *The Social Consequences of Literacy in Medieval Scandinavia*, Turnout, Belgium: Brepols Publishers, 2005.
12. John Higgitt, 'The Murthly Hours', *CHB Newsletter*, 2001. See also his book, *The Murthly Hours: Devotion, Literacy and Luxury in Paris, England and the Gaelic West*, London: British Library Publishing, 2000. The Murthly Hours can be viewed at http://digital.nls.uk/murthlyhours/ (accessed Jan. 2012).
13. Fischer, *History of Reading*, p. 188.
14. Sarah Salih and Denise Nowakowski Baker, eds, *Julian of Norwich's Legacy: Medieval Mysticism and Post-Medieval Reception*, New York: Palgrave Macmillan, 2009.
15. Linda Olson and Kathryn Kerby Fulton, eds, *Voices in Dialogue: Reading Women in the Middle Ages*, Notre Dame, IN: U of Notre Dame P, 2005; Liz Herbert McAvoy, ed., *A Companion to Julian of Norwich*, Cambridge: D.S. Brewer, 2008.
16. David N. Bell, *What Nuns Read: Books and Libraries in Medieval English Nunneries*, Kalamazoo, MI: Cistercian Publications, 1995.
17. Rosalind Brown-Grant, *Christine de Pizan and the Moral Defence of Women: Reading Beyond Gender*, Cambridge: CUP, 1999.
18. For examples of Matheolus's tirades, see Karen Pratt, *Woman Defamed and Woman Defended: An Anthology of Medieval Texts*, Oxford: OUP, 1992. This book also contains Le Fèvre's translation (*c.* 1371–72) of a subtle poem, the *Liber lamentationum Matheoluli*, written around 1295 by Mathieu of Boulogne. Christine de Pizan, *The Book of the City of Ladies*, trans. Rosalind Brown-Grant, London: Penguin Books, 1999.
19. Brown-Grant, *Christine de Pizan*, pp. 5–6.
20. Christine's skilful use of persuasion and style came from her study of the classical philosophers, rhetoricians and poets, and from her familiarity with medieval rules for eloquence. In her own writing she occasionally referred to rhetoricians, and to rhetorical eloquence as a goal of the accomplished speaker and writer. Sometimes she presented herself as a fully qualified participant in literary exchanges; at other times, she mentioned rhetoric in delightfully artful apologies, denying her own eloquence while preparing to verbally demolish her opponents.
21. Charity Scott Stokes, 'Margery Kempe's Family Background and Early Years, 1373–1393', *Mystics Quarterly*, no. 25 (Mar./Jun. 1999); Janel M. Mueller, 'Autobiography of a New "Creatur": Female Spirituality, Selfhood, and Authorship in *The Book of Margery Kempe*', *New York Literary Forum* (1984), pp. 12–13, 63–75.
22. Raymond A. Powell, 'Margery Kempe: An Exemplar of Late Medieval English Piety', *The Catholic Historical Review*, vol. 89, no. 1 (2003), pp. 1–23, 7, 11.
23. John Foxe, *Actes and Monuments*, 1576 edn, book 8, p. 970.
24. Susan Powell, 'Lady Margaret Beaufort and her Books', *The Library*, 6th ser., vol. 20, no. 3 (Sep. 1998), pp. 197–239.
25. Cited in ibid., p. 198.
26. Yu-Chiao Wang, 'Caxton's Romances and Their Early Tudor Readers', *Huntington Library Quarterly*, vol. 67, no. 2 (Jun. 2004), pp. 173–88.
27. Kenneth Charlton, ' "False fonde bookes, ballades and rimes": An Aspect of Informal Education in Early Modern England', *History of Education Quarterly*, vol. 27, no. 4 (Winter 1987), pp. 449–71.
28. N.F. Blake, ed., *Caxton's Own Prose*, Oxford: Clarendon Press, 1973.
29. Rebecca Warren Davidson, *Unseen Hands: Women Printers, Binders, and Book Designers*, Princeton University Library, Graphic Arts Collection, http://libweb2.princeton.edu/rbsc2/ga/unseenhands/ (accessed Nov. 2005).
30. Ibid.

31. Deborah Parker, 'Women in the Book Trade in Italy, 1475–1620', *Renaissance Quarterly*, vol. 49, no. 3 (Autumn 1996), pp. 509–41.
32. Ibid., p. 512.
33. Ibid., p. 515.
34. Vincent Ilardi, *Renaissance Vision from Spectacles to Telescopes*, Philadelphia, PA: American Philosophical Society, 2007.
35. Burgess and Busby, trans., *Lais of Marie de France*, p. 87.
36. There is no agreement as to who the artist or artists responsible for the decoration of Mary's Book of Hours might have been.

5 'To Reade Such Bookes . . . My Selfe to Edyfye'

1. Moderata Fonte, *The Worth of Women – Wherein is Clearly Revealed Their Nobility and Their Superiority to Men*, ed. and trans. Virginia Cox, Chicago: U of Chicago P, 1997, pp. 76–7.
2. This has been mapped with a high degree of accuracy by Philippe Nieto, 'Géographie des impressions européennes du XVe siècle', *Revue française du livre*, nos 118–21 (2003), pp. 118–73.
3. Steven Roger Fischer, *A History of Reading*, London: Reaktion Books, 2004, p. 224.
4. Ibid., pp. 224–5.
5. Miriam Usher Chrisman, *Lay Culture, Learned Culture: Books and Social Change in Strasbourg, 1480–1599*, New Haven and London: Yale UP, 1982, pp. 69–70.
6. See http://en.wikipedia.org/wiki/Bible_translations_by_language (accessed Feb. 2008).
7. E.E. Reynolds, *Margaret Roper: Eldest Daughter of St Thomas More*, London: Burns & Oates, 1960, p. 38.
8. Ibid., p. 227; Alberto Manguel, *A History of Reading*, London: Flamingo, 1997, p. 270.
9. Jeremy Munday, *Introducing Translation Studies: Theories and Applications*, Abingdon, Oxon: Routledge, 2001, p. 24.
10. David Norton, *A Textual History of the King James Bible*, Cambridge: CUP, 2005, p. 5.
11. The Council of Trent, Fourth Session, *The Canons and Decrees of the Sacred and Oecumenical Council of Trent*, trans. J. Waterworth, London: Dolman, 1848, pp. 17–21.
12. Manguel, *History of Reading*, p. 271.
13. Tyndale's preface to his translation of the Pentateuch, 1530, quoted in Manguel, *History of Reading*, p. 272.
14. Ibid., p. 273.
15. Ibid., p. 275.
16. Randall Martin, ed., *Women Writers in Renaissance England: An Annotated Anthology*, 2nd edn, London: Longman, 2010, p. 45.
17. Janel Mueller, 'Complications of Intertextuality: John Fisher, Katherine Parr and "The Book of the Crucifix"', in C.C. Brown and A.F. Marotti, eds, *Texts and Cultural Change in Early Modern England*, Basingstoke: Macmillan, 1997, pp. 15–35.
18. Elaine V. Beilin, ed., *The Examinations of Anne Askew*, New York and Oxford: OUP, 1996, pp. xv–xxiii; Elaine V. Beilin, *Redeeming Eve: Women Writers of the Renaissance*, Princeton, NJ: Princeton UP, 1987, pp. 36–7; Janet Clare, 'Transgressing Boundaries: Women's Writing in the Renaissance and Reformation', *Renaissance Forum*, vol. 1, no. 1 (Mar. 1996); Martin, ed., *Women Writers*, introduction to 'Anne Askew, *The Examinations* (1546, 1547)', pp. 58–71; Diarmaid MacCulloch, *The Reformation*, New York: Penguin Books, 2003, p. 205; Felicity Heal, *Reformation in Britain and Ireland*, Oxford: OUP, 2003, pp. 323–30.
19. Beilin, *Redeeming Eve*, p. 99.
20. Pat Cunningham, *Blind Faith: Joan Waste, Derby's Martyr*, Derby: Pecsaeton Publishing, 2008.

21. Thomas Freeman, '"The Good Ministrye of Godlye and Vertuouse Women": The Elizabethan Martyrologists and the Female Supporters of the Marian Martyrs', *The Journal of British Studies*, vol. 39, no. 1 (Jan. 2000), p. 17.

22. Alison Plowden, 'Grey, Lady Jane', *ODNB*.

23. Lady Jane Grey, letter VI to Heinrich Bullinger, before 1553, *Original Letters Relative to the English Reformation* . . ., ed. Hastings Robinson, Cambridge: CUP, 1847.

24. Freeman, '"The Good Ministrye"', p. 11.

25. Ibid., p. 11.

26. Ibid., p. 11.

27. Ibid., p. 17.

28. Martin, ed., *Women Writers*, p. 27.

29. Ibid., p. 80.

30. Elizabeth Otten Delmonico, review of *Defences of Women: Jane Anger, Rachel Speght, Ester Sowernam and Constantia Munda*, sel. and intro. Susan Gushee O'Malley, *The Sixteenth Century Journal*, vol. 30, no. 2 (1999), p. 610.

31. Martin, ed., *Women Writers*, p. 81.

32. Ibid., p. 91.

33. Allegorical readings have been proposed, thereby sidestepping the question of Boccaccio's possible misogyny.

34. Carol Thysell, 'Gendered Virtue, Vernacular Theology, and the Nature of Authority in the Heptameron', *The Sixteenth Century Journal*, vol. 29, no. 1 (1998), pp. 39–53.

35. Alice T. Friedman, 'The Influence of Humanism on the Education of Girls and Boys in Tudor England', *History of Education Quarterly*, vol. 25, nos 1/2 (1985), pp. 63–4.

36. Kenneth Charlton, *Women, Religion and Education in Early Modern England*, New York: Routledge, 1999, p. 106.

37. See http://www.oocities.org/boleynfamily/transcripts/elizabeth.html (accessed May 2009).

38. Suzanne W. Hull, *Chaste, Silent and Obedient: English Books for Women, 1475–1640*, San Marino, CA: Huntington Library, 1982, p. 77.

39. Laurie Ellinghausen, 'Literary Property and the Single Woman in Isabella Whitney's "A Sweet Nosegay"', *Studies in English Literature 1500–1800*, vol. 45, no. 1, *The English Renaissance* (2005), pp. 1–22.

40. Wendy Wall, 'Isabella Whitney and the Female Legacy', *English Literary History*, vol. 58, no. 1 (1991), p. 52.

41. Fischer, *History of Reading*, p. 236.

42. Manguel discusses Rilke's fascination with Labé's poetry at some length: *History of Reading*, pp. 261–70.

6 Competing for Attention

1. N.H. Keeble, ed., *The Cultural Identity of Seventeenth-Century Woman*, London and New York: Routledge, 1994, p. 76.

2. Ibid., p. 77.

3. Lukas Erne, 'Shakespeare and the Book Trade', The Lyell Lectures, University of Oxford, 2012.

4. Susan Gushee O'Malley, sel. and intro., *Defences of Women: Jane Anger, Rachel Speght, Ester Sowernam, and Constantia Munda*, The Early Modern Englishwoman: A Facsimile Library of Essential Works, part 1, vol. 4, New York: Scholar Press, 1996; Ester Sowernam, *Ester hath hang'd Haman*, 1617, ed. R.S. Bear, Renascence Editions, 1998.

5. Sowernam, *Ester*, p. 21.

6. Rachel Speght, *A Muzzle for Melastomus*, London: Thomas Archer, 1617, p. ix.

7. Elizabeth Otten Delmonico, review of O'Malley, *Defences of Women*, *The Sixteenth Century Journal*, vol. 30, no. 2 (1999), pp. 609–12.

8. Rachel Speght, *Mortalities Memorandum*, 1621, Renascence Editions, The University of Oregon.

9. Constantia Munda, *The Worming of a Mad Dog*, 1617, p. 5.

10. Katherine Usher Henderson and Barbara F. McManus, *Half Humankind: Contexts and Texts of the Controversy about Women in England, 1540–1640*, Champaign, IL: UI Press, 1985, p. 239.

11. Patricia Fumerton and Anita Guerrini, eds, *Ballads and Broadsides in Britain, 1500–1800*, Farnham, Surrey: Ashgate, 2010, p. 1.

12. Dianne Dugaw, *Warrior Women and Popular Balladry, 1650–1850*, Cambridge: CUP, 1989.

13. *Règlemens pour la communauté des filles établies pour l'instruction pauvres filles de la paroisse Saint-Roch*, Paris, 1688, quoted in *A History of Women in the West*, vol. 3, *Renaissance and Enlightenment Paradoxes*, ed. Natalie Zemon Davis and Arlette Farge, Cambridge, MA: Harvard UP, 1995, p. 104.

14. Marquise de Marie de Rabutin Chantal Sévigné, *Recueil des lettres de madame la Marquise de Sévigné, à madame la Comtesse de Gignan, sa fille*, Paris, 1774, pp. 177–8.

15. Kenneth Charlton, *Women, Religion and Education in Early Modern England*, London: Routledge, 1990, pp. 217–18.

16. Suzanne W. Hull, *Chaste, Silent and Obedient: English Books for Women, 1475–1640*, San Marino, CA: Huntington Library, 1982, pp. 65–6.

17. June Taboroff, '"Wife, Unto Thy Garden": The First Gardening Books for Women', *Garden History*, vol. 2, no. 1 (Spring 1983), pp. 1–5.

18. Sarah G. Ross, *The Birth of Feminism: Women as Intellect in Renaissance Italy and England*, Cambridge, MA: Harvard UP, 2009, pp. 209–11.

19. Claude Fleury, *Traité du choix et de la méthode des études*, Paris, 1686, p. 270.

20. Keeble, ed., *Cultural Identity*, p. 286.

21. Ibid., p. 286.

22. Ibid., pp. 286–7.

23. Ibid., p. 287.

24. Ibid., p. 287.

25. Ibid., p. 287.

26. *The Paradise of Women: Writings by English Women of the Renaissance*, ed. Betty Travitsky, Westport, CT: Greenwood Press, 1981, pp. 60–3.

27. Louise B. Wright, 'The Reading of Renaissance English Women', *Studies in Philology*, vol. 28, no. 4 (1931), pp. 671–88.

28. Ibid., p. 680.

29. Ibid., p. 681.

30. Victoria E. Burke, 'Manuscript Miscellanies', in *The Cambridge Companion to Early Modern Women's Writing*, ed. Laura Lunger Knoppers, Cambridge: CUP, 2009, p. 34.

31. Victoria E. Burke, 'Contexts for Women's Manuscript Miscellanies: The Case of Elizabeth Lyttelton and Sir Thomas Browne', *The Yearbook of English Studies*, vol. 33, *Medieval and Early Modern Miscellanies and Anthologies* (2003), pp. 316–28.

32. *The Conway Letters: The Correspondence of Viscountess Anne Conway, Henry More and Their Friends*, ed. Sarah Hutton and Marjorie Hope Nicolson, Oxford: Clarendon Press, 1992, p. 12.

33. Natalie Zemon Davis, *Women on the Margins: Three Seventeenth-Century Lives*, Cambridge, MA: Harvard UP, 1995.

34. Keeble, ed., *Cultural Identity*, p. 264.

35. Lucy Hutchinson, *Memoirs of the Life of Colonel Hutchinson: With a Fragment of Autobiography*, ed. N.H. Keeble, London: Dent, 1995.

36. Dorothy Osborne, letter to Sir William Temple, 14 Apr. 1653, in Kenneth Parker, ed., *Dorothy Osborne: Letters to Sir William Temple*, London: Penguin Books, 1987, p. 75.

37. Quoted in Hull, *Chaste, Silent and Obedient*, p. 26.
38. Janet Todd, *The Critical Fortunes of Aphra Behn*, New York: Camden House, 1998.
39. Virginia Woolf, *A Room of One's Own*, London: Harcourt, 1989, p. 66.
40. María de Zayas, *The Enchantments of Love: Amorous and Exemplary Novels*, trans. H. Patsy Boyer, Berkeley, CA: U of California P, 1990, p. 172.
41. *The Puritans: A Sourcebook of Their Writings*, ed. Perry Miller and Thomas H. Johnson, Toronto: General Publishing Company, 2001, p. 140.
42. P.F. Kornicki, 'Unsuitable Books for Women? "Genji Monogatari" and "Ise Monogatari" in Late Seventeenth-Century Japan', *Monumenta Nipponica*, vol. 60, no. 2 (2005), pp. 147–93.

7 Answering Back

1. Anna Laetitia Barbauld, ed., *The Correspondence of Samuel Richardson*, 6 vols, 1804, rpt. 1966, vol. 6, pp. 178–82, cited by John August Wood, 'The Chronology of the Richardson-Bradshaigh Correspondence of 1751', *Studies in Bibliography*, vol. 33 (1980), pp. 182–91.
2. Steven Roger Fischer, *A History of Reading*, London: Reaktion Books, 2004, p. 256.
3. Sarah Kofman and Mara Dukats, 'Rousseau's Phallocratic Ends', *Hypatia*, vol. 3, no. 3 (1989), p. 135.
4. Jean-Jacques Rousseau, *Émile*, quoted in John Darling and Maaike Van De Pijpekamp, 'Rousseau on the Education, Domination and Violation of Women', *British Journal of Educational Studies*, vol. 42, no. 2 (1994), p. 120.
5. Anne L. Schroder, 'Going Public against the Academy in 1784: Mme de Genlis Speaks Out on Gender Bias', *Eighteenth-Century Studies*, vol. 32, no. 3 (Spring 1999), p. 377.
6. Ibid., p. 380.
7. Magdi Wahba, 'Madame de Genlis in England', *Comparative Literature*, vol. 13, no. 3 (Summer 1961), pp. 221–38.
8. Massimo Mazzotti, 'Newton for Ladies: Gentility, Gender and Radical Culture', *British Society for the History of Science*, vol. 37, no. 2 (Jun. 2004), pp. 119–46.
9. Elizabeth Griffith, extract in Brian Vickers, ed., *William Shakespeare: The Critical Heritage, 1774–1801*, London: Routledge, 2003, vol. 6, p. 138.
10. Abby Hunt and Paul Everson, 'Sublime Horror: Industry and Designed Landscape in Miss Wakefield's Garden at Basingill, Cumbria', *Garden History*, vol. 32, no. 1 (Spring 2004), pp. 68–86.
11. Vivien Jones, ed., *Women in the Eighteenth Century: Constructions of Femininity*, New York: Routledge, 1990, p. 3.
12. Barbara Maria Zaczek, *Censored Sentiments: Letters and Censorship in Epistolary Novels and Conduct Material*, Cranbury, NJ: Associated UP, 1997, p. 24.
13. *Selected Letters of Samuel Richardson*, ed. John Carroll, Oxford: Clarendon Press, 1964, p. 336.
14. Lady Bradshaigh, letter to Richardson, 11 Jan. 1749, *Correspondence of Samuel Richardson*, ed. Barbauld, vol. 4, pp. 240–1.
15. *Selected Letters of Samuel Richardson*, ed. Carroll, p. 319.
16. Alexander Pope, *The Poems of Alexander Pope*, ed. John Butt, New Haven and London: Yale UP, 1963, pp. 384–5.
17. Kate Williams, 'The Force of Language, and the Sweets of Love: Eliza Haywood and the Erotics of Reading in Samuel Richardson's *Clarissa*', *Lumen: Selected Proceedings from the Canadian Society for Eighteenth-Century Studies*, vol. 23 (2004), p. 311.
18. Stephen Szilagyi, review of Claudia N. Thomas, *Alexander Pope and his Eighteenth-Century Women Readers*, *South Atlantic Review*, vol. 60, no. 1 (1995), p. 181.

19. Roger Chartier, 'Richardson, Diderot et la lectrice impatiente', *MLN*, vol. 114, no. 4, p. 654.
20. Anna Barbauld, 'On the Origin and Progress of Novel-Writing', *The British Novelists: with an Essay, and Prefaces, Biographical and Critical*, 50 vols, London: Rivington, 1810, vol. 1, p. 61.
21. Ibid., p. 61.
22. Ibid., p. 26.
23. Ibid., pp. 58–9.
24. Ibid., p. 47.
25. Ibid., pp. 56–7.
26. Ibid., p. 2.
27. Ibid., p. 60.
28. William Moy Thomas, ed., *The Letters and Works of Lady Montagu*, London: Bohn, 1861, vol. 2, p. 305.
29. H.J. Jackson, *Romantic Readers: The Evidence of Marginalia*, New Haven and London: Yale UP, 2005, pp. 177–8.
30. Ibid., pp. 180–1.
31. Quoted in Miriam Rossiter Small, *Charlotte Ramsay Lennox: An Eighteenth-Century Lady of Letters*, Hamden, CN: Archon Books, 1969, p. 64.
32. Charlotte Lennox, *The Female Quixote: or, The Adventures of Arabella*, ed. M. Dalziel, London: OUP, 1970, p. xviii.
33. Lisa O'Connell, 'Gender, Sexuality and the Family: Women's Writing, Language and Readership in *The Lady's Magazine*, 1770–1832', in *Defining Gender, 1450–1910: Five Centuries of Advice Literature Online*, ed. Sara Mendelson, Claire Walsh, Jeremy Black and Erika Rappaport, Marlborough: Adam Matthew Publications, 2004, n.p.
34. Susan E. Whyman, 'Letter Writing and the Rise of the Novel: The Epistolary Literacy of Jane Johnson and Samuel Richardson', *Huntington Library Quarterly*, vol. 70, no. 4 (Dec. 2007), p. 586.
35. Ibid., p. 590.
36. Bethany Wiggin, 'Dating the Eighteenth Century in German Literary History', *Eighteenth-Century Studies*, vol. 40, no. 1 (Fall 2006), p. 131.
37. *A History of Reading in the West*, ed. Guglielmo Cavallo and Roger Chartier, trans. Lydia G. Cochrane, Oxford: Polity Press, 1999, p. 285.
38. Hannah More, *The Works of Hannah More*, 7 vols, New York: Harper & Brothers, 1835, vol. 2, p. 356, More's emphasis.
39. Quoted by Reinhard Wittmann in *The History of Reading: A Reader*, ed. Shafquat Towheed, Rosalind Crone and Katie Halsey, London and New York: Routledge, 2011, pp. 41–2.
40. James Harris, *Hermes: or, a Philosophical Enquiry concerning Language and Universal Grammar*, London: H. Woodfall, 1751, p. 424.
41. Elizabeth Carter, *Letters from Mrs. Elizabeth Carter, to Mrs. Montagu, between the years 1755 and 1800 chiefly upon literary and moral subjects*, 3 vols, London: F.C. & J. Rivington, 1817, vol. 1, p. 69.
42. *The Letters and Works of Lady Mary Wortley Montagu*, ed. Lord Wharncliffe, London: Richard Bentley, 1837, vol. 1, p. 323.
43. *The Letters and Journals of Lady Mary Coke*, Edinburgh: David Douglas, 1889, vol. 4, p. 26.
44. Letter to Mrs Dewes, Aug. 1750, *The Autobiography and Correspondence of Mary Granville, Mrs. Delany: with interesting reminiscences of King George the Third and Queen Charlotte*, ed. Lady Llanover, 3 vols, London: R. Bentley, 1861, vol. 2, p. 582.

8 Books of Their Own

1. Jennifer Phegley, 'Clearing Away "The Briars and the Brambles": The Education and Professionalization of the *Cornhill Magazine*'s Woman Readers, 1860–65', *Victorian Periodicals Review*, vol. 33, no. 1 (Spring 2000), pp. 22–43.
2. Both were published in the Jan. 1861 number: ibid., p. 25.
3. Ibid., p. 32.
4. Ibid., p. 38.
5. Martyn Lyons, 'Fires of Expiation: Book-Burnings and Catholic Missions in Restoration France', *French History*, vol. 10, no. 2 (1996), p. 248.
6. Martyn Lyons, *Readers and Society in Nineteenth-Century France: Workers, Women, Peasants*, New York: Palgrave, 2001, p. 12.
7. Robert Brudenell Carter, *On the Pathology and Treatment of Hysteria*, 1853, quoted in Kate Flint, *The Woman Reader, 1837–1914*, Oxford: Clarendon Press, 1995, pp. 58–9.
8. Flint, *Woman Reader*, p. 4.
9. Charles Fletcher Dole, *Noble Womanhood*, Boston: H.M. Caldwell Co., 1900, pp. 10–12.
10. Elizabeth Fry, *Memoir of the Life of Elizabeth Fry*, 2 vols, London: Charles Gilpin, 1847, vol. 1, p. 12.
11. Revd Thomas Timpson, *Memoirs of Mrs. Elizabeth Fry: including a history of her labors in promoting the reformation of female prisoners, and the improvement of British seamen*, New York: Stanford and Swords, 1847, p. 44.
12. Fry, *Memoir*, vol. 1, pp. 12–13.
13. H.J. Jackson, *Romantic Readers: The Evidence of Marginalia*, New Haven and London: Yale UP, 2005, p. 86.
14. http://www.historyonline.chadwyck.co.uk/pfto/ (accessed Feb. 2009).
15. Steven Roger Fischer, *A History of Reading*, London: Reaktion Books, 2004, pp. 274–5.
16. Marie Corelli, '*A Romance of Two Worlds*', in *My First Book*, ed. Jerome Klapka Jerome, London: Chatto & Windus, 1894, pp. 206–10, my emphasis.
17. Philip Waller, *Writers, Readers, and Reputations: Literary Life in Britain, 1870–1918*, Oxford: OUP, 2006, p. 557, n. 57.
18. Margaret Oliphant, *The Life and Letters of Mrs M.O.W. Oliphant*, ed. Annie Coghill, Leicester: Leicester UP, 1974, p. 434.
19. Gertrude Bell, letter to her mother, Feb.(?) 1892, Gertrude Bell Archive, Newcastle University Library, http://www.gerty.ncl.ac.uk (accessed Feb. 2012).
20. Janet Penrose Trevelyan, *The Life of Mrs. Humphry Ward*, London: Constable, 1923, p. 119.
21. Jane Austen, letter to Cassandra Austen, 22 Jun. 1808, *Jane Austen's Letters*, ed. Deidre Le Faye, Oxford: OUP, 1997, p. 131.
22. Fischer, *History of Reading*, p. 273.
23. Harriet Martineau, *Harriet Martineau's Autobiography*, London: Smith, Elder & Co., 1877, vol. 1, p. 429.
24. Quoted in Q.D. Leavis, *Fiction and the Reading Public*, London: Chatto & Windus, 1965, p. 155.
25. Tess Lewis, 'Once is Not Enough; Rereading and Remembering', *Hudson Review*, vol. 55, no. 3 (2002), p. 505.
26. Vera Brittain, *Testament of Youth*, London: Virago, 1978, p. 84.
27. Mary Brown, *Memoirs of Friendship*, 1923, quoted in *The Literary Utopias of Cultural Communities, 1790–1910*, ed. Marguerite Corporaal and Evert Jan van Leeuwen, p. 206; Flint, *Woman Reader*, p. 244.
28. Quoted in Waller, *Writers, Readers, and Reputations*, p. 230.
29. *A History of Reading in the West*, ed. Guglielmo Cavallo and Roger Chartier, trans. Lydia G. Cochrane, Oxford: Polity Press, 1999, pp. 402–3.

30. J.S. Allen, *In the Public Eye: A History of Reading in Modern France*, Princeton, NJ: Princeton UP, 1992, p. 207; François-René de Chateaubriand, *Mémoires d'outre-tombe*, 1848, part 1, book 12, ch. 3.
31. Quoted in David Gilson, *A Bibliography of Jane Austen*, New Castle, DE: Oak Knoll Press, 1997, pp. 152–3, translator's emphasis.
32. Elizabeth Barrett Browning, letter to Mary Russell Mitford, 19 Dec. 1846, *The Letters of Elizabeth Barrett Browning*, ed. Frederic G. Kenyon, 2 vols, London: Smith, Elder & Co., 1897, vol. 1, p. 313.
33. *The Brownings' Correspondence*, ed. Philip Kelley and Ronald Hudson, 18 vols, Winfield, KA: Wedgestone Press, 1985, vol. 3, p. 191.
34. Martin Garrett, 'Mitford, Mary Russell (1787–1855)', *ODNB*.
35. Mary Russell Mitford, *Recollections of a Literary Life: or, Books, Places, and People*, London: Richard Bentley, 1857, vol. 1, p. vii.
36. Leavis, *Fiction and the Reading Public*, pp. 164–5.
37. Henry Ludlam, *A Biography of Dracula: The Life Story of Bram Stoker*, London: W. Foulsham & Co., 1962, pp. 108–9.

9 Nation-Building

1. Alberto Manguel, *A History of Reading*, London: Flamingo, 1997, pp. 280–1. Interestingly Douglass uses the root 'master' twice.
2. Celeste-Marie Bernier and Judie Newman, '"The Bondwoman's Narrative": Text, Paratext, Intertext and Hypertext', *Journal of American Studies*, vol. 39, no. 2, *Nineteenth-Century Literature* (2005), pp. 147–65; Gill Ballinger, Tim Lustig and Dale Townshend, 'Missing Intertexts: Hannah Crafts' "The Bondwoman's Narrative" and African American Literary History', *Journal of American Studies*, vol. 39, no. 2, *Nineteenth-Century Literature* (2005), pp. 207–37; Shirley Wilson, review of *In Search of Hannah Crafts*, *Legacy*, vol. 22, no. 2 (2005), pp. 209–10.
3. Catherine Kerrison, 'The Novel as Teacher: Learning to be Female in the Early American South', *The Journal of Southern History*, vol. 69, no. 3 (2003), p. 524.
4. Ibid., pp. 525–6.
5. Susan L. Tolbert, 'Reading Habits of the Nineteenth-Century New England Girls', http://philandsusantolbert.com/research/millgirl.html (accessed Oct. 2004).
6. Ibid.
7. Catherine J. Golden, *Images of the Woman Reader in Victorian British and American Fiction*, Gainesville, FL: UP of Florida, 2003, p. 17.
8. George Eliot, *Silly Novels by Lady Novelists*, London: Penguin Books, 2010.
9. Letter to Harriet St Leger, 27 Jun. 1835, *Fanny Kemble's Journals*, ed. Catherine Clinton, Cambridge, MA: Harvard UP, 2000, p. 84.
10. B.C. Southam, ed., *Jane Austen: 1811–1870*, London: Routledge, 1979, vol. 1, p. 50.
11. W.H. Auden, *Collected Poems*, ed. Edward Mendelson, New York: Modern Library, 2007, p. 84.
12. Virginia Woolf, 'Jane Austen at Sixty', *The Essays of Virginia Woolf*, ed. Andrew McNeillie, 4 vols, London: Hogarth Press, 1994, vol. 4, p. 155.
13. Charlotte Bury, *The Diary of a Lady-in-Waiting*, ed. A. Francis Steuart, London, 1908, vol. 2, p. 251.

10 The Modern Woman Reader

1. Wendy Lesser, *Nothing Remains the Same: Rereading and Remembering*, New York: First Mariner Books, 2003, p. 3.
2. *Daily Telegraph*, 29 Jul. 2009.
3. Boris N. Mironov, 'The Development of Literacy in Russia and the USSR from the Tenth to the Twentieth Centuries', *History of Education Quarterly*, vol. 31, no. 2 (1991), p. 245.

4. Sreemati Chakrabarti, 'Women and Adult Literacy in China', in *Across the Himalayan Gap: An Indian Quest for Understanding China*, ed. Tan Chung, New Delhi: Sundeep Prakashan, 1998, p. 32; UNESCO, Institute for Statistics, Data Centre.

5. Fred M. Leventhal, 'British Writers, American Readers: Women's Voices in Wartime', *Albion: A Quarterly Journal Concerned with British Studies*, vol. 32, no. 1 (2000), pp. 1–18.

6. '"Deathly Hallows" Film Breathes Life into Harry Potter Book Sales', Nielsenwire, 17 Nov. 2010.

7. BBC News, 1 Mar. 2007.

8. *New York Times*, 12 Jun. 2005.

9. Alison Peden, 'Contextual Bible Study at Cornton Vale Women's Prison, Stirling', *The Expository Times*, vol. 117, no. 1 (Jan. 2005), pp. 15–18.

10. Jenny Hartley, *The Reading Group Book*, Oxford: OUP, 2002, p. 123.

11. Bill Costello, 'America's Reading Gender Gap', *TCS Daily*, 21 Oct. 2009; Myra Barrs and Sue Pidgeon, eds, *Reading the Difference: Gender and Reading in the Primary School*, Centre for Literacy in Primary Education, 1993.

12. Shelly Higginbotham, 'Reading Interests of Middle School Students and Reading Preferences by Gender of Middle School Students in a Southeastern State', Master's Thesis, Mercer University, 1999.

13. UNESCO, Institute for Statistics, Data Centre.

14. http://www.en.wikipedia.org/wiki/Literacy (accessed Feb. 2009).

15. http://www.asiahumanrights.com (accessed Jan. 2009).

16. OpenNet Initiative, 'A Report of the Status of the Internet in Iran', Nov. 2005, p. 7.

17. Ibid., p. 12.

18. OpenNet Initiative, 'Iran', 16 Jun. 2009.

19. Natalie Dixon, 'Iranian Censorship of Women's Online Magazines', 17 Nov. 2010, http://www.owni.eu (accessed Jan. 2009).

20. Cecil Hewitt Rolph, ed., *Lady Chatterley's Trial*, London: Penguin Books, 2005.

21. Azar Nafisi, *Reading Lolita in Tehran: A Memoir in Books*, New York: Fourth Estate, 2004, p. 35.

22. Ron Synovitz, 'Afghanistan: Author Awaits Happy Ending to "Sewing Circles of Herat"', *Payvand Iran News*, 4 Jan. 2004.

Index

bestsellers 105, 123, 133, 157, 186, 192, 202, 240, 241, 252, 254, 263, 264, 280, 282, 291
Bhagavad Gita 262
Bianzago, Angela and Laura 106
Bibesco, Elizabeth Asquith 9
Bible 47, 69, 83, 86, 94, 105, 115, 118, 119–22, 140, 219, 258, 267, 278
  Esther, Book of 147
  Geneva 120
  King James version 122
  New Testament 126, 147
  Old Testament 119, 147
  readings 284–5
  Revelation, Book of 46
  Septuagint 119
  translations of 47, 62, 119, 121, 122, 166
  Vulgate 62, 119
Bibliotheca Hagiographica Graeca 74
'Bibliothèque bleue' 143
Black Death 97
Black Lace 290
black people 257–60
Blackwell, Elizabeth, *A Curious Herbal* 194
Blackwood's Magazine 242–3
Blanchardyn and Eglantine 104–5
blogs 288
  in China 289
Blount, Martha 201
Bluestockings 187, 195, 211, 220
Boccaccio, Giovanni 176
  The Decameron 106, 132
Boethius 83
Bohemia 120
Boke his Surfeyt in Love 130
Boniface, St 59–60, 96
bonkbusters 290
Bonner, Bishop Edmund 125
Book at Bedtime 282–3
book-burning 5, 233, 291
book clubs, TV 283
book-ownership patterns 117–18
book pedlars 142, *142*, 143, 267
book trade, women in 106–7
Books of Hours 94–7, 109, 111, *112*
Boston, Massachusetts 178, 179, 262
  Brook Farm 262
Boston Recorder 263
Boswell, James 212, *213*, 221
  Life of Samuel Johnson 212–13
Bowdler, Henrietta 242–3
Bowdler, Thomas 242–3

Bowes, Elizabeth 129–30
Bowyer, Ann 161
The Boy's Own Paper 253
Bradford, John
  'The Defence of Election' 129
  'The Hurt of Hearing Mass' 129
  'The Restoration of All Things' 129
Bradshaigh, Lady 184, 197, 198–200, 206
Bradstreet, Anne, *In Honour of that High and Mighty Princess Queen Elizabeth of Happy Memory* 166–7
Brendan of Clonfert 58
breviaries 94
Bride and Prejudice (film) 283
Bridget of Sweden, St 50, 57, 103
Bridgettine Order 104
Bridgewater, Frances Egerton, Countess of 145
Brigit of Ireland 57, 58
Brinon, Madame 179
British Ladies' Society for Promoting the Reformation of Female Prisoners 236
Brittain, Vera, *Testament of Youth* 246
broadsides 143, 150, 153
Brontë, Charlotte 244, 259
  Jane Eyre 270, 277, 286
Brontë, Emily 259
Brooke, Frances 273
  History of Lady Julia Mandeville 208
Broughton, Hugh 122
Brown, Gordon 295
Brown, Louise 277
Brown, Mary 246
Brown, William Wells, *The Escape, or a Leap for Freedom* 260
Browne, Mary (sister of Elizabeth Lyttelton) 161
Browning, Elizabeth Barrett 244, 246, 248–9, 250
  'Lord Walter's Wife' 233
Browning, Robert 249
Brucioli, Antonio 119
Bruto, Gian Michele, *La Institutione di una Fanciulla Nata Nobilmente* (*Mirrhor of Modestie*) 136
Buddhism 49, 68–9
Buisson, Marie 166
Bullinger, Heinrich 127
  The Christen state of matrimony 136
Bulwer-Lytton, Edward (1st Baron Lytton) 240, 244, 251–2
Bunyan, John, *Pilgrim's Progress* 173

Niagara Gloss Starch (advertisement) *269*
Nielsen BookScan 283
Nightingale, Florence 244
Noailles, Anna, comtesse de 179
Nonaka En 3, 182
Nordhausen 64
Norfolk 102
Norfolk, Thomas Howard, Duke of 137
Norton, Caroline 34
Norway 94, 101, 278
Norwich 153
   Church of St Julian 98
novella 176
novels 113, 150, 152, 172–7, 184, 195,
      197–211, 214–17, 222, 224, 248,
      270–1
   American 261–2, 265–6
   French 184, 249, 254–5
   German 184, 222, 255
   Gothic 209, 247, 248, 272
   men's and women's choices 286–7
   serialised 231–2, 247, 253, 284
   suspicion of 182–3, 195, 197, 211, 222,
      224, 229–30, 233–5
   theory of 189–90, 210
nuns, nunneries 44, 50–1, 52, 53–61, *53*,
      64–6, 71, 85–7, *87*, 106, 146, 151,
      164, 165–6
   Byzantine 72–4
   libraries 49, 85, 86, 87–8, 98
Nuremberg, St Catherine's Convent 86–7

O'Casey, Sean, *Juno and the
     Paycock* 278
occasionnels 143
Octavia (sister of Augustus) 40, 42, 43
Oecolampidius, Johannes, *A sermon, . . .
     to young men and maydens* 136
Office of Strategic Services 278
Ohio 255
Okumura Masanobu, *Sweets from a
     Temple 183*
Oliphant, Margaret 240
Olive Branch 263
Olivétan, Pierre-Robert 119
Olivier, Jacques, *Alphabet of the
     Imperfection and Malice of
     Women* 8
Olney, Buckinghamshire 219
ONI (OpenNet Initiative) 290
Opie, Amelia 208
The Oprah Winfrey Show 283
Opuscula philosophica 162–3

oral literature 89–90
Orkney 284
Ortúñez de Calahorra, Diego 140
   *The mirrour of princely deedes and
     knighthood* 137–8
Osborne, Dorothy 171
Osborne, John 201
Oswald, King 58
Otto I (the Great), Holy Roman Emperor
   65, 66–7, *67*
Otto II, Holy Roman Emperor 66
Ottoman Empire 5
Ottonian Renaissance 66–7
Overbury, Sir Thomas, *Characters* 160
Ovid 7–8, 10, 33, 37–9, 65, 83, 170, 291
   Ars Amatoria 38
   Epistles 172
   Heroides 55, 139
   Medicamina faciei femineae 38
   Metamorphoses 37–8, 175
   Remedia amoris 38
   Tristia 38
Oxford
   Bodleian Library 139
   Brasenose College 161
   Christ Church 161
   University of 122
     former women's colleges 158
   libraries 124
Oxford Companion to the Book 18

Padua 106
Paine, Thomas, *The Rights of Man* 237
Pakistan 23, 294–5
Palaemon, *Grammar* 40
Palaeolithic art 22
The Pall Mall Gazette 31, 246
pamphlets 119, 123, 143
   pamphlet wars 146–9
   see also treatises and manuals
paper, manufacture of 98
paperbacks 280
papyrus 28, 32, 35–6
Paraclete, abbey of the 80
parchment 98
Paris 140, 179, 186, 194, 223, 254, 288
   Bastille 190
   Comédie-Française 206
   Hôtel de Rambouillet 175
   Les Halles charity school 151
   Port-Royal 164
Parliament 191
   House of Commons 149

Parry, James, *The True Anti-Pamela: or,*
Memoirs of Mr James Parry 202–3
Parton, Ellen Eldredge, drawing of Sara
Willis Parton (Fanny Fern) *264*
Paul 148
Epistles of 4, 11, 120, 137
Corinthians 120, 130
Paul IV, Pope 121
Peabody, Elizabeth 179, 262
Pearson Education 287
Pearson PLC 287
Pech Merle cave, France 21
Penguin Books 280
Penguin Group 287
Penny Blood series 253
Penny Sunday Times 253
La Pensadora Gaditana 189
People's Police Gazette 253
Pepys, Samuel 150
periodicals 157, 188–9, 202, 217, 284
specialist 255
in US 260, 262, 263, 266
see also magazines
Perpignan, Siege of 141
Peru 286
Peter Lombard, *Sententiae* 83
Peter Pindar (John Wolcot), *Bozzy and*
Piozzi 213
'La Petite Anglaise' 288
Petrarch (Francesco Petrarca) 82,
97, 106
Petronius 83
Petrus Pictor 89
Philadelphia 257
Philipaut, Julie, *Racine lisant 'Athalie'*
devant Louis XIV et Madame de
Maintenon 180
Philip of Novara 93
Philips, Katherine ('Orinda') 34, 158,
174, 177
Philiscus of Thessaly 42
Philomela, Ovid's story of 37–8
philosophers, women as 163–4
Philostratus, *Life of Apollonius* 42
Philpot, John 129
Phoenicians 30
pictograms 23
Pine, Robert Edge, portrait of Catherine
Macaulay *192*
Pinianus 44
Piozzi, Gabriel Mario 212
Piozzi (earlier Thrale), Hester 211–13
Anecdotes of Samuel Johnson 212–13

Piramus, Denis 91–2
Pizzano, Tommaso di Benvenuto
di 99
Placcius, Vincent, *Theatrum Anonymorum*
et Pseudonymoron 177
Plantin, Christophe 106
Plat, Hugh
Delightes for Ladies 157
Floures of Philosophie 139
Plato 71, 220, 262
Phaedrus 30–1
Plautus 65
The Pleasures of Conjugal Love Explained:
In an Essay Concerning Human
Generation 195
Pliny the Younger 39–40
Plutarch 106, 162
Lives 220
Pocket Books 280
Poe, Edgar Allan 254
poetry 3, 70–1, 152, 181–2, 195, 234,
267–8
Poitiers 54–5
Poland 83, 120, 267
Polynesians 22
Pompeii 43
Villa of the Mysteries *41*
Ponson du Terrail, Pierre Alexis,
Rocambole 247
Pope, Alexander 34, 198, 201, 235
The Dunciad 201
The Rape of the Lock 222
translation of *The Iliad* 201
pornography 290
Powell, Thomas, *Tom of all Trades* 160
prayer books 94
prayers 82, 103, 105
précieuses 177
Presbyterianism 123, 149, 261
presbyters 47
Prévost, Antoine François (Abbé), *Manon*
Lescaut 254–5
Pride and Prejudice (TV adaptation) 283
Prierias, Sylvester 118
Priestley, J.B. 6
Primrose, Lady Diana, 'A Chain of Pearl
. . .' 167
printers, women as 105–7
printing, print culture 105–7, 115–20,
145, 188
Priscian (Priscianus Caesariensis) 83
Privy Council 122
Propertius 55

Volckmann, Anna Helena 222
Volmar *78*
Voltaire, François-Marie Arouet de 11,
    187, 226, 233, 248
    Nanine 206
Vonnegut, Kurt, *Slaughterhouse-Five* 286

Wace 111
Waddell, Helen 277
Wakefield, Priscilla Bell, *An Introduction to
    Botany* 194
Walker, Anthony, *The Holy Life of Mrs
    Elizabeth Walker* 153
Walpole, Horace 10, 211
Warburton, Bishop William 216
Warcup, Anne 128
Ward, Mrs Humphry (Mary Augusta) 239,
    240–1
    The History of David Grieve 240–1
    Lady Rose's Daughter 241
    The Marriage of William Ashe 241
    Milly and Olly 240
    Robert Elsmere 241
    Sir George Tressady 241–2
Waste, Joan 126
A Way to Get Wealth 155
Webb, Beatrice 241–2
Webb, Mary 278
websites, blocked 290
Webster, William, *The Most Pleasant and
    Delightful Historie of Curran, a
    Prince of Danske, and the fayre
    Princess Argentile* 160–1
Wellden, Elizabeth 161
Westminster Review 270
Whigs 191, 201–2, 208
Whitby 58–9
    Synod of 58
Whitney, Isabella 138–40
    Copy of a Letter 139
    A Sweet Nosegay 139
The Whole Duty of Man 10
Wiertz, Antoine, *The Reader of Novels*
    229–30, *230*, 290–1
Wilcox, Ella Wheeler
    Poems of Passion 240
    'Solitude' 240
Wilde, Oscar 241
Wilkinson, Joan 128
William of Gellone 62
William of Septimania 62, 63
Willis, Sarah Payson (Fanny Fern; later
    Parton) 263–4, *264*

Fern Leaves from Fanny's Portfolio 263
    Ruth Hall 263–4
wills 117
Wilson, Revd Thomas *192*
Winchilsea, Anne Finch, Countess of 174
    Poems 171–2
Winfrey, Oprah 283
Winthrop, Adam 178
Winthrop, John 178, 181
Winthrop family 178
Wolfreston, Frances 145
Wolfreston, Standford 145
Wollstonecraft, Mary 226
    Thoughts on the Education of Daughters
        196, 226
    A Vindication of the Rights of Woman
        188, 227
'woman question' 226
Woman's Hour 282
women, rights of 244, 289
Women's Liberation Movement 226
Women's National Anti-Suffrage League
    242
Woolf, Virginia 174, 274
    The Common Reader 6, 196
Woolworth's 280
Wordsworth, Dorothy 207
Wordsworth, William 207, 234, 262
Wren, Sir Christopher 161
Wroth, Mary 139
Wu Wushan 181
Wüchterin, Barbara 118
Wyatt, Sir Thomas, the younger 127
Wyer, Robert 134

Xenophon 224
    Economicus 136
    Xenophon's Treatise of Householde
        (tr. Hervet) 133

Yamaga Soko 3
Yaroslav I, Prince of Kiev 75
Yedingham, Yorkshire 103
Yousafzai, Malala 294–5

Zäunemann, Sidonia Hedwig 222
Zayas y Sotomayor, María de 176–7
    Desengaños Amorosos 176
    Novelas Amorosas y ejemplares 176
Ziegler, Christian Mariane von 222
Zimbabwe 2
Zola, Émile 255
Zurich 119